The IEA Health and Welfare Unit

Choice in Welfare No. 45

How To Create a Competitive Market in Pensions:
The International Lessons

Michael Littlewood

IEA Health and Welfare Unit
London

First published July 1998

The IEA Health and Welfare Unit
2 Lord North St
London SW1P 3LB

© Michael Littlewood, 1998

ISBN 0-255 36437-7
ISSN 1362-9565

Typeset by the IEA Health and Welfare Unit
in Bookman 9 point
Printed in Great Britain by
St Edmundsbury Press
Blenheim Industrial Park, Newmarket Road
Bury St Edmunds, Suffolk IP33 3TU

Contents

Figures

Tables

Foreword

How to Create a Competitive Market in Pensions draws on the experience of several countries—especially the United States, the UK, Chile and New Zealand—to make a convincing case for increased competition in provision for retirement income. The author, a pensions expert from New Zealand, demolishes the case for compulsory pensions. They are not justified—whether they are European-style unfunded state pensions; or funded state schemes in the manner of Singapore; or compulsory funded private pensions on the Chilean model so much admired by Britain's Minister for Welfare Reform, Frank Field.

Michael Littlewood also argues powerfully against tax breaks and for the tax regime to treat all savings schemes equally. Tax concessions invariably go to the wrong people, he says, and there is strong evidence that their impact on total savings has been exaggerated. In both Britain and the United States it may be necessary for governments to face down the tax-favoured private pension providers and to reverse the tax treatment of pensions. Payments into pension schemes should have the same standing as ordinary savings. Payments should not be exempt from tax, as they are at present; instead of exempting the investment income of pension companies it, too, should be taxed; but pension benefits should no longer be subject to taxation.

Britain's State Earnings Related Pension Scheme (SERPS) should be abolished after honouring current obligations and the regulatory regime for the pensions industry should be simplified. Excessive regulations add to costs and create entry barriers which diminish the competition that is ultimately the consumers' best protector.

Littlewood accepts that the government must perform some key tasks. Its role is important but limited to maintaining an assured national minimum, sustaining tax neutrality, minimising regulation, and controlling inflation.

Michael Littlewood's argument may seem vulnerable to criticism by those who draw attention to the danger of 'free riding'. They argue that some people who could afford to save for retirement will choose instead to rely on the taxpayer. Such people, so the argument runs, can properly be forced to pay into a pension scheme. However, it would be a case of 'overkill' to compel *everyone* to buy a government-approved pension merely in order to reach a minority of potential free-riders.

People are different, and we each have our own legitimate preferences. The step-by-step building up over 30-40 years of a capital sum which must be spent on an annuity at retirement may not be the best method of saving for many, perhaps the majority. There is inherent uncertainty about any long-term investment and, far from it being a sign of irresponsibility to steer clear of schemes requiring long-term lock-in, it could just as well be a sign of prudence. Compulsion requires people to tie themselves to a scheme that may not turn out to be a good bet. Indeed, for much of this century investing in our own home has proved to be a better investment than a pension.

Moreover, the risks we face change over the lifecycle. For example, a married couple with children to support may wish to give priority to provision against the early death of the breadwinner or incapacity for work and then switch to a pension when the children are grown up. A scheme on the Chilean model which requires 10 per cent or more of income to be paid into a pension throughout our working lives crowds out any such alternative.

The pattern of work is also changing. Earlier in the century, it was possible to assume that most people were the employees of a large corporation, but this is no longer true. Far fewer workers now expect to spend their career with one employer and many more prefer self-employment. A self-employed person, for example, may prefer to invest in his own business and such an investment may well prove to be a more sound method of provision than a deferred annuity. Low earners might be forced to save when they could well prefer a lower income in retirement. They might also prefer to carry on working.

Rather than compel the majority who do not need compelling, the lesser evil would be to expect those who have not made provision to continue working so long as they are fit. Incapacity Benefit would continue to be available for those too ill to work, just as it is for the younger age group. There is, in any event, much to be said for 'working till you drop'. Not everyone wishes to 'retire' in the modern sense. Throughout history it has commonly been supposed that individuals would work, leading a 'useful life', until illness or death intervened. The idea of retirement was partly a product of early industrialisation which involved sustained heavy work that was beyond the capacity of men in their mid-60s. Today work is not physically so demanding and many more people can carry on for longer.

Michael Littlewood has produced a very readable book on a complex subject that will be of value, not only for teaching in sixth forms, colleges and universities, but also for those who work in the financial services sector.

David G. Green

The Author

Michael Littlewood graduated from Auckland University in New Zealand (Arts 1967, Law 1969).

Michael worked a total of 14 years as an employee-benefit consultant, first as legal counsel and then as a senior consultant for what is now Watson Wyatt in the UK. On his return to New Zealand he was a senior consultant with what has since become Watson Wyatt New Zealand.

In 1988, Michael joined Fletcher Challenge Limited (a New Zealand-based multi-national with interests in forestry, pulp & paper, building materials and construction) as its Employee-Benefits Director. He remains an adviser to Fletcher Challenge and now also part-owns a personal financial planning business that helps employers help their employees take control of their financial lives.

Michael was a member of the New Zealand Government's Task Force on Private Provision for Retirement in 1991-92 and was a councillor of The Association of Superannuation Funds of New Zealand for six years until 1992, including three years as its chairman.

He has written numerous articles for newspapers, business journals and specialist magazines on issues relating to retirement provision, financial planning and public policy.

Michael lives in Auckland and is married to Vivien. They have four children.

Summary

This book aims to help countries redesign their public and private retirement income systems.

- **Common problems**: The retirement income policies of nearly all developed countries are in terrible shape. The problems these countries face are universal and offer us lessons on how not to do things.

- **Welfare isn't working**: Most people reach retirement age and need income to support them in their non-earning years so retirement income is a major component of the welfare state. Changing patterns in population growth and mortality and the cost of welfare systems have made these systems unsustainable. Substantial, radical, reform is required but politicians respond with erratic, incremental, 'sticking plaster' changes.

- **Tax incentives don't work**: Tax-based incentives are used in nearly all countries to encourage people to save for retirement. Of the three main policy strategies (tax incentives, compulsion and voluntary) tax incentives are the least effective. They don't work and cost more than they recover. They are also inequitable, distortionary, inefficient, and increase the tax burden elsewhere.

- **Compulsion not much better**: Compulsory private saving schemes have advantages and disadvantages. Some models work better than others. However, it is more efficient for the economy as a whole (and for individuals) if savers are left to make their own saving decisions in a voluntary environment.

- **An efficient welfare net is first**: Without a stable foundation at Tier I (public, welfare-related provision), citizens can't know how to behave sensibly at Tiers II and III. We must design a state pension scheme that operates as efficiently as possible, sends the right signals to savers and is flexible and robust enough to allow for non-disruptive change over decades rather than sudden change.

- **The state's role in a voluntary environment**: In the end, citizens must look after their own retirement needs. The state's primary role is to provide a safety net, but there are other ways it can help itself and its citizens. These include ensuring that the economy is sound; that savers have choices and the information they need to make good decisions; that investments are treated equitably and that the regulatory environment provides transparency without being restrictive.

- **Employers' role is vital**: Employers are involved in retirement saving schemes but there is often misunderstanding about the role such schemes play within the general retirement saving framework or their costs and benefits. Employers can co-operate with the government in a mutually beneficial relationship in which employers help the government to implement public policy.

- **How would your country adjust?** Developed countries face the same structural problems and behavioural roadblocks when trying to reform their existing retirement schemes. The book paints a brief picture of how the retirement income systems of six different developed countries—the US, the UK, France, Australia, Germany and Chile—would look under the new regime.

Introduction

The staple conversation on the farms around was on the uselessness of saving money; and smockfrocked arithmeticians, leaning on their ploughs or hoes, would enter into calculations of great nicety to prove that parish relief was a fuller provision for a man in his old age than any which could result from savings out of their wages during a whole lifetime.

Tess of the D'Urbervilles (1891)

The retirement-income policies of nearly all developed countries are in terrible shape. Fortunately, the issues these countries face are universal, although you might not think so from the diversity of the 'answers' from around the world.

Someone could be right—the trick is finding out who that might be.

Enter 'Homo Economicus'

People generally won't do the things they don't like doing. Retirement is one of life's passages—it's a form of financial death when we can expect to lose our economic place in the world. Saving for retirement is therefore an intrinsically negative project that we prefer to put off for one very excellent reason or another. This throws a significant challenge in the path of public policies achieving their policy objectives.

However, the response of individuals to public policy is, or should be, the touchstone against which its success is judged. If people respond to policy in a way that is contrary to a government's intention, then it's the policy that's wrong, not the people.

That's why I've introduced *homo economicus* as one of the main 'characters' of this book. It's a Latin tag often used by economists to explain how people react to 'signals' that government policy or economic conditions send to a country's citizens. When a government proposes a change to policy, or if conditions change, a good test is to ask, 'how would (or should) I behave if I were acting rationally in response to this signal?'

Governments often won't like the answer. However, there is usually a good reason for the way people behave and it's mostly to do with self interest. And that's the best reason of all. *Homo economicus* is generally a force for good that should be developed, not fought.

Bold Antipodean Beginnings

Public debate on the most appropriate policies for a country is bound to consider the merits of retirement income policies around the world. It's logical to turn to the experience of others grappling with the same issues, if not for answers at least for options. Although New Zealand is young, small and at the bottom of the world, it has come to some interesting conclusions in the public policy area. The lessons have been painful and the solutions are far from bedded down. But whatever happens next, I hope that this book will help you see why I think New Zealand has come closest to finding the right way.

The Road to Damascus

I am an employee benefits practitioner, not an academic. The views I express are largely the result of my practical experience in the employee benefits field and involvement in the policy development process in New Zealand. In fact, this has over time led to a fundamental shift in my thinking. And, in that way, the book chronicles a personal experience.

Although I had developed an interest in public policy issues, I remember when my head was really turned—both the date and the circumstance. I was working for a firm of actuaries—it was 17 December 1987. I was driving to collect an outfit for a pre-Christmas costume party and was listening to news of a special announcement. The Government had, among other things, just decided to withdraw all tax concessions for retirement saving, starting that day. In New Zealand's unicameral system of government, once the executive branch had made its decision, that was it—no more debate.

I thought that was the beginning of the end of my current career. Who would save for retirement without tax concessions? Why would my customers (employers) want to hear what I had to say any more? I pulled to the roadside and listened transfixed.

Over the last ten years, I've discovered I was wrong. I now think tax concessions are more a distraction than an incentive. They hinder rather than help savers to make the 'right' decisions.

In any event, the Government's 'Economic Statement' was, in retrospect, the beginning of my own road to Damascus.

Time for Change

I hope you will find this book thought-provoking and practical. It began life as a contribution to the debate in New Zealand which preceded a 1997 referendum on the compulsory privatisation of the government pension arrangements. This proposal was massively defeated by 92 per cent of voters. The present book is a much-revised version of that early draft. I want to present a coherent framework through which we can all contribute to a sustainable, comprehensive and comprehensible public policy on retirement incomes. For all the obvious reasons, we can't leave it to the politicians. We all have an individual responsibility to make it work.

I will be pleased if you agreed with the policy framework I suggest, but you don't have to for this book to be useful. I will be content if it simply makes you wonder whether the old way of doing things is likely to withstand the coming pressures.

Then, like me, you can change your mind.

Technical Terms and Other Data

Book-reserved schemes: In most developed countries private pensions tend to be pre-funded—i.e. the liability for the future benefits is supported by a pool of assets that are, to a greater or lesser extent, roughly equal to the present value of the future benefits. In Germany, however, tax and accounting practices have supported the notional setting aside of assets within the accounts of the employer to pay for future benefits. These are known as 'book-reserved schemes'. Although the pre-funded model is becoming more common in Germany, book-reserved pensions still cover about 54 per cent of occupational scheme benefits.

Currency: Throughout this book, the 'base currency' is in US dollars converted, where necessary, at the exchange rate on 24 October 1997. In some cases where conversion doesn't make sense (such as describing tax bands) I've used local currency.

Defined-benefit retirement saving scheme: A defined-benefit scheme usually calculates a retirement benefit by reference to the pay of a member at retirement and the length of membership over which the benefits have been earned. defined-benefit schemes need not be prefunded (most Tier I social security schemes run by governments are defined-benefit) but they always need another party to underwrite the benefits—that could be the government, the employer or a financial institution like an insurance company that sells an annuity.

Defined-contribution retirement saving scheme: A defined-contribution retirement benefit scheme calculates its benefits by reference to the contributions paid in by the member and the employer, where appropriate. Interest is usually added to the accumulating contributions and the final benefit is based on the total.

Population statistics: I've used the international convention of describing the 'working age population' as everyone between ages 16-64, inclusive. 'Young dependents' is everyone under 16 while the 'retired' is everyone 65 and over. In most developed countries these days, the younger age should probably be 18. Like most statistics, these divisions are rough and ready—not all over-65s are 'non-producers' (which is what really matters in the context of the issues discussed in this book); not all between 16-65 are producers, especially when the unemployed and caregivers are allowed for.

Statistics New Zealand: you will find a lot of information in this book about our experiences of pension management in New Zealand. A lot of that information is attributed to Statistics New Zealand which is the government department responsible for producing our official numbers.

Acknowledgements

Anyone who has written a book will know what a time consuming business it is. For that reason, the first thank you is almost always to the author's family and that is the case here. Without Vivien's urging and support, it simply wouldn't have happened.

Other people have helped me with different contributions. They include Catherine Judd for a great editing job; Angela Ryan, Susan St John, Roger Kerr and David Green for support and challenging views; and my previous employer, Fletcher Challenge Limited (and its previous Employee Relations Director, John Hart) for giving me the chance to learn about new ways of doing things.

But, as they say, the conclusions are all my own.

Michael Littlewood
Auckland, New Zealand
April 1998

1

The Present Mess

Summary

Retirement income policy is a huge subject which impacts on all sections of the population and affects economic viability. It is one area that requires informed debate and long-term, consistent strategies. However, history has proved that it is also an area that has been used for political leverage, leading to erratic changes, inconsistencies and the absence of strategic, long-term thinking.

****

Most articles or books about retirement income policy start with tales of woe about the coming demographic deluge—we are all apparently on the point of disappearing under an economic tidal wave of elderly indigents. Tomorrow's taxpayers will not want (or be able) to finance this onslaught. Like King Canute, the authors of these doom-laden tracts think that the tide will be unstoppable.

There is some point in looking ahead at what might happen, if only to give us the shock we seem to need in democratic societies before real change takes place. Retirement income policy is a huge subject, involving billions of dollars of current expenditure and, in some countries, trillions of dollars of liabilities. It's all fertile ground for the alarmists.

If ever there was a public policy issue that needed a commitment to research, informed debate and long-run, consistent strategies, the retirement income issue is it. There are several very substantial reasons for this.

First, the amounts of money involved are huge whether you are looking at private savings (New Zealand has about 17 per cent by value of Gross Domestic Product [GDP] in private retirement schemes[1] while the international champion—the Netherlands—has about 124 per cent) or the value of state-provided benefits. The present value of the unfunded, 'off-balance-sheet' liabilities for pay-as-you-go state schemes in the developed world is generally huge, dwarfing what most people think of as the national debt.

Second, the number of people affected is huge and they fall into a number of categories:

The old

In New Zealand, about 13.5 per cent of the whole population (21 per cent of the working age population[2]) is over the age of entitlement for the age-based benefit (the 'state pension age'). Although that age is increasing (it will be 65

---

[1]   At December 1995, according to survey results issued by the Government Actuary's office.

[2]   *Demographic Trends 1992*, Statistics New Zealand.

1

for men and women by 1 April 2001), the proportions over that age will increase from about 2011 as the baby-boomers start reaching 65.

The soon to retire
Most employees start to think seriously about retirement saving in their late forties. In New Zealand, about 15.4 per cent of the total population is between ages 45 and 60. A lot of them are concerned both about the viability of the state-provided pension and the adequacy of their own savings. The number of them who are actually doing something about it is quite another matter. About 20 per cent of working age New Zealanders belong to a formal retirement saving scheme—relatively low by international standards.

Employers
People who employ people should be concerned about the welfare of their employees—it's in their own economic interests.

Savers
Savers are or should be vitally concerned at what society intends to deliver when they themselves retire and about how that will be delivered, now and then.

The managers of money
The economic welfare of money managers depends on a clear understanding of their own sources of new business. Public policy plays a crucial role in their strategic plans.

The users of capital
That includes a number in the groups already mentioned. In the end, society can only deliver a 'fair' share to the retired if society itself is economically successful. If savings are to deliver at least part of that economic well being, they must be successfully deployed. That should be as much a part of a country's retirement income policy as the amount of the state's benefit or the age from which it's payable.

Taxpayers
This isn't an exclusive group—you'll find them among the old, the soon to retire and all the other members on the list of those most affected by policies on retirement income.

Society in general
One measure of a civilised society is how we treat the economically deprived, including the old, the young and the disabled. Retirement income policies are an important part of society's glue because of a common feeling that the old have 'done their bit' for society. It's now society's responsibility to return the favour. Politicians find it difficult to argue with that notion, particularly as the old have plenty of time to remind them about it.

This book touches on all these groups because they all have a part to play in the very large puzzle that is public policy on retirement incomes.

The third 'big' reason for developing a well-informed and long-term strategy on retirement income is that, of all long term projects, this one takes the longest. It makes retirement saving an important issue for us all individually. For each of us, it takes so long to get there and then another age to enjoy the fruits of our thrift. And, if it doesn't work for us all individually, then it won't work for the country as a whole.

For commitment, both in time and money, saving for retirement beats raising children, educating them, training for a career and retraining for a new one. The saving period will usually be longer than retirement itself.

The last 'big' reason is that most of us will make it to retirement. At any age, in developed countries, we all have a better than 75 per cent chance of making it to retirement age in a reasonably healthy state. The other 25 per cent will either die or become disabled before reaching retirement age. Direct insurance can cover the needs of that 25 per cent—the rest will have to depend either on their own savings, or on the government's ability to extract tax from its citizens' pockets.

Retirement income policy is a vital project for every country—in the end, most of us (the 75 per cent) will benefit from policy that works. We will all pay the price if it doesn't.

Lessons from Developed Countries

We can all draw from the various experiences of the world's developed countries. I'll use their different ways of addressing policy issues on retirement income as illustrations and, in some cases, as lessons on how *not* to do things. Nearly all developed countries face major change in this expensive area of public policy—other countries needn't follow them.

One of the best things about the retirement income 'industry' is that, despite significant cultural and regulatory differences among developed countries, the broad issues are much the same the world over. That makes the 'solutions' relatively easy to compare even though it may take some years or even decades to see if they actually worked.

The same will not be true of what are sometimes euphemistically called 'developing' countries. Those countries will probably get there in due course but I can't hope to deal adequately in this book with the issues they face now and in the future.

I want to focus this book on the problems faced by the retirement income systems of the countries in the developed world. They have, after all, made the biggest mess of things.

2

Democracy, Demography
and the Welfare State

Summary

Most people will reach retirement age and require income to support them in their non-earning years. So, governments around the developed world have become involved in providing some degree of support to their retired citizens. This government intervention has arisen for a number of reasons including the need to prevent poverty, capital market failures and the lack of forward planning by many.

Governments use an array of tools to intervene in this area, including tax incentives, regulation of private saving schemes and a range of compulsory saving régimes. The classic retirement income régime has a three-pillared structure: basic government provision, workplace schemes and all other forms of voluntary saving.

However, Pillar I schemes are now failing or becoming unsustainable, due in large part to slower population growth, longer life expectancy and reduced economic growth.

The rising costs of welfare systems cause a rise in the cost of labour as social security contributions increase. This has become an important and unpalatable issue for politicians. Response has been piecemeal and inconsistent. Change has often been introduced by stealth. Substantial reform is now needed with possible solutions including raising taxes (with or without welfare cuts) modifying benefits and private provision.

****

The state is the great fictitious entity by which everyone seeks to live at the expense of everyone else.

Frederic Bastiat (1801-1850)

Modern economies have developed quite sophisticated ways of pooling risk. We take relatively for granted insurance against the unexpected, like fire, theft, accidental damage or injury. Governments often play no direct role in these other than as the consumers' watchdog. There are exceptions (such as New Zealand's 'no fault' Accident Compensation Scheme for personal injury following an accident), but, generally, citizens are left to make their own arrangements with the private risk-poolers of the insurance markets. The alternative is to face the financial consequences of carrying our own risk.

The Expected Risk of Retirement

Retirement is a condition rather than an event. The 'retirement' event rarely occurs at a precise moment, nor can it be precisely defined; retirement has almost as many definitions as there are retirees. However, from a financial

4

viewpoint, 'retirement' is relatively clear. Retirement is also an expected risk—in New Zealand, more than 80 per cent of people at *all* ages will make it to an age when they can realistically contemplate stopping all or most paid employment and then start to depend on their stored-up financial resources. Figure 1 shows the chances of a male New Zealander making it to age 60 (or of dying or becoming disabled before then):

Figure 1
Probability of Need for Financial Provision: New Zealand

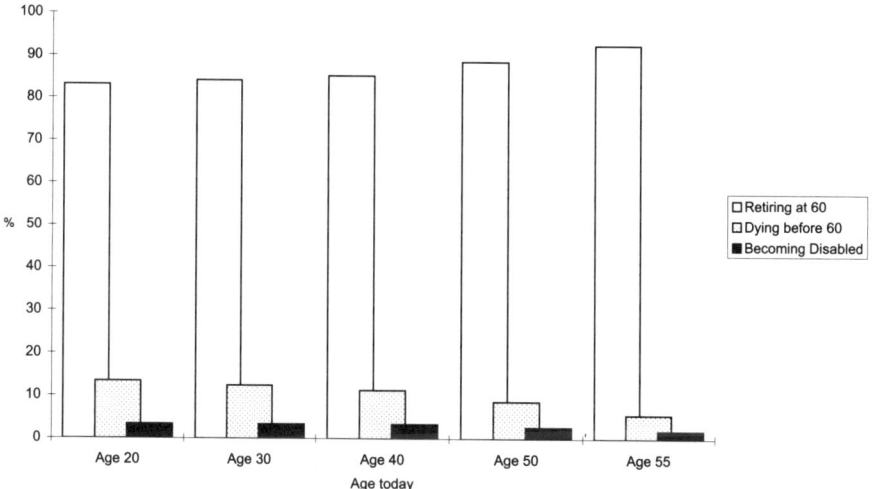

Source: Watson Wyatt New Zealand Limited, 1992

All developed countries will show a similar pattern.

Given this relative certainty (and the fact that we routinely insure ourselves against the other two risks of death and disability), why have governments of developed countries become so heavily involved in delivering retirement income?

Part of the explanation is that retirement is the most certain of the three conditions and, for that reason, is the most expensive. Figure 1 shows that death and disability during working years are relatively unlikely, so the cost of protection against their happening is quite low. That doesn't stop governments from getting involved in the financial exigencies that follow death or disability. Usually, though, they deal only with the real economic disasters and not the run-of-the-mill cases.

On the other hand, the prospect of building up a pool of assets that's sufficient to last for all our retirement years as well as for those of our 'significant others' is too daunting for most even to start the task.

So Why Have Governments Become Involved?

'Developed' governments at first provided only the ambulance and stretchers at the bottom of the retirement cliff, probably because most people (for that, read most voters) prefer that their old don't starve. Chapter 3 looks at the appropriate role for governments. But to make sense of that discussion, we need to understand why we have got to where we are and the imperatives for reform which that implies.

There are several explanations for the now heavy involvement of the governments of developed countries in the delivery of retirement incomes.

Protecting the Disadvantaged

There was much poverty among the old before and after the First World War, and governments had a legitimate interest in its alleviation. It was the genesis of the concepts of redistribution that underlie the modern welfare state.

When governments first got started in the retirement income business, old age was almost synonymous with poverty. In part, that followed the breakdown of traditional family and community networks (with consequential social dislocation) caused by the Industrial Revolution. 'Old age' became equivalent to 'can't work' and therefore 'poor'. The concept of an age from which a person was no longer economically useful grew out of a physically demanding, increasingly factory-based, urban work environment. A 'retirement age' was a new idea driven by the more institutional environment of the industrial employer.

However, financial markets weren't sophisticated enough to deliver efficient vehicles that allowed citizens to defer consumption from their working years to the period when they were 'retired'. It took some time for industrial societies to develop a replacement for the commitment that rural individuals got from their families in a working lifetime.

At first, the 'society' that gave the indigent old some security was quite local. The church and the community in which the poor lived were primarily responsible. For example, England's first Poor Law Act of 1601 put the onus on the local parish to look after those in need, including the old. The extent of the industrial revolution's change meant, however, that the focus for responsibility had to become a wider 'society'. Individuals lost contact with their small local societies. The towns and cities to which they now belonged were too large for the old sense of community to translate into financial support for the 'can't work' period of old age.

Employment-based pension schemes first emerged in the early 1800s—and banks led the way. One of the first recorded employer-sponsored pension schemes started in 1808[1] and was sponsored by the Bank of France—somewhat surprising, given that in the second half of this century France's retirement income structure has been entirely dominated by the state.

The state took a little longer to become involved. Bismarck started the first contributory, old-age 'insurance' scheme for Germany in 1889 as part of a broad programme of social insurance that had gradually evolved in the 1880s. It was the first of many, but they mostly had quite limited financial objectives, certainly by comparison with today's standards. Bismarck's scheme offered no more than a minimum subsistence level, but on a basis that connected benefits with contributions in the insurance mould.

New Zealand chose a different route when its first old age pension was introduced in 1898. Its modest objectives were quite specific—a small, means-tested, flat-rate pension was provided on grounds of residency for New

---

[1]   Quigley, N.C., in *Private Superannuation in the Banking Industry*, Bank of New Zealand Officers' Provident Association, 1988.

Zealanders aged 65 or more 'provided that they were of good repute, sober, and had not deserted their family or been recently in gaol'.[1] No specific contributions were required for those benefits.

Non-contributory 'welfare' schemes spread. The UK introduced a non-contributory, income-tested pension for the over 70s in 1908. Again, some citizens were excluded on moral grounds, and also if they had received past poor relief. But the means-tested benefits of these schemes placed them apart from the Bismarckian breed that provided the model for Rumania, Sweden and the Netherlands before World War I. After the war, contributory schemes took off and most European countries installed them.

The Depression

Some social welfare programmes really got moving after the Depression in the late 1920s and early 1930s. This period saw widespread economic dislocation, including the loss of savings and significant hardship. Social Security started in the US in 1935; the New Zealand programme had its genesis in the Labour Party's victory in the same year. Though still modest by today's standards, these systems started a significant state involvement in the financial lives of all retired citizens, not just the poor. The UK's watershed came in 1925, consolidated by the Beveridge report of 1942—again, a system of modest state benefits that Beveridge saw as a stimulus, not a replacement, for additional private provision.

Post-War Economic Growth

State intervention would flower because of the baby boom, rapid growth and prosperity after World War II. Politicians could offer large increases in state entitlements and buy much voter satisfaction in exchange for quite modest increases in the amount governments took from their taxpayers. Often, governments dressed up the schemes in the language of insurance with 'premiums' creating 'entitlements' to 'protection' against both the foreseeable and the unforeseeable. That made the new or larger structures look a little less like a tax and a little more like sensible advance provision—a quite saleable proposition.

Little wonder then that such schemes were flavour of the post-war period among politicians of many countries. From the perspective of retirement provision, they were certainly not insurance; but they were vote-winners.

Storing up a 'Bargain'

The last reason that caused governments to become more and more involved derives from the intergenerational 'bargain' that developed. Governments did not have to work hard to convince current taxpayers that the state should relieve them of direct financial responsibility for the care of the elderly. Those taxpayers, especially if they were close to retirement, were also looking after themselves. So, despite their apparent benevolence to older citizens, tax-payers' self-interest seeded this new breed of scheme. These taxpayers stored

---

[1]   Sinclair, 1991 cited in St John, S. and Ashton, T., *Private Pensions in New Zealand: Can they Avert the Crisis?*, Wellington, NZ: Institute of Policy Studies, 1993.

up claims against the next generation of taxpayers—the classic inter-generational 'contract' which was nothing of the kind.

The natural attraction of politicians to policies that win votes underlies most explanations for the involvement of governments in the delivery of retirement incomes. There are, however, some more technical reasons for the involvement of governments, though some of these seem to me to be *ex post facto* rationalisations. These reasons include:

Myopia or Short Sightedness

People seemingly don't look ahead (or don't start looking ahead soon enough) and therefore don't understand how much they need to save for their retirement. While short sightedness is certainly a problem, it's another step to say that it requires the state's involvement to the extent common today. A state 'solution' implies we should give up before we have even started—that only the state knows what's best. This 'nanny state' kind of thinking seems less fashionable these days.

Information Gaps

People don't get the right information, even once they have made the decision to start saving. The answer to that should be to improve the flow and quality of information.

Capital Market Failures

People try to save but their money is stolen or their saving vehicle fails through poor strategy or bad investments. The state can justify picking up some of the pieces of a failed scheme but that's scarcely a reason to replace or crowd out individual citizens' own responsibilities to look after themselves.

Insurance Inadequacies

If the government makes everyone, including the young (who are assumed to be indifferent to early provision) join mandatory retirement income arrangements, the costs for all will be less over the long term. This argument, of lower costs, is at best superficial.

'Good' and 'Bad' Annuity Risks

Market-related programmes don't work because those who are 'bad' retirement risks (because they think they will live a long time) opt in. Those who are 'good' retirement risks, because they won't live long, opt out and drive up the cost of life annuities for the 'bad' risks. That's because the 'profits' the annuity pool would have earned on the 'good' shorter living risks will not subsidise the annuities of the 'bad' longer living risks.

This issue, however, arises only at the point of retirement, which is when a saver must buy the retirement annuity. That can't justify intervention from the time a citizen first enters the workforce.

Government policy

Then, finally, there is the self-inflicted damage done by governments themselves. Governments need an anti-inflation lobby if they want to maintain a sustainable retirement income policy. Inflation is a tax on saving. Governments can't expect citizens to save (to buy insurance against their retirement needs, if you like), unless they can offer them the reasonable possibility of long term, *real* rates of return. If a government's policies allow a redistribution of wealth from savers to earners (or from lenders to the owners of 'real' assets like land and shares) through inflation, it must not be surprised if those who thought they had everything under control, even if they didn't, look to the government to fix things when they reach retirement. Where else can they go? Who else has the power to right the wrongs of the past?

All of these reasons need a closer look and I have more to say about them later. The general conclusion we can draw at this stage is that some form of intervention is inevitable. The issue is: what sort?

How Governments Can Intervene

Governments that intervene in the provision of retirement incomes for their citizens have a number of potential tools to choose from. Most countries use most of them and some even try all of them. The following list is in approximate order of popularity among developed countries:

'Insurance Premiums' and Benefits

State-run schemes collect contributions from citizens' pay and distribute them to those who have paid their contributions in past years.[1] 'Entitlements' accrue based usually on periods of contribution but there is almost always no pool of assets to draw on—as money comes in, it mostly goes straight out again. In many cases, taxpayers also chip in because today's contributions aren't enough to pay today's benefits.

Taxes and Transfers

Governments collect money under regimes that normally ask higher earners to pay more than lower. Governments then pay some of that to the older but not necessarily needier citizens or deliver goods (through devices like food stamps) or services (like health benefits) at the expense of all taxpayers. Over recent decades, these have grown—according to the International Monetary Fund, transfers and subsidies rose in industrial countries from eight per cent of national incomes in 1960 to 21 per cent in 1992.[2]

Though the language and rules of the 'insurance premiums and benefits' option seem different from 'taxes and transfers', for all practical purposes, interventions 1 and 2 are the same and I will treat them alike. A government can run both types and change the rules for both, either opportunistically or when circumstances require. Also, until the point of retirement, there is none of the risk-sharing that insurance demands. From the state pension age, they both look the same.

---

[1]   But benefits are not just paid to contributors—there are usually complex rules about the spouses of contributors and about 'approved' absences from employment. Benefit entitlements also often accrue when contributions are not paid.

[2]   'World Economic Outlook', *The Financial Times*, 18 April 1996.

Incentives

The tax system lets you reduce your otherwise taxable income by your contri-butions to approved schemes. The investment income earned by those savings is treated favourably and the eventual benefits are usually taxed as ordinary income. All taxpayers, including the old, help pay for that help.

Regulation of Private Schemes

Governments write books of rules to regulate private saving schemes of all kinds. There is an element of consumer protection in this (sometimes with a 'fair play' slant), but mostly such regulation protects the tax system's investment in concessions for the favoured schemes. The rules make sure that pensioners eventually pay tax on the benefits they receive.

Industry Regulation

The major players in the saving industry tend to be heavily regulated, mostly with an eye to consumer protection. In some countries though, like Japan and Finland, regulation also intentionally limits competition. The rules affect insurance companies, fund managers, the securities markets, banks, 'fiduciaries' and those involved in selling saving vehicles.

Compulsory Private Saving

More and more countries look to compulsory private provision as an appropriate form of intervention—the so-called 'privatisation of social security'.

Benefit Guarantees

Sometimes, governments give direct guarantees to privately organised benefits—the UK's 'Guaranteed Minimum Pension'[1] and its relationship with the State Earnings Related Pension is an example.

Underwrites

There are indirect underwrites of the kind that usually accompany a compulsory private saving scheme. These provide a minimum social welfare benefit if a saver's scheme falls over or if the saver doesn't have long enough to build up a reasonable level of income. This could be caused by a short work history or a short membership period.

Deposit guarantees (such as the UK's deposit protection scheme) are a more direct form of underwrite. Investor insurance (such as is provided by the Pension Benefit Guarantee Corporation of the US) is a more indirect type of underwrite. This taxes (charges a premium to) sound pension schemes to pay the benefits of the badly-run schemes that go broke. A similar insurance scheme got under way in the UK in 1997. The UK version is not insurance in the usual sense—the Occupational Pensions Regulatory Authority (OPRA) waits until a scheme falls over from fraud or theft before billing remaining schemes. It's a 'post event' compensation financed by law abiding schemes.

---

[1]   The benefit that is equivalent to the State Earnings Related Pension and that a private scheme promises to pay in exchange for contracting out of the state scheme.

The Three Pillars of Retirement Income Provision

The 'classic' retirement provision structure has three 'pillars':

Pillar I: basic government provision—a tax-financed, mandatory, welfare-related income of, normally, modest proportions. The payment is usually calculated on defined-benefit principles and is unfunded though there may be an identified tax or 'contribution' (as in the UK's National Insurance, or Social Security in the US).

Pillar II: occupational schemes—delivered by or through the workplace and most commonly financed by contributions from employers and employees, with all taxpayers chipping in through tax concessions. Benefits can build up either on the defined-benefit or defined-contribution basis, or both. They are not necessarily funded (where a pool of assets is built up ahead of the obligation to deliver the benefit), particularly if they are run by a government agency or through the book reserve system common in Germany. They may be entirely run by the government, even for private sector employees (such as in France).

Pillar III: all other saving—by definition, these are voluntary, funded and, in retirement income terminology, operate on defined contribution principles —that is, the accumulated savings build up with accumulated investment earnings.[1] They are often tax subsidised—the UK's Additional Voluntary Contribution (AVC) programmes, Canada's Registered Retirement Saving Plans (RRSPs) and the US's Individual Retirement Accounts (IRAs) are all examples. They don't, of course, have to be in such formal arrangements. Pillar III includes things like bank deposits, listed shares, trading down the family home at retirement, selling a business or owning it for the income. All are part of the retirement saving structure.

So What Has Gone Wrong?

The retirement income policies of nearly all developed countries are in serious trouble, despite decades of change. In fact, the trouble is as much to do *with* the decades of change as anything else. But that is not all.

The World Bank in its 1994 Policy Research Report[2] summed up what has gone wrong for Pillar I, the piece which is delivered directly by the state and which is supposed to be the foundation for everyone's retirement income planning:

The public pillar is supposed to :

- *Redistribute to the poor.* But many rich people get back in pensions more than they have contributed, while many poor people do not collect any benefits.

- *Augment the income of the old who can no longer work productively.* But many recipients are middle-aged and still capable of working.

---

[1]   They will be on the defined-contribution basis during the saving period. At retirement, they could be replaced by a private annuity which is a personal, defined-benefit saving product.

[2]   *Averting The Old Age Crisis: Policies to Protect and Promote Growth*, The World Bank Policy Research Report, Oxford University Press, 1994, pp. 101-02.

- *Protect the old against inflation.* But many governments have failed to index fully, using inflation to reduce their real costs.

- *Be a remedy for myopia among workers.* But the programmes' implementation often demonstrates the myopia of politicians, in some cases causing the old age system to collapse.'

In most developed countries, 'old' is no longer synonymous with 'poor'. Averages by their nature disguise extremes, but they show a marked improvement in the incomes and wealth of the old and in the value of their claims on public services over the last decades. The following two examples illustrate this:

The UK

Figures prepared by the UK government[1] show that the unemployed are replacing pensioners in the bottom 10 per cent of the income scale. This seems to be attributable to a growth in private savings because the state pension barely changed in real terms.[2]

Over the 14 years between 1979 and 1993, pensioner couples saw their average real incomes rise by 53 per cent, the highest increase for any of the 'family types' published by the Department of Social Security. The proportion of pensioners in the bottom 10 per cent of the income scale has dropped by about half over the same period and stood at only 20 per cent in 1993.[3]

The US

US Census Bureau figures[4] show that median household incomes for the old have risen a lot over the period 1965-1992. An elderly man's median income, for example, has gone from $8,691 to $14,789 in 1992 money (a total increase of 70 per cent or 3.2 per cent a year). Those income figures don't count the value of the elderly's claims on Medicare, the tax-funded health care programme which started in 1965 and is available to all the old, regardless of income or wealth—a significant exclusion in the context of the cost of health care in the US.

This means the spending power of the old has increased. In 1960, the average 70-year-old US male spent only about two-thirds as much as the 30-year-old male. By 1990, the 70-year-old male was spending 25 per cent more than the 30-year-old. The relative spending of elderly women had also increased, but not by as much.[5]

---

[1] *The Financial Times*, 3 June 1995.

[2] A survey published by the UK's Government Statistician on 2 August 1995, reported in *The Daily Telegraph*, 3 August 1995.

[3] Though the gap between UK's wealthiest and poorest pensioners widened sharply over the last decade according to a survey by The Institute for Fiscal Studies, reported in *The Financial Times*, 22 November 1995. That doesn't change the point I'm making.

[4] Cited in an editorial of *The Wall Street Journal*, 22 June 1995.

[5] From a study by Auerbach, A.J., Kotlikoff, L.J. and others, reported in *Business Week*, 24 July 1995.

An increasing emphasis on annuities (including Social Security pensions) means that today's expenditure can be higher at the expense of future inheritances, because that part of a pensioner's wealth disappears on death when the annuity stops. Annuities pay out the pensioner's capital during his/her lifetime as part of the annual income. According to one group of commentators,[1] this has contributed to falling US saving rates.

Census Bureau figures show that wealth has also risen for the old in the US by comparison with other groups. The over-65s' household median net worth was $88,000 in 1992; it was $31,000 for the 35-44-year-olds. Excluding the value of the family home, the bottom 20 per cent of the old were 25 times as wealthy as the poorest 35-44-year-olds.

All these figures count wealth in traditional ways; if measures of wealth also included Social Security and Medicare benefits, the change and the contrast would be even more dramatic.

Now, 'children' are more synonymous with 'poor' than 'old' and that shift has significant implications for what we call civilised society. This book deals only, however, with the older end of the population's age structure.

Increasing State Involvement

History shows that what started as public schemes designed to provide a subsistence level of income and to alleviate poverty have grown somewhat over the last 40 years or so, as Table 1 shows.

Figure 2 shows what has happened to New Zealand's old age benefit for single people since it was improved in 1938.

Just looking at the amount paid as a pension doesn't always give the full picture. There are some 'extras' in New Zealand, though we're not in the same league as, for example, Australia. There, pensioners get a 'concession card' with access to discounted travel and medicines, and there is a pharmaceutical allowance, rent assistance, telephone allowance and a 'remote area allowance'.

Much the same kind of change has happened the world over. In 1930, the average for all countries of the minimum pension for single pensioners was 10 per cent of an average production worker's wage. This reached 19 per cent in 1950 and 25 per cent in 1965. By 1985, the average of the minimum pension had reached 37 per cent.[2]

This taxpayer-supported munificence wouldn't have been possible in a traditional, pre-funded retirement scheme where assets are built up ahead of benefits. The only way these increasingly generous schemes could work was through the power of governments to tax and redistribute.

The success of unfunded 'Pillar I' schemes depended on two further conditions, but not many politicians or voters understood them. The schemes first depended on population growth or, more accurately, on a relatively young average population with a relatively small retired population. For example,

[1] Gokhale, J., Kotlikoff, L.J. and Sabelhaus, J., in 'Understanding the Postwar Decline in US Saving', Brookings Papers on Economic Activity, 1996.

[2] Palme in 'Pension Rights in Welfare Capitalism', SOFI Stockholm, 1990 cited by Einar Overbye in a contribution to the Pension Reform Interest Group run on the Internet at 'prig@fsu.edu'.

when the US Social Security system started in 1940, there were 16 workers for each beneficiary. Now, the ratio is 4.7 to one and by 2030, the projection is 2.8 workers for each beneficiary. In Portugal, the ratio is already 1.5 workers (or, more accurately, contributors) for each pensioner, and is expected to be 1.1 by 2010.[1]

Table 1
Ratio of average pension to average wage in some OECD countries 1939 and 1980

Country	1939[1] % (actual)	1980[2] % (synthetic)
Australia	19	25[3]
Belgium	14	-
Canada	17	34
Denmark	22	29
Italy	15	69
The Netherlands	13	44
New Zealand[4]	29[5]	44[6]
Norway	8	-
Sweden	10	68
Switzerland	-	37
UK	13	31
USA	21	44
Average	**16.5**	**42.5**

Source: Averting The Old Age Crisis: Policies to Protect and Promote Growth, The World Bank Policy Research Report, Oxford University Press, 1994.

Notes:
1. Source cited by the World Bank as SSIB data files, Esping-Anderson, 1990.
2. Source cited by the World Bank as Aldridge, 1992. The 'synthetic' reference is to a simulated percentage of final salary for single workers with average wages in manufacturing.
3. Source Australian Bureau of Statistics.
4. Author's figures.
5. Choosing 1939 means the New Zealand figure was the then new Social Security pension.
6. 1980 was the peak year in New Zealand for what had become known as 'National Superannuation'. An equivalent figure for 1998 would be 41 per cent.

Unfunded state schemes also depended on real economic growth feeding through into real wage growth. Most of these schemes based the contributions on wages, so increasing wages meant increasing scheme contributions. As Paul Samuelson said 30 years ago in a 1967 Newsweek editorial:

The beauty of social insurance is that it is actuarially unsound. Everyone who reaches retirement age is given benefit privileges that far exceed anything he has paid in... How is this possible? It stems from the fact that the national product is growing at compound interest and can be expected to do so for as far ahead as the eye can see. Always there are more youths than old folks in a growing population. More important, with real incomes growing at some three per cent a year, the taxable base upon which benefits rest in any period are much greater than the taxes paid by the generation

---

[1]   IBIS Review, February 1995.

now retired... A growing nation is the greatest Ponzi[1] game ever contrived.[2]

It is not just the contributions that are based on increasing wages—the benefits are usually tied to them as well, either directly or indirectly. Expanding post-war populations coupled with economic growth lulled governments into a false sense of security. The music is now beginning to slow down and the chairs are being withdrawn, one at a time.

Figure 2
New Zealand's Pillar I (Single) as % Average National Wage, 1940-95

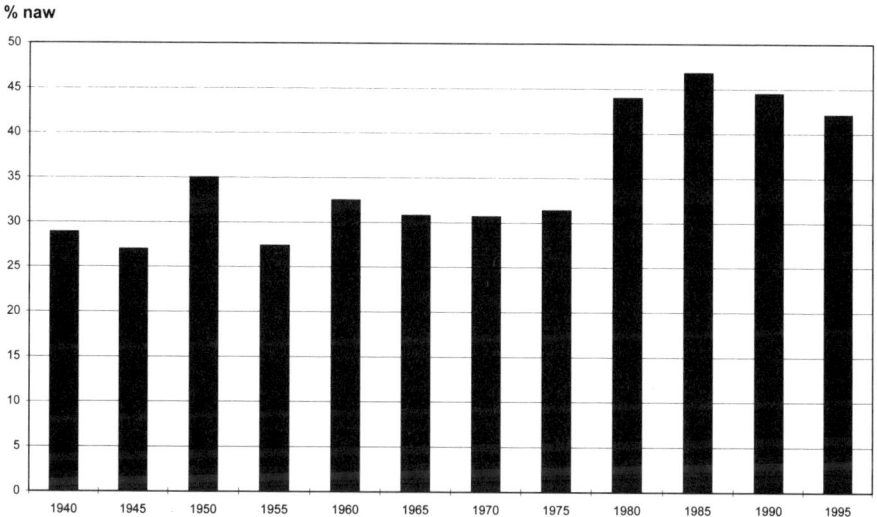

Source: New Zealand Year Books; government statistics.
Notes:
1. The figure shows what happened when 'National Superannuation' started in 1977 but disguises the effect of the increase in value because the qualification age fell from 65 to 60. That increased the benefit's actuarial value at age 60 but not the figure's nominal value. The qualification age is now increasing to 65 for men and women.
2. The 1990 and 1995 figures are for the then new 'single, living alone' benefit.
3. The figure shows pre-tax benefits in relation to pre-tax incomes.

There are several reasons for this. First, from the early 1960s, baby-boomers could decide how many children they wanted, and they decided to stop having them at previous rates. Not only did that affect the future numbers of new entrants into the work force but it also freed women to enter the workforce on roughly equivalent terms to men. That was to change the workforce for ever.

Next, economic growth and increasing real wages were no longer givens. Contribution rates (the balancing item needed to pay for today's beneficiaries) started to increase, so politicians are now feeling the heat. As the baby-boomers move in a gentle demographic tidal wave through to retirement, it's not difficult to predict unsustainable contribution rates and/or reductions in benefits.

---

[1] A 'pyramid' style of scheme that depends on numbers continuing to be added at the bottom to support the relatively smaller number at the top.

[2] Quoted in the World Bank report, 1994, op. cit., p.105.

Figure 3
Population over 65 as a Percentage of Those 16-64

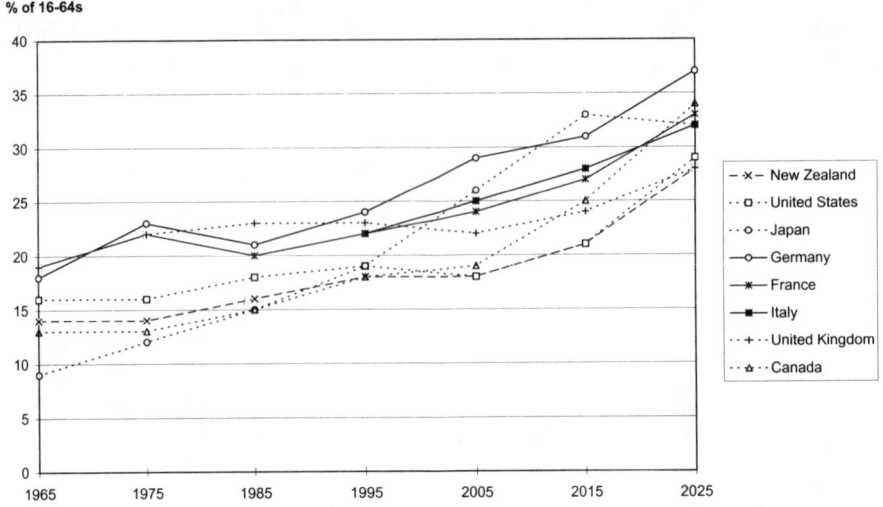

Source: OECD figures, 1995; New Zealand data from Statistics New Zealand
Note: Italy's information is only from 1995.

Figure 4
Population Under Age 16 as Percentage of Those 16-64

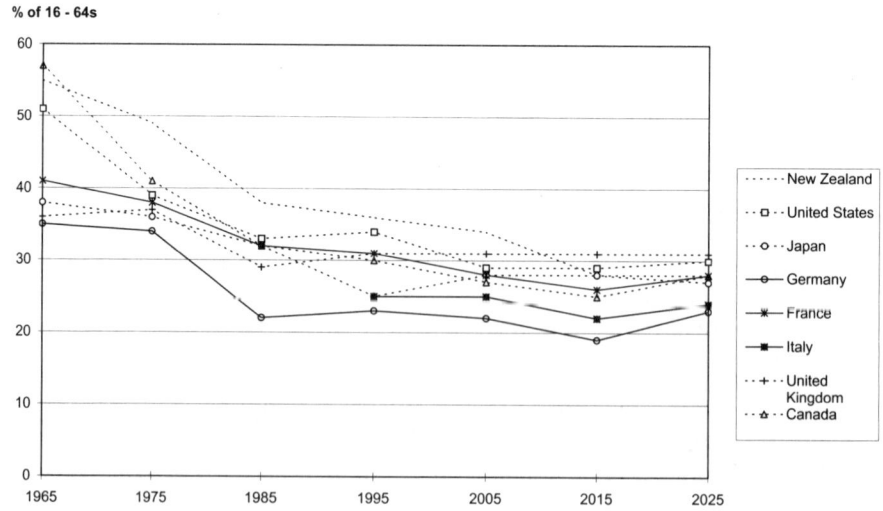

Source: OEDC figures 1995; New Zealand data from Statistics New Zealand
Note: Information for Italy is only from 1995.

Figures 3, 4 and 5 give an international snapshot of the usual way that people see the unstable demographic foundation of Paul Samuelson's Ponzi game. They show how the old and the young relate to those aged 16-64 who, in international statistics, are assumed to be the productive members of society.

Figure 3 shows the old steadily increasing in relation to the working-age population in a selection of developed countries. The old are not the only dependents who get support from the working-age population. Figure 4 shows a corresponding reduction in the proportion of the young.

All developed countries have varying welfare obligations to the young and the old. From a social welfare perspective, the extra costs of the old to tomorrow's taxpayers should be partly offset by the lower costs of a relatively smaller population of young.

Figure 5 shows the changes we can expect in the *total* dependency ratios over the coming years.

Total dependency ratios look more comfortable than those just for the old, but we can't equate the cost to the taxpayer of one old person with one young person. Pensions and medical care will, on average, cost considerably more than education and medical care for the young. The World Bank's report *Averting the Old Age Crisis* puts the cost of social outlays on the over-65s at between 2.1 times the under 15s for the UK and up to 3.8 times for both Italy and the US.[1] The multiple in Australia is 2.3, according to the National Commission of Audit.[2]

In part, these differences can be explained by the fact that the costs of young dependency are often borne privately by families, whereas a greater proportion of the costs of age dependency comes from the public purse. However, some commentators suggest that the young absorb more than their fair share of policing and emergency hospital costs.

Total dependency ratios are, however, more important than the old age dependency ratios normally used in discussions of this kind. Also, we should have much better information about actual, rather than assumed, dependency ratios—who is working and producing the wealth at all ages by comparison with who is not working or producing wealth. In the UK over the period 1931-1981 socio-economic developments (that altered the propensity of people to engage in paid employment) have had almost double the impact of purely demographic effects in increasing male economic dependency rates.[3]

The Figures give us some indication of general trends and the message is plain enough—welfare systems are set to become more expensive for all the countries shown in the Figures. Though it's mostly to do with the expected rise in the cost of pensions, the cost of health care will also make a significant contribution.

On top of the demographic shifts, unemployment has compounded the pressures felt by welfare schemes. This combination of factors has been particularly difficult for the unfunded welfare schemes of developed countries. Not only does the number of welfare beneficiaries increase, usually at a time

---

[1]   Based on OECD data for 1988, p. 34.

[2]   Reported in *The Australian Financial Review*, 24 June 1996.

[3]   According to Johnson, P., in 'Grey Horizons: Who Pays for Old Age in the 21st Century', *The Australian Economic Review*, 3rd Quarter 1996.

when the nation is facing economic difficulty, but also the contributions to the 'pay as you go' retirement income scheme start falling away. Employers and governments, in the face of mounting unemployment, started using early retirement or disability benefits to disguise publicly unpalatable statistics, like the number of the unemployed. But that only compounded the problems. Public schemes began offering expensive bribes to encourage older workers to leave their jobs. Politicians thought that younger workers would replace the old. However, employers took the opportunity to reduce their work forces and replace unskilled workers with technology, rather than with the young, unskilled, now unemployed school-leavers.

Figure 5
Total Dependency Ratios

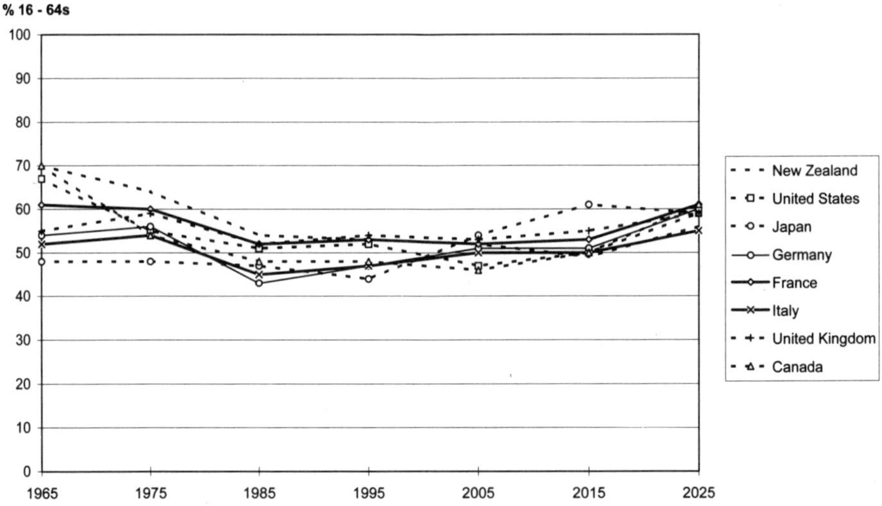

% 16 - 64s

Source: OEDC figures 1995; New Zealand data from Statistics New Zealand

On top of all this, people are, inconveniently, living much longer than when the schemes started. In New Zealand, the population aged 80 and over will treble from the 1994 total of 89,000 (2.5 per cent of the population) to 259,000 (5.9 per cent) by 2031.[1] They are also dying in much more expensive ways than in the past. While this last has nothing to do directly with retirement incomes, it changes the cost of health schemes and multiplies the mounting pressures on increasingly limited government resources.

---

[1]   *Demographic Trends 1995*, Statistics New Zealand—the future population assumes medium fertility and mortality.

The Impact of These Changes on Employment

Increasing contributions to state welfare schemes, as well as being unpopular, have some unfortunate side effects. New Zealand got rid of the separate Social Security tax in 1969 when it was merged into the general tax rates.[1] However, most governments collect the schemes' costs through pay-related contributions, so increasing them has the same economic effect as a tax increase. In fact they are often worse than a tax increase, because they are calculated on an employee's full income without the deductions normally available in the tax calculation—that's the position in the UK. Social security contributions tend to be regressive (the lower paid are relatively worse off than the higher paid), especially if, as is usually the case, the pay on which they are collected is subject to an upper limit.

Increasing contributions to pay for increasingly expensive welfare systems has a perverse effect—it makes them less secure at a time when the need for security is greater. As the cost of labour increases through higher social welfare contributions, the relative cost of automation (or the cost of moving production to another country) decreases, so increasing the risks of higher unemployment. Having fewer employees increases the burden on those still in the system and the upward spiral continues.

Taxpayers don't like paying more than their fair share, particularly if they think they won't get the same benefits when they retire, so they will naturally try to avoid or evade taxes. Employers, who are being asked to pay an increasing share, in a world constrained by global competition, treat employment taxes as another part of the cost of labour and will tend to reduce the quantity of labour they need.

With an increasing black economy and reducing employment, the burden for those who still choose to participate in the system, or who can't avoid it, becomes higher again. German labour is now the most expensive in the world—the average hourly rate (including non-wage costs like social security taxes) is $27 in Germany, $17 in the US, $14 in the UK and Australia, $9 in New Zealand and $5 in Hong Kong.[2] Social security contributions in Germany are now 40.8 per cent of wages (with pensions costing 19.2 per cent), and the social security system was expected to run a deficit of $600 million in 1996/97. So it's no surprise to hear that German employers are looking eastwards to cut costs. Germany's gross domestic product rose 61 per cent in real terms between 1970 and 1994 but the amount of labour needed fell to 80 per cent of its 1970 level. Unemployment grew 17-fold over the same period.[3]

High non-wage costs also seem to contribute to long periods of unemployment. According to the OECD, in 1992 42 per cent of the European Union's unemployed were out of work for a year or more. The corresponding figure in the US was 11 per cent. Not only are the generous European benefits a disincentive to the unemployed to find new jobs, they also raise the hurdle rate for employers to take on new staff.

All this has its own impact on economic growth and turns the screw further on politicians.

---

[1]   New Zealand's Social Security 'Fund' had already disappeared in 1964.

[2]   US Labour Department figures cited in *The Economist*, 9 December 1995.

[3]   From a report cited in *The Financial Times*, 20 May 1996.

These pressures seem to be coinciding with (or even causing) a growing disaffection among voters with big governments. In fact, Robert Samuelson puts a lot of US disgruntlement down to the 'Age of Entitlement' as citizens come to realise that society can't deliver on the promises made by their political leaders. He said the American dream has turned out to be a fantasy:

> Our imagined society was a utopia. It was too perfect to happen, and the belief in its practicality has created the social equivalent of the mechanical bunny—something constantly chased and never caught.[1]

A growing unease compounds this disappointment as wages fluctuate more than they used to, employees have more part-time jobs than before, employers are more willing to lay employees off when times are tough and as more work is contracted out. It's taken about 50 years for voters to discover that big government may actually harm more than it helps. The ultimate expression of that disaffection was the collapse of communism. But nearly all democracies now face their own less dramatic but insidiously significant versions of the fall of the Berlin Wall.

The one policy that affects people for the longest period and costs the most is the retirement income policy. So that's the one that faces the greatest fiscal pressure.

The Certainties of Demography

There is at least one certainty that helps in the development of a retirement income policy. Once people are born, everyone knows roughly when they're going to retire. We also have plenty of notice—60 to 70 years. Once people are born, they're on the road to retirement.

In days gone by, the demographic picture of the populations of developed countries had a classic pyramid shape, with a large young population supporting a relatively small old population. In all developed countries, the pyramid is developing more precipitous sides as the numbers become more even in each age group. The rate of change and its extent varies by country but there's a similar pattern throughout the developed world. For example, in the US, the population of over 65s doubled every 30 years from 1900 to 1990. Despite this, population growth kept the proportion of over 65s manageable. Now, a much reduced growth in the total population means that doubling the over 65s again over the 35 years from 1990 to 2025 changes the picture for the future.[2]

This change worsens an already growing problem faced by the richer countries. As they grow richer, voters tend to demand more of their political leaders. They want more (and more expensive) health care, more expensive education and better pensions.

The state provides most of these services in most developed countries. Richard Darman, head of former US president George Bush's Office of Management and Budget, described this as 'the ultimate Cookie Monster... Its motivation is clearly not malevolent... What harm it may do is largely unintended.'[3] That doesn't, however, change its cost.

---

[1] *The Good Life and its Discontents*, Times Books, 1995.

[2] Longino, C.F., 'The Myths of an Aging America', *American Demographics*, August 1994.

[3] Quoted by Barr, N., in, *The Economics of the Welfare State*, Stanford University Press, 1993.

A Potential Political Nightmare

Politicians now face a real problem. Around the developed world, it's clear that they find it very difficult to face up to voters with this problem. A 1995 report of a select committee of the UK's House of Commons agreed that something had to be done about welfare spending in general and that the 'something' had to be radical. In the UK, the cost of the welfare state grew from about six per cent of national income in 1920 to 10 per cent in 1948 and on up to about 24 per cent in 1992, with 'social security' itself running at 12.6 per cent.[1]

Retirement pensions are a big and increasing part of the problem.

In Italy, the need for change has been apparent for nearly 20 years but the highly charged nature of the debate on the subject has obstructed change. A December 1994 demonstration in Rome on the reform of social security attracted more than one million participants. Those who wanted the *status quo* found themselves defending a system that had allowed the income replacement ratio to rise to 80 per cent of a retiree's average revalued earnings in the last five years after a full career.[2] The pension started at age 60 for men and 55 for women. A package of changes introduced in 1995 has started to chip away at these generous arrangements, and more will be required.

Politicians around the world are responding to the retirement income issue in similar ways. Reform is piecemeal and inconsistent. Stealth rather than open discussion marks 'progress' today. The tools of change are now income or asset tests, longer qualification periods, longer averaging periods for pay-related benefits, and higher contributions or taxes or both (since social security contributions don't seem like taxes). However, in 1990, the French government collected 44 per cent of its total revenues from the payroll taxes used to finance social security. The equivalent German figure was 36 per cent.[3]

Germany illustrates the new process. Changes to the social security system in the 1990s included changing the benefit base from gross earnings to net, increasing the retirement age, limiting the periods that can count without contributions and reducing government subsidies. Despite all this, the Bundesbank still thinks that more change is imperative because the present 19.2 per cent of covered earnings now required for retirement pension contributions will still rise to 21 per cent or 22 per cent by 2010, and on up to 27 per cent by 2030.[4] In pension planning terms, that's just around the corner. And even though there is a large 1997 deficit expected in the social security system, Germans seem unconcerned: 'There are problems, but the existing system still has the overwhelming support of the German people' according to Peter Blank, head of planning at the Department of Health and Social Affairs in Berlin.[5]

---

[1]   *The Financial Times*, 24 January 1996.

[2]   Lower proportions accrued on pay above the 'INPS salary ceiling' of $37,800 a year.

[3]   From *Oxford Analytica*, 2 August 1996.

[4]   Reported in the *IBIS Review*, September 1995.

[5]   Reported in *The Financial Times*, 24 April 1996.

He did have the grace to go on: 'I don't know exactly how they will do it, but the state is obliged to find a solution'.

However, whether the Germans like their system or not, it's unsustainable, and more change is inevitable. The only issues that must be resolved are how and when.

Stealth and inconsistent changes in the rules that govern retirement incomes tend to dilute trust. In that regard, it seems difficult to support *The Financial Times* in an editorial[1] that praised the 'commendably incremental approach' of the then Social Security Secretary, Peter Lilley. While such an approach may work for immediate benefits like those for the unemployed or lone parents, it's a disaster for retirement benefits. That much was virtually acknowledged by the same journal in an editorial only a week later when it said that: 'It is important that people are given the chance to plan properly for retirement'. Retirement income policies have to operate over very long periods so trust is an important part of the policies' 'glue'.

All over the developed world, substantial change is imperative:

- **Austria:** State pensions already cost nearly 15 per cent of GDP.[2]

- **France:** The OECD predicts that pension spending will see government debt rise from 40 per cent of GDP in 2000 to between 90 and 105 per cent in 2030. There seems no immediate prospect of the state pension age increasing from its present 60 for both men and women.[3]

- **Italy:** Despite a crisis that included a public sector deficit of 14 per cent of GDP, Italy's 1995 reforms won't take full effect until 2030, and that won't stop the deficit increasing in the meantime. There is one thing of which Italians can be absolutely confident—the 1995 reforms won't suffice until 2030. Further changes will be needed long before then.

- **Japan:** The Japanese face an increase in their pension contributions from today's 16.5 per cent of pay to around 35 per cent by 2025, by which time Japan will have a higher proportion of elderly people than any other developed country.[4] The OECD says that rising pension spending could lift Japan's deficit from its present 3.5 per cent of GDP to 20 per cent by 2030. Italy's deficit, by contrast, will be 'only' 12 per cent. The only alternative is a reduction in benefits, but there is no serious present discussion of that.

- **US:** The present surplus in the Social Security 'Fund' will disappear by 2013 and retirement pensions will have to be cut by a third by 2022 if the 'Fund' is simply to stay out of debt. The 75 year 'solution' to Social Security funding, agreed in 1983 will be run off its legs after only 30 years.

In a democracy, an elected government can't really be expected to make enormously unpopular moves on its own. The International Labour Office is

---

[1]   12 September 1995.

[2]   By contrast, it's only 6.5 per cent in the US. New Zealand's state scheme costs 5.7 per cent and is expected to fall to 4.5 per cent by 2001 when the state pension age reaches 65.

[3]   *The Financial Times*, 6 October 1995.

[4]   *The Economist*, 3 August 1996.

similarly constrained, which is probably why it also endorsed the incremental approach in a 1995 report.[1] Even the ILO can't really criticise the governments on which it depends.

Change, even if it is incremental, should get voters to think and talk about the issues. The US Social Security's old age pension system will need reform. But in all the talk about the debilitating effects of big government and the cries for 'welfare that works', the comparative silence on serious cuts to both Social Security and Medicare (universal health cover for the old) has been striking :

> The fundamental problem in American politics is that the most costly of welfare programs are not regarded as 'welfare' by the American voter... Public choice theory tells us that nothing much will change here. Just as thieves rob banks because that is where the money is, politicians appeal to the middle classes because that is where the votes are.[2]

This also explains why the public broadly supports the welfare state and favours higher taxes to 'improve' social services. A UK survey[3] found that 58 per cent of the public think taxes should be raised as long as they pay for health, education and social benefits, and 33 per cent thought the current level should be maintained. Only four per cent thought that welfare cuts should be used to reduce taxes.

So, tinkering and piecemeal reform is much more appealing than directly confronting the issues. While there may be an increasing distrust of politicians, voters still expect their own economic bailiwicks to be defended. However, the demographic imperative means that politicians won't be able to keep their heads in the fiscal sand too much longer.

> For the near future, then, discretion will continue to be the better part of policy. In the more successful countries, the costs of the welfare state will be kept down. But it is hard to see how a welfare system suited to the next century can be created with its current incarnation.[4]

Private Provision to the Rescue?

With governments failing to come to grips with the problems of sustaining public provision, it's difficult to see how they could do better on private provision. And they haven't. Chapters 4 and 5 look at the two methods governments often use to encourage or require their citizens to behave 'sensibly' (tax incentives and compulsion).

Governments are (or should be) interested in whether or not their citizens save for retirement. Democracy, demography and the welfare state will see to that because if people don't save, our modern tax-derived system of income distribution may not cope. All developed countries are ageing at various rates and no democratic state that calls itself civilised can contemplate widespread

---

[1]   'Report of the Director General', 5th ILO European Regional Conference, September 1995.

[2]   Barry, N., 'The Conservative Revival in America', *Agenda*, Vol. 2, No. 3, 1995.

[3]   Cited in *The Financial Times*, 23 November 1995.

[4]   *The Economist*, 26 August 1995.

poverty among elderly voters. There will be so many of them and they will each have a vote.

In every developed country, something has to be done—the question is 'What?' Before looking at the main options, it's as well to look at some principles on which a government might build its policies.

3

First Principles

Summary

How do governments develop a sustainable retirement income policy?

In terms of the shape of policy, there are three philosophies behind the ways in which governments manage society: 'command and control', market-based incentives and the free market. As far as retirement income policy is concerned, governments around the developed world employ the first two methods, but none go as far as to rely on the free market.

Governments are also interested in the mix between the two extremes of retirement income delivery: from wholly private provision at one extreme through to wholly public on the other.

Retirement income comes from two main sources: today's resources—collected and delivered today, and private savings, i.e. yesterday's stored-up financial assets. Governments should link these two sources to ensure that the system works. Underlying these considerations is the debate about which comes first—savings or growth, and the absence of satisfying information to answer this question.

If a retirement income policy were to be developed from scratch, what are the options? This gives rise to a 'first principles' approach based on the three-pillar structure outlined in chapter 2 (p. 11) and translates into a three-tiered hierarchy: Tier I being the state welfare or safety net; Tier II, employment-related schemes; and Tier III private savings. There are strong links between these three tiers which vary as employment relationships and demographics change.

Governments have a crucial role in deciding what the state should do in terms of providing a safety net. Other roles for the government include getting the economy right, information and education, achieving consensus and, within the concept of 'generational accounting', ensuring that the burden of the policy strategy falls equitably.

Governments also have an interest in delivering more than the minimum in Tiers II and III, and modifying behaviour in these areas through 'bribing' (i.e. tax incentives), 'bludgeoning' (i.e. compulsion) and laissez faire (i.e. voluntary saving).

****

The Income Support 'Cake'

This book is about retirement incomes which is a big enough subject on its own. However, the incomes received by old people are only part of the range of issues that should make up a coherent, sustainable policy of support for those who have reached the end of their working lives. Financial support in retirement is really one large topic that touches a number of different bases. *State age-based benefits*—for example, Social Security in the US, National Insurance in the UK and New Zealand Superannuation in my part of the world.

State 'welfare' benefits—for example, special-needs grants, food stamps and other direct transfers to the really needy. They usually exclude income 'entitlements'.

Occupational retirement scheme benefits—incomes and lump sums from employment-related schemes.

Other private savings—such as shares, government bonds, real estate and bank deposits.

Housing provision—which might involve state-provided subsidies such as cheap rentals, rates relief and tax deductible mortgage interest. From a private perspective, it also includes trading down the home to one more suited to retirement needs.

Health services—the retired population is clearly a big user of the health system, and someone has to pay for it. It isn't usually the old.

Subsidised public services—such as bus fares, television licence fees and telephone rentals. In Australia, for example, the Pensioner Concession Card, that provides discounted travel and medicines, is worth $1,330 a year to the average user.[1]

Advance private provision—for retirement consumption, for example, replacing household appliances before retirement or saving for the retirement trip. This last is a significant part of New Zealand culture.

The whole goes to make up a complex, inter-connected structure in which change to one part tends, over a period, to produce a compensatory change in another part. I think that's because, in the more developed countries which are my focus, society has an intuitive notion of what, on the whole, constitutes 'fair' treatment of the old.

Whatever the reason, this natural tendency will make the size of the income support 'cake' for a given retired population in a community relatively constant. However, as policy on the individual elements changes, the sizes of the individual slices also change. And, as the size of the retired population changes, there is a natural pressure for the size of the cake to change.

So, reducing the state's age benefit is likely to produce a countervailing pressure on one or more of the other parts of the structure. Some of the pressure points will also be state-funded so that the taxpayers' initial 'savings' will be illusory in the long run.

The Three Big Ones

The three biggest retirement issues for governments are housing, health and income. I will only look at the last of these, though the other two are very important if a government's retirement policies are to work over the long term.

For example, the retired can more easily provide for themselves (and a government can more easily deliver a reasonable standard of living in retirement) if people usually retire with a mortgage-free home.[2]

---

[1] Reported in *The Australian Financial Review*, 3 November 1995.

[2] This book is not the place to discuss ways in which governments might get involved in housing issues though housing is a vital topic—some commentators now see housing ownership in general (not state housing provision or subsidies in particular) as a major component in the

Similarly, the retired don't need to save as much for retirement income if the state delivers a 'free' health system. Nothing, of course is 'free' if the government is expected to pay for it because the 'government' is a synonym for 'all us taxpayers', including the retired.

Housing and health are both vital retirement issues, but how a government might develop a sustainable retirement income policy is quite enough to deal with in one sitting.

Three Philosophies of Government

According to Michael Kellogg,[1] a Washington lawyer, there are three ways in which a government might manage individual aspects of a modern society:

Command and control: regulators write and enforce rules and standards.

As a philosophy of government, 'command and control' suffers from a number of disadvantages. It tends to be slow because it relies on a single bureaucracy to learn and understand everything there is to know about a problem and then to prescribe a solution.

It also tends to be adversarial and the rules imposed tend to be inefficient and expensive because everyone, despite different needs, has to behave in the same way.

Market-based incentives: the government shapes policy but uses market incentives to implement it.

According to Kellogg, 'the idea, in short, is to let government steer and the market row'.

Free market: market forces act without government intervention and people are left to pay for their own mistakes.

And so it is for retirement incomes.

Different governments around the world use two of Kellogg's three philosophies to develop retirement income policies. Most adopt shades of the 'command and control' method though some stray into aspects of 'market incentives'. None is brave (or rash) enough to use just the 'free market'. Hong Kong came closest but is buckling in the face of the uncertainties it faces with China's resumed control.

Expressions of Interest

For the reasons discussed in chapter 2 all developed governments have a view on the way in which their retired are or should be treated financially. Governments express those views through the way they treat institutional

---

sustainability of state-provided income benefits for the old. Among 13 developed countries, where home ownership rates are high, the earning replacement level (social transfers relative to the average earnings of males aged 25-54) of old age pensions tends to be low and vice versa. High home ownership among the retired also means higher inheritances go to the next generation to help pay for their own retirement incomes; and so the links go on. Castles, F. and Mitchell, D., cited in Castles and Ferrera, 'Home Ownership and the Welfare State: Is Southern Europe Different?', *Southern European Society and Politics*, 1996.

[1] In the Cato Institute's quarterly magazine *Regulation*, No. 1, 1994.

forms of benefit provision. Welfare, 'social security' and group saving instruments of various kinds are the most powerful vehicles for that expression.

Retirement incomes are delivered through a spectrum that stretches from the wholly private vehicles at one end to the wholly public at the other end. There will always be some who, for whatever reason, are unable to save. For them, wholly public provision is inevitable. However the way in which the 'public' delivers that provision is not.

At the other end of the spectrum is a group that can be self-sufficient and 'needs' no support from the public.

There's a point between these two extremes when wholly public provision of retirement incomes starts to have elements of private provision in the mix. That mix will include more and more private provision as it moves towards the other end of the spectrum.

Governments should express their interest by agreeing on the shape of the extremes and then discuss where the transition from public to private begins and how it moves from one to the other. Not many developed countries do that at the private end of the spectrum—almost all of them deliver some public provision even if the retiree doesn't, on any reasonable measure, 'need' it.

The Spectrum from Wholly Private to Wholly Public

Most discussions on retirement income policy assume that 'public provision' is about welfare or 'social security' (which, in the US, doesn't seem to count as welfare) while 'private provision' includes everything the individual or the employer does. It's not as simple as that.

As Susan St John and Toni Ashton have pointed out,[1] most governments are almost as much involved in private provision as they are in public provision. Tax incentives for private savings are the most common thread amongst the policies of developed countries, but there are other, more subtle, forms of intervention. The state puts money into retirement incomes in a variety of ways.

St John and Ashton described the spectrum in a nine step progression from private to public (the comments and examples that follow are mostly mine).

1 Private voluntary savings—all countries use private voluntary savings for Pillar III (private individual savings—see chapter 2 from p. 11 for an explanation of the three 'Pillars'). New Zealand also uses them for Pillar II (employment-based arrangements). New Zealand is alone in that regard among developed countries.

2 Private, tax-encouraged savings—all developed countries except New Zealand encourage private savings for Pillar II with tax incentives.[2] Some developed countries use also them for Pillar III (IRAs, AVCs, RRSPs, TESSAs and so on).

---

[1]   *Private Pensions in New Zealand : Can they Avert the Crisis?*, Institute of Policy Studies, 1983, starting from p.105.

[2]   For example, the cost of tax incentives for retirement savings in Australia is about half the cost of the age pension—based on Australian 1997-98 Budget information and cited in the New Zealand Periodic Report Group's July 1997 Interim Report, p. 103.

3 Compulsory, private savings—in Chile, private savings are run by private, heavily-regulated, institutions. Even here, there can be state involvement if those private savings have an underwrite in the form of minimum welfare benefits (as is the case in Chile—see item 9 below).

4 Compulsory, state savings scheme—for example, Singapore and a number of South East Asian and Pacific states. The usually single, central scheme is run by the state.

5 Social insurance—this mimics private insurance but it is generally designed to achieve specific social goals. Citizens' 'premiums' go straight to the already retired. There may be a 'fund' (such as for the OASDI in the US) but the pensions are not pre-funded to the extent that today's contributors are paying for their own benefits.

6 Pensions from earmarked taxes—this identifies, in an accounting sense, that a piece of the ordinary income tax goes to meet the cost of pensions for the currently retired. New Zealand tried it briefly in 1989-90. Linking part of tax payments to the current cost of retirement pensions attempted to create some linkage between taxes ('contributions') and benefits. The trouble is that a lot of people get the pension but don't pay taxes. That artifice died in 1990.

7 Non-contributory, tax-funded, *flat-rate* pensions—money disappears as the link between contributions and benefits, and is replaced by some version of the 'social contract'. Denmark's 'FP' benefit is an example; New Zealand also had this before 1984 when an income test was introduced.

8 Non-contributory, tax-funded, flat-rate, *income-tested* pensions—as for 7 but now the benefits are reduced if the recipient has other income (Canada and New Zealand) or income *or* assets over a particular level (Australia). New Zealand's income test disappeared in 1998 when New Zealand Superannuation moved back up to Category 7.

9 Welfare benefits—delivered by the state on the basis of some measure of poverty. Several countries (such as the US, the UK and New Zealand) have income and/or asset-tested supplements to basic entitlements.

As St John and Ashton pointed out, only item 1 (private voluntary savings) can be called completely 'private'. Even here, though, there are regulatory requirements (such as securities legislation or accounting standards), where the state has a role and a consequent cost to taxpayers, and, presumably, a benefit for savers, though some may argue with that.

> But it should be clear that state intervention cannot be captured by a single measure. Expenditure, regulatory control, compulsion, implicit guarantees and the provision of tax incentives are not easily aggregated but should be seen as different dimensions to the complex issue of assessing the state's role.[1]

Different countries use different mixes of various elements of the spectrum. Table 2 (drawn from St John and Ashton) shows a summary of the way that a range of countries create their versions of the mix:

---

[1]   St John and Ashton, *op. cit.*, p.108.

Table 2
Spectrum of Private and Public Provision of Retirement Income

Country	UK	US	Australia	New Zealand	France	Germany
1 Private savings	✔	✔	✔	✔	✔	✔
2 Tax favoured private	✔	✔	✔		✔	✔
3 Compulsory private			✔			
4 Compulsory state						
5 Social insurance	✔	✔			✔	✔
6 Earmarked taxes						
7 Flat rate universal				✔		
8 Flat rate income test			✔			
9 Welfare benefits	✔	✔		✔		

Source: after St. John, S. and Ashton, T.

Where Does Retirement Income Come From?

Retirement income has two main sources: the government through transfer payments—a 'today' resource—collected and delivered today; and private savings through stored-up financial assets, also called 'claims'. These are yesterday's potential consumption stored up until today.

I have left out the expenses avoided by retirees by, for example, having a mortgage-free home or a new (and less costly) car or home appliances. These have an opportunity cost in economic terms but would not be seen as 'negative expenses' by retirees. I have also disregarded the financial savings that retirees achieve from government-provided health care or housing.

The nine alternatives described by St John and Ashton offer various shades of state involvement in these two main themes.

Each supplier of each part of the retirement income 'service' (from the government through the private saving institution to the individual paying off a house mortgage) has a different motive for its involvement. The question that society must resolve is whether all of those motives allow the community to deliver an 'acceptable' standard of living to those who are no longer participating in paid employment, but who are drawing either on their own stored-up resources or society's income. How should they be linked, how monitored and how can we make sure that the whole thing actually works?

This shouldn't be a debate about increasing the amount the country as a whole saves.[1] While the amount the country as a whole saves is an important issue, it's a distraction to decisions on a workable and consistent retirement income policy.

---

[1] The Mexican government has introduced compulsory private provision that is supposed to lift personal savings from about 16 per cent in 1994 to 24 per cent by 2000, reported in *Business Week*, 20 November 1995.

Economists have long debated the apparent link between low levels of personal saving and high social security benefits. The vaunted thrift of some Asian nations could be linked to a low level of state-provided benefits. However, that does depend a bit on how you define 'private'—Singapore's compulsory Central Provident Fund or the equivalent in Malaysia may be called 'private' by economists, but who makes the rules? They don't look very private or personal, especially if most of the money is borrowed by the government, as happens in both those cases.

Private savings won't work unless there is a successful economy somewhere (not necessarily where the savings are made) that delivers a good return on those savings to justify their existence. Successful economies depend at least in part on someone's savings, whether the government's, the corporate sector's, households' or other countries' savings, and on how well they are invested.

More private saving for retirement may mean more savings overall. They could, however, simply mean lower savings elsewhere, like in the government sector if expensive tax incentives are used to encourage those savings. More saving may also lead to more and better investment, though it need not, as New Zealand demonstrated in the 1980s.

However, there is considerable debate about these issues in economic circles—which comes first, savings or growth? Does a higher rate of saving lead to growth or does growth allow a higher saving rate? The traditional definitions of 'saving' in each of the three major sectors (government, corporate and private) seem so unsatisfactory that I think we need to change the way we look at them. An individual's ability to be financially independent in retirement depends not on the sum of each year's 'saving' (as defined by economists) but on the individual's wealth at and in retirement.

It's impossible even to begin to answer the question of measuring saving unless the nation has access to proper studies of national wealth. There's no point in measuring flows without also working out where everything ends up.

The questions about saving, investment and growth and their relationship can't be answered because the information on which they are based is so unsatisfactory. But anyway, does it matter? The current view of economists seems to be that savings and investment tend to follow, not precede growth.

A country's attitude to saving and the development of its retirement income policies should be treated as two separate issues though they are often linked by populist politicians—'we've got to do something (anything!) about the bad saving habits of our citizens—don't you worry about the economy, leave that to us.'

In particular, encouraging or requiring private provision for retirement should not be seen as a way of fixing a country's poor saving record, at least, not in a 'command and control' mode. Chile illustrates this point—a study[1] showed that the Chilean compulsory scheme contributed to dissaving (measured in the traditional way) for the first seven years of its life.

Retirement income policies won't fix the country's housing or health problems either; all these should be designed in their own right. These various elements are all related to the extent that they are all important to retired people. And changes in one might provoke change in another.

---

[1]   Holzmann, R., 'Pension Reform, Financial Market Development, and Economic Growth: Preliminary Evidence from Chile', IMF Working Paper, August 1996.

Having said that, economics have a lot to do with the long-run picture. People need income to live on and a place to live in and that all costs money. If the retired are no longer helping to produce society's wealth and are now starting to spend it, the money has to come from stored-up resources, from other producers of wealth (like those citizens who are still in work and producing) or from savers in other countries, though that can't go on for ever.

The stored-up resources of the currently retired are things like shares, deposits, bonds and investment properties.[1] The income they deliver to the retired owner comes from the economies in which they are invested—either domestic or overseas. Unless those economies can use those resources and give a good return to the savers who invest in them, private saving won't actually achieve much. They may, as has been the case in New Zealand, act as a vehicle for passing wealth from savers (who include the retired) to earners through inflation. That's one effect of a combination of inflation, pay increases that match or beat inflation and negative real returns on investments.

Despite what some proponents of tax incentives or compulsion might have us believe, more saving doesn't let you move responsibility for pensions from one period to another—from this generation of workers to the next of retirees. What is a stored-up resource for one person is a potential source of capital for another, but still in today's economy—not tomorrow's. Saving won't work unless investment does—today's economies have to be successful for that, not tomorrow's.

In most developed countries, the money that the retired spend comes largely from the rest of society in the form of income transfers through one form of tax or another. Relatively little comes from the previous, or even present, savings of the retired themselves.[2] In most countries, the state is the dominant provider of retirement income.

So it's important that the producers of wealth (generally, that's taxpayers) can afford those transfers *and* feel happy about them, otherwise that part of the retirement income policy will keep changing.

The state is dependent on a strong economy for its own income and to keep its expenses down on things like unemployment benefits and disability benefits. They tend to increase in incidence and cost at times of economic pressure. The retired are also dependent on that same economy to protect the income they get from the state.

So, from the economy's overall perspective, it doesn't really matter whether the retired get their spending money directly from the state or from their own resources. In the end, it all ultimately comes from the same place. That's not to say, however, that the income's immediate source and the mix between public and private are unimportant. They are important and that's one of the reasons for this book.

---

[1]   They also include the houses the retired live in and the home appliances and motor vehicles they use in retirement. Some countries count the money spent on these last as 'saving', though I would regard them as more like extended consumption.

[2]   The position in the US is a little different from most—of 9.5 million couples and 14 million singles age 65 and over, 40% of income comes from Social Security, 21% from asset income, 20% from private pensions, and 17% from earnings. Cited in 'The Road to Retirement', Compensation & Benefits Review Special Report, 1996, data from US government sources.

People often justify the complex structures (and expense) of tax incentives and compulsory saving schemes by saying that they encourage private provision. The next two chapters spend some time on these ideas.

Decision Strategy

Retirement income policies are complex and touch a number of different aspects of our developed societies. One of the dangers of dealing with any complex issue is that we tend to be captured by its current complexities. Dealing with those on a piecemeal basis tends to become fire-fighting rather than a 'first principles' process. The history of change around the world shows that very few countries have asked themselves some basic questions about the respective roles of the major players.

For the moment, let's ignore what we do now and ask the question: if we had no state or private provision for retirement income (and, by implication, no currently-retired citizens) what would we want to do?

What are the respective roles of the state (that's all us taxpayers), employers, employees, the self-employed, all other citizens, the financial institutions and anyone else who can contribute to people making appropriate decisions about their financial futures? Again, let's leave out of the discussion the currently retired and those who are so close to retirement that they don't really have much of a chance to do anything about their financial position. They will have a part to play in the debate (apart from anything else, most of them will be taxpayers and voters) but not just at the moment. They are too close to the subject.

Once we have decided on a 'cleared decks' strategy, we can then turn our attention to issues of the transition—how do we get from here to the ideal retirement incomes regime? First, a word about the roles of the main players.

The Retirement Income Hierarchy

There's an established hierarchy that should drive how people behave in making decisions about their own retirement income needs:

Tier I:[1] The role of the state ('Pillar I')

No-one (employers, employees or other individuals) can make any decision about their long-term needs until they know, or can make a reasonable guess, about what will emerge from the state.

---

[1] I think that it's more useful to talk about 'tiers' rather than the traditional 'pillars'. A 'tier' fits the concept of an hierarchical decision rather than a 'pillar' (the concept of which originated in Switzerland where contributions to each of the three 'pillars' were, in 1992, approximately equal). The decisions about the shape of Tiers II and III should follow the pattern established at Tier I. The 'three-legged' stool is another often used but less than useful analogy. It also implies that each of the legs should be about the same length or of the same importance. You'll see I don't agree with that.

Planning for retirement income is a long-run process, so savers won't welcome constant change and, therefore, uncertainty, about what the state might deliver to them when they reach retirement. Constant change stops savers placing a realistic value on this first layer in the hierarchy. It may even encourage savers to discount the value of the state's potential contribution altogether. That's economically inefficient and could lead to intergenerational conflict. Worse, it could lead to a development of the 'possum in the headlights' syndrome[1] where, despite compelling imperatives, people refuse to do anything.

One of the most important objectives in settling the future of a country's overall strategy should be to allow employers and employees to place an accurate value on the role that state provision will play in citizens' total retirement incomes. That assessment will then help them to make sensible decisions about the second and third tiers of the hierarchy. That's why the reform of the state system by stealth (seemingly the most popular technique in developed countries) is a risky strategy. If the state wants to back out of Tier I, it can achieve its objectives only by encouraging provision at Tiers II and III. How can people respond 'sensibly' at Tiers II and III if they don't have a clear idea of Tier I's future? For that, we need more honesty from our leaders—a scarce commodity in retirement income policies.

Tier II: Employment-related retirement benefits ('Pillar II')

Most citizens are employed at some or even most stages in their productive lives, so employer-sponsored retirement schemes represent the next most powerful layer in the hierarchy.

An employer has a closer financial relationship with an employee than anyone else and the state should consciously capitalise on that relationship. In many, mainly European, countries the state does much more than that—it gets involved in the design, administration, financing and delivery of Tier II as well as Tier I—France and Denmark are two examples.

Tier III: Private savings ('Pillar III')

Once savers know what the first and second layers of the retirement income hierarchy will produce, they can then make sensible, informed decisions about the third layer. Private savings can take a number of forms, for example:

- direct personal retirement provision
- paying off a mortgage on the home
- private investments (shares, property, etc), and
- reducing post-retirement financial commitments.

The three layers of the hierarchy are inter-connected and the mix will change as public and private policies and behaviour change. The whole

---

[1]   The possum is an imported pest in New Zealand. When caught in the headlights of an on-coming car, it's mesmerised before it's flattened. It doesn't get much chance to practise getting out of the way. Most savers first face up to the implications of their saving habits on the relative eve of their retirement.

hierarchy is fluid and inter-dependent. Its respective components and their contributions to the whole will change as the economy contracts and expands, as employment relationships change and as the demographic make-up of the country changes.

This probably explains the diverging conclusions that academics have reached on the relationship between public and private spending on pensions. Some argue that reducing public spending isn't compensated by extra private spending but just increases the retiree's economic insecurity. Others say public and private spending are negatively correlated. Both could be right—these views have been developed in the context of much change and uncertainty and only provide a helicopter view of a country's habits. I'm suggesting that we should concentrate on what should be an individual saver's logical approach to the retirement saving decision—the 'ground zero' view.

The response of individuals to changes in economic and political conditions should be hierarchical, but pressures on any individual layer are likely to create reactive change in the layer above *or* below the one directly affected. So, removing or reducing tax incentives for Tier III will increase the pressure on employers at Tier II and on the state at Tier I. The reduction or withdrawal of the employers' role at Tier II will have knock-on effects at both Tiers I and III. Signals embedded in the design of Tier I have a powerful effect on employment patterns and, eventually, on the sustainability of Tier I itself.[1]

The New Zealand Hierarchy - to 1987

In New Zealand, the 50 years to 1987 saw a reasonably logical retirement income hierarchy develop. The broad 'bargain' saw the state's first encouraging the purchase of a home which should be paid off by retirement age. By retirement age, about 84 per cent of New Zealanders live in their own homes with about 74 per cent having paid off their mortgage. This policy is helped by the absence of capital gains tax on the sale of a home and by its exclusion from now abolished death duties. New Zealand has never given tax relief on mortgage interest.

Governments then effectively discouraged the accumulation of private saving for cash income by the provision of a reasonable, but not generous, indexed pension paid out of general tax receipts. High rates of inflation and low or even negative net real rates of return on savings put off all but the most determined saver. Only the better-off, who needed additional retirement income, tended to make use of tax-favoured retirement schemes. The health system was largely 'free'.

Though each element of this structure could be criticised, the whole presented a reasonably coherent, though intuitive answer to the retirement income issue—as long as we were content with a closed economy.

During a long period of relative economic prosperity, the old hierarchy served New Zealanders well. However, governments of the last 50 years had

---

[1]   In *Passing the Torch* by Quinn, Burkhayser and Myers 1990, W.E. Upjohn Institute, the authors argue, after reviewing the literature, that retirement patterns can be explained by the financial incentives 'embedded' in the US Social Security system. It seems that people respond rationally in the US to the signals they are given by the state and by their employers.

unwittingly painted New Zealand into a policy corner, one that gave governments of the 1980s and early 1990s few choices in our recently acquired policy of fiscal honesty.

Kellogg's Three Philosophies[1]

As must be obvious by now, the main problem faced on the retirement income issue is that ultimately it has to be resolved by politicians. The temptation to bend policies to current exigencies is enormous. The time horizons of successful politicians and successful retirement income policies are like oil and water. Also, large amounts of money sit around in private saving schemes; and money is the thing most governments in most developed countries need but don't have.

So how do the state's retirement income policy options fit with the three philosophies of government described by Kellogg?

Command and Control

Governments favouring the 'command and control' philosophy need regulators who write and enforce rules and standards. In a retirement saving context, they can't let people do the things they want. The regulators know what's best. This means preventing citizens from doing things that come naturally to them and requiring them to do things they would prefer not to, because it's in their own best interests.

As a retirement income policy, 'command and control' has been the prevailing fashion in Europe for many years where the state has tended to sideline private provision at Tiers II and III to the edges of public policy. Unfunded state schemes are the dominant influence in most of continental Europe. This is evident from the statistics on the amounts different countries have in funded schemes at Tiers II and III. The pension scheme assets (mainly Tier II arrangements) in Belgium, France and Portugal are all less than 10 per cent of one year's GDP. All of them have much central planning through generous state schemes. The pension assets of The Netherlands (equivalent to 124 per cent of GDP) and the UK (76 per cent of GDP) both reflect their relatively less centralised retirement income planning.[2]

The modern incarnation of state intervention, the compulsory *funded* scheme, is attracting a lot of interest and even some activity.

If a government wants to make sure all its citizens have at least something to live on in retirement (the welfare 'safety net'), it really has no choice —'command and control' is the only realistic option for Tier I. However, the issues for Tiers II and III are rather different.

Free Market

As the foundation of a government's retirement income policy, 'free market' forces would see the government standing to one side for Tiers I, II and III. There would be no safety net—no Tier I. Everyone would have responsibility for their own retirement needs. But such a pure approach won't work in the long run. That's because of the democratic dimension.

---

[1]   See p. 27.

[2]   NRJ Research cited in *Marathon London's Investment Review*, 30 September 1995.

Each person's vote is worth as much to the political process as anyone else's, regardless of their age. By the time retirees find out the consequences of the free market on their own retirement incomes (meaning they don't have enough), it will be too late for them to do anything about it. However, it won't be too late for them to punish their political leaders through the ballot box. It's human nature to pin the blame on someone else when some part of your life is out of control—'it's not my fault'.

Market-based Incentives

The concept of market-based incentives, on the other hand, does seem to have potential for the development of a government's retirement income policies.

The market-based incentives concept sees the government's role as shaping policy but then using the incentives to implement it. The government 'steers but the market rows'. The long-run nature of a government's policies in this area makes it quite difficult to see where the policy boat is headed from any point along the way. It's even quite difficult to tell whether they've worked once people make it to retirement.

The government must have a clear, and clearly sustainable, set of objectives —that's the responsibility of the central authority. And those objectives must be communicated in a way that lets people see their relevance and their place in the individual's own personal financial plans. That's where the regulators meet the savers face to face.

Market-based incentives are a mixture of scene setting (the government's responsibility), minimum standards (another role for the regulators), communication (a two-way process) and action.

A modern democratic government cannot abandon its overall responsibility to alleviate poverty among its citizens, including the old. That should form the foundation of all the government's retirement income policy initiatives. That's why I'm an advocate of the 'tax transfer' school of state-provided retirement incomes.[1] The current capacity of a government to deal with the income needs of the poor depends on the current capacity of the government to raise revenue.

The safety net at Tier I mustn't get in the way of Tiers II and III, so great care should be taken in its design. Chapter 6 provides a suggested shape of that minimum provision.

In all of this, governments must try to shape policy over long periods from a point in time at which, by definition, there is much uncertainty. Even if a government can't be certain about a specific future, the framework it creates must be stable. To do that, a government must take its citizens along with it.

The First Decision

The first, biggest and most difficult question of all to answer is what the state should do for all its citizens, regardless of the reason for their financial

---

[1] The three schools were explained by Thompson, L.H., in 'The Social Security Debate', *Journal of Economic Literature*, Vol. XXI, December 1983. The other two schools are the insurance model (where the risk of losing income for any reason, including retirement, is shared among all workers) and the annuity-welfare model (where there are two elements, part social adequacy and part individual equity).

dependency—ill health, unemployment, permanent disability or 'retirement'. The answer to this 'big one' establishes a floor or safety net that applies to everyone, including the old. As *The Financial Times* put it, 'First, social security is about mitigating social distress'.[1]

Most state systems then go further for the old. This raises three basic questions:

- Should age on its own be sufficient to qualify for any benefit? All developed countries say 'yes'.
- Should the benefit paid to the old be different in principle from the benefit paid in other circumstances? Again, developed countries tend to say 'yes' and pay more to the old than they do to others.
- Should the benefit be paid to all the people who qualify, regardless of their other income or assets? Again, in developed countries, the answer is usually 'yes'.

There is no reason why this should be so, but these answers will be a powerful influence on everyone's behaviour as *homo economicus* reacts to the state's signals.

Once 'society' has decided on the minimum acceptable standard of living for the old, there are two crucial, further decisions for policy makers:

- Should the minimum be delivered by the state, privately or by a mix of both?

- Does the state have a role in the delivery of anything over the minimum?

In nearly all countries, the state dominates the provision of the minimum and also plays a large part in the delivery of incomes above that minimum.

The Retirees' Share of the Economy's Cake

The annual Tier I pension in any year for an individual pensioner has been, is and will continue to be the total figure that taxpayers as a whole are prepared to pay in that year divided by the number of pensioners eligible in that year to receive it.

The only issues that then remain to be resolved are:

- the size of the overall cake—how many dollars?

- the eligibility conditions—who's entitled to get it?

- the slope of its distribution—is it universal or will it be weighted to the lower-paid, either directly or indirectly, through income- or asset-testing?

From the country's perspective (at the macro level) it doesn't really matter what the rules are on the way that the agreed slice of the economic cake is shared out among all those who are entitled to receive a benefit. In New Zealand there are no rules about a minimum number of years a person has to work and pay taxes. A ten-year period of residence is all that's required, with at least five years after age 50. This is the 'tax and transfer' model of state-provided retirement incomes.

The contrast with, for example, the UK and the US is quite stark. In both of those countries citizens (and their employers) must pay their dues over their working lifetimes to get the full benefit—the 'insurance model'.

---

[1]   Editorial, 12 September 1995.

While that sounds fair and equitable, I think contribution rules (that create 'entitlements' purchased from the contributions) get in the way of a successful Tier I benefit, particularly where that extends into what would in most countries be regarded as Tier II territory (employment-related benefits). France discovered the truth of that in 1995 by taking on private-sector workers who belong to the state's defined-benefit, salary-related Tier II pension scheme. It didn't dare try the same move with public-sector employees, especially those in jobs where strikes would really annoy voters, like train drivers.

Like all aspects of a government's operations, retirement income policies need to adapt to changing conditions. The rules in the US and the UK (and in a number of other countries) that deliver Tier I 'entitlement' benefits affect the process of change, but in the end can't stop it; they just make change more difficult.

Politicians around the world are now beginning to understand that what matters most is growth and employment (not 'entitlements'), and that they can't deliver either of them directly. If taxpayers as a whole don't like the size of the slice going to the retired, regardless of how it's calculated, the slice will be made bigger or smaller. In the UK, it's getting smaller despite the 'entitlements' created by complex National Insurance arrangements. The Social Security system in the US will also face the same pressures, despite the complex system of 'entitlements'.

A successful retirement incomes policy must be adaptable. That's achievable even while maintaining a stable framework. The government must be fair to all its stakeholders and it must react to changing conditions, particularly those over which it has no control, like the 'oil shocks' of the 1970s. A government's resources are finite—its capacity to raise revenue through tax is limited, as some Eastern bloc countries have now discovered. While efforts have to be made to protect the most vulnerable, in the end, those most dependent on the government, like the retired, will suffer the most if governments are weakened by economic dislocation.

The economic reality of the amount spent by the government on Tier I may be a year-by-year 'bearability' test, but that's a short-run view of the issues that should drive a country's design policy. The size of the retirees' slice delivered by the state at Tier I could in theory be set each year.

However, we can't set the size of the Tier I benefit based on what we can afford today, because the vital ingredient of sustainability must be added to the recipe. Without sustainability there won't be stability. Without stability, people can't be expected to behave 'sensibly' over the long periods affected by retirement income policies. A key government objective for the development of Tiers II and III should be to get people to behave 'sensibly', however society defines that.

Further Roles for the State

We have seen that the shape of Tier I has 'knock-on' effects on the behaviour of voters, employers and individual savers (who also happen to be voters). Once everyone has agreed on the design of Tier I, is that the end of the state's role?

While it's vital to get Tier I right, that's only the start of the state's involvement. Partly, that's because the success of Tier I will depend in large part on 'successful' behaviour at Tier II (employment-related schemes) and Tier III (all other private saving). There is, therefore, a symbiotic relationship between Tier I, on the one hand, and Tiers II and III on the other. Each of the two is dependent on the other if the whole structure is to work or be 'successful'.

In this context 'success' can be measured in a number of ways. Do voters think Tier I is fair? If they don't, it will be changed. Is it sustainable? If not, then it certainly will be changed. Is it easy to understand? Again, complexity makes the scheme vulnerable to change. Does it work? A democratic system can't tolerate starving voters, particularly those like pensioners with a lot of time on their hands.

Does it leave room for individuals and employers to make their own decisions, if that's what they want? Generally, a vibrant market is vital to a successful economy—if the state crowds out private provision for retirement saving, that reduces opportunities. Public and private provision have their strengths and weaknesses and, intuitively, it seems sensible to combine their respective strengths and reduce their weaknesses.

So, what's next on the state's agenda? Governments around the developed world do much more—some of it is useful, but a lot is not. The next two chapters look at some direct (and expensive) strategies—tax incentives and compulsion.

Governments have one vital role—getting the economy right—and a number of important but less vital tasks.

Getting the Economy Right

No public or private system of provision for retirement stands any chance of working unless the government gets the economy right. There are some things the government has no (or only limited) influence over, but it can make a difference with others.

Controlling Inflation

Take inflation as an example. Tier I may be sustainable today but if the benefit were linked to inflation, it might not be in 20 or 50 years. Too much inflation tends, from a retirement income perspective, to create state dependency. The state is the only national institution with the power to protect people's income from the adverse effects of inflation. It simply takes money from us all to pay for it. However, its power to do that is limited; it's not just the direct cost to the taxpayer of the higher retirement incomes. That's because inflation has knock-on effects.[1]

Not only does excess inflation drive up the cost of Tier I, it also makes it more difficult for the private sector to supply the services needed at Tiers II and III. Employers and other saving institutions can't afford (or find it

---

[1]   Apart from the long run damage it does to the value of money. Inflation of 1% a year halves the value of money over 70 years (about the period that a well disciplined and long-lived saver will be building up and then running down retirement savings). Increasing inflation to 2% reduces the years to 35. Inflation of 'only' 3% a year halves the value of money in 23 years—that's a better performance than a number of OECD countries manage at the moment.

impossible) to deliver credible vehicles at Tiers II and III if they can't earn a net real rate of return—that means after tax *and* inflation. If the private sector can't do its job, voters will look to the state to expand Tier I or deliver taxpayer-funded clones of the private schemes that should be there at Tiers II and III.

Inflation tends to crowd out private provision because private providers can't deliver. It also seems that the level of saving in a richer country is more affected by the size of the real return by comparison with the position in a poorer country. In an International Monetary Fund study,[1] saving in the poorest countries rose by 0.1 per cent for each one per cent rise in the real return. In richer countries (described in the study as 'middle-income countries') saving went up by 0.67 per cent for each one per cent rise in the real return.

Failing to reward savers appropriately, of course, only makes it worse for the taxpayers—they are punished twice for inflation. Not only does Tier I become more expensive but also the state finds itself involved in areas that should really be the responsibility of the private sector.

The final knock-on effect from a savings perspective is that a combination of inflation and taxes tends to distort savings decisions, particularly where tax is charged against nominal and not real returns. As inflation rises, savers are discouraged by falling net real returns.

The trouble with inflation is that, while it makes state benefits more expensive, the value of government debt (contributed to by the same state provided benefits) tends to fall in real terms, as does the real cost of servicing it. That makes inflation attractive to governments.[2]

With significantly reduced rates of inflation among developed countries since the mid-1980s, there are some who think that inflation is dead and that the globalisation of the world's economy has changed things forever.

International markets are now a lot more open than they were in the 1960s, so governments will be punished more swiftly than was the custom then. But the danger remains. Maybe it will be easier for governments to keep their heads in the fiscal sand and not address the demographic issues we are discussing. Why not allow debt to balloon and then kill it with a dose of unexpected inflation? This would also be the surest way to kill confidence, stop saving in its tracks and undermine confidence in the financial structures on which the savings culture of society is now being rebuilt.

Saying we want to keep inflation under control is one thing—knowing what inflation is, is another. We need to be confident that current measures of inflation fairly state changes in the value of money. Leonard Nakamura[3]

---

[1]   Reported in *The Economist*, 9 March 1996.

[2]   'The last time industrial countries sprang the inflation surprise, in the 1960s and 1970s, they eliminated indebtedness accumulated up to and during the Second World War. In the UK, which had enjoyed a long period of price stability, post-war inflation reduced gross public indebtedness from 300% of gross domestic product in 1945 to 50% in 1980, a default equivalent to £500 - 600 billion at 1995 prices.' *The Financial Times*, 23 April 1996.

[3]   In, 'Is US Economic Performance Really That Bad?', Federal Reserve Bank of Philadelphia working paper No. 95-21, cited in *The Economist*, 28 September 1996.

estimates that the US inflation rate has been overstated by two to three percentage points a year since 1974. Others suggest a much lower overstatement. Given the importance of the inflation measures to savers (particularly those saving for retirement), this doubt isn't good enough, despite the difficulties of measurement in increasingly services-based economies. We need good information on this and, generally, more effort from governments, because only they are in any position to provide it.

Good Returns

The next part of the state's responsibility to the economy is related to the last—if private provision for retirement is to play a role in the agreed structure, savers need to be confident that their savings will be there when they need them. Part of that is about information, education and regulation; the rest of it is about people's perceptions of the place their savings will have in the future economy. In other words, is it worth saving? Will the rewards justify the risk of deferring today's consumption for tomorrow's security? Where will the savings go? Are they likely to make the economy stronger so that tomorrow's consumers will be able to deliver the returns needed by tomorrow's retirees?

The ability to get a reasonable return on savings seems a fundamental right. However, the prospect of good returns seems to reduce with extended periods of inflation. Though some asset classes (shares and property) have the potential to keep up with inflation over the long term (40 to 70 years), the same is not necessarily true over shorter periods. Savers must get compensation for inflation over short as well as long periods. The most practical way for governments to achieve that goal is to keep inflation low in the first place.

Government Saving

It seems that if governments don't save (that is, they run deficits), everyone pays more for their money. A study for the G10 group of large industrial countries[1] found that the real rate of interest has risen by one percentage point (from three per cent to four per cent) over the last 35 years, seemingly because of a decline of about five percentage points in the national saving rates of the G10. It seems that the main reason is the decline in saving by governments, though personal saving has fallen as well.

Higher real rates of interest may be good for savers, but they cost everyone in the productive sector more than is necessary. They also cost taxpayers more than is otherwise required. So it's in everyone's interests to get governments to save.

Accessible Markets

The government must also make investment markets as accessible as possible, including overseas markets. They should make it easy for people to save and to join with others in saving together. Barriers to entry should be reduced or, preferably, eliminated.

It's in the government's, i.e. all taxpayers', interests that these things are so. The retirement income 'slack' created by and in private markets must be

---

[1]   Reported in *The Financial Times*, 9 October 1995.

absorbed by someone, and that usually means taxpayers. They will eventually have to pick up the pieces of capital market failures, so that should be sufficient incentive to get it right from the first.

Having said that, a growing economy makes the government's job easier. Growth happens for reasons that have only passing connections with the state. A growing labour force with improving skills, the capital available to that labour force—and the technology associated with it—will all help the economy and help make our retirement more secure.

Intergenerational Equity—Political Sustainability Over Time

Having got the economy right, governments have a second important role in making retirement income policies work: to ensure government spending programmes stand the test of equity over time. 'Generational accounting' is one way of testing the equity of government spending programmes over the very long run. It tries to measure the burden of today's financial strategy, not only on today's teenagers but also on their children.

There's a practical reason for this kind of test—if today's and tomorrow's taxpayers think they're not getting a fair share of the available resources, there's a risk that they'll simply change the rules. Constantly changing the rules is bad news for retirement income policies.

Alan Auerbach (from the University of California at Berkeley) helped develop the concept of generational accounting.[1] This measures the lifetime taxes of all kinds paid by a generation of taxpayers, including income taxes (both wage and non-wage) corporate income taxes, consumption taxes, excise taxes, and local taxes. Transfers are then deducted from this—retirement income, health and unemployment benefits, family and housing benefits and also education. All of these amounts are discounted to present values so that the 'fairness' of relative burdens can be compared. The discount rate obviously has a crucial influence on the process and very small changes in the rate have considerable leverage in the outcomes so the findings must be treated with some care.

Generational accounts do not track the relative rewards different generations get for the money the government spends on them—they simply track income and expenditure incurred during each generation (with the exception of money spent on education which is treated as a transfer payment).

Auerbach argues that a sustainable policy is one in which the present value of all future taxes is equal to the present value of future spending plus the current stock of debt (that has to be paid back by someone at some stage). He says that today's deficit or level of borrowing is a relatively poor gauge of an economy's health because neither of them take account of future commitments to older populations. Governments will find it much more difficult to fool voters if the long-term implications of today's decisions are open and understandable.

One of the government's responsibilities is to inform its citizens about the future political sustainability of current policies. Generational accounting lets policymakers check the political temperature of tomorrow's outcomes today.

The US developers of the concept recently carried out such an exercise in

---

[1] As reported in *The Economist*, 9 September 1995.

New Zealand. The report by Auerbach, Baker, Kotlikoff and Walliser[1] looked at New Zealand's position and compared it with a number of other countries. Figure 6 summarises their six-country comparison:

Figure 6
Generational Accounts

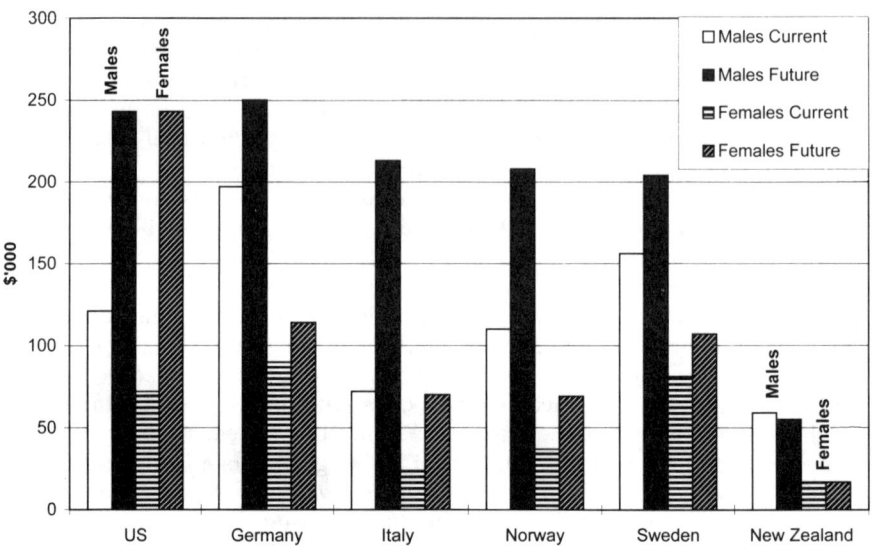

Source: Auerbach, Baker Kotlikoff and Walliser

In all cases (including New Zealand) everyone pays more over their lifetimes than they get back—the higher the bar in figure 6, the greater the overpayment. The greater the overpayment, the more likely will be future change to tax and redistribution policies.

In all cases (*except* New Zealand) the next generation pays significantly more than the current. The greatest difference in this comparison is for US females.[2]

As the New Zealand report says: 'Generational accounting emphasises the importance of implicit as well as explicit government commitments'. Figure 6 shows that New Zealand has a sound long-term picture. However the US, Italy (under a more generous assumption about future fertility and mortality) and

---

[1]   *Generational Accounting in New Zealand: Is There Generational Balance?*, New Zealand Treasury, July 1995.

[2]   The reason that females do better than males in all the comparisons is because of their lower lifetime incomes and therefore their lower taxes, the social welfare benefits they receive during their child-bearing years, and the more health care and pensions they receive because they live longer than men.

Norway all have current policies that place large burdens on young generations. That doesn't necessarily make them unsustainable, but it does make them vulnerable to future change.

Many in New Zealand suggest that tomorrow's taxpayers will get a worse deal than today's retirees despite paying more tax today to support the currently retired. The numbers produced in the report don't support that. As the report said:

> ... perhaps the most salient observation to make is that [its results] indicate that future generations will bear a lower lifetime net tax burden than current new-borns.

New Zealand is in the happy position of being able to improve what is already a healthy long-term political future. The report says that if individual income taxes were reduced by 2.2 per cent, the results would be roughly balanced between the generations. Income taxes are to be reduced by somewhat more than that over the next two years.[1]

Having produced the 1995 report, future governments should re-do the numbers to ensure New Zealand stays on track. Any change in the results is unlikely to be dramatic unless policy itself shifts dramatically. Re-doing the numbers should be a condition of adopting any new policy, so that voters and taxpayers can see what they are getting themselves into.

Governments that make generational accounting a regular part of their policy review process will find that the debate on retirement income issues will put the focus where it must lie—on the long term. Alternative strategies can be tested to see if they meet the tests of fairness and political sustainability. Policy will be made in a more considered way rather than on the hoof as tends to be the case in most democracies. Individual taxpayers don't have even the remotest idea of whether they are getting good value for the taxes they or their employers are paying on their behalf today. Governments can, however, use this discipline to explain the long-run impact of current policies and of proposed changes to those policies. It's all part of the confidence-building process that the government should lead.

It's easy to criticise generational accounting because of its long-run guesses, its concentration on current government strategy (and its assumption that current policy will be there for decades) and its sensitivity to the discount rate. Generational accounting is a tool, just one of a number that should be used to measure possible outcomes of a government's long-term strategy.

Fiscal Sustainability

Generational accounting measures fairness at an individual level by tracking the lifetime taxes and transfers of an average voter. A larger and, in some ways, more important issue is whether the government can afford to maintain its strategy over the very long term.

Many of the expenses faced by governments with ageing populations are, themselves, age-related; the costs of health care and retirement pensions are the biggest age-related expenses, but not the only ones. Voters need to know from an overall perspective whether current policies will stand up to those age-related strains.

---

[1]   A similar exercise in Australia shows an average contribution by the current generation is $15,700. By contrast, today's new-borns have a total positive contribution of more than twice that at $36,200.

One measure of sustainability is to look at the amount of tax that tomorrow's governments will need to raise in order to balance their budgets. It doesn't matter if the budget doesn't balance now—a current deficit that is covered by borrowing will, in this exercise, be treated as though it had been raised through extra tax.

A model should be developed to predict future budgets over the next 50 or 60 years. The process should test a number of scenarios—in part to see what might constitute a reasonable 'central' scenario, but also to test the sensitivity of variations in individual guesses from what might be seen as the reasonable best guess. Because of the very long periods over which such a model has to operate, relatively small changes in any guess can produce quite large changes in the outcomes.

New Zealand has such a model—it emerged from work done in 1992 by the Task Force on Private Provision for Retirement. Despite all the changes that had happened in New Zealand over the 20 years to 1992 no-one had looked at the long-run fiscal implications of our ageing population. There had been much hand-wringing but no real work.

The main purpose of the 1992 study was to see if New Zealand faced a fiscal crisis over the following 15-20 years because of the ageing population. It took account of all the changes that might follow New Zealand's changing age structure, including the reducing numbers of young people. The Task Force used an accounting framework to calculate an annual balanced budget tax path ('ABT').[1] Once the government's budget was balanced so that expenditure equalled income, the average tax rate was then changed each year to maintain the budget balance at zero. The projections over the 60 years to 2051 rested on some crucial guesses about the future. The key ones were:

- productivity growth of one per cent a year
- unemployment reducing from 10 per cent in 1992 to five per cent by 2001
- a real interest rate of six per cent a year
- the government achieving a balanced budget by 1997
- the state's age benefit maintaining its real value in relation to wages (at the time, the benefit increased in relation to prices).

The 1992 study influenced the deliberations of the Task Force and significantly shaper of its final recommendations. It was updated by the Retirement Commissioner in 1995 and again by the Periodic Report Group in 1997—Figure 7 shows the 1992 results with the 1997 calculations. The later work refined and updated the guesses on which the ABT calculations were carried out. Some of the changes were prompted by New Zealand's improved fiscal and economic position; others followed the availability of better public data on the government's financial position. Productivity growth was increased from one per cent to 1.6 per cent; unemployment was to stay at about six per cent (compared with falling to five per cent by 2001). More

---

[1]   An alternative technique was also used—the long-run balanced tax rate ('LBT')—struck a single fixed tax rate that will generate budget equilibrium at the end of the study period. This implied a higher tax rate than ABT at the beginning but one that generated a fiscal surplus to repay debt and generate reserves. LBT produced a lower tax rate than ABT at the end of the period and is, in fact, closer to current government policy than ABT.

sophisticated allowances were made for taxes, interest rates, employment participation rates and health, education and welfare costs.

Figure 7
Tax Revenue as a %GDP: New Zealand

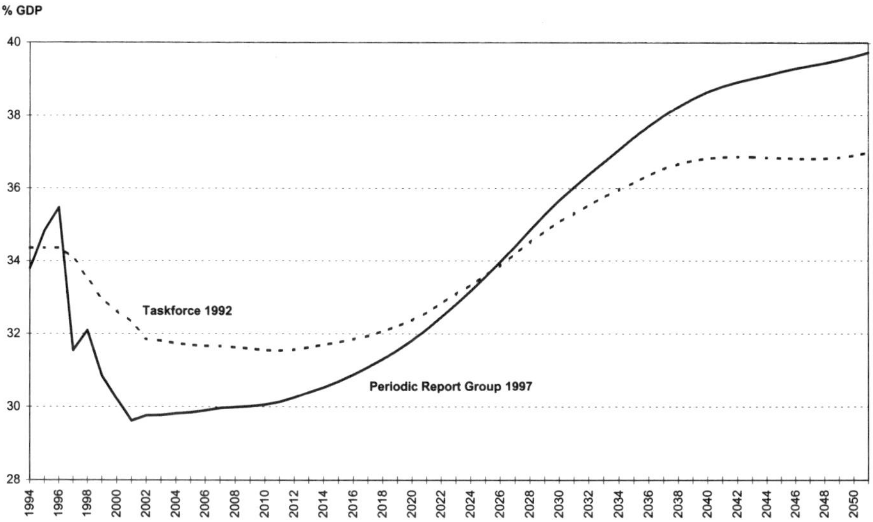

Source: Task Force on Private Provision for Retirement, 1992; Period Report Group, 1997.

ABT holds debt at a constant level so interest costs are also held level at the assumed interest rate.

The 1997 study was able to use better information now available from the government's new accrual accounting system. The New Zealand government now runs its accounts on 'Generally Accepted Accounting Principles'—the same principles as a trading company with a traditional balance sheet and income/expenditure accounts.[1] The new GAAP accounts let the researchers take today's balance sheet and run it forward over the coming 55 years. The 'GAAP indicators' are the new way of measuring the fiscal sustainability of New Zealand's ageing population.

The Periodic Report Group expects the net cost of the old-age pension to rise from four per cent of GDP to nine per cent in 2050/51. This is about the same as the average paid by OECD members in 1990.[2]

---

[1]   According to the Periodic Report Group's July 1997 report, the change in the government's accounting policies explained about 0.5% of the roughly 2% of GDP difference in the end points shown in Figure 7. The rest was largely attributable to better information about expected mortality and age related health costs and also the removal of the income test on New Zealand Superannuation from 1 April 1998.

[2]   *Averting The Old Age Crisis: Policies to Protect and Promote Growth*, The World Bank Policy Research Report, Oxford University Press, 1994,

Meanwhile, health costs (for everyone, not just the old) are forecast to approximately double by 2050/51 from about five per cent of GDP today to about 10 per cent.

The eventual results will be very sensitive to labour force participation rates, unemployment, productivity growth, expenditure discipline and economic cycles.[1] Despite all these uncertainties, we need to keep the forecasts current and in the public eye. Voters may then understand that small but significant changes at the start of such a long period can multiply to levels that will threaten their retirement security. We may then stand a chance of keeping governments honest.

Information and Education—the Seatbelt Syndrome

The government cannot afford to stand to one side and hope that retirement incomes, or the policies that produce them, will get 'better', however that is measured. We all need to address this subject in the same way that most countries agreed on the compulsory wearing of seatbelts in cars.

In theory, each person should decide individually whether or not to wear a seatbelt because, when an accident happens, that individual will bear the consequences of the decision not to wear one. However, that is not an holistic view of the seatbelt issue. The reality of consequential loss is that, while the individual may be injured and suffer physical pain, the *financial* consequences of damage and medical expenses will be borne eventually by the whole community. So, the community has a stake in the decisions on whether or not cars are fitted with seatbelts, on their safety standards and on whether or not they are worn. For the relatively small cost of fitting the belts and the relatively minor inconvenience of buckling up, the community obtains a potentially significant financial benefit.

No taxpayer is immune from the consequences of the debate on retirement provision that is now running in all developed countries. *All* taxpayers have a stake in *each* taxpayer's decision on whether or not to save for retirement. If voters decide not to save and arrive at retirement with no income on which to live, it's politically unlikely that they will suffer the full financial consequences of their decisions not to save.

With 14 per cent of the population (about 20 per cent of voters) currently entitled to the Tier I pension in New Zealand, governments cannot be exposed to the political risk of people who reach retirement without savings also being without 'enough' income. Even if governments could say that those voters should have saved when they had the opportunity, they cannot ignore 490,000 votes in 1995 (1,130,000 votes in 2031 or about 34 per cent of voters).[2]

All this imposes an obligation on governments to tell voters about the

---

[1]   In Brown, R.L. and Bilodeau, C., 'The Canadian Wealth Index Transfer Index', (Canadian Institute of Actuaries, to be published in Proceedings) a model predicts the impact of the baby-boomers on the cost of social security programmes. The state pension age is used as the variable to control the index so that sustainability can be measured.

[2]   Based on medium fertility, medium mortality and a net annual immigration of 5,000 a year—figures produced by Statistics New Zealand based on the 1991 census.

issues; to let them see what the country's policies mean for them as individuals. Information can lead to informed decisions. That won't necessarily happen, but people who know what's going on tend to behave 'sensibly'. And how much should they save if they're behaving 'sensibly'? The answer, inevitably, will be a very individual one:

> The right level—at least to a first approximation—is the level that would emerge if all the separate households were free to divide their income between current and future consumption in accordance with their own values, provided only that the terms on which they do so were not distorted and did not impose uncompensated costs or benefits on other households.[1]

And who are we to argue otherwise or to impose our views as to what might suit someone else?

Part of the information and education responsibility involves the government telling us what's realistic. Calculating what the numbers will be in the future and presenting the future in terms that ordinary savers can understand and adjust to will help make a retirement income policy successful.

Governments must also produce proper information about their own financial affairs so that we know what's actually going on rather than what they would prefer us to think. The first step should be the adoption of accrual accounting according to the 'generally accepted accounting principles' (GAAP). This would see a proper balance sheet with assets and liabilities and income and expenditure accounts. Depreciation would be seen as an expense of the same kind as civil servants' salaries. Pension liabilities (both social welfare and the benefits for civil servants) could be accounted for (though not pre-funded) in much the same way as private employers show them. The emphasis on the cash deficits and surpluses would diminish and be replaced by a focus on whether the government was behind or ahead of the game on its *recurrent* operations. GAAP accounts are not the be all and end all but they are light years ahead of what pass for government accounts in nearly all developed countries.

Getting the Politics Right

For the reasons discussed in chapter 1 politics and the way developed societies make their decisions have a big part to play in a successful retirement income policy. Getting the politics right is not something to be left to chance. Winning a majority in the elected assembly is not enough—that's just winning the battle; it doesn't remotely approach the requirements to secure the war. Elections happen too often in democracies for a stable retirement income policy.

Though I have expressed doubts about governments' time or capacity to grasp the complex interconnected facets of a retirement income policy, I also think that if citizens, who basically want to get things right, are given believable and useful information by people they trust, they will do the right thing and end up acting in the country's best interests. They will do this because it's in *their* best interests that it should be so.

Everyone must be involved in this process—not just the elected representatives but those in the savings industry, employers, employee representatives, the already retired and anyone else who has an interest in

---

[1]   Friedman, M., 'What is the "Right" Amount of Saving?', *Policy*, 6 Spring 1990, pp. 52-54.

the issue. All the politicians, not just the winning group, must have the opportunity to join in the process and a framework should be built to achieve that if one doesn't already exist.

The political objective should be consensus—the agreement of all politicians to the proposed strategy. I don't count as consensus the policies of a democratically elected party that just happens to have the support of a majority of the voters who turned out on election day. Consensus means the agreement of everyone who matters in the retirement income industry. That may be a tall order, but it's a risk-free strategy for a government. If it works, that's great—if it doesn't, the government is unlikely to attract much opprobrium for trying. Anything less than consensus will be less than ideal; but a government shouldn't give up if it doesn't achieve consensus the first time around. It must do what it can—it simply can't make the big calls without widespread support.

Delivering More than the Minimum—The Three Regimes

Then there is the question of further direct involvement in Tiers II and III—it's a favourite global strategy for governments so there must be something in it.

Governments are—or should be—interested in whether their citizens save for retirement at Tier II (employment-based schemes) or Tier III (other private savings). As emphasised in chapter 2, democracy, demography and the welfare state will eventually see to that.

There are three main ways that governments express their interest in Tiers II and III. In descending order of global popularity, they are:

Bribing (a.k.a. tax incentives)
Taxpayers are encouraged with their own and other taxpayers' money to save in acceptable ways and for acceptable purposes. Internationally, this is by far the most popular way. The next chapter looks at whether this is a good idea.

Bludgeoning (a.k.a. compulsion)
Earners are told what to do and where to go to do what they have to do. A small, but increasing, number of countries are going down this road. In some cases, bludgeoning is stepping down into the business of providing Tier I (for example, in Chile). Chapter 5 looks at this option.

Laissez faire (a.k.a. voluntary)
By far the least popular way things are done—the government sets the 'tone' and then lets the people decide. Chapter 7 considers how that might look.

A number of countries mix bribing and bludgeoning—their citizens are all forced to save and then they are all rewarded for that intervention by an incentive provided from their own tax dollars. Australia and Chile, among others, both do that.

Governments have no choice as to whether they should be directly involved at Tier I though they have much choice on the style of involvement. However, the choices multiply at Tiers II and III. Chapters 4 to 7 look at how most governments have missed the boat in all three Tiers.

The Current Unrest

There is much international dissatisfaction with the unfunded state schemes that have provided the backbone of social 'security' schemes of the last 50 years. In most countries, these have grown up alongside an increasingly complex web of tax-induced Tier II and III arrangements. In some cases, links have been established between the two systems but they have usually developed in an uncoordinated fashion.

There are increasing signs of regulators wanting to get out of Tier I, or at least assigning responsibility for Tier I provision to Tiers II or III. Governments are particularly looking to employers to step into the demographic gap. Much of the debate takes the present framework for private provision at Tiers II and III pretty much as is and tries to graft new structures on to the present tax-funded regimes that are themselves built on the shaky foundations of unsustainable social welfare arrangements.

I think it's time we looked at everything we do, not just the bits we don't like.

4

Tax and Level Playing Fields

Summary

Governments around the world spend billions of dollars on tax incentives. In view of the large amounts of money in tax-favoured vehicles around the world, it would be easy to conclude that tax incentives for retirement savings are successful. However, there is very little evidence to support this.

There can be only two reasons to justify tax incentives for retirement:

- *to improve personal provision so that people have more to live on in retirement and are therefore likely to be less dependent on the state, or*

- *to reduce the amount of income that would otherwise have been paid to a retired person through the welfare system.*

Some further reasons are put forward, with a common reason being that tax incentives increase the amount of capital available for investment. Others say that retirement savings have a different quality from other, shorter-term savings and unless the state intervenes to promote retirement savings with tax incentives, the country will be poorer in the long term.

All these reasons are difficult to support. The evidence suggests, in fact, that tax incentives don't work and cost more than they recover. There are also other reasons for abandoning them:

- *they are inequitable*

- *they have a distortionary effect*

- *they are inefficient*

- *they are expensive to administer*

- *it is not possible to allow savers a concession without increasing the tax burden elsewhere.*

'Bribing' people into saving for retirement is a thoroughly bad idea.

∗∗∗∗∗∗∗∗∗∗∗∗∗∗∗∗∗∗∗∗∗

No Need For Concessions

In my introduction I spoke of my shock in December 1987 on learning of the New Zealand government's decision to remove all tax concessions for retirement saving, and my belief at that time that people would not save for retirement without incentives. My views on this have changed. While saving for retirement is clearly a 'good thing', that does not mean the state should pay its citizens to do it.

There can be only two reasons to justify tax incentives (that's taking money out of all taxpayers' pockets) for retirement saving. These are:

- **to improve personal provision** so that people have more to live on in retirement and are therefore likely to be less dependent on the state. That, indirectly, should save governments money by relieving future pressure on age-related welfare budgets, particularly in relation to non-cash benefits, or

- **to reduce the amount of income** that would otherwise have been paid to a retired person through the welfare system. This will be a direct saving and can be done through some form of income and/or asset test that links public and private provision.

In fact, decreasing dependency on future state benefits (not just increasing future total retirement incomes—state plus private) is the only strong reason for having tax incentives. That means today's governments are giving up tax revenue in return for a saving in tax tomorrow with reduced state benefits.

However, both reasons imply that the state has a view on its overall obligations to old people, and not only in relation to income levels. I've already discussed that in chapter 3.

Some people suggest further reasons. A common one is that tax incentives increase the amount of capital available for investment. This implies that the market cannot fill the gap between the returns it requires and what it's actually able to deliver, without dipping into taxpayers' pockets. That doesn't sound very sensible.

Others say that retirement savings have a different quality from other, shorter term savings. Unless the state intervenes to promote retirement savings with tax incentives, the country will somehow be the poorer in the long run. Again, that's difficult to support.

I'll look at these two reasons later but first, a reminder of the tax architecture of retirement saving schemes.

EET ⇒ TET ⇒ TTT ⇒ TTE: New Zealand from 1987 to 1990

There's a set of acronyms that help focus the debate on the tax treatment of retirement savings. They were designed mainly for formal retirement saving structures like pension schemes, or what we, in New Zealand and Australia, call superannuation schemes. They apply to all forms of saving.

There are three major movements of money in a retirement scheme. The initials 'T' (for taxed) and 'E' (for exempt) tag the tax treatment of each and help explain New Zealand's changes between 1987-1990.

Contributions

Employees, employers (or both) and members of the public contribute money to a scheme. If those contributions are deductible for tax purposes, they are 'exempt' from tax ('E'). That was the position in New Zealand until 17 December 1987. From then, contributions effectively lost deductibility and so had to be paid from after-tax income. The tag changed to 'T' or 'taxed'.

How the contributions are treated by the person or institution that pays them is only part of the tax story. If the employer's contributions confer no taxable benefit on the employee in respect of whom they are paid, that is also concessionary by contrast with money that could have been paid as salary. More accurately, it preserves the concessionary treatment intended by the legislature.

When New Zealand first withdrew the concession for contributions, they were initially subject to a fringe benefit tax, paid also by the employer. Now, more sensibly, they are subject to a withholding tax that reduces the amount actually received by the retirement saving scheme. Both types of tax are proxies for the tax that employees would have paid had the contributions come directly as income. It's as though the employees had paid the contributions themselves from after-tax income.

Investment Income

In a funded scheme, trustees usually invest the contributions. If the investment income is tax-free, it is 'exempt' or 'E'. That was the case in New Zealand until 31 March 1988. From then, a retirement saving scheme has paid income tax of 33 per cent which is the top marginal rate of personal income tax (and the corporate tax rate as well). The investment income is now taxed or 'T'. Once again, that tax is really a proxy for what each of the scheme's beneficiaries would have paid had they invested the money directly.

Benefit

The eventual retirement benefit was largely taxed as income. Until 1990 in New Zealand, most retirees received a pension, though it was possible to have lump sum schemes. In a pension scheme, a retiree could exchange up to 25 per cent of the future pension value for a tax-free lump sum, but the remainder was then taxed in the normal way. From 1 April 1990, all benefits from a retirement scheme (lump sum or pension) became tax-free. So 'T' became 'E'.

In summary, New Zealand went from EET to TTE in a three step process:

EET: the position before 17 December 1987 for pension schemes (by 1987, lump sum schemes were ETE but with significant controls on the deductibility of contributions)
TET: 18 December 1987 to 31 March 1988
TTT: 1 April 1988 to 31 March 1990
TTE: the present position for *all* retirement schemes, both lump sum and pension.

Nearly all developed countries give tax incentives for retirement savings. Table 3 shows the position for a selection:[1]

The most valuable of the Ts or Es is the middle one—the tax status of the saving scheme's investment income. That reflects the power of compound interest over the long saving periods involved with retirement saving. Even a lower concession, such as exists in Australia, confers a significant benefit on the taxpayer who makes use of the tax-favoured vehicle.[2]

Why the Change?

The change was made in New Zealand because a recent government was persuaded that formal retirement schemes were only one way New Zealanders

---

[1]   Details of the tax treatment in the countries noted come from *International Benefit Guidelines*, 17th Edition, William M. Mercer Companies.

[2]   Denmark has partly recognised this with a tax of about 50% on real interest of more than 3.5% a year. However, that tax was introduced in 1992 to raise money, not to change the philosophy of the way funded schemes were treated.

saved for retirement. Not many actually used them (the best guess then was only about 30 per cent of employees). Also, the tax concessions were expensive, and most employees resigned before reaching age 50. This last was significant because, inexplicably, no tax applied to the early withdrawal benefit, so the tax system's investment in the savings built up was lost: EET became EEE.

People also saved for retirement through bank accounts. Those operated under a TTE tax regime—amounts were saved from after-tax income (T); the account-holder paid tax on interest (T); withdrawals were not taxed (E). This meant the government was telling people, through the tax system, that an approved scheme was a 'better' investment than a bank account. One vehicle was tax-preferred, the other was tax neutral.

Table 3
Comparison of Tax Incentives for Retirement Savings

	Contributions	Investment income	Benefits
Australia[1]	t	t	t
Canada	E	E	T
Chile	E	E	T
France	E	E	T
Germany[2]	E	-	T
Italy[3]	t	E	t
Japan	E	E[4]	T
New Zealand	T	T	E
Sweden	E	E[5]	T
United Kingdom	E	E	T
United States	E	E	T

Source: William M. Mercer Companies, 1995.

Notes:

1 Australia's lower case 't t t' indicates that some tax is applied at each stage of the money's movement into and out of a retirement scheme. Each of the tax rates is generally somewhat less than 'normal' hence the 't' rather than the 'T'.

2 German retirement schemes are usually financed by book reserves in the employer's accounts. Amounts set aside in respect of book reserve schemes are deductible and don't confer a taxable benefit on the employee. The growing value of the benefit isn't taxed in the employee's hands but, as there aren't any identified assets, the tax status of the assets isn't an issue. However pension liabilities are now moving off the balance sheets of employers and into Spezialfonds and other external vehicles that receive special tax treatment on earned income but are less favoured than the traditional reserves. About 54% of occupational pension benefits and pension rights are now covered in book reserve schemes.[1]

3 Italy has recently (1995) adopted a new tax regime for private pension plans that has limited deductibility for contributions (hence the 't'), a flat tax of only $6,300 on all the investment income of a scheme (no more than an annual registration fee), and tax on only 87.5% of the final pension (hence the 't').

4 Japan imposes a nominal income tax on the assets of 'tax qualified pension schemes'. Though the emerging benefits are taxed, there are concessionary deductions that don't apply to earned income.

5 Sweden also imposes a nominal tax on 'occupational pension insurance' and the capital income of a 'pension foundation'.

---

[1]   According to Peter Ahrend in 'The Role of Book Reserves', Benefits & Compensation International, July/August 1996.

Tax Neutrality

Tax neutrality is an important concept in this debate. In New Zealand 'neutrality' is defined by reference to the tax treatment that would apply if the member invested the money directly, rather than through an approved retirement scheme. An ordinary, interest-bearing bank account is a convenient model. This form of neutrality is identified with income tax.

The other form of neutrality is identified with expenditure and is often used to justify the almost universal EET tax model. This says that tax should be applied only when the savings are spent, in retirement. If all, or even most government revenue were raised by expenditure taxes like Europe's Value Added Tax or New Zealand's Goods and Services Tax, there would be some sense in applying the expenditure tax model to retirement savings. However, most governments raise most of their money through income tax, so the concept of tax neutrality seems more naturally aligned with the income tax model. (In OECD countries, an average of 60 per cent of 1995 governments' revenues came from taxes on income and profits and also from social security taxes. An average 32 per cent came from consumption taxes).[1]

A neutral *income* tax system neither favours nor penalises additional income generated from retirement savings compared with income earned from other savings or through additional work. The model requires that contributions to a retirement scheme receive no special tax treatment by comparison with investing the money directly. Also, the investment income the scheme earns on assets attributable to the member should be taxed at a rate that is equivalent to the individual's own marginal rate in the year. The benefits (or withdrawals) should not be taxed, because they are tax-paid capital.

As nearly all developed countries have a progressive tax system where lower income earners pay less tax than higher income earners, the income tax neutrality requirement is difficult to meet. A saver's marginal tax rate at the date of saving will usually be more than the rate that applies when the saving scheme pays the benefit so the tax system can't be neutral about the saving decision.

There's another form of *income* tax neutrality we could apply to retirement savings to reflect their special character. The TTE bank account model used in New Zealand can be equivalent to ETT, where the contributions are deductible but the benefits are taxable. However, for the two to be equivalent, the tax rates when contributions are made would have to be the same as the rates charged on the benefits—the front 'E' in ETT would then be the same as the back 'E' of the TTE version. Although an ETT system would send a signal that saving for retirement is 'a good thing' (that is, better than saving for other things), it would require regulatory walls to be put up around the retirement saving system to ensure that the eventual benefits were taxed. Those walls are costly and inefficient. So, if we're going to have tax neutrality, I think it has to be TTE, not ETT.

In practice, complete neutrality is unattainable, particularly if the retirement saving scheme provides defined benefits that are subsidised on an unallocated basis by the employer. The compromises adopted in New Zealand included a withholding tax on the employer's contributions and income tax charged at the *top* personal marginal rate, rather than the saver's own

---

[1]   Reported in *The Economist*, 13 September 1997.

marginal rate. Although that sounds penal, there's a relatively small difference in New Zealand between the average personal marginal tax rate on income (24 per cent) and the top rate of 33 per cent.[1]

So how do governments lose money from incentives?

Tax incentives cost money. Tax incentives for retirement savings cost lots of money but you wouldn't think so to read comments by some people who should know better. For example:

> What's needed [to correct a bias in the tax system that 'punishes thrift'] is a far-reaching overhaul of the nation's tax system and a more effective deployment of the savings incentives Congress has now in place. A broad expansion of IRA and 401(k) schemes would be a good place to start. Surprisingly, such a change would cost the government nothing over the long run, and it would correct a big inequity in our tax system.[2]

The article concentrates on the relative inequities of US tax concessions. Incentives are the given starting point. In a moment, I'll demonstrate that author's mathematical inexactitude. But why do we even think about encouraging individuals to save for retirement, or encouraging others, like employers, to do it on their behalf?

The author of the above quote has been captured by a simple concept: if an individual's marginal rate of tax remained the same during the savings period and into retirement, and if the government collected tax on all the money that came in from a retirement scheme, then exempting contributions and their build-up would only be a tax deferral, not an incentive. However, the tax deferral argument is wrong.

The government, on average, never gets back all the money it gives away to those who save for retirement through approved schemes, even if all the money that emerged were taxed. (Though that's not always the case—in the UK, part of what would otherwise be taxable pension can be a tax-free lump sum; in Australia the saver can take much or even all of the benefit as a lump sum.)

To see how this works, we need to make some economic and tax guesses to compare the internationally typical EET regime and the New Zealand's TTE version. (I use the term 'guess' deliberately because we can't possibly know what the out-turn on these sorts of calculations will be over such long periods.) Let's take a model, in more senses than one, male employee who saves for his whole working life and then buys an annuity on his life at retirement with all of the savings he has built up.

For this calculation, I'll use the following guesses:

- **interest** (including realised and unrealised gains) before tax of seven per cent a year on the savings (also used as the underlying rate for the annuity in retirement).

---

[1]   The penalty is real but, in any event, is diminished significantly, if not eliminated for low income families by the abatement regime inherent in the Family Support Tax Credit. This is a state-provided supplement to low incomes introduced when the New Zealand consumption tax—GST— started in 1986. FSTC reduces as family income increases. The more recent Independent Family Tax Credit is similar. The 24% is reduced to 21% from 1 July 1998.

[2]   Ehrbar, A., 'How Washington Can Stop Its War On Savings', *Fortune*, 6 March 1995. IRAs and 401(k) schemes are tax-favoured saving vehicles.

- **income tax** (on the *interest* in the hands of the trustee in the TTE model and on the *annuity* in the hands of the retiree for the EET model) of 33 per cent.

- **inflation** of two per cent a year both during the build up of savings and during the retirement period—this rate is used to bring all future dollars back to today's money so we can talk about 'real' money.

- **savings** of 10 per cent of the earner's income, starting at age 20 in 1998 and ending at age 65 in 2043. We'll say that his income, at age 20, is $20,000 a year. At age 65, it will be $31,000 in today's money.

- **the full amount** of savings reaches the trustee in the EET model while only 6.7 per cent of pay (10 per cent less tax on the contributions of 33 per cent) is paid to the TTE scheme.[1]

  Paying the contributions out of after-tax income has the same effect as a direct tax on the contributions themselves.

- **the employee's pay increases** at three per cent a year.

- **the accumulated savings** at the employee's retirement age of 65 are used to buy an inflation-proofed annuity that stops when the retiree dies.

- **the annuities** for both the EET and the TTE models are priced using the English mortality table for annuitants called PA(90) with no allowance for expenses (or profit for the supplier of the annuity). Though that last guess (no expenses or profit) is a bit unrealistic, as long as it applies to both sides (EET and TTE) it won't matter too much. Any advantage will accrue to the EET model where the initial pension will be higher.

The combined impact of these guesses is that the TTE scheme's net real rate of return is a little over 2.6 per cent a year (seven per cent after tax of 33 per cent is 4.7 per cent, less inflation of two per cent). Also, the employee's pay goes up at a real rate of almost one per cent a year.

As long as the same pre-tax interest and inflation guesses are used on both sides of the comparison, it doesn't much matter what they are.

Under both models, the same total pre-tax contributions of $76,067[2] will be paid. Because of the different tax treatments, only $50,965 actually reaches the TTE scheme. The rest goes to the government in tax.

Again, because of the different tax treatments, the final accumulations at retirement differ somewhat. Under the TTE scheme, they amount to only $135,946 because of the tax paid by the trustee on the scheme's investment income. Under the EET scheme, the retirement accumulation is $365,559 (some $229,613 or 169 per cent more).

---

[1]   At $NZ20,000 a year, the New Zealand marginal rate of tax is actually 24% (it reduces to 21% in 1998/99)—it becomes 33% at $NZ34,500 ($NZ38,000 in 1998/99). However, if the employer pays the contributions, withholding tax of 33% would be deducted regardless of the employee's income. For simplicity, I'll use 33% in the interests of symmetry with the tax on the build-up.

[2]   The actuarial calculations in this analysis were done by Watson Wyatt New Zealand Limited—the guesses on which the calculations are based are mine. All the results are expressed in 1997 dollars.

The annuity bought with the accumulated savings is:

- **in the TTE scheme,** $11,824 a year. Though this annuity is exempt from tax in the hands of the retiree under the TTE model, the trustee of the scheme (or the insurance company concerned) still pays tax on investment income earned on the purchase price of the annuity.

- **in the EET scheme,** $37,886 a year. This annuity is taxable but the price of the annuity (represented by the assets that support the annuity) is still invested on a tax-free basis by the annuity provider.

So what does this amount to for the two main parties interested in all these transactions—the employee and the government?

The employee pays the same before-tax amount in both cases but, by the time he dies, eventually receives quite different amounts because of the different tax treatments:

- **in the TTE scheme,** the employee gets a total of $135,946 in 1998 money;

- **in the EET scheme,** the employee gets a total after-tax amount of $244,925 in 1998 money (80 per cent more).

The government's collections under the two models were:

- **in the TTE scheme,** tax of $233,427 in 1998 money;

- **in the EET scheme,** tax of $120,634 ($112,793 or 48 per cent less than under TTE).

The difference between the values of the tax collected by the government is actually clouded by the impact of the interest rate guess on the tax collected under the TTE model. The value of the tax collected under TTE assumes that the government is able to earn the same return on the collections as the individual saver (seven per cent in my example). If the government were running a budget deficit during the 45-year saving period, it would be reasonable to substitute the government's cost of money for the interest rate guess. That would reduce the value of the tax collected under TTE where the tax is paid earlier than under EET.

So, to summarise all those figures:

	TTE ($)	**EET** ($)	**Difference** %
Contributions	76,067	76,067	-
Received by scheme	50,965	76,067	+50
Amount at retirement	135,946	365,559	+169
Annuity	11,824	37,886	+220
Total benefits received	135,486	244,925	+80
Government collects	233,427	120,634	-48

At this point, I'm not arguing whether that loss of tax revenue is good or bad (I'll come to that shortly)—all I'm saying is that the traditional EET treatment of retirement schemes is concessionary in a world based on income tax. If we compared the expenditure tax's EET with the income tax model (TTE), it would cost today's and tomorrow's generations of taxpayers real money. That advantage is conferred on savers who use the tax-favoured vehicles—everyone pays for it, including those who save *and* those who don't.

This way of looking at the advantage conferred on tax-favoured schemes puts to one side the argument[1] about the relative returns the tax-favoured savings earn by comparison with the interest the government pays on debt to finance the concession. The proper initial comparison should be between a world where the concessions don't exist and the world where they do. Only when we've established the true cost of the concessions can we start a discussion as to whether they actually achieve anything (and at what cost) and how to pay for them.

Can Governments Ever Make Money with Tax Concessions?

Governments have only two ways to pay for a tax concession to savers:

- collecting more tax from all taxpayers than would otherwise have been necessary without the concession, or

- borrowing more to fund a larger deficit than would have occurred without the concession. Borrowing only puts off the day when the cost of the concession will be paid for and puts that cost off to a new generation of taxpayers to meet, leaving the cost of carrying that additional debt to today's taxpayers.

The only other possibility is a mixture of the two.

Both methods have a cost by comparison with a concession-free zone. If we preferred higher taxes for all, the costs would be hidden but nevertheless real and we would all pay for them (taxpayers, savers and all the other citizens), even if we didn't choose the method of saving favoured by the concession.

Borrowing more to fund a larger deficit has more apparent direct costs as well as the damaging less obvious ones. Let's assume for a moment that the government has no money to pay for the concession and has to borrow the lot. At the moment, that applies, at least in part, to nearly all countries.

Because actuarial mathematics is such an elegant subject, there is an interest rate on the accumulating savings in the approved vehicles (and on the run-down during retirement) at which the compounding cost to the government of funding an EET version of tax concessions will be less than the long-run benefit of the extra tax collected when the pension emerges. (I'll leave out, at the moment, any recoveries the government might make through income or asset testing of EET savings against state-funded benefits—more on that later).

To work that balancing interest rate out for my example, we must make a guess about the cost of money to the government.

If the total return to the saver is seven per cent (leaving a net 4.7 per cent, after tax of 33 per cent) then 4.5 per cent a year would be a reasonable guess about the cost of money to the government. This takes into account the probability that the government won't be investing in the shares and real estate favoured by pension schemes. The rate paid by the government will therefore be less than the seven per cent used to build up the private tax-favoured savings. So, 4.5 per cent is 2.5 per cent ahead of inflation (at two per cent a year) and a net after-tax return to the government's lenders about one per cent more than inflation.

Using the guesses in my example, that 'balancing' interest rate is 8.03 per cent a year. So, if the long term return to savers through the tax-favoured

---

[1]   Run in the *Fortune* article of 6 March 1995 already referred to.

EET pension system on the savings during the build-up and then on the run down during retirement is more than 8.03 per cent a year, then the government might collect more than the cost of funding the concession. That required rate is 3.53 per cent more than (or 1.8x) the assumed cost of money to the government. It's also 1.03 per cent more than (or 1.15x) the seven per cent rate I assumed the ordinary investor would earn. If the saver expected seven per cent at the outset, there doesn't seem to be any sensible reason to expect that it will actually turn out to be 15 per cent greater. If there were such a reason then all the guesses in the example should be adjusted upwards.

However even if the 8.03 per cent a year were a sensible proposition, remember what's happening. The government has borrowed today's money and effectively 'lent' the full amount of the loan (the cost of the concession) to the saver on the security of the future tax to be collected tomorrow from the emerging benefit. That's not a risk-free strategy—it only means the government may be no worse off.

The main risk for tomorrow's governments of adopting this shaky strategy is that the savings may not achieve the 8.03 per cent a year long-run yield, especially if we have to add a piece to allow for the extra risks involved. Also, given the infinite inventiveness of taxpayers and their highly-paid advisers, can I be sure that the government will actually get the tax at the end of the day? And what about the transaction costs involved? In the US, ERISA[1] and the enforcement of the Inland Revenue Service's Code come at a large cost. I would want to see a further element built into the 'balancing' interest rate to pay for these costs as well.

That discussion can also include the additional risks governments run through financing the concessions by borrowing. The very act of borrowing incurs economic costs beyond the actual interest paid. New Zealand is much more aware now of the risk premium that taxpayers (and all borrowers in our economy, including companies and home owners) pay if their country borrows more than the world thinks it could reasonably support. According to the IMF[2] each increase of seven per cent in the ratio of national debt to output puts the cost of money up by one per cent. The IMF said that the increase in the US public debt between 1981-93 added 1.4 per cent to long term rates. That affects the rates that the whole community pays for money.

How Can This Be?

It doesn't really make sense, does it? If the government taxes everything that comes out of the favoured scheme, surely the government would be left in a neutral overall position, wouldn't it?

The answer to this apparent paradox goes back to the point I made earlier in this chapter about the power of the concessionary treatment of the middle 'T' or 'E'. The concession by giving a tax deduction to the contributions (the capital contributed to the scheme) is matched by the tax on the benefits that come out at the other end. So movements into and out of the tax-favoured fund are balanced.

---

[1]   The Employees Retirement Income Security Act which governs retirement schemes.

[2]   Cited in *The New York Times*, 10 March 1996.

However, any concession on the treatment of the build-up (the middle 'E') operates for such a long time (45 years in the example during the build-up and a further 14 years for a male during the retirement run-down), that the annual amount of the pension produced is much higher when it starts than the pension under the alternative, neutral TTE model. In the example, the 33 per cent tax collected during the payment period of 14 years under the EET model never has a chance to catch up with the taxes the government would have collected under the TTE method of taxing ordinary savings that are treated neutrally.

Increasing the tax rate in retirement could leave the government in a neutral position overall. In my example, the tax rate on the pension in retirement would have to be increased, from the 33 per cent I have used, to 69 per cent, or more than twice the ordinary rate. The retirement tax rate in the TTE model on the savings supporting the tax-free annuity would remain at the assumed 33 per cent.

That 'balancing' tax rate of 69 per cent would again have to be increased to allow for the government's exposure to risk and the transaction costs involved.

Putting up taxes on retirement savings for retirees as a class would be highly unpopular—New Zealand has experienced the political problems that brings.[1] However, if a country has progressive income tax rates (rather than the flat rate of 33 per cent in my example), the top rates would have to be increased by even more than the 69 per cent to ensure that an average of 69 per cent was actually collected.[2]

Also, we need to recognise that the income of retirees will usually be lower than when they were working. In a progressive tax system, the cost of making money for the government over the cost of the concession would be higher (expressed in terms of the percentages of tax to be paid on the emerging EET pensions) than the tax on 'ordinary' earned income from a 'retirement' job or interest received from a TTE investment. That's because, in a progressive tax system, the value of the concession during employment will be higher for the higher paid because it has been claimed on the top slice of taxable incomes that will be nearly always be higher than they become in retirement.

A change of that nature would be even more politically explosive.

---

[1]   New Zealand had a surcharge on the 'other income' of a person who is entitled to receive the state-provided age benefit—New Zealand Superannuation. See chapter 6 for more on this income test.

[2]   Much the same kind of analysis can be applied to the UK Labour Party's notion (in opposition) of tax incentives that are designed to encourage people to help pay for the costs of illness and old age called 'Individual Savings Accounts' (reported by The Financial Times, 3 May 1996). If the benefits drawn from an ISA were taxed as income, they would be the same as tax-favoured pensions. On the other hand, if the state reduced its expenditure on health care by the full amount of the benefit taken out of the ISA, that would be an effective tax rate of 100% (the cost the state would otherwise have paid would be reduced by the full amount of the private income) and so incentives could, in that case be justified on fiscal grounds. I wonder if anyone would care to lay bets on the probable tax treatment of ISA benefits (assuming they become law)?

The concessionary treatment in the EET model continues right up to the pensioner's death, because the assets supporting the annuity are still favourably treated. Although the pensioner pays tax on the return of capital in the EET model (it comes back to the pensioner tax-free under the TTE model), the income received by the pensioner is higher if the funds supporting the pension still earn more tax-free income than would be the case under the TTE model. The pension provider will price the EET pension using the tax-exempt seven per cent rather than the tax-paid 4.7 per cent in the TTE model.

Tax, Saving and Level Playing Fields

Why Has New Zealand Adopted Such an Unusual Approach?

Why hasn't anyone else followed New Zealand's unusual approach? Is there something the rest of the world doesn't know?

Tax incentives are traditional—the Task Force on Private Provision For Retirement (which looked at the appropriate role for New Zealand governments in retirement income provision) thought they were the worst of the three main alternative interventions. How come something so popular came third, after voluntary and compulsory provision?

The Cost of Tax Incentives

Tax incentives cost governments a lot both directly and indirectly. The US Treasury[1] put the nominal cost in the US at over $50 billion in one year alone. That's just for the loss of personal income tax receipts and it should be reduced by the eventual tax on pensions paid out. However, the price of the concessions should then be increased by the enormous transaction costs involved in the US retirement saving industry.

Actually, though, tax incentives don't cost *governments* anything.

The 'government' is a synonym for 'all taxpayers'. So it's 'all taxpayers' who provide the incentives. In practice, tax incentives tend to be driven by the needs of the vocal middle classes. Incentives to save for retirement are a good example of middle-class welfare—saving for retirement and retirement benefits generally are probably the most costly middle-class welfare.

In developed countries there are more taxpayers than savers so the smaller group (members of whom behave in a way that is 'acceptable') collects money from the larger group (some of whom behave in the 'acceptable' way, but many of whom do not).

Do Tax Incentives Work? The Saving Quantum Conundrum

Incentives are designed to change behaviour. Saving for retirement is a good thing, and tax incentives encourage saving for retirement, don't they? Or do they?

The New Zealand Task Force spent a lot of time on this question. It concluded that tax incentives certainly encourage savings in a *particular* direction but no-one anywhere seemed to know whether they actually increased savings overall.

---

[1]   Noted in Munnell, A.H., 'Current Taxation of Qualified Pension Plans: has the time come?', *New England Economic Review*, March/April 1992.

One study[1] suggested that most of the money flowing into tax-favoured Individual Retirement Accounts (IRAs) in the US comes from existing savings. Using 1982-1986 data, the authors estimated that only 20 per cent of IRA contributions were additions to national savings. Another study[2] concluded that most of the money flowing into tax-favoured schemes in the US was not new savings but a substitute for other forms of savings. The authors noted particularly that the personal savings rate in the US that averaged about seven per cent in the 30 years to 1980 has fallen to about 4.5 per cent just as tax-favoured savings have taken off.

A contrary indication seemingly comes from studies done by Wise and Venti and cited in the *Fortune* article already referred to.[3] These showed that families who had IRAs and savings in 401(k) schemes had more financial assets than others who didn't. While that may be true, it's another step to suggest that the tax-favoured families wouldn't have saved if the tax concessions hadn't been there. Anyway, looking only at the families' financial assets isn't the whole story. Yet another US study[4] found that increases in 401(k) scheme assets were approximately matched by increases in mortgage debt (reduced equity in houses). In fact, the 401(k) increases seemed to occur only where the household owned the family home. Over the 1984-1992 period, 401(k) assets went up by about $310 billion while housing equity fell by about $295 billion. The conclusion, according to *Business Week*, is that:

> ...wildly popular 401(k) schemes could be costing the government hefty revenues with negligible impact on consumer savings and debt.

Alicia Munnell, in the paper already cited (see note 1 p. 63) concluded it is 'at best unclear that taxpayers are getting their money's worth' from the huge expenditures in the US.

The following is a little simplistic but shows why it's so difficult to support incentives.

From a retirement saving perspective, society can be divided into three groups:

Group A: **savers**—those who would save for retirement even if there were no incentives.

Group B: **vacillators**—those who might or might not save.

Group C: **immovable**—those who won't be swayed even by the most generous incentive and the most pressing salesperson.

For the sake of our example, we'll assume that all members of all three groups are taxpayers.

Incentives won't change the behaviour of Group C. They may be too poor to save in the acceptable way demanded by the incentive, or they may prefer to save in 'unacceptable' ways like buying their own shares (rather than letting the trustee of their retirement scheme do that), building up a business,

---

[1]   By economists Orazio Attansio of Italy's University of Bologna and Thomas DeLire of Stanford University.

[2]   By economists Eric Engen, William Gale and John Scholz published in *The Brooking Papers on Economic Activity*.

[3]   See p. 57.

[4]   Engen, E. and Gale, W., reported in *Business Week*, 11 December 1995.

getting an education, paying off a farm or reducing the home mortgage. For whatever reason, the incentive doesn't encourage them to save any more.

Group A would have saved even without the incentive. The incentive may mean they save more in the acceptable way, though that could be at the expense of other 'unacceptable' saving methods.

This leaves us with Group B, some of whom will be persuaded by the incentive and some not. This then is really the incentive's target. However, even those whose heads are turned might have preferred to save in unacceptable ways rather than in the way demanded by the incentive.

It's true that anyone can advance from Group C to Group A (or at least to the 'well behaved' section of Group B)—the incentives are accessible to all. But that's not the point. Some can't (because they can't afford to) and some of the rest won't because either they don't see the need or they prefer to save in other ways. That may help explain why only two thirds of US employees who are eligible to participate in a 401(k) scheme (employer-provided, often subsidised and always tax-favoured) choose not to according to a US Labor Department survey.[1]

All members of all three groups pay for these incentives through their taxes. So my first reason for a tax incentive (increasing self-provision to reduce, indirectly, future reliance on the government) seems at best doubtful and at worst unproved. Logic says that there should be more saving with tax incentives (because of the vacillators who say yes) but I haven't seen the proof of it. A. Lans Bovenburg said of the US:

> ...while the effect of tax policy on the level of private saving is relatively small and uncertain, it nevertheless has a powerful effect on the composition of private saving and investment.[2]

And, in his view, some of that wasn't in the national interest.

That was also the conclusion of the New Zealand Task Force.

The second reason to justify tax incentives for retirement saving (reducing the amount paid by the State to retired persons) is manifestly unsatisfied. This is clearly not one of the reasons most countries use to justify the huge direct and indirect cost of incentives because so few developed countries reduce the state's age-related benefit on account of income from private saving (whether tax-subsidised or not). New Zealand, Australia and Canada are the only developed countries that have an income or asset test for Tier I benefits, though New Zealand has, inexplicably, got rid of its 'surcharge' (from 1 April 1998).

Australia, however, lets even tax-favoured savers off the income-tested hook by allowing them access to incentivised (and compulsory) savings well before the state pension starts. This gives them plenty of time to spend those savings before having them would affect their entitlement to the state benefit. In Australia, that's called 'double dipping'—making use of the tax concessions and collecting the state benefit.

---

[1] Reported by *Dow Jones News*, 26 February 1996. The same survey showed that 79% of employees who withdrew savings before retirement didn't roll them all over into a new fund despite the tax penalties imposed. So the savings weren't really for retirement income.

[2] 'Tax Policy and National Saving in the United States', *National Tax Journal*, Vol. XLII, No. 2, June 1989.

A hot topic among the economists who have looked at whether incentives actually work is to see if people adjust their saving level to compensate for the concession. In other words, do people save less to achieve a given level of retirement income in a concessionary environment than they would if there were no incentives? Economists call this the 'income effect'. On this, Jane Gravelle concluded, again in the US context:

> The conventional analysis, that IRAs either reduced savings or at least increased it very little seems more compatible with actual savings behaviour during the early 1980s.[1]

The income effect sounds sensible, particularly if we start with a concession-free environment. The greater sophistication of computer-based personal financial planning packages makes this an even more attractive explanation.

Suppose a saver (this time a model female earner) decides she wants to retire with a total after-tax retirement income of 60 per cent of her net pay near retirement. She loads all her assets and liabilities into the modelling software as well as her existing saving arrangements and her cash needs at retirement. In a world where there are no tax incentives for retirement saving, the computer tells her that she needs to increase her savings from, say, 10 per cent of her net pay to 15 per cent in order to reach her objective. She's happy about that and makes the necessary arrangements.

The government then decides that its citizens are not saving 'enough' for their retirement and that more people need to be convinced to save. It introduces a concession. Our saver must now get her computer programme updated for the new environment. She reruns her figures and is pleasantly surprised.

If she keeps up her existing savings, she would be able to look forward to a total net retirement income of 75 per cent of her net pay near retirement—up by 25 per cent. She now has two choices:

1. She can keep saving 15 per cent (this now costs her less on a net basis) and look forward to a richer retirement than she expected. Result: no new saving; higher taxes (or a bigger deficit); reduced national savings and a happy saver.

2. If she wants to stick with the original 60 per cent net retirement income objective, the computer tells her that she can reduce her 15 per cent savings down to, say, 11 per cent. Result: reduced saving; higher taxes (or a bigger deficit); reduced national savings and a happy saver.

I don't think this level of sophistication sounds idealistic and I have more to say about this in chapter 9.

Even if other citizens don't have access to a computer programme like the one used by our saver, they can make adjustments to their own behaviour after thinking about the government's new signals. They'll probably get it wrong either by over- or under-estimating the impact of the new tax concession. My point is that a large share of the new expenditure won't reach its target.

Why is there endless debate about the efficacy of incentives? Why, given the number of countries that bribe their citizens to save for retirement, don't we now know whether or not they work?

---

[1]   'Do Individual Retirement Accounts Increase Savings?', *Journal of Economic Perspectives*, Vol. 5, No. 2 Spring 1991, pp. 133-48 at p. 147.

We can't know without good longitudinal studies of wealth, that is, tracking people's spending behaviour through their economic life cycles.

All the studies I've seen on this rely on the snapshot approach of measuring economic behaviour—taking slices through the population at given moments, rather than following particular populations through their economic lives. The trouble with snapshots is that they miss the migration of people from one group to another. They assume that the people in the bottom group at one snapshot are the same as the people in the same group at the next. A 1992 study by Isabel Sawhill and Mark Condon[1] looked at income growth and mobility in the US for the periods 1967-1976 and 1977-1986. They concluded that about half of those who began in the bottom quintile moved into the higher quintiles (some all the way to the top), and about half of those in the top quintile moved down, some all the way to the bottom. More than two-thirds who started out in the middle moved up or down.

A US Treasury study cited in the same article found that 86 per cent of those in the bottom income quintile in 1979 had moved up by 1988 and, of those, 40 per cent reached the top two quintiles. Only 33 per cent of those in the middle quintile stayed there while 19.7 per cent fell and 47.3 per cent moved up. A more recent study[2] reached much the same kind of conclusion —only 5 per cent of those in the bottom quintile in 1975 were still there in 1991; 29 per cent of them had reached the top quintile; fewer than 0.5 per cent showed up in the bottom quintile in each of the years 1975-1991.

If we were cynical about this state of affairs, we'd say that the fact that taxpayers don't demand good longitudinal studies of economic behaviour as justification for the continuation of tax incentives is probably a reflection of the fact that the normally vocal middle-class beneficiaries of those incentives would stand to lose most from their demise.

However, the more probable explanation is that with so much money in tax-favoured vehicles around the world, politicians probably think that the incentives are working.

When you think how much governments spend on tax incentives, this lack of curiosity seems odd. There are however increasing concerns around the world about the cost of tax incentives, about their fairness and about whether governments actually get good value for them. The World Bank in its recent report said:

> ... the evidence is inconclusive on whether tax preferences stimulate people to save more—and, if so, whether these benefits exceed the costs.[3]

Again:

> ... it is not clear whether tax incentives have increased aggregate saving, and most of the tax benefits have gone to high-income households, many of which would have saved in any event.[4]

---

[1]   For the Urban Institute in the US and cited by Craig Roberts, P., in *Business Week*, 13 July 1992.

[2]   Cox, M. and Alm, R. of Federal Reserve Bank Dallas, 'By Our Own Bootstraps', reported in *The Financial Times*, 4 March 1996.

[3]   *Averting the Old Age Crisis, op. cit.*, p. 183.

[4]   *Ibid.*, p. 201.

You have to wonder why, given their popularity, tax-based policies were ignored in the World Bank's report. There was no discussion about the relative merits of income and consumption taxes or why the World Bank's customers should move away from the widespread use of payroll taxes.

Other Problems with Incentives

If tax incentives don't work and cost more than they recover, that should be sufficient reason to abandon them. But those are by no means the only problems for incentives. There are several others:

Inequities

Most countries give tax incentives for retirement saving by making the contributions deductible and either by exempting or favouring the build-up of assets.

Both are regressive forms of income redistribution. That's because high income earners have more disposable income and so tend to save more both in proportional and dollar terms.

That also defines the electorate of supporters for tax incentives—they tend to be rich, articulate and have close connections with the political process. They also know how to organise themselves.

Concessions for higher earners let them gain relatively more from an incentive—they can contribute more to the favoured scheme and, with a larger amount at stake, will benefit more from the advantages given to the build-up of investment income on the favoured basis. To illustrate, census data show that people in the US without tax-favoured IRAs or employer-sponsored savings or pension plans have median incomes of $15,000 a year. By contrast, those *with* IRAs etc have median incomes of $44,500 a year.[1]

One way of limiting the advantages conferred on the concession at the front end is to restrict the amount that can be paid to the scheme or limit the amount that can be claimed as a deduction from tax. If the limitation is linked to the pay of the employee (say, 15 per cent of pay as is the case in the UK) that has the curious effect of reinforcing the regressive nature of the concession on contributions. The higher the income, the higher the maximum dollar value of the exemption, both on the contributions and the build-up.

If the limitation is a monetary one, that would put an upper limit on the inequity, but would suffer from a further problem. Savers are likely to take the limit as a signal from the government that this is all they need to put aside. In New Zealand, until 1987, contributions to tax-favoured retirement schemes and life insurance policies were limited to $NZ1,400 ($NZ1,200 for employees).[2] Anecdotal evidence from advisers indicates that contributions to personal arrangements actually increased once the limit was removed.

Monetary caps on contributions or on a pension scheme member's pay that qualifies for tax-favoured saving treatment are used by a number of countries. They are also vulnerable to change when governments need to cut spending. Canada reduced the nominal amount of contributions allowed between 1995

---

[1]   According to Karen Ferguson of the Pension Rights Center in a letter to *The Wall Street Journal*, 11 January 1996.

[2]   Respectively 6.6% and 5.6% of the 1987 national average wage.

and 1996 by 13 per cent—they won't return to their 1995 nominal level until 1998; the UK reduced qualifying pay for lump sum benefits by 40 per cent in 1989 and introduced monetary pension limits for the first time; the US reduced qualifying pay by 36 per cent in 1994.

Some countries (the US is a good example) have books of rules to limit inequities that are inevitable with any form of bribery designed to influence behaviour. Fairness *should* be a key objective for any tax system, so deliberate (or accidental) slopes in favour of the more highly paid should be avoided, if at all possible. But it's a forlorn hope because regulators are always three steps behind the advisers.

There are other potential inequities besides those that can be measured by income. Why not, for example, offer women a greater incentive than men? They live longer so a given level of incentive will deliver them a smaller annual retirement income, though it will have a similar overall value.

Distortions

A further problem with tax incentives is their distortionary effect. All countries that favour saving for retirement through the tax system impose rules about where or how those savings should be invested.[1] There are several different types of distortions created:

Trusteed Arrangements

Trusteed arrangements are usually mandated so that assets are kept separate from the saver's other savings or from the employer's business assets. The tax system needs that separation to protect its investment and to ensure it gets the tax recoveries when benefits are paid 30 or 40 years later. The concessions are to help people save for retirement. They're pointless if retirement income doesn't appear and get taxed.

Assets

Other restrictions can apply to the assets approved schemes can buy—Canada has direct investment restrictions. No more than 20 per cent can be invested in overseas assets.[2] Both New Zealand and Australia had similar restrictions until fairly recently (1984); approved schemes had to invest a minimum proportion of their assets in local and central government securities at less than market rates.

---

[1] I come from a country that gets a lot of its income from farming activities that *aren't* subsidised by taxpayers so I see parallels with the insanities of farming subsidies around the world. If 85 per cent of the average farmer's income comes from taxpayers (Switzerland); if farmers have to supply map references for all their fields and then tell the government three times a year what they are doing in those fields (Europe); if there is one bureaucrat for every five farmers (the US), you can be sure that a lot of farming activity is about protecting the tax base and not about growing things that consumers might actually want. The same thing applies to tax-driven saving schemes.

[2] However, one scheme manager told me that the restriction now has little practical effect as it can be avoided (if a scheme really wants to) by the use of derivatives.

In Japan, at least 50 per cent of a pension scheme's assets must be in yen-denominated fixed interest securities (including cash) but only up to 30 per cent can be invested in overseas' assets and only up to another 30 per cent in local shares. These restrictions disappeared in 1997 for employee pension schemes, but not for 'tax-qualified' pension schemes, another type of retirement saving arrangement.

Austria, Belgium and Switzerland all have similar types of detailed requirements as to the proportions that can be invested in different asset classes. Switzerland's restrictions are a regulator's dream—not more than 30 per cent of cash can be foreign and there can be no more than: 75 per cent in loans on property; 30 per cent in foreign Swiss franc loans; 20 per cent in foreign loans in foreign currencies; 50 per cent in Swiss property; 5 per cent in foreign property; 30 per cent in Swiss equities; 25 per cent in foreign equities; 50 per cent in all equities; 30 per cent in foreign currency assets; 70 per cent in real assets and 30 per cent in foreign exposure.[1] Now, doesn't that make you feel secure!

It's no wonder that Swiss funds scored seventh out of seven, both on nominal and real rates of return, in an EU country comparison of the real returns over 1984-93 (run by the European Federation for Retirement Provision).[2] The two countries with the fewest restrictions (Ireland and the UK) were first and second.

Cartels

Japan has another type of control—conniving cartels. For reasons best known only to the regulators, the investment of the privately owned retirement funds of Japanese citizens was totally controlled by the life and trust companies, but not because they gave the best return. One commentator[3] suggested that this was part of a government-driven strategy to increase exports by extracting savings from workers at low cost and giving them to 'export-oriented manufacturers who put market share above profits'. Savers probably wouldn't support such a strategy by choice. The position is easing a little but, even now, a private pension scheme can give a maximum of only one half of its assets to a private fund manager (as opposed to a life insurance or trust company) and then only after it has been going for three years. Happily for Japanese investors, this type of control will disappear in 1999.

Economically targeted investment

A third type of potential control goes under the seemingly innocent title of the 'economically targeted investment' (or ETI). These are investment opportunities, usually dreamed up by politicians rather than investment managers, that are designed to win votes and improve the lives of voters, not savers. Examples of these have surfaced in the US (public housing), Australia (infrastructure development and revitalising distressed industrial areas) and

---

[1]　　According to Kuhn, E., in 'Pension Fund Investment in Switzerland', *Benefits & Compensation International*, November 1995.

[2]　　Reported in *The Financial Times*, 24 June 1996.

[3]　　Taggart Murphy, R., author of 'The Weight of the Yen', reported in *The Economist*, 20 April 1996.

Ireland (job creation, particularly in manufacturing). Collateral 'benefits' cited by ETI advocates include the creation of jobs, extended home ownership, developing affordable home ownership, revitalising neighbourhoods, directing investment to capital-poor areas and offering home ownership benefits to members. In the traditional trusteed schemes of English-speaking countries, it's difficult to see how any of these 'benefits' can be supported as a justification for an ETI. That especially applies to allowing some members the chance to buy a home, presumably at the potential expense of other members who can't afford to buy a home or who choose not to do it through the scheme.

'Approved' Vehicles

Another structural distortion created by subsidies is that 'approved' vehicles are favoured for new savings business over other vehicles that might actually be better for the country. While there may be competition between suppliers of services to approved vehicles, competition between approved vehicles as a whole and all other 'unfavoured' vehicles is reduced. The need for approved vehicles to perform well (by comparison with 'unacceptable' saving alternatives) will reduce. That may explain the growth of tax-favoured pension funds in the UK, apparently at the expense of other saving institutions. Table 4[1] shows the picture:

Table 4
Percentage Shares in Total Financial Institutions' Liabilities: UK

	Banks	Building Societies	Insurance Companies	Pension Funds
1913	64	4	32	-
1930	61	8	31	-
1939	55	12	32	na
1960	43	12	32	14
1970	32	17	27	16
1980	30	20	25	21
1990	28	17	26	26
1994	27	16	25	27

Source: Rose, H.

There are different possible explanations for the decline in the share of liabilities attributed to banks. One suggestion is that it was the loss of advantages enjoyed by banks as financial intermediaries. I think the more likely explanation for the rise of pension funds and the relatively smaller reduction in the market share held by the life insurance companies is the significant tax advantages enjoyed by those institutions.

Encouraging Inefficiencies

In fact, tax incentives may actually encourage inefficiencies and allow savers to be more tolerant of performance inadequacies and administrative

---

[1]   From data provided by Harold Rose in The Financial Times, 24 November 1995.

shortcomings. Perhaps that explains why Japanese institutions have been able to avoid competing among themselves for tax-favoured business. Until recently, cartels of the insurance and trust companies decided on the appropriate (low) rate to be credited to savers' accounts so there was only a limited amount of competition, even among the favoured vehicles. Those poor returns have also hurt employers' schemes; thanks in part to the controls imposed by Japan's Finance Ministry, the big companies' schemes may be as much as $200 billion underfunded.[1]

However, I think there's a more direct explanation for the inefficiency. To illustrate: let's assume that savings for retirement were still deductible for tax purposes in New Zealand. Taxpayers would then pay savers roughly 33 cents for every dollar they saved. So the investment manager could lose 33 per cent of the saver's money before the saver ran the risk of being worse off following the decision to save. Alternatively, the seller of the saving product could charge the saver 33 per cent of the amount invested for setting up the deal before it touched the saver in the pocket. In both of these cases, the saver is relatively less sensitive to poor returns or to high administration costs than would be the case if the first dollar of net returns went into the saver's pocket or if the first dollar of costs came out of the saver's pocket.

For much the same reason, I think savers are relatively less sensitive to inflation on the returns they receive. A tax-free return (that would have been taxed had it been directly received by the saver) is more robust to the effects of the 'tax' imposed by inflation. A tax-free return of, say, seven per cent a year can withstand inflation of up to that amount before the saver is actually affected in the pocket by inflation. Real rates of return mean much more to a saver paying tax on the nominal return than they do to the sheltered investor in an approved retirement scheme.

The Mere Existence of Tax-favoured Vehicles

The last institutional distortion is at the 'micro' level—the mere existence of tax-favoured vehicles will attract savings, not because they are the best (however that is defined) but because they are subsidised by all taxpayers. 'Labor-sponsored venture capital funds' in Canada are a case in point. Special tax breaks that are supposed to insulate investors from the high risk of venture capital (at the cost of all taxpayers) have passed the tax benefit over but most of the money has actually gone into government bonds. Now there's a neat circle.[2]

New Zealand's recent financial history has also been littered with the ruins of schemes that made sense from a tax perspective in times of high marginal rates (racehorses, films, goats, grapes and leveraged listed shares) but did not withstand the ultimate test of economic sense.

Other Controls

Then there are the controls that are imposed by the state supposedly to protect savers from mismanagement. The latest version of these are the UK's requirements that approved schemes must 'have a written statement of the

---

[1]   According to a report in *Forbes*, 15 July 1996.

[2]   According to a report in *The Financial Post*, 20 February 1996.

principles governing decisions about investments' and must 'obtain and consider written advice of a person who is reasonably believed by the trustees to be qualified by his ability...'[1] and so on. Though this is ostensibly about consumer protection, the cynical might think these controls are really to protect the governments from having to compensate savers who are locked into programmes by the rigidities of a tax-driven regulatory system, who can't vote with their feet and so find it more difficult to keep fund managers honest.

All these absurd conditions can be tolerated only because of the significant financial advantages the tax system confers on retirement savings. They can't be justified on any economic basis—quite the contrary, actually. Because the controls prevent investors from making optimal economic choices, they will reduce returns to the savers in the long term. That will water down whatever contribution those savings will make to future taxpayers and increase the pressures faced by tomorrow's welfare system. But then, they are tomorrow's voters not today's. The rational response must be to remove distortions caused by the different tax treatments.[2]

With both broad types of control that I've described (the 'where' and the 'how'), some forms of saving are favoured by weight of money over others. The requirements of trust law, for example, structurally favour listed shares over investment in small businesses. Ownership of big, liquid investments will be naturally preferred by favoured vehicles over small start-ups.

That doesn't necessarily mean we will get more big, liquid investments for the favoured vehicles to choose from. It may only bid up the prices of the existing ones. Just to demonstrate that point in the context of Chile's compulsory environment, on the day that Chile's Central Bank allowed approved schemes to increase their holdings of local shares from 30 per cent to 37 per cent of total assets, the 40-stock selective IPSA index rose 4.4 per cent. Analysts believed that the effect of the new rules on shares that are heavily weighted in the index would see increased demand for them by the approved schemes.[3] Where's the new investment?

Former Australian Prime Minister, Paul Keating, wanted the burgeoning compulsory schemes in Australia to concentrate less on buying the shares of the large listed companies, like BHP, Westpac and National Australia Bank, and look at 'bringing the new companies to market'.

Inefficiencies

The tax system has a large investment in the tax-favoured savings locked up in approved schemes. That investment is the present value of the future tax

---

[1] Section 35, Pensions Act 1995.

[2] The Editor of *The Financial Times* (editorial, 5 October 1995) saw that: 'Among the chief priorities [in the taxation of savings and investment] should be an attempt to restore neutrality between different types of saving, so that resources flow naturally towards the highest pre-tax returns.' I have no problems with that as an objective. But wait; three paragraphs later: 'Another temptation that the chancellor should continue to resist is a revenue-maximising raid on pension funds.' So, does that mean that all savings should get the same treatment as tax-subsidised pension schemes? Or getting rid of incentives altogether?

[3] Reported by *Dow Jones News*, 18 May 1995.

receipts the government will collect when the benefits are paid. It belongs to tomorrow's taxpayers and it has to be locked up, being let out only under controlled conditions.

Commentators boast about the size of this tax-leveraged industry. Assets in heavily subsidised UK schemes grew from the 1994 equivalent of $53 billion in 1975 to $468 billion in 1994.[1] The numbers in other favoured jurisdictions are apparently as impressive. But, as these bits of the market grow, relative to the rest, so too do the problems multiply.

Economic Inefficiency

'Locking-in' creates economic inefficiencies. Markets become less responsive both to individual savers' needs and to the needs of the economy at large.

Inflexibility

Individuals also face costs through loss of flexibility. Savings for retirement might be better spent on an earlier financial crisis (like ill health) or on an alternative more productive investment.

Some of this can be avoided by having a system that allows for the repayment of the concessions if they are not applied to their intended purpose. Precedents for that exist in the US (with IRAs) and in the UK (with Tax Exempt Special Saving Accounts—TESSAs) but it's all a costly and inefficient process, incurring considerable transaction costs.

Nearly all tax systems require that benefits emerge as a pension or annuity.[2]

The pension requirement carries with it further costs for individuals through loss of flexibility. It makes the tax concession less attractive, particularly for low-income earners who have less capacity to save in different ways so as to preserve flexibility. They are forced to trade off the tax-favoured income for the more flexible but unfavoured lump sum. However, that decision is not made at retirement (when the price of the trade-off could be better assessed) but when the saving starts and when the employee would have little idea of his or her future needs.

The constraints even create problems for people who had opted for retirement pensions but, after they retired, wanted access to their savings for reasonable reasons. A recent example of this showed up in the UK when the government's 1995 budget proposed special conditions for people receiving tax-favoured pensions who wanted to provide for possible rest-home costs. The industry wanted the government to go further by offering tax-favoured saving for rest home costs.

Benefit Inequities

'Locking in' also creates downstream benefit inequities that the system has tried to fix in many jurisdictions. There are books of rules about vesting, preservation and the protection of preserved benefits against the impact of

---

[1]   Reported in *IBIS Review*, October 1995.

[2]   Australia is the exception to this—tax-favoured savings can 'disappear' from the system through payment of benefits as a lump sum, with a modest recovery to taxpayers through a concessionary tax levied on the saving scheme's benefit.

inflation—the UK and the US rules (all 600 pages of them in the case of the US) are outstanding examples of this. Some of those rules have been driven by consumer protection legislation but a lot have fallen out of the tax system's justified paranoia about 'leakage'. The up-front subsidies and the favours conferred during the build-up can only be justified if fences around the system prevent the escape of the favoured funds or their misdirection away from ordinary citizens to the relatively favoured few.

Cartels

There's another more subtle form of inefficiency that's encouraged by this cosy system. Closed systems tend to produce cartels—groups that act for their own benefit rather than for the good of their ultimate customers (the people who save for retirement). Tax subsidies tend to insulate these players from the judgements of markets, partly because money is locked in but also because tax subsidises the returns earned on the money invested, as well as on the contributions made.

Compliance Costs

As well as being inefficient, tax incentives are expensive to administer. Bureaucracies are created both by gamekeepers and poachers but the gamekeepers start from behind and are likely to stay there. The economic imperative is much stronger for the poachers, whose job is to maximise the after-tax value of income for their fee-paying clients. The whole process makes the walls around the tax-favoured funds grow ever higher.

Regulatory supervision creates another compliance cost. New Zealand's regime provides a practical illustration. Our approved ('registered') tax-neutral retirement schemes are administered by the Government Actuary under the Superannuation Schemes Act 1989. That Act contains only 20 pages. And that's it! There are no regulations, 'practice notes', 'memoranda' or 'binding rulings'. The neutral regulatory regime is much simpler than those that apply in countries with tax concessions.

The US contrasts sharply with New Zealand in this regard. Life is now so complicated there that a new service has started—a company that specialises in auditing the calculation of a beneficiary's entitlements. It keeps half of anything it recovers. The company claims that it finds mistakes in 50 per cent of the cases it investigates.[1]

Under US law, a member of a tax subsidised 401(k) plan can lose the tax-favoured status of the benefit because of the plan's failure to comply with the rules.

> Next time you run into your resident pension management person, casually ask whether he or she has read Announcement 94-101, 1994-35 I.R.B. 1, 08/12/94 IRC Sec.401. Got that? It's an IRS-issued set of guidelines that tells 401(k) auditors what to pounce upon.[2]

Everyone pays for the costs of compliance, even if they aren't saving—who do you think pays for the salaries of all those regulators? Savers also meet the costs of those who clip the tickets in the private sector.

---

[1] Reported in *The New York Times*, 4 June 1995.

[2] *Fortune* magazine.

Income Tax Rates

Higher than necessary income tax rates are another cost of tax incentives. It's not possible to give a concession to savers without either increasing the tax burden elsewhere, increasing government borrowing or reducing the government's expenditure in other areas. The first two of these responses directly increase present or future taxes while the third reduces the worth of government services that would otherwise have been supplied.

The shift to TTE in New Zealand has been part of a consistent drive towards a broad-based, (relatively) low-rate system where inconsistent treatments are driven out. The general approach has been to deny all claims for special tax treatment in the interests of keeping the rate relatively low for everyone. So a New Zealand taxpayer can't claim a deduction for a spouse, children, house mortgage interest, education, life insurance, disability insurance, medical insurance or anything else of any consequence, unless it is directly connected to the production of taxable income.[1] Tax as a share of the New Zealand economy is falling. It was 36.5 per cent of GDP in 1995/96 and, according to the government, should be 33.4 per cent in 1999/2000. Tax rates in New Zealand are still too high, but they are lower than they would be if the government offered tax incentives.

Getting taxes down also saves on what the economists call the 'dead-weight cost of taxation'. This cost measures the value of the opportunities that are effectively lost when taxation diverts labour, land and capital from their best uses. A 1994 New Zealand report[2] suggested that the marginal dead-weight costs of tax on income from labour have increased over the last 20 years in New Zealand from five per cent to 18 per cent.

Levelling out tax treatments of different forms of saving has an investment-related implication. It concerns what are known as 'tax wedges'.[3] The marginal tax wedge is the real difference between the pre-tax business return and the post-tax lender's return. Where individuals face alternative investment possibilities (such as direct saving vs. retirement schemes vs. life insurance policies), the closer the wedges are together, the better. In New Zealand there is now no practical difference between these three forms of saving. Individuals will now choose the most appropriate form of saving for the best reasons—return, security, flexibility and so on. Tax is no longer an issue.

The cost of a retirement saving incentive does not, by itself, mean that it is a bad idea but it does mean that the benefits from the concession must outweigh the cost. I haven't read of a cost/benefit analysis for tax incentives carried out by any country. That's something of a puzzle. Most of the recent studies I have seen have concentrated on whether tax concessions increased

---

[1]   Though, to be fair, there is a welfare-related income support system that reduces the tax burden for families in the lowest income groups.

[2]   Diewert, E. and Lawrence, D., 'The Marginal Costs of Taxation in New Zealand'.

[3]   The New Zealand Task Force used a discussion of tax wedges from a paper by Michael Rich of the New Zealand Treasury 'Neutrality of Taxation on New Zealand Business Investment 1984-90', prepared for the New Zealand Association of Economists' Conference, Lincoln University, 1991.

saving. I would have expected that point to have been demonstrated before the concession was even introduced. The real debate should be about whether the government is getting good value for the cost of the concession.

A tax concession that has the government taking some money out of the pockets of every single taxpayer (even from the lowest paid who have no hope of saving for retirement) helps institutionalise all these problems. That money is then given to those who behave 'appropriately'.

This long litany of difficulties with tax incentives can be summed up by saying tax incentives don't work. I have seen no proof anywhere that tax incentives increase a country's overall savings. They certainly don't save the government money directly, they are unfair, distortionary, inefficient, cost a lot to administer and everyone pays more tax with the extra dead-weight costs that implies.

They therefore trip at three of the four hurdles Adam Smith developed to judge any tax system—they are inequitable, have high compliance costs and are economically inefficient. I also think they trip at the fourth (certainty)—because of their high cost and indifferent outcomes, someone will wonder why we still have them. Tax incentives for retirement saving are (or should be) inherently uncertain.[1]

This long litany of difficulties with tax incentives earned them a distant last in the three horse race run by the New Zealand Task Force between the three main options for retirement income provision—voluntary, compulsory and tax concessions.

Four Final Arguments

Quality

There are four final arguments that some raise in favour of tax incentives. The first concerns the 'quality' of savings for retirement by contrast with savings accumulated for other reasons. They argue that the long-term purpose of savings for retirement gives these savings a more desirable character. Other less subtle proponents of tax-subsidised saving think that they 'benefit the stock market by stimulating share dealings...'[2] Whatever the mechanics, because such savings can take a longer view, they will apparently be less sensitive to the ups and downs of the short-term market fluctuations.

There seem to be two things wrong with that argument:

Theory
Economists debate whether the market needs that kind of 'improvement'. Even if markets need it, there are countervailing difficulties. Locking the savings of our future retirees into tax-favoured vehicles carries with it the danger of distorting market signals on the 'correct' relative returns between long- and short-term savings. It also assumes that governments know better than the market what the economy needs.

---

[1] More evidence of this uncertainty emerged in the UK's 1997 Budget with the news of the removal of the Advance Corporation Tax relief for tax subsidised schemes. We can expect more of that kind of incremental attack on those schemes' privileged positions.

[2] A study by Deutsche Bank reported in *The Financial Times*, 24 November 1995.

Practice

It seems to me that the institutional focus of money managers over the years has actually become shorter rather than longer. While I know that pension plan trustees try to focus on the medium to long term, the league tables run by the asset strategists and pension consultants emphasise the latest quarterly returns almost as much as the last year, never mind the last three to five years. We all know that the longer-term view is the more appropriate but that's not the way the public gets this news presented.

It seems sensible for businesses to have access to long-term capital so that they can invest in long-term projects with, presumably, better long-term returns. It's another question whether governments should become an intermediary in that process at the potential cost of us all through higher taxes. Shouldn't that intermediation be left to financial markets?

If money can be invested profitably, markets have a tendency to match supply and demand at a price that reflects the risks involved. Financial markets tend to be particularly inventive. They have developed many ways to link the needs of savers with a short-term horizon to businesses that have long-term needs. Listed shares are a case in point. They are, effectively, an investment in perpetuity and, being publicly traded, usually give individual investors the liquidity they need.

Locking up savings imposes a cost on savers who naturally want to be compensated for the loss of liquidity. They'll tend to want a higher return to compensate them for the relative inflexibility and for the risks of mismanagement, and also for being denied the ultimate choice of being able to take their money out and invest elsewhere. This means that, over time, businesses may actually pay a higher price for funds from a locked-in source than they would from a more flexible (but initially more demanding) source.

On this issue, the New Zealand Task Force concluded that markets are likely to know better than governments what the markets want and how that should be delivered.[1]

Raising the Cost of Capital

If tax incentives for retirement are such a bad idea, then withdrawing them sounds like the logical next step. But won't that raise the cost of capital for companies? That's the flip side of the argument that tax incentives tend to de-sensitise savers to lower than optimal returns. If savers don't mind lower pre-tax returns (because they are tax free) then the users of capital get their capital at a potentially lower cost.

That's not the case in New Zealand, though it would be in other countries without changes to the way company tax works. In New Zealand, companies pay tax on their incomes—any dividends paid to shareholders carry 'imputation credits' that reflect the company-paid tax. When shareholders return the dividends in their personal tax returns, the imputation credit reduces the income tax that they would otherwise have paid. Only one lot of tax is effectively paid on the company's income at the investors' own rate.

So, where imputation exists, the retirement saving scheme's tax position depends on the tax environment in which it operates:

---

[1]   'Private Provision for Retirement—The Options', August 1992.

EET: because there is no tax on the scheme's investment income, the imputation credits are lost. The tax paid by the company would be the final payment.

TTE: as a taxpayer, the scheme will claim the imputation credit against the dividends received.

In both cases, only one lot of tax would be paid.

However, without imputation, changing the tax status of retirement saving schemes might increase the cost of capital (though tax-favoured retirement saving schemes are not the only owners of shares).

Tax Implications of Deferring Consumption

Some suggest a third justification for the special tax treatment of retirement savings—it has to do with the impact of income tax on investment earnings.[1] The argument, briefly, runs that income that is deferred for retirement is subjected to higher rates of tax than the income that is consumed immediately. That's because the saver pays tax on the bit of the investment income that compensates for the impact of inflation. Over the long periods that retirement savings accumulate and are then spent, this can produce some potentially startling numbers, especially if the inflation rate were fairly close to the earning rate. New Zealand's top marginal rate of 33 per cent would rise to an effective 58.3 per cent after 30 years (assuming five per cent interest and five per cent inflation) and up to a numbing 73.1 per cent with a 10 per cent interest rate and 10 per cent inflation.

The real problem here is inflation. Governments would be better employed getting that under control rather than compensating a special group of the population—those who save in favoured vehicles—at the expense of all taxpayers.

Even if there were merit in the argument, exempting *all* investment income is a weak justification for the EET treatment savers get in most developed countries.

The Information Gap

The fourth argument is the common response to all this—'But people don't understand. Without incentives, people won't save for retirement; governments of tomorrow will face a tidal wave of elderly indigents. We must have tax incentives so that we don't need to explain the actuarial niceties of pre-funding future retirement incomes to those who, unlike us, aren't equipped to make sensible decisions.'

An alternative equivalent argument runs that people need to be protected from their own profligacy. Retirement savings need to be locked out of reach behind the high walls erected by governments to protect their investment in the tax incentive. No-one makes them put the money behind those walls but, once they do, they won't be able to get at it.

---

[1] See, for example, 'Comments on issues related to retirement income provision in New Zealand' prepared for The New Zealand Business Round Table by Schieber, S.J. of Watson Wyatt, Washington, DC.

I think both these arguments are a touch arrogant—they smack of 'mother knows best'. You'll know that a supporter of tax incentives is really scraping the barrel if he uses these arguments against you.

Tax incentives are no substitute for information but there is undoubtedly an information gap. The argument about the information gap led to what the New Zealand Task Force thought was the key to a government's proper involvement in retirement saving. More on that later.

Conclusion

Tax incentives seem to be a big part of the problem rather than part of the solution. Tax-based regulation is becoming increasingly complex and specialised. Governments that offer tax incentives are entitled to protect their investment, but I think their efforts are driving a wedge of incomprehension between savers and savings and even between employers and savings.

There is no doubt that saving for retirement is a good idea. But there is something wrong if all taxpayers are forced to 'bribe' their fellow citizens into behaving 'sensibly'. In any event, throwing public money at a problem won't solve it. And it seems that tax incentives cost more than they recover.

The bulk of evidence shows that tax incentives do not work. So, why do governments keep using them? Even the reasons that supporters of tax incentives give don't stack up.

Those who spend my money to provide incentives for other people to save should supply proof that tax incentives really do work.

If they don't work, incentives should go.

5

What About Compulsion?

Summary

Compulsory, contributory, funded schemes (as opposed to compulsory, contributory but essentially unfunded systems) are found in a number of countries. Of these, the Chilean model is recognised as being the best designed scheme and attracts international attention. However, this regime has encountered 'delinquency' problems and its long-term viability in its present form is uncertain.

Compulsory schemes offer a number of features including the need for central government support, defined contributions, pooling of assets into a specific fund, and a requirement that the economy perform well to provide satisfactory returns.

Such schemes generally form part of the 'command and control' approach to government. They have a number of disadvantages and advantages. The former include the cost and complexity of the structures required for administration of such schemes, economic costs, lower returns and difficulty in achieving consensus. Advantages include a probable increase in total savings, and a reduction in the incidence of 'free-riding'.

The disadvantages heavily outweigh the advantages. A more efficient alternative would be to create an environment that allows and encourages individuals to modify their savings behaviour without compulsion.

****

Compulsion is catching on. More and more countries seem to see forced saving as one way of coping with the coming demographic deluge. Some have made the change while more are looking at it seriously.

Before we look at the relative merits and problems of the compulsory option, we need some definitions. There are two types of compulsory regime: contributory, but essentially unfunded, and contributory, funded systems.

The contributory but essentially unfunded system of income redistribution is common in many countries (like the OASDI, 'Social Security' in the US and National Insurance in the UK). The benefits can build up in different ways, such as by the period of compulsory contributions (the UK's basic state pension). They can be pay-related (such as in France and with the UK's State Earnings Related Pension Scheme or SERPS), or they can be both pay and contribution-related (the US system).

A tax-funded welfare benefit that depends on periods of residency or low incomes for the old is also a compulsory regime. However, the absence of an identified 'social security' contribution distinguishes this type of compulsion from the contributory, unfunded regime already described. Its cost comes simply from general tax revenues.

81

The contributory, funded system involves 'real' assets (including government bonds which have many of the characteristics of unfunded future pensions) built up from the contributions of members and, sometimes, their employers. Again, there are two main types—first, the centrally-run 'provident funds' of Singapore, Malaysia and some of the small Pacific Island countries. Japan's national pension contributions are also run on a similar, though partly funded basis, with a central body (the Finance Ministry) responsible for its investment. About three quarters of Japan's pension funds of $1,770 billion are in the public sector.[1]

Then there are the systems modelled on the Chilean example where the government says what has to be paid but the member or the employer/manager chooses where the money goes. This model has recently been attracting the attention of policy makers around the world. A number of countries have introduced such a system.[2]

This chapter is devoted to the contributory, funded model. The unfunded version only raises revenue from taxpayers and pays it to the old who are alive today. It's mostly about income redistribution, not saving for retirement.[3] The contributory, unfunded model is discussed in chapter 6.

A number of countries (for example, Australia, Singapore and Chile) inexplicably mix incentives and compulsion—earners (and their employers in the cases of both Australia and Singapore) are forced to save and then they are all rewarded for that with a tax incentive, paid for by themselves. There's some point in enticing people to save through a tax incentive but, if they are *made* to save, the incentive seems particularly pointless.

Who Uses the Compulsory Funded Regime?

Compulsory funded regimes are the flavour of the decade. Peru, Colombia, Argentina, Mexico and Poland have all looked at them. Some have already begun.[4] They are all different, giving their own twists to a common theme. A brief sampling illustrates the diversity.

---

[1]   From a report in *The Financial Times*, 2 May 1996.

[2]   Out in left field is Finland's funded, defined-benefit, compulsory Työntekijän eläkelaki or TEL. This delivers a top up to Tier I equal to 60% of covered pay after 40 years. Each employer has its own plan (no choice to savers) but the final employer delivers the full pension. A central clearing house collects the vested entitlements from earlier employers. The employer's cost is fixed centrally because, for some reason, all employees cost the same.

[3]   Though, in the US, it's also used as a way of monitoring future governments' obligations to the old. The regular actuarial valuation attempts to measure future outgoings and to show the amounts that will be needed to meet that. The money collected is then 'invested' by lending it all back to the government and reducing the deficit for today's taxpayers.

[4]   The latest is Hungary which, from 30 June 1998, will require all new entrants to the workforce to have a personal pension. Accruals under the social security system will reduce by 26% according to William M Mercer's 'Market Alert', 11 August 1997.

Singapore

The government-run Central Provident Fund (CPF), set up in 1955, requires total contributions of 40 per cent of covered pay up to a maximum of $45,800 a year. Of this, 20 per cent comes from employees, 20 per cent from employers. However, only four of that 40 per cent has to go into a special account for old age and 'contingencies' and even this can be drawn on to buy a home if the amounts in the 'Ordinary Account' have been spent. A minimum level of pension must be secured on retirement—the balance can be taken as a lump sum at retirement.

The bulk of the CPF is a major source of housing finance,[1] health insurance and education funds, so it's not just about retirement. It's mostly invested in securities issued by the government so politicians have a passing interest in the CPF as well. 96 per cent was in domestic bonds at the end of 1996.[2] A lot of that was then invested by the government in overseas' equities where the returns went to the government and not the members. The position has 'improved' a bit in the last three years by offering choices to members.

What distinguishes the Singapore model from the notionally funded Social Security in the US is that Singapore runs budget surpluses, so doesn't actually need to borrow the money from the CPF. That doesn't prevent the government from offering savers a poor return—3.6 per cent per annum over 1983-1993 (a real return of just two per cent per annum). Some things don't change. Having said that, a central fund that's invested wholly in government securities is really no fund at all. A government can achieve the same end by putting up taxes and changing its own accounting systems from cash accounting to proper 'Generally Accepted Accounting Practices' where the accumulating obligation for the future retirement benefits is recognised as a contingent liability on the country's balance sheet.

There is only one fund or accumulation of money in this version of the model and savers don't run it. Unelected officials normally have a large say in how the savings are spent, often for reasons that would seem to be more about winning votes than increasing the future incomes of retirees. Take this, for example, from Malaysia's Deputy Prime Minister, talking about the idea that savers might want to invest their own savings:

> The whole arrangement is to protect the very poor. How do you protect them if you allow them to take out the money and invest, when we cannot guarantee returns?[3]

In Singapore's case, there are signs that things will eventually get better for savers. The government announced in 1994 that the CPF will gradually increase the choices savers have. However, the change seemed more to do with building Singapore's status as a financial centre than with the security of savers' benefits or the returns they might get in the future. Savers will be able to put some of their money with approved managers but the only qualifying managers will be those who, among other things, have been in Singapore for at least three years, run at least $318 million, have at least three professional managers, invest at least 10 per cent in banks or

---

[1] New housing loans took 33% of new contributions in 1994/5 according to the CPF's 1995 annual report.

[2] *Pension Fund Indicators*, PDMF Limited, May 1997.

[3] Reported in *Business Times*, 5 January 1996.

government bonds and so on. When Lee Kuan Yew[1] announced the changes, there wasn't a word in his speech about improving the lot of the saver and no embarrassment at the poor past returns.

Australia

In Australia, an 'accord' between unions and the government established a network of privately managed, mostly (by weight of members) union award-based retirement schemes. They were introduced to give a pay rise without that feeding through into spending at an economically and politically tender time in Australia's recent past (1986). The fact that the regime was sold as a retirement saving issue just confused things. Employers were made to pay the initial three per cent of pay on the basis that the compulsory contribution was in exchange for 'productivity improvements'. That excuse was dropped in 1992 when the 'superannuation guarantee charge' was introduced and, by law, applied to all employees, not just union members. The rationale is now that forced saving will improve Australia's national savings, an objective that's hindered by the cost of tax concessions—estimated by the Department of Treasury at $5.6bn for 1993/94.

Australian employers currently pay a compulsory contribution of six per cent of pay, but this will grow to nine per cent by 2002-3. They pay it for all employees, not just union members as originally required. Employees were to contribute at a rate that would have reached three per cent by 2000. A further layer of complexity was to be added with an income-tested contribution from the government (paid for by all taxpayers) to match the employees' contributions—an idea that drew criticism before it even started. However, the 1997 Budget announced that both these extra contributions will not proceed.[2]

Despite the compulsory scheme, Australian household saving rates have continued to fall and are now among the lowest in the OECD. According to the Australian Bureau of Statistics, the saving rate has been decreasing for more than a decade after having peaked at 16 per cent in the mid-1970s.[3]

In the Australian model, there are separate funds (or pools of money) in which a member's contributions may be invested. Typically, the member doesn't choose where they go because, by weight of numbers of members, that's done by the trustees of the scheme to which they belong. Most schemes, again by weight of member numbers, are union related and many award agreements with unions specify where the money must go. The new Australian government intends to let members have more choice about where their money is invested. That new complexity was supposed to begin in 1998 but will probably be delayed until 1999.

Chile

In 1981 the Pinochet government introduced a privately-funded replacement for a bankrupt web of social welfare benefits. Thirteen per cent of pay is paid by employees to a fund of their choice. Of that, about 10 per cent goes to the member's individual retirement saving account. The other (approximately)

---

[1]   Published in *The South China Morning Post*, 27 September 1994.

[2]   The government had already announced that the compulsory contribution threshold was to rise from $A5,400 a year to $A10,800.

[3]   Report in *The Sydney Morning Herald*, 30 May 1996.

three per cent is used by the approved fund, the Administradora de Fondos de Pensiones (AFP) to pay for survivors' and disability insurance and administration expenses.

The now 15 AFPs (down from 21 in the early 1990s) are tightly controlled and money can be shifted without charge from one to another on 30 days' notice from the employee.

In the Chilean model, the member chooses the institution that invests the compulsory savings. Countries that have adopted or are installing versions of this model include Argentina, Hong Kong, Mexico, Poland and Uruguay.

Sweden and Italy

And then there are the hybrid schemes which fail the 'market test' (there is no choice about where the money is invested) and where the state decides the basis on which the pension conversion works at retirement. In Sweden personal pension accounts that will receive only two per cent of each employee's pay (up to a ceiling) will live alongside the massive, unfunded defined-benefit system. Though the existing benefits won't be reduced by the compulsory accounts, the government managed to reduce the cost of social security by a little more than the amount to be paid to the new system (18.86 per cent down to 16.5 per cent).

Italy is trying to constrain its future pension liabilities with a similar hybrid approach. In 1996 the social security system started individual accounts for members' contributions as the price for eliminating special discriminatory provisions that existed in the state scheme.

The US and the UK

There are signs of interest in compulsion in the US and UK. The pension lobby group in the UK, the National Association of Pension Funds (NAPF), has called for a clone of the Chilean model to be considered.

The Financial Times supports the idea:

> While the insistence on compulsion will not appeal to libertarians, it is the only practical means of addressing the problem of moral hazard inherent in the continuing state safety net. If they know the state will not leave them in penury many will opt for improvidence rather than thrift.[1]

The Chilean experience has been noted with approval in the US. *Business Week* supports a 'fully-funded pension system' to partially replace Social Security. The present contributions of 12.4 per cent should, according to *Business Week*,[2] be divided into a smaller pension for five per cent and a 2.4 per cent survivor's and disability benefit (the same as now); the final five per cent should go into 'Personal Security Accounts', where earners have a say over where the money is invested. There has even been a suggestion that the expected increases projected for the future in the US Social Security system should be invested in 'real' assets by the Fund's Trustees.[3]

---

[1]   Editorial, 1 May 1995.

[2]   8 July 1996. See also Roberts, P.C., 'It's time to privatise Social Security', *Economic Viewpoint*, in *Business Week*, 27 February 1995.

[3]   See, for example Bosworth, B., 'Putting Social Security to Work', *The Brookings Review*, Fall 1995.

More on the Chilean Model

Compulsion may address the moral hazard that citizens will refuse to behave sensibly and will prefer to rely on the state, but does that, on its own, make it a good idea? Is that the only thing that compulsion achieves? Before looking at this, I want to describe the Chilean model more fully, for two reasons:

- it's attracting quite a bit of international attention and there are already several similar versions based roughly on the model

- I think that, with a few shortcomings, it's a well designed compulsory scheme and illustrates both the advantages and disadvantages of the genre.

The scheme is replacing a complex web of failed social welfare arrangements. In 1981 Chileans were given five years to choose whether to stay with the existing benefits or shift to the new. It helped that the new scheme cost employees less than the old and that they then had accounts supported by 'real' assets that they owned. The money no longer vanished into bottomless government coffers—the benefits would now be 'secure'.

In order to achieve this piece of fiscal magic (better and larger benefits for less money) the government gave some inducements. First, for employees who chose to switch to the new system, the 'past service liability' that the old benefits represented was turned into a 'real' liability by the issue of government securities equivalent to their then value (plus a real return to cover the period to state pension age). That made the benefits *seem* more secure—it didn't actually make them more secure because the same government was still making the promises. Those promises are still costing a lot.[1] The transition costs from the old to the new regimes are, after 15 years, still five per cent of GDP and there is disagreement as to when that figure will decrease. The change both forced the government to run budget surpluses and to redirect spending away from other areas of need. Some commentators[2] are now saying that the transition costs will never disappear despite the fact that some pensions are already more under the new regime than they would have been under the old.

Next the government promised that the new scheme would never give the member less than the old, relatively miserable (for most) scheme—in that way it gave a modest underwrite to the investment performance of the members' new savings.

Lastly, the government made employers increase their employees' pay by about 18 per cent so their take-home pay wasn't reduced. However, this change was not that onerous for employers—their labour costs were reduced by five per cent overall because of the elimination of employer-paid social security contributions which had, by then, grown to 65 per cent of pay. Average real pay fell by nearly 15 per cent between 1981 and 1987[3] and that also helped reduce expectations and employers' costs.

---

[1] According to Kay, S., of UCLA in 'Unexpected Privatizations: Politics and Social Security Reform in Argentina, Brazil and Uruguay' 1996.

[2] United Nations Development Programme, reported in *The Economist*, 18 April 1998.

[3] According to *The Economist Intelligence Unit*, 1 February 1996.

The Chilean regime now focuses on the individual saver. From 1981 employees became the sole contributors to social security—apart, that is, from the government which still supports the age benefit's underwrite and the financial performance of the institutions that invest savers' money.

The contributions are paid to the AFP chosen by the saver. Apart from evasion, this was the only choice given to earners.

Employees pay a total amount of 20 per cent of qualifying pay. But seven per cent of that goes on health insurance and about three per cent goes to pay for the saver's disability insurance benefits (about 0.7 per cent of pay) as well as administration expenses. That leaves about 10 per cent for compulsory retirement savings. Employees can choose to pay more—up to 20 per cent of capped earnings qualify for a deduction from taxable pay.

On retirement, the employee must use the savings to buy a lifetime annuity, indexed to inflation, of at least the minimum benefit underwritten by the government. Other choices are available, especially if the employee's benefit exceeds 70 per cent of covered average earnings, measured over the 10 years before retirement.

The government has licensed, now, 15 AFPs to receive the compulsory contributions.[1] The AFP manager must observe solvency rules as well as intricately detailed regulations governing where it can invest the AFP's money. Among other things, these include a limit on how much of the AFP's assets can be invested in shares (up to 40 per cent, with no more than five per cent in any one share), and a restriction on how much can be invested overseas (no more than 12 per cent). Other limitations apply to government bonds, corporate and state bonds, 'personality investment fund shares' and hedging instruments.

Some of the licensing and investment regulations are to protect the security of members' benefits but not all. The restrictions on the amount that can be invested internationally protected Chile's balance of payments by limiting the flow of funds to international investments. Unfortunately, they also limit the AFPs' ability to diversify their assets away from the Chilean economy.[2]

The very existence of restrictions implies that the AFPs and their members might prefer to invest their retirement savings somewhere else. The suggestion that savers aren't sophisticated enough to decide an appropriate mix comes out of the command-and-control school of government, as does the whole structure of compulsion.

Each Chilean AFP must report to its members on a quarterly basis. A key part of the regime allows members to transfer from one AFP to another every six months with only 30 days' prior notice and only a nominal transfer charge. This was intended to provide a balance to the power of the AFPs

---

[1] Despite the choice, the market is in fact quite concentrated—the largest three AFPs in 1995 had more than two thirds of contributors and half the funds.

[2] The new Mexican compulsory scheme (constructed largely according to the Chilean model) also has this problem but in larger measure—all money must be invested in Mexico. Not only that but the 'AFOREs' (the Mexican equivalent of an AFP) will be '...obliged to use their resources primarily for:—the development of national productive activity; employment generating schemes; house-building, and regional development'. Reported by Oxford Analytica, 6 May 1996.

which were delivered a large captive market and a potential licence to print money. AFPs now have 4.9 million members and control assets worth $33 billion or 40 per cent of GDP.[1]

However, some things don't change. AFPs sell memberships in much the same way as insurance contracts are sold in other countries—introducers get commissions from the AFP. There are rules about this—overall administration expenses are limited but are high. Sales costs have risen from eight per cent of the AFPs' trading incomes in 1991 to 26 per cent in 1995.[2] The average administration expenses are 3.22 per cent of a contributor's pay, including the cost of disability insurance.[3] Of this, an average of about two percentage points is a commission to the AFPs.[4]

By contrast, the US Social Security programme cost 0.08 per cent of participants' taxable wages to administer.[5] That wouldn't allow for the employer's costs in administering the collection and payment of contributions but neither would the Chilean numbers.

The rules on transfer were designed to protect the consumer. I asked a major AFP manager why savers changed their allegiances—was it because of superior investment performance? They had looked at this issue and discovered that most members moved because of a persuasive seller rather than through dissatisfaction. About 10 per cent of all members shifted in a year at the time of my conversation (1992). About 1.4 million a year (25 per cent) changed AFPs in 1995[6] and the proportion is rising. AFPs with the largest sales forces (more than 70 per cent of whom are apparently young women) are the most successful at getting and keeping contributors. Marketing costs have risen significantly.

The Chilean regime enjoyed a favourable investment climate in its first 14 years, closely linked to a strong and growing economy. The returns were spectacular, at least until fairly recently. Eleven of the AFPs averaged 14.1 per cent per annum for the 13 years to 1994. The top AFP earned an average of 14.9 per cent per annum while the bottom one earned 13.7 per cent per annum[7]

---

[1]   According to *The Economist*, 13 September 1997.

[2]   From the *New Zealand Press Association*, 21 June 1996.

[3]   Johnathan Kandell in 'Very Social Security', *Worldbusiness*, Jul/Aug 1996.

[4]   This is a regressive element in the Chilean scheme—over the three years to 1997 workers on minimum salaries received an after-expenses return of 3.7% while the system as a whole returned 6.1% according to Veronica Jacobsen in 'Paying For Pensions', a report for the New Zealand Business Roundtable, July 1997.

[5]   From 'Principles of Financing Social Security Pensions' by Lawrence H Thompson, July 1995. The equivalent figure in New Zealand has been estimated (by the Periodic Report Group in its July 1997 'Interim Report') as 0.04% of the average income of the population aged 16+.

[6]   Veronica Jacobsen again.

[7]   Based on those numbers, it's not easy to see why you would pick one AFP over another. However, the reason for their similarity is intended. By law, the average return, each *month*, must be no more than 2 percentage points

However, returns fell dramatically in 1995. In the year to 31 October 1995, AFPs lost an average of 3.7 per cent and achieved only 3.5 per cent in 1996. One of the reasons for the poor returns is the set of rules that tell AFPs where to put their money.

The average asset allocation of all AFPs at 31 October 1995 was:

Government Bonds[1]	40.3%
Chilean Shares	29.1%
Corporate Bonds	5.5%
Bank Instruments	22.3%
International Bonds	0.3%
Local Unit Trusts	2.5%[2]

There's considerable evidence that the scheme has changed the attitudes of Chileans towards saving and retirement. However there are now also signs of dissatisfaction, despite the fact that pensions now emerging after only fifteen years are greater than under the old system. Perhaps the bankrupt, politically manipulated social welfare schemes are far away enough to have lessened the influence on Chileans' behaviour today.

The IBIS Review[3] reported that the superintendent of the Chilean system is a worried man. According to him, 45 per cent—nearly half—of the 4.9 million contributors are 'delinquent' in paying their required contributions towards their retirement savings.[4] The problem is apparently persistent—28 per cent are more than 13 months behind. They don't know what the reason is but the suspicions centre on high fees. Perhaps employers are part of the

---

below the rolling 12 month average of all AFPs or, if less, at least half of the last 12 months' returns of all AFPs. Each AFP must have a 'fluctuating profit reserve' and a 'guarantee reserve' to make sure the minimums are achieved. If they don't, the government makes up the difference and the AFP is dissolved! The 'guarantee reserve' makes it difficult for new AFPs to start because the reserve has to be available from the outset. Those that started in 1981 could build the reserve gradually. The statutory requirement for broadly similar returns probably also encourages switches (limited investment return penalties) and indirectly boosts management expenses. It may also lead to relatively passive investment strategies and lower than optimal long-term returns.

[1] That 40% of the 'private' AFPs' money is lent to the government does nothing more for the ultimate security of members than the traditional unfunded PAYG arrangement. Both depend on future governments meeting their contractual obligations.

[2] In any developed country, I would be concerned about that average mix. Under English trust law, a locked in retirement income portfolio that had 68.4% invested in bonds would leave the trustees potentially open to action for breach of their fiduciary duties.

[3] October 1994.

[4] Colin Gillion and Alejandro Bonilla, 'Analysis of a national private pension scheme: the case of Chile', International Labour Review, Vol. 131, 1992, No. 2, report that the proportion of AFP members who paid contributions regularly went from 76% in 1983 to 71% in 1988 and down to 53% in 1990.

problem—they are supposed to make the deductions and send them to the chosen AFP. If they don't, they can be sued by the superintendent, and there are 150,000 such actions pending.[1] Official explanations of this 'delinquency' concentrate on the increasing proportions of self-employed (who don't have to contribute), women who have left the workforce and employees who have moved overseas. There may be one or two people who have just stopped paying.

One possible solution being mooted is to 'target new labour force entrants with enticements to commit to the system'. Something to do with 'mortgage accrual credits' has been mentioned. Sounds like more good old fashioned bribery to me. Chile is also looking at offering savers a bonus to stick with one AFP and so reduce the rising marketing costs. An alternative suggestion is to pass a law limiting switches to no more than one a year. Needless to say, the surviving AFPs are welcoming the changes.

So, not only are tax incentives insufficient to persuade the recalcitrant 45 per cent but there now seems to be a need for some real encouragement—in a *compulsory* scheme!

What struck me about the *IBIS Review* article was that no-one seemed to question the notion of incentives in a compulsory scheme. Nor did they know why so many people were opting out illegally and for so long.

There is clearly much interest around the world in the compulsory funded model, where people are forced to save for their own retirement.

Key Features of Compulsion

There are some common characteristics of compulsory regimes:

Centrally Designed

All compulsory regimes require the government to make a lot of rules. These lay down how much must be saved; where the savings are put; often, where they are invested; how they are supervised and when and how they are paid out. Having lots of rules means that changing lots of rules is also a constant.[2]

Funded

A pool of assets is set aside specifically for retirement income. These compulsory regimes have actual assets earning actual investment income.

Defined Contribution

Compulsory regimes are usually run on a defined-contribution basis, where amounts paid to the scheme accumulate with interest until retirement. The accumulated savings must then usually buy a pension for the member's life. During the build-up, the contribution is defined but the eventual benefit cannot be predicted because that depends on the investment return earned

---

[1]   *The Economist Intelligence Unit*, 1 February 1996.

[2]   According to Brian Scullin, formerly Executive Director of the Association of Superannuation Funds of Australia, in a speech 'The Australian Corporate Superannuation Scene: Current Developments', August 1996, '...there have been something like 2,000 substantive rule changes in the last 10 years.' A lot of that was self-inflicted because no-one had a clear idea of what the Australian scheme was all about when it started.

on contributions.[1] It also depends on interest rates predicted at the point of retirement and for the whole pay-out period. That's because interest rates are one of the two key drivers in the pricing of pensions bought by a given lump sum.[2]

Government Support

Most Western-style countries have a version of the 'social compact' which says that citizens have a safety net if they do not have enough to live on. The benefit usually applies only when people reach the state pension age.

If the compulsory regime didn't deliver the agreed minimum, for whatever reason, the state would top up the compulsory benefit to that minimum. The justification for a safety net doesn't change with the introduction of compulsion.

Success Depends on the Economy

A 'successful' compulsory regime, no matter how you measure success, depends on good investment returns. That, again, is because it's founded on the defined-contribution principle where the member's benefit depends, in part, on the contributions paid, but crucially on the returns earned on those contributions.

Those returns will usually depend on a healthy local economy[3] and, if the regime can invest overseas, on other healthy economies.

Vesting, Preservation and Portability

Compulsory regimes usually require:

- members' benefits to be theirs from the outset—no 'vesting schedules' where entitlements are earned over periods of membership or employment
- for members' benefits to be kept until retirement or 'preserved' for the purpose for which they were put aside
- for benefits to be taken from job to job—they must be 'portable' from one scheme to another.

Most of these rules make sure the member actually gets the intended benefit but is not allowed to spend it before retirement other than in the approved way.

---

[1] The NAPF has suggested that the UK use the existing defined-benefit pension scheme structure to cope with its recommended compulsory regime. Perhaps this is because most of NAPF's members are the largest defined-benefit schemes. This won't work. If the UK introduced compulsion, it would have to redesign the existing funded retirement income structure first.

[2] The other key driver is mortality or the expected time for which the pension will be paid.

[3] Martin Feldstein (in *The Economist*, 24 June 1995) emphasised the importance of the local economy to the returns on funds invested for retirement. He argued that international capital flows don't really help a country's investment programme if the country isn't saving enough itself. That's because most investment capital stays 'at home'. That increases the dependence of a compulsory regime's success on the performance of the country's own economy.

A Long Timeframe

Compulsory regimes have to work for a long time. An employee, who joins the workforce and an approved scheme at age 20, may save for 45 years and then draw down on those savings for another 15 years or so after retirement at age 65. Sixty years is a long time for any sort of regime to maintain its integrity. It needs wholehearted community support over very long periods. Such a scheme was introduced in New Zealand in 1975—it lasted only nine months before it was dismantled by the populist leader of a new National Party government (Robert Muldoon). New Zealand has just finished a debate on yet another type of compulsory scheme, this one being closer to the Chilean model. It was the subject of a referendum in September 1997.[1]

Advantages of Compulsion

Compulsion does have some apparent advantages.

It Limits 'Free-riding'

In theory, the citizens of developed countries can be divided into three broad camps:

Group 1 who *can't* afford to save *and don't*

Group 2 who *can* afford to save *but don't*, and

Group 3 who *can* afford to save *and do.*

Group 1, the bottom group (the poor non-savers), is a problem for a compulsory regime. If they don't earn enough to save now, a compulsory regime won't help them. They're probably already receiving some form of tax-subsidised income support. That support would need to increase if the compulsory contributions weren't to reduce their standard of living today below the level already established by the community as the acceptable minimum. Even if the government chose to impose a compulsory scheme without that compensation, the problem of high effective marginal rates of tax would be magnified by the compulsory contribution.

Low income means low contributions, no matter how you work them out. Low contributions mean relatively high costs in a defined-contribution environment unless some deliberate cross subsidies are built into the system. In fact, it's not hard to imagine circumstances where low-paid earners will actually be worse off with a compulsory scheme than they are with their existing state entitlements and whatever small amounts they can put aside on a voluntary basis.

The really poor who are wholly dependent on the state for whatever reason—illness, disability or an absent parent—are another problem. Unless the state came up with the full amount of the compulsory contribution, they wouldn't stand a realistic chance of participating.

That means that taxpayers as a whole will end up paying for the compulsory contributions of the poor. The really poor are still on welfare but now part of

---

[1]   The referendum was part of the price the previous National government had to pay to secure a coalition with the New Zealand First party in the new proportional representation parliament. It was soundly defeated—on an 80% turn out in a postal ballot, only 8% favoured the compulsory scheme—92% voted against the idea.

the money they receive from taxpayers is being managed by the private sector. That may make the really poor feel a bit better but I'm not sure what it does for taxpayers.

This group, if it continued to be dependent until 'retirement', would qualify for a state-provided benefit whether it's pre-funded (through the compulsory regime at our expense) or delivered on a 'pay as you go' basis through a more traditional kind of welfare benefit (still at our expense). Unless the compulsory scheme earned a better after-tax (and after expenses) return than the cost of money to the state then taxpayers would pay more for a compulsory scheme than for a traditional unfunded arrangement.[1] That means taxes must be higher to pay for all this.

Group 2—those who can afford to save but don't—is sometimes called the 'free riders' because its members seemingly decide to depend on taxpayers as a whole for retirement income. A compulsory regime could help protect taxpayers from 'free riders'. This implies that the eventual retirement benefits obtained directly from taxpayers through transfers are both income- and/or asset-tested so that extra saving through the compulsory regime actually reduces the state-provided benefit.

Much middle-class angst focuses on free riders. The general idea of free riding is easier to describe than to deal with. We can describe the group's characteristics but it's a bit more difficult to say who individually is a free rider and who isn't. If a farmer chooses to buy a needed tractor rather than start a retirement saving account with a life insurance company, would that make him a free rider? When we decide that people can afford to save but don't, we beg some important questions:

How do we know they can afford to save?
You can't answer that unless you have good information about wealth and income. This won't be the usual 'snapshots' that emerge from the five-yearly census.[2] Unless you can see when individuals can afford to save at the various stages in their lives and then what they do with their money once they reach that happy state, you can't make informed judgements as to who are the free riders and what turns them into this bane of taxpayers' lives.

How do we know they're not saving already?
When middle-class people talk about saving for retirement, in the context of a discussion about free riders, they normally mean in arrangements that are with banks, insurance companies or pension schemes. The money is locked away for retirement 'for their own good'. These are quite easy to measure and track over time but they are not the only way that people save for retirement.

Farmers save by paying off debt, investing in improved stock or buying new equipment. Workers can save by taking time out to invest in education to

---

[1]   They would also pay more because the compulsory scheme would deliver even if the beneficiary didn't 'need' the retirement benefit or if the beneficiary died before making it to retirement. There would also have to be allowance made for the dead-weight costs imposed on taxpayers for the collection of the money needed to provide beneficiaries their retirement savings.

[2]   These studies miss migrations from one wealth or income class to another between each census—see chapter 4, p. 67.

improve their earning capacity (and their future ability to save). Small business owners might save by opening a new branch and hiring new staff to improve the leverage of their management expertise. Entrepreneurial savers might go into a joint venture with someone who has a good idea or may even decide to build their own portfolio of directly owned shares. Someone else may decide to buy a second home, not to live in but to rent out as an investment. The rent will pay off the mortgage by the saver's retirement.

How do we propose measuring those other ways, many of which will be better for the country than a traditional saving scheme? This leads me to the last important question...

Who says financial instruments are the best?
Lending a nation's retirement savings to the government (through government bonds or treasury bills) may actually be a bad idea—it may simply encourage the government to spend it or to run bigger deficits than would otherwise have been the case. Even putting it all into the share market may not be a great idea if that only bids up the value of existing shares. Letting farmers invest in new machinery, employees in further education or the small business in new staff may all be much better for them (and for the country) than forcing people to behave in a single approved way.

We need to understand why so many people worry about free riders —because it's these worriers who seem most likely to promote compulsion (and vote for it) as the answer to this 'problem'.

The concept of free riding relies on the presence of a state benefit that people collect even when they haven't done the 'right thing'. People who for whatever reason fail to get a job are compensated with a state-provided income called the unemployment benefit. If they get pregnant even though they haven't enough to support a child, they are again apparently 'rewarded' by a state-provided income.

People all round the world are becoming resentful about that kind of state dependency and are turning their attention to those who depend on the state when they are old though not necessarily 'retired'. Past critics of state spending have tended to avoid the old. That is still the case in the US where 'social welfare' (spending on the poor) doesn't include 'social security' (most of the spending on the old). Politicians there can still reliably criticise welfare dependency without prejudicing the grey vote but that can't last much longer.

If bribery (as in tax incentives) hasn't made free riders get serious about saving for retirement, the obvious solution is force them—and everyone else—to save. But that doesn't mean getting rid of the tax incentives (even though they haven't worked);[1] it means instead that everyone ends up taking advantage of them.

There are two possible solutions to the free rider problem. The first is to have a compulsory scheme that totally replaces state provision.[2] The other is to keep the present unfunded arrangements already in place but to have a more complete system of testing beneficiaries' entitlements to the state benefit by both income and asset tests.

---

[1]   No country that has a compulsory scheme has got rid of tax incentives for retirement saving.

[2]   As in Chile—the trouble is that, in most developed countries with flat-rate retirement benefits, that imposes a significant saving burden on middle- and low-income earners.

This second solution seems a more promising approach to free riders than the complexities and distortions that come with a compulsory scheme. That's because any new compulsory scheme will take years to deliver a benefit that's equal to or greater than the existing state benefit. In the meantime, *homo economicus* will ensure that his assets are structured in a way to maximise his entitlements to state benefits while at the same time arranging his income to minimise his exposure to the compulsory contributions. A complete set of tests will identify those who could support themselves but choose not to.

Group 3—those who can afford to save and do so—won't be much affected by the compulsory regime. They are already saving and will probably reduce the amounts they put away now to allow for the amounts the state forces them to save.

However, even for this group, the picture is not as simple as that. For instance, the well-behaved well-off could also choose to save in ways that preserve their maximum entitlement to the state-provided benefits. This problem could again be eased by strengthening the asset and income tests but the resourceful and resource-rich *homo economicus* will often find some way of optimising his economic advantage.

Meanwhile, at the bottom of the economic heap, the less well-off usually have fewer opportunities to rearrange their affairs both to maximise their state entitlements and minimise their compulsory contributions. Their best option might be to enter the 'informal' economy.

Reduces Myopia

The second apparent advantage of compulsion is that it should reduce myopia. The ability to save enough for retirement seems to be a function of income and length of time to retirement. People who decide to save later than they could are short-sighted or myopic. Making them save sooner could help them to look after themselves.

A compulsory regime does have some potential to reduce myopia. Its existence may help people think about the issue a lot earlier than if left to their own devices. Thinking about it could let them see that they are able to do something about the need to save for retirement.

However, compulsion also has the potential to introduce its own form of myopia. Existing savers might think that the compulsory amount is all they need to save for retirement, because someone who knows a great deal more about these things than them has decided so. That could encourage them to reduce their existing savings. I think there's an element of *myopia compulsoria* about the recent Australian experience.

Education and better information could reduce myopia by as much as the more invasive and expensive compulsory savings scheme.

Increases Total Savings

The next apparent advantage of compulsion is that, because a compulsory scheme catches the free riders and the myopic, more citizens will probably save more under a compulsory regime than under either a voluntary regime or one that is founded on tax incentives. Savings as a whole should be greater.[1]

---

[1] Though we can't be too certain about that. The Deputy Governor of the Australian Reserve Bank was reported (in *The Australian Financial Review*, 21 May 1996) as saying that he believed Australia's system of compulsory

That can't, of course, be measured just by looking at the amount of money that flows into the compulsory arrangements which is almost a national fixation in both Chile and Australia. The questions are the same as I have suggested for tax incentives—without compulsion, how much money would have been held in those arrangements? How much in the compulsory schemes has been transferred there from other forms of saving? In other words, do we have new savings or are they just substitutes for others? And lastly, are the economic and transaction costs in having such a regime justified by the increase?

In Chile, compulsion has added to domestic savings but not by as much as many expected. Figure 8 shows the pattern of the scheme's first 15 years:

Figure 8

Contribution to Chile's Domestic Savings
from the Compulsory Scheme

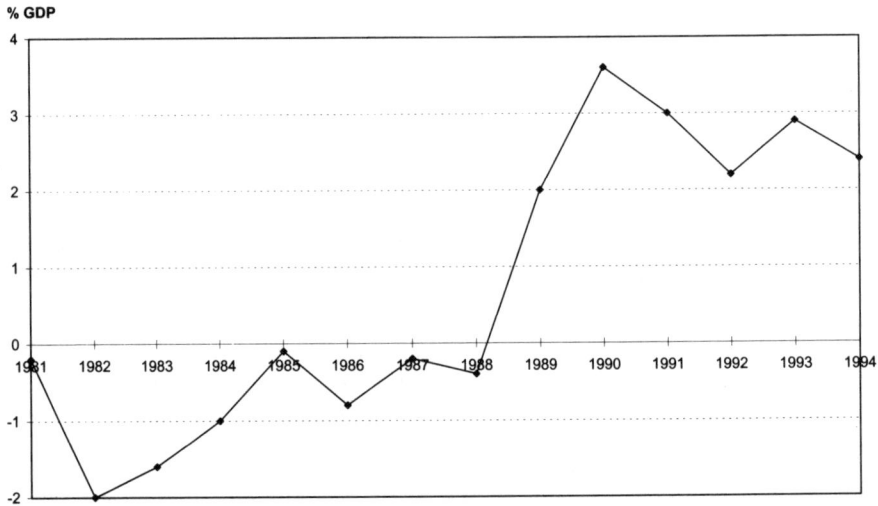

Source: Holzmann, R., in 'Pension Reform, Financial Market Development and Economic Growth: Preliminary evidence from Chile', IMF Working Paper, August 1996.

The combined compound effect of the positive and the negative contributions to domestic savings over 13 years was a little over 10 per cent of one year's GDP. If Chile wanted to improve personal saving, one might wonder whether it was all worth the trouble, particularly as the now positive contribution seems to be decreasing.

Reduces Future Expenditure

The last advantage of compulsion is the reason for the compulsory regime's introduction—future government expenditure will be reduced, but only if the age-related welfare benefit is reduced by the annuity produced by the compulsory scheme. Reducing the cost to the government of those who are

retirement saving would eventually boost the country's total level of savings, although 'at the moment it's very hard to judge.'

earners and who are forced to save will give others who can't save greater security for their own benefits.

Some people also argue that there are further advantages. Martin Feldstein, in an article already cited,[1] suggests that a compulsory regime is one way to insulate an economy from the slings and arrows of outrageous international capital flows. He says (in relation to the Mexican crisis of 1994-5[2]) that countries must:

> ... concentrate on raising national saving. The Mexican government has been developing laws to establish a mandatory private funded pension system ... If that system had been expanded more aggressively, the national saving rate would have been substantially higher in 1994 ... As a result, the economic crisis might well have been averted.[3]

This begs a number of questions about the effectiveness of any compulsory regime, most of which I hope I will answer shortly. On the specific issue of whether a strong compulsory regime could have helped Mexico, there seem to be two possible responses.

First, would a strong, locally invested[4] compulsory regime have simply disguised Mexico's underlying problems rather than bringing forward the day when international capital markets forced the government to face up to the real issues? Again, the issue is not how much Mexicans will save (or are forced to save), it's surely what happens to the money that really matters.

Secondly, if Mexico were not paying its own way, the concept of a 'strong' compulsory regime might be oxymoronic. The scheme would be infected by the problems of its host.

Another apparent advantage is that retirement savings are long-term savings. A larger pool of retirement savings may give more balance to everyone's overall investment portfolios. There would certainly be a larger pool of savings specific to retirement incomes with a compulsory regime, compared with either a tax-subsidised or purely voluntary scheme. However, the issue is the same as the 'quality' argument addressed in the last chapter about tax incentives.[5]

In a compulsory regime, there is another twist to this argument. With tax incentives, you don't have to save through the favoured regime. You could choose to skip the bribe and save in the way that best suits your needs. That,

---

[1]   'Too little, not too much', *The Economist*, 24 June 1995.

[2]   When a loss of confidence in the Mexican government and currency led to a huge outflow of money and a collapse in the peso.

[3]   *Business Week*, 20 November 1995, also thinks that: 'Pension fund reform is the cornerstone of an effort to raise the national savings rate, reducing Mexico's dependence on the fickle foreign capital that helped cause last December's meltdown'. Even if *Business Week* were right, and I don't think it is, the Mexican government faces the major hurdle of convincing about two thirds of Mexican workers (23 million out of 36 million, according to *The Economist*, 9 December 1995) to leave the black economy and come out into the light. The new scheme with compulsory contributions of 6.5% of pay plus an additional 5.5% of the minimum wage coming from the government is more likely to make that problem worse than better.

[4]   Feldstein argues that most of a country's savings are invested locally.

[5]   See pp. 77-78.

by its very nature can't apply under compulsion. If your capital were diverted away from areas where there is no ready replacement, there would be direct costs both to individuals and to the economy as a whole.

The self-employed must be part of the compulsory arrangements. In New Zealand the self-employed make up a significant and growing part of the numbers in work.[1] The small business owner's source of equity is mostly from personal saving. A compulsory regime can't offer a substitute because savings will be managed in large trusteed arrangements. I've already covered this issue in relation to tax incentives.[2]

The last 'macro' argument supporting compulsion is that a compulsory regime could change the way people think about cash incomes in retirement. A compulsory regime may help to educate the whole country about the importance of saving for retirement and so allow individuals to take collective ownership of the solution.

I think there are other ways of addressing both of these last two issues. These are discussed in chapter 7.

Disadvantages of Compulsion

There are advantages of compulsion (beyond just resolving the moral hazard issues), but I think the disadvantages are more numerous and outweigh the advantages significantly.

Size, Cost, Complexity

The administrative structures needed to support any compulsory regime must be large, complex and rigid.[3] That's because there is so much about the natural preferences of our citizens that will need to be controlled or suppressed.[4] There will be significant compliance costs, particularly at the start, and they will be paid for in the end by the members, either directly or indirectly, either through reduced returns or higher taxes to pay for the regulators.

The collection and administration of small contributions from the low-paid present particular problems. Part-time employment, or low pay generally, must generate low contributions. Unless the compulsory regime creates deliberate cross-subsidies, many contributors will find their savings

---

[1]   In New Zealand, they are 12% of the total employed, up from 11% in 1990, according to the New Zealand Official Yearbook, 1996. In Chile, 25.9% of the workforce was self employed in 1995 (National Employment Survey Statistics cited in *AFP: The Chilean Private Pension System, 1980-2010*, London: Genesis Investment Management, 1996. The self-employed don't have to contribute to an AFP and 95.9% of them didn't in 1995.

[2]   See pp. 73-74.

[3]   The Chilean compulsory scheme's administrative costs are somewhat more expensive (17-20% of contributions) than the complex, bankrupt scheme it replaced (5-10%) according to Veronica Jacobsen in 'Paying For Pensions', a report for the New Zealand Business Roundtable, July 1997.

[4]   'Delinquent' Chilean citizens and their employers have either decided they don't need to save or that they can save in other ways and for better returns.

struggling to earn enough to administer them. The nominal cost of collecting and tracking $100 is broadly the same as collecting and tracking $1,000 or $10,000, but the relative cost is significantly higher. This problem can be alleviated by having a threshold below which no compulsory contributions are collected, but then, once the threshold is reached, requiring contributions on all income. That solution carries with it some more problems.[1]

Multiple accounts for employees who have several employers in their working lives (or, even, contemporaneously) creates another complexity. Even though Australia's compulsory arrangements have been in place for only ten years, there are an estimated 11.6 million memberships of compulsory schemes for a total workforce of about 8.3 million.[2] Keeping track of those growing records won't be cheap and someone must pay. Multiple accounts also mean that savers are paying more than they need in investment management fees. Mr Scullin (see note 2 on p. 90 above) quoted the case of his own 23 year old son who already had eight retirement saving accounts and, according to his father, didn't care about any of them.

State Intervention in the Employment Relationship

The compulsory regime is often imposed on the relationship between the employer and employee. Economic costs are imposed on employers and, therefore on the whole community. The cost of employment increases without a commensurate rise in productivity.

Employers usually have to contribute to the regime in respect of their employees (such as in Australia and Singapore) and they also face the costs of collecting the employees' own contributions.

In fact, if the compulsory regime were *not* enforced through the employment relationship (or through the income tax system), the costs of collecting the contributions would be borne by the contributors through reduced returns on the savings. Involving the employers in the collection process is easier and has the added attraction of having them subsidise the regime's administration costs.[3]

Most compulsory schemes are founded on the traditional view of relatively stable employment in an industrial environment with relatively large employers. With employees staying put, it's easier to keep track of them; to make sure they do what they are told.

However, the workplace is changing and that 'industrial' model is becoming less important as a source of new employment. In the US, 97 per cent of businesses[4] have fewer than 100 employees while 83 per cent have fewer than

---

[1] Australia's answer is a taxpayer-subsidised 'Superannuation Holding Accounts Reserve' plus rules that prohibit schemes from charging administration or investment fees on small balances if the investment income didn't meet the cost. Other members must subsidise the small saver.

[2] From a speech by actuary Colin Grenfell reported in *The Australian Financial* Review, 21 November 1995.

[3] Though, in the end, employees will 'pay' those costs through the impact of employment costs on jobs.

[4] Out of a total of 5.7 million companies with at least one employee.

20. Only 70,000 companies employ more than 100 people with a mere 14,000 having more than 500.[1]

Imagine that you are one of those small employers in the US—you're already moaning about the cost of government regulation and the amount of form filling you have to do.[2] Along comes a bright-eyed official to tell you about the new compulsory saving scheme you now have to implement for your employees and here's a book of new rules you must comply with. You don't have an employee benefits manager you can turn the problem over to. Will you really take on that new clerk to help out in sales or would you prefer to 'hire' a computer where there's no cost of regulation? Your customers won't pay you any more just because someone has decided your employees aren't saving enough.

The necessary regulatory intervention in the employment relationship created through the introduction of an employer-based compulsory saving scheme will cost more and will cost jobs—regardless of its impact on the country's retirement income policies and outcomes. It may even make a country less competitive by comparison with the countries that don't have such a regime.

A government could choose to run the collection mechanism as an add-on to the income tax system. That also poses a threat, this time to the integrity of the tax system itself. It doesn't matter how the compulsory contributions are described on employees' pay slips; they will be seen as another tax despite the connection between those contributions and the benefit that eventually emerges. There is only so much 'tax' that citizens are prepared to pay, particularly if the eventual benefits reduce their existing 'entitlements'.

Employers are then faced with an additional hazard. Though the compulsory contributions can be seen as part of the employees' overall remuneration, employees will tend to place a lower value in pay negotiations on the deferred pay represented by those contributions. They will naturally look for compensation through direct, immediate cash. There is, therefore a danger that employers may pay twice for at least a part of the compulsory contributions.

Another intervention in the employer/employee relationship is more subtle—compulsory regimes really have to be on a defined-contribution basis. The regulatory costs of monitoring the build-up of defined benefits and the administrative burden on the schemes themselves make them unsuitable for the forced marriage of public and private provision. Problems in the linkage between the UK's Guaranteed Minimum Pension and the State Earnings Related Pension are a good example.[3] If the employer wanted, in our model compulsory scheme, to offer defined benefits, the employer's preferred basis will have to live on top of the mandated coverage. Australia shows why

---

[1]   US Small Business Administration statistics cited in 'The Wonderland Economy' John Case, *Inc.*, *The State of Small Business*, June-July 1995.

[2]   According to a survey of 2,100 small manufacturers by the US National Association of Manufacturers in January 1994 (cited in 'There are no Simple Businesses Anymore', Edward O Welles, *Inc.*) 41% rated government regulation as their companies' most serious problem.

[3]   Now made even worse by allowing defined-contribution schemes to contract out of a defined-benefit state scheme.

compulsory regimes should stay away from defined-benefit schemes—it has created an expensive regime to administer.

The swing to defined-contribution arrangements in a compulsory environment carries with it another, potentially more damaging threat, this time to the economy. The investment strategies of defined-benefit and defined-contribution retirement schemes tend to be very different. The trustees of a defined-benefit scheme can take a more sanguine view of short-term fluctuations in returns when an employer underwrites the contributions needed.

In a defined-contribution scheme, the investment risk lies with members because they take the advantages of good returns and the disadvantages of poor returns. The effect on the investment strategies of trustees is usually marked. In Australia, for example, a 1995 study[1] showed that defined-contribution schemes (most of which are the ones Australians are forced to join) had about 32 times the level of short-term investments as defined-benefit schemes over any of the previous three years. That emphasis will eventually be bad for Australians and bad for Australia.

Compulsory regimes around the world also face a threat from the increasing tendency for traditional employment relationships to be replaced by self-employment. The integrity of a compulsory regime depends on making the self-employed pay but that will become increasingly expensive to administer.[2] There will be more people to check up on and the system will depend more on reporting integrity. The potential advantages of joining the black economy are increased if compulsory contributions *and* tax can be avoided.[3]

Regressive

The third disadvantage of compulsion is that if all earners paid compulsory contributions based on all earnings, that would be regressive, because low earners don't have as much disposable income as higher earners. It will also be inequitable for many. The promoters of compulsion need reliable information on whether low income earners can afford such a contribution. The issue was avoided in Australia by imposing the initial contribution burden on the employer. In Chile, the 'incentive' was a reduction in the contributions payable to the tottering, existing social security system. They're now trying the same incentive system in Sweden.

---

[1] By actuary Colin Grenfell—reported in *The Australian Financial* Review, 21 November 1995. Australia doesn't have investment restrictions for its compulsory schemes so investment patterns are the result of trustees coming to their own conclusions.

[2] The self-employed don't have to contribute in Australia. Though two-thirds of them belong to funds (not necessarily making the minimum contributions that employers have to pay for employees) we can expect that proportion to fall and the number of self-employed to increase as the required contribution reaches the now intended 9%. Employers will play a role in this as the tendency to contract out services grows.

[3] One of the successes of the Chilean model is that only 20% of the work force are not included in the 'official economy' (according to *The Economist*, 9 December 1995). It would be interesting to track that figure since 1981 and over the future.

The regressive tendencies of compulsory regimes are particularly acute in the modern welfare state where tax-funded benefits for those who don't work (or who don't earn 'enough') are income-tested. This creates two problems for the compulsory regime:

Barriers to entry

Unless the welfare benefit is increased so that the beneficiary is no worse off after allowing for the compulsory contributions, a further structural barrier is erected in the way of encouraging the beneficiary to return to work.

In fact, taking money out of workers' pockets (through tax) to pay to welfare beneficiaries only to take it away from them to lock away for retirement is a bit pointless. The state would probably have delivered a retirement benefit to them anyway (because they were the low-paid and may remain so for their working lives) but only if they actually made it to retirement and didn't die or pair up with someone rich (or get rich) before then. The compulsory regime should end up costing the community more on this score alone by contrast with the unfunded alternative. Savers' accounts will either find their way into the pockets of the beneficiaries of the deceased (in the case of death) or the pockets of someone who didn't need it once they reached retirement.

Effective marginal tax rates

This is another slant on the point just made but this time it applies to those already in work. Most countries have an elaborate system of tax-funded income support systems or tax deductions for dependents, mortgage payments, education, health care, childcare support or whatever. The income support systems often abate with increasing income and can create high effective marginal tax rates (EMTRs). In New Zealand, it's possible for that to be as high as 94 per cent through a combination of income tax and lost benefits.[1] High EMTRs are economically destructive because they distort the work/benefit trade-off or encourage attempts to beat the system, legally or illegally.

Most compulsory regimes define 'income' for the compulsory contributions in a different way from 'income' for tax purposes. Tax is often paid on something less (sometimes a lot less) than the base used for the compulsory contributions. In a way, that needs to be the case if the compulsory regime is to be effective. Anyway, those contributions tend to worsen an already bad situation where there are high EMTRs and may require that the contributions be excluded from 'income' for the purpose of working out abatement rates for welfare benefits.

According to the OECD, the best way to reduce unemployment is to make labour markets work more efficiently, with more flexible wages, lower minimum wages, less generous jobless benefits and a better trained workforce.[2] At least two of those conditions would be compromised by a compulsory retirement saving scheme. That will tend to increase the 'natural' rate of unemployment and so increase unemployment permanently.

---

[1]   The same is true elsewhere—for example, in the US, the EMTR can exceed 100% with the loss of the Aid to Families with Dependent Children, Medicaid, food stamps and low rents for housing.

[2]   The report 'Jobs Study' cited in The Economist, 25 November 1995.

Economic Costs

Another disadvantage of compulsion is that it makes people save in a particular way (rather than in ways that best suit their needs) and this imposes economic costs on the country as a whole. It also imposes costs on savers through lower than optimal returns. Locking funds into a compulsory regime carries with it the same economic costs as locking them into a tax-favoured regime (see pp. 73-75 for the tax argument). These costs can only be avoided by allowing savers more choice than a compulsory regime can permit.

Most compulsory regimes by implication recognise that economic cost to the country by limiting the required contributions to a flat percentage of capped income. However, that's a fairly blunt instrument because the regime has no clear objective and no clear relationship to the government's own commitment to the elderly.

The government can limit the economic damage more directly by identifying a target benefit that it wishes to emerge from the scheme at the end of the contributory period. That target should be related to the government's obligation for a tax-funded welfare benefit paid to the old. For example, if the Tier I benefit were, say, 30 per cent of the national average wage then, once the compulsory savings had built up to an amount that would yield a pension of 30 per cent, the compulsory savings could stop. In principle, a government should find it difficult to justify interfering in its citizens' economic lives to a greater extent than it will deliver on when they retire. If the government would otherwise pay a welfare benefit to an old person, it can substantiate a stake in the saving decisions of its citizens up to the value of that benefit.[1]

The regime can then set compulsory contributions on a basis that will achieve that target, but no more than that target.[2] That also implies an income test on the compulsory scheme's benefits that would reduce the Tier I benefit. While that overall structure may limit the damage caused by constrained choices, you can imagine the detailed rules required to administer such an arrangement.

For example, how does the system know when an individual saver reaches the target? What if the regime allowed (as it probably should) savers to choose more than one manager of the compulsory savings? How do you cope with married couples (where the government's Tier I benefit is usually less than twice the single person's rate) or where only one of the couple is in paid employment? What happens when they are not married but act as though they are? What happens when they stop being married (or acting as though they are)? Is the government allowed to increase the compulsory scheme's target as the community becomes better off (and it increases the Tier I benefit)? What about a run of disastrous investment returns once a saver has reached the target? How do you cope with non-cash fringe benefits that are likely to become popular if contributions were based on taxable income? What about savers who emigrate? ... and then return?

---

[1] Chile has yet to discover this truth—perhaps that explains its scheme's high 'delinquency rate'.

[2] This would also allow additional discretionary savings into the sectors of the economy that would be denied access to funds accumulated from the compulsory regime, like education or small businesses.

Because women live longer, does the regime target the value of an annuity based on the life of a male or a female citizen, or neither? Who supplies the annuity and on what terms? How should the annuity suppliers be regulated? What happens if the saver becomes disabled before the state pension age, or dies, leaving a surviving spouse or partner? Given the link between the state's welfare benefit and the compulsory regime's annuity, how is that regulated during retirement?

Each of these questions can be answered but only at the expense of complex rules that will be needed to protect the compulsory regime's integrity. The only alternative is to develop a 'one-size-fits-all' regime that slides past any logical connection with the government's own welfare obligation to the elderly.[1] That will send its own message to citizens or, at least, disguise the message the government wants to send by demanding that we all behave in a particular way.

Natural Flows Distorted

With the government setting the rules as to what constitutes 'acceptable' behaviour, market signals as to what might actually be desirable (as opposed to 'acceptable') are immediately affected. Australia is beginning to discover this—compulsory retirement savings are now the biggest single flow of household financial saving (outside of housing), exceeding the flow into bank deposits and similar traditional forms of household saving.[2]

There has been a call for more tax incentives, and now there is a call for other financial savings of the kind that 'flows most directly into financing Australia's business investment and job creation'.

Perhaps letting the markets resolve that might be better than Australia's 'command and control' approach. Once you paint yourself into a regulatory corner, more paint is an easier response but it's not usually the best answer.

Lower Returns

In the long run, compulsory regimes will tend to produce lower returns to savers than voluntary ones. There can be choice among various bits of the compulsory system, such as in Chile for the individual saver, or in Australia for the trustees of the individual schemes, where they, and not the members, make the investment decisions. But there will be no competition between the compulsory regime as a whole and alternative forms of saving.

---

[1]   Australia is an example of such a scheme.

[2]   According to Dr Vince FitzGerald, writing in *Decisions*, December 1995. Paradoxically, Dr FitzGerald was one of the Australian government's key advisers on savings and played a prominent role in developing Australia's compulsory regime. The Managing Director of the Australian Stock Exchange was quoted (the *New Zealand Press Association*, 12 June 1996) as saying that the domestic market couldn't absorb the expected inflow from compulsory savings. 'There isn't enough product in this country to absorb that. I would think inevitably we're going to have more than half of it go off-shore, but that will be if we're lucky.'

Wholesale fund managers will be the winners, with retail fund managers, small businesses (that's most businesses) and the economy the losers.[1]

There's another more practical effect that applies in New Zealand because of the tax-neutral treatment of retirement and other savings, particularly saving through paying off your house mortgage. Interest earned in New Zealand on retirement savings is taxed while interest paid on a house mortgage comes from after-tax income. Let's say the interest paid on a house mortgage is 10 per cent a year. The tax paid return on compulsory savings would have to be greater than 10 per cent (15 per cent before tax if the marginal tax rate were 33 per cent). That means the compulsory savings scheme's return would have to beat the cost of a mortgage by more than 50 per cent for the New Zealand saver to be as well off, compared with using those compulsory savings to reduce the amount owing on the mortgage.[2]

In New Zealand the average diversified retirement portfolio achieved 6.4 per cent a year after tax in the ten years to 31 March 1996.[3] Over the same period, house mortgage interest rates averaged about 14 per cent a year or a full 7.5 per cent more than the retirement saving returns. New Zealand has been through a significant restructuring programme over the last 12 years so that difference shouldn't last, but some difference is likely.

Let's assume for an illustration that we have a 7.5 per cent gap between the cost of a mortgage and the after-tax return on the retirement saving portfolio. A saver has taken out a $100,000 mortgage that will be repaid over 20 years. A new compulsory saving scheme requires the saver to pay $200 a month.

If the 10 year gap experienced in New Zealand persisted for the next 20 years, our saver would be 46 per cent worse off by being forced to save in a diversified portfolio rather than reduce the mortgage. Even at a 1.5 per cent gap, the saver will be 12 per cent worse off.[4]

Government Underwrite

Governments usually underwrite the performance of the compulsory regime as a whole because those who don't save enough or whose own scheme fails will need some form of basic welfare provision. The government is effectively contracting out part of its future welfare obligation while retaining ultimate responsibility for its delivery.

That underwrite could inspire fund managers to take risks they wouldn't contemplate without the underwrite—the Savings & Loan debacle in the US

---

[1] In Australia, traditional single policy savings with life insurance companies have, according to a survey by Rice Kachor, a local investment research firm, slumped because of the emphasis on compulsory retirement saving programmes (the *New Zealand Press Association*, 27 November 1995). Rice Kachor also blamed 'the lack of incentive for people to save in other ways'.

[2] The same effect applies in countries that allow a tax deduction for mortgage interest and don't tax the investment returns on compulsory retirement savings.

[3] According to actuaries Watson Wyatt New Zealand Limited. Performance figures for periods before 1986 are less reliable in New Zealand because of the strong regulatory controls on both portfolio composition and interest rates.

[4] Calculations by Watson Wyatt New Zealand Limited.

shows what can happen in another field of regulatory endeavour. That mess can be directly traced to the deposit insurance provided by the government for 'small' savers. The insurance encouraged the managers of savings and loans institutions to take unacceptable risks because they knew small savers couldn't lose in the end.

To a greater or lesser extent and either directly or indirectly, the state underwrites the investment performance of the compulsory regime. Allowing the saver the right to shift from one manager to another at relatively short notice (such as in Chile) limits the state's exposure a bit. The intense competition that can create is the government's best available insurance against failure but it must be accompanied by extensive reporting requirements (with rules to ensure comparability) and a sophisticated financial press. This should be supported by an information and education campaign to ensure that the public understands what it's told.

The competition would be further intensified if there were no regulatory requirements for the investment of the money collected by the compulsory regime.[1] Chile has not felt able to go that far because the compulsory funds (the AFPs) are constrained by regulatory requirements.[2] Chile presumably imposes those rules to limit the government's potential exposure to failure. The unintended consequence of those rules is that they probably increase, rather than decrease, that risk. Compulsory funds should be allowed to fall over so that savers lose money. The regime will be more effective if the markets are allowed to manage risk as a proxy for the government. Savers would pay more attention to their chosen AFP if they knew that the government wouldn't bail them out.

A final piece of competitive pressure to help a government keen to introduce a compulsory regime would be if the savers had something at stake. If, at the end of the day, your total retirement income (state plus compulsory) were likely to be better than if there were no compulsory scheme, there would be an incentive for savers to monitor the performance of their chosen managers and to change when they failed to perform.

This means that the compulsory regime's expected benefit (when mature), plus whatever the government delivers in welfare, must be more than the welfare benefit on its own. That may require the government to reduce its future commitment to old-age welfare for those who don't save enough or whose savings fail. That must be announced at the outset and won't be popular because it will affect everyone, including those who aren't able to

---

[1]   Other than the normal fiduciary obligations similar to the rules under which trusts operate in legal systems derived from the English Law of Equity.

[2]   These get intimately involved in the AFP's internal affairs. *AP-Dow Jones News*, 29 April 1996, reported that Chile's 'Risk Classification Commission' authorised AFPs to invest in two more local shares (Empresas Conosur S.A. and Forestales S.A.) as well as bonds issued by Santander Leasing S.A. A number of foreign mutual funds (two Citimarket and four Templeton funds) were also approved. According to Valdes, S. and Diamond, P., cited by Jacobsen, V., 'Paying For Pensions', a report for the New Zealand Business Roundtable, July 1997, experience shows that when AFPs are allowed to buy an individual share for the first time, its price rises by 10-20% in anticipation of the competition from the AFPs to buy.

reach the target benefit under the compulsory scheme, for whatever reason.

If savers have something at stake in the whole process, they should be allowed to choose which investments the manager buys with their compulsory contributions. Different savers have different risk preferences and they should be allowed to express them through the portfolio that they choose. The Chilean model is deficient in this regard—though savers can switch from one AFP to another, each AFP can run only one fund that must be all things to all savers.[1]

However, the government may intend that the mature compulsory scheme leaves the individual saver no better off, taking the welfare and compulsory scheme's benefits together. If the government were the only party that gained from the whole process (through reduced future welfare benefits) then the government should set the investment scene rather than the member. That doesn't imply rules about permitted investments, only that the member shouldn't have any say in the process.

Illusion of Security

Having a parcel of money with one's name on it looks safer than an unfunded welfare benefit like New Zealand Superannuation, the OASDI of the US or National Insurance in the UK. However, that parcel of money doesn't guarantee security. That can only come from a strong and growing economy. The parcel of money may affect the question 'who pays for my retirement income?' but doesn't of itself make an individual's income more economically secure. It simply switches the future claim for retirement income from the public purse to the private sector. That switch may make it slightly safer from political interference, though the Australian model doesn't give rise to confidence in that regard.

This leads us to a very important point. Forcing people to put money aside in accounts they 'own' doesn't necessarily do anything for today's or tomorrow's producers of wealth; nor does it necessarily help tomorrow's generation of taxpayers face the demographic deluge. It also fundamentally misunderstands the economic processes that underpin pension promises for society as a whole:

The widely held (but false) view that funded schemes are inherently 'safer' than PAYG[2] is an example of the fallacy of composition.[3] For individuals the economic function of

---

[1] The Chilean government says that, given the large number of unsophisticated investors, it's more important to keep the system as simple as possible. That's acceptable for a while but has the potential to create significant tensions and impose real economic costs in the long term. The rules that the government imposes on the returns AFPs must achieve (see note 7 p. 88 above) are also part of that simplification process. But, while they may protect the government against the possibility of paying up under its social welfare underwrite, savers pay for that with less than optimal returns and the country pays with a less than optimal allocation of resources.

[2] Pay as you go (or unfunded) state pension schemes.

[3] It is a fallacy of composition to assume that because something is true for an individual it will necessarily be true on aggregate. For instance, if I stand on my seat in the theatre I will get a better view, but if everyone does so, nobody will get a better view.

a pension scheme is to transfer consumption over time. But (ruling out the case where current output is stored in holes in people's gardens) this is not possible for society as a whole; the consumption of pensioners as a group is produced by the next generation of workers. From an aggregate viewpoint, the economic function of pension schemes is to divide total output between workers and pensioners, i.e. to reduce the consumption of workers so that sufficient output remains for pensioners. Once this point is understood it becomes clear why PAYG and funded schemes, which are both simply ways of dividing output between workers and pensioners, should not fare very differently in the face of demographic change.[1]

Nicholas Barr argues that huge funded schemes could, in fact, be a source of intergenerational conflict rather than contribute to the security of future retirement incomes. That's because their presence doesn't guarantee access to the goods that retirees need to live on when they stop producing. Inflation has the potential to match up the available financial resources with the available production that workers don't consume. Alternatively, there could be intergenerational conflict as the pensioners try to sequester current production with the purchasing power of their pool of savings. Again, inflation could be the result, as workers deny pensioners access to the consumption they wish to keep for themselves.

By contrast, under a PAYG welfare benefit, poorer pensioners could force workers politically to give up more production than they would have preferred by choice. However, workers could again force inflation up through wage demands to deny pensioners their claims and force pensioners to reduce their standard of living.

In either case, the result is more likely to end up between the two extremes. The distance between those two positions can be summed up by the difference between the side that produces the wealth and the one that decides how it's spent. On the one hand, there are the workers who can decide where their output (the community's wealth) goes and how it gets there because they own that production, and, on the other hand, the potential voting power of the large block of older people with the apparent ability to vote themselves a larger share of that wealth than they could otherwise justify.

Either way, private savings (whether those are compulsory or voluntary) can't help, unless in the meantime they contributed to improved productivity in the economy to compensate for the rising number of (unproductive) pensioners relative to the smaller number of (productive) workers.

I've seen no evidence to suggest that forced savings will increase future pensioners' security by improving the productive quality of the community's wealth. From an economic perspective, that's the only way that forced savings could be justified in the context of concerns about the ageing population.

If that weren't enough, compulsory schemes suffer from a further potential insecurity—contributors may complain that, as they are forced to save in a particular way, the government should guarantee their savings. Governments should resist that pressure. The implied underwrite created by the link between the state's welfare benefit and the compulsory regime is quite enough.[2]

---

[1]   Barr, N., *The Economics of the Welfare State*, Stanford University Press, 1993.

[2]   Though the government could help by insisting, as in Mexico, that the fund manager provide proof of its 'economic and moral solvency'. I'm not sure how 'moral solvency' would be measured.

However, the more intimately the government becomes involved in the regulation of the compulsory schemes, the more difficult it will be to avoid coming to the rescue of a scheme that falls over—that's what happens in Chile and it's a good reason for the government to stay away from detailed regulation as much as it can, given the compulsory regime.

Political Pressure

Another disadvantage of a compulsory regime is that it will be politicised and so requires complete and lasting consensus among the law makers. In some ways, that consensus will be more important than is needed for the state-provided safety net at Tier I.

The large pool of assets will look like a political honey pot and will be subjected to politicians' views as to what might be seen as 'appropriate' investments.[1] From Australia come the reported comments of the self-styled 'Minister for Superannuation' in the previous Labor Government, Mr Sciacca.[2] He said that Australian companies have an obligation to borrow in a way that allows offshore debt to be supplanted by local, compulsory superannuation savings. As he put it:

> There is little point in creating a new national savings pool if in the end it simply means we add wealth to our competitors overseas.

It's difficult to know how to respond to that.

Political pressure from those who are the ultimate beneficiaries of the compulsory regime's pensions will not necessarily reduce by comparison with a pension regime without a compulsory element. This kind of pressure results from perceptions of fairness. Future retirees will look at the rest of the community and judge whether they are being treated well in relation to the standards of the day and not those that are relevant when the compulsory regime was first designed. A successful compulsory regime won't eliminate political pressure on tomorrow's governments from tomorrow's pensioners. This is especially true if the savers don't have anything at stake because their total retirement income (Tier I plus the compulsory Tier II) is much the same once they retire.

Contractionary

Starting the compulsory regime and extracting spending out of the economy will be contractionary at the outset. Paradoxically, most countries look at

---

[1] There was a great example from Malaysia of what politicians think are good investments. The government decided that the compulsory Employees' Provident Fund (EPF) should bail out the financially troubled *government*-owned steel-maker, reported in *The Australian Financial Review*, 2 April 1996. Private investors had turned the deal down. The compulsory EPF was already facing questions from members about inadequate returns and I'm sure they weren't asked about this deal. Nor about the next one—the EPF is venturing into low-cost housing and a local survey was 'confident that the EPF can be effective in carrying out its multiple role to help the government control the escalating prices of houses, particularly in the low- and medium-cost range', reported in *The Business Times*, 1 April 1996.

[2] From *The Australian Financial Review*, 21 November 1995.

compulsion only when the economy is already in trouble. Introducing a compulsory regime at that time will usually make things worse.[1] It will tend to reduce demand and output though, for the same reason, it will tend to improve the current account balance.

These effects can be lessened by introducing the regime gradually or, better still, waiting until the economy is growing strongly before starting.

According to Don Harding,[2] there's another, much longer term effect signalling 'appropriate' economic behaviour that may not be in the country's best interests. Forcing people to save in a particular way reduces the money they have to spend on other things. This is called liquidity constraint. It means that people may prefer to get money today rather than tomorrow. According to Harding, people may tend to prefer careers with higher short-term incomes, to those where the short-run incomes look lower than the future potential. Harding says that, because about one third of GDP relates to salaries, wages and the like, it follows that compulsory saving would need to have only a small effect on human capital accumulation to reduce GDP by an amount that is relatively large compared to the alleged gains from a compulsory policy.

> Clearly the magnitudes are such that any positive effect of compulsory saving on GDP could easily be reversed by adverse human capital effects. The net effect of the [compulsory regime] could even be to reduce total wealth.

There is, apparently, no direct evidence of this effect—the Australian scheme has been going for only 10 years—but the idea does illustrate the potentially pervasive and sometimes unintended consequences of such a large intervention in the economic lives of a nation's citizens.

Consensus is Compulsory

A new compulsory regime must have complete and lasting consensus among not only the politicians (as mentioned) but also among all the key players in the industry. In the adversarial style of government common in developed countries, such a deep consensus is unusual for any issue or for any period, let alone for the length of time required for a successful retirement income policy.

The 'sandwich generation' argument makes consensus more difficult. The sandwich generation is the one 'squeezed' between the growing number of over 65s and the reducing number of new entrants to the workforce. This argument has it that those who are now paying taxes to provide today's retirees with benefits have an informal inter-generational bargain with tomorrow's taxpayers to do the same for them. Introducing a compulsory regime part way through that process breaks the bargain. Today's taxpayers (and contributors to the compulsory regime) will be paying twice for their retirement income—once for their parents and once for themselves. There's not

---

1   Sweden and Chile attempted to avoid this by offering a 'better' (more expensive) scheme for less. That's OK if you have undemanding voters or a crisis on your hands. It doesn't, however, make logical or fiscal sense.

2   An economist writing in 'Public Policy and National Saving', *Agenda*, Vol. 3, No. 1, 1996.

a lot that can be done about that practically,[1] so the political consequences just have to be faced.

'Consensus vulnerability' is a systemic disadvantage of compulsion. I don't count as 'consensus' the fact that a political party scoring the most votes in an election happens to be in favour of compulsory private provision for retirement. That's only the first requirement.[2]

A compulsory scheme will not last without consensus not just among the political parties, but among all citizens. That dependence is more acute than for the other two main contenders for the private provision of retirement incomes—tax incentives and a voluntary regime.

The compulsory regime's benefits, if any, will emerge only very slowly as assets build up. The political temptations to interfere with the process or to unwind it for short term advantage will make it vulnerable. In that regard, a compulsory scheme is different from other government policies, such as the unemployment benefit. In this instance, if a new government didn't like the policy of its predecessor, it would change the rules and, from then on, the new rules would apply. The changes may advantage the new generation of the unemployed (if the benefit increases) or they may create hardship (if, as is more likely these days, the benefit were reduced); but most people are relatively unaffected by the change which can take effect straight away. In both these regards the compulsory scheme is different. Every earner will be affected; the loss of income will be immediate but the reward will be off in the distant future.

There's an inherent conflict between the modern style of democratically elected government and a compulsory, funded retirement saving regime. Most western style governments don't have the declared support of most of the country's voters, let alone most of its citizens. Don't look for policy stability if a government that's supported by only a minority of voters introduces a scheme that requires the support of *all earners* and their employers for the 40 to 60 years the compulsory regime needs before it delivers on its promises. You can forget about it entirely if the politicians don't even agree amongst themselves.

Dictatorship is a good start for a compulsory regime—perhaps that's why Chile began so well.[3] The hard part for Chile is just beginning. The first 16 years were probably the easiest as they are finding out now.

---

[1] Unless you adopt some transparent 'fiscal mirrors' such as those suggested by one of the minor political parties here in New Zealand. This converts unfunded liabilities into 'assets' by issuing debt (shades of Chile) and then requiring the purchase of an annuity. An alternative approach is to make the employer, not the individual, pay the compulsory contributions (Australia). Take home pay may not go down, but the individual is, of course, still paying for it.

[2] Australians are quite supportive of their compulsory regime—according to a survey carried out in 1995, reported in *The Weekend Australian*, 29-30 July 1995. 65% of respondents thought that people should be forced to join a scheme. However that support was qualified by a wish from supporters that the funds management industry be closely supervised.

[3] It also helped that the Pinochet Government exempted the generous pensions of the military and the police when it introduced privatisation in 1981—very sensible.

Avoiding Compulsory Provision

A further disadvantage of forcing people to do something that doesn't fit into their plans is that they will find ways of compensating for it or avoiding it.

Though a democratic government can force people to do lots of things, in the long run, it's quite a difficult feat to achieve for retirement savings. That's because the compulsory regime has to operate successfully for such a long time before it starts to deliver on its objectives. There is therefore considerable potential for slips 'twixt cup and lip. *Homo economicus* is not far away from the problems—and there are several of them.

The 'Income Effect'

First, there is the 'income effect', which could see people reduce their other savings. This is the compulsory regime's version of the same issue that applies to tax incentives.[1]

Let's say a group of savers has already decided on an appropriate level of income in retirement. The government then introduces a compulsory scheme. The savers' natural reaction is to reduce their voluntary savings to take account of the now mandated element of their provision for retirement.[2]

Even if savers didn't have access to a sophisticated personal financial planning package, I think it would be unrealistic to expect no change to other saving programmes, particularly if the employer had to make the contributions on the employees' behalf, as in Australia. That's because the saving need (i.e. the *employee's* future retirement income) is divorced from the action taken to satisfy that need (i.e. money put aside by the *employer*).[3] Employees will tend to think that the compulsory scheme will take care of that problem—they don't need to worry about it any more. That tendency may help to explain Australia's falling household saving rates, even after the compulsory scheme was introduced.

'Not My Problem'

One of the welfare state's problems is that more and more of the things we used to look after ourselves have been subsumed by the state. A compulsory private savings scheme seems to be another in the long line of personal responsibilities that someone has decided would be better satisfied through state agency rather than by private action.

Clearly, there are problems with state-run Tier I schemes and, apparently with our saving habits. The natural reaction of the advocates of 'command and control' is not to explain things and let people make their own decisions

---

[1]   See p. 65 onwards for the tax-related discussion.

[2]   Australian officials estimate that about one third of the amounts put into the compulsory scheme will come from reductions to other savings. Some private commentators say the proportion switched may be higher than that. For example Vince FitzGerald, 'Public Policy and National Saving', *Agenda*, Vol. 3, No. 1, 1996, thinks that the offset could be as high as 50% and that 'whatever the offset is in the short to medium term, it is likely to rise significantly over the long term as people's superannuation balances rise'.

[3]   Chile's decision to require employees, not employers, to pay was the right strategy.

but to take charge and tell us what's good for us. In the long run, that's created a disconnection between the problem and a rational response. More and more, what should be the individual responsibility has become 'not my problem'. Forcing people to save for their own good is a natural part of that world.

The 'Early Retirement Effect'

I don't think it's possible to force people to save more than they think is necessary. If the 'income effect' or the 'not my problem effect' didn't achieve the saver's wishes, the 'early retirement effect' might.[1] As soon as savers think they have enough, they'll stop working and so avoid the compulsory regime altogether. The temptation to do this will be at its greatest when, as in Australia, the compulsory savings are available before the state pension age (especially if that can be as a lump sum) and the state pension itself is income-tested.

Increased Borrowing

Another way for people to compensate for unwanted compulsory savings is to increase their borrowings.[2] In the family's balance sheet, that will have the effect of offsetting the state-mandated asset and nothing has been gained from forced personal saving. In fact, the family's risk profile has probably worsened because the investment income earned on the compulsory savings may not be more than the cost of the extra borrowings.

All of these are legitimate ways of compensating for being forced to do something that doesn't fit in with your plans. The final, and less subtle, way is to evade the forced savings altogether by joining the black economy. If a country already has problems with the size of the black economy, the compulsory regime can be expected to worsen things, not improve them.

Can Compulsion Ever be Justified?

The concept of compulsion is part of the 'command-and-control' philosophy of governing which says that democratically elected leaders can solve everything, given time and bureaucratic resources.

Sometimes, I think compulsion can be justified and Chile in 1981 was probably a case in point. Things were in very bad shape and, in a way, anything would have been an improvement.[3] However, the Chilean experience was a bit like forest fire-fighters lighting a new fire to stop a much more

---

[1]　See Note 5 on p. 126 of chapter 6. Angela Ryan looked at a combination of age- and tax-based signals and the value Australians put on leisure. To that can now be added the benefits they think they will get from compulsory saving. In fact, the compulsory regime may encourage earlier and earlier retirements as the balances build up.

[2]　Australians do this. The Australian Bureau of Statistics report that, as at March 1996, people have borrowed nearly 90% of their after-tax income, up from 70% ten years ago, report in *The Sydney Morning Herald*, 30 May 1996.

[3]　And compulsory saving has probably had more of a political than an economic effect anyway.

damaging one in its tracks. That doesn't make the second fire good, only better than the alternative.

I think the better approach is to stop the first fire or, at least, deal with it before it becomes a problem.

6

Let's Start With Tier I

Summary

There are several factors to consider when designing a Tier I scheme. The first step is to set an objective for public provision. The recommended objective of 'preventing poverty, plus a margin' seeks to create an affordable and sustainable scheme and to encourage private saving without marginalising those on low incomes or who spend time out of the paid workforce. In line with this objective, the benefit is set at 55 per cent of the national average wage for couples (35 per cent for single people). The qualifying age would be 68. The scheme, however, allows an element of choice with early payments available from age 60 (with the flat-rate benefit reduced by 0.5 per cent per month) and late payments whereby the pension is increased by 0.5 per cent for each month after age 68 that the pension is deferred.

For reasons of affordability and fairness, the benefit should be subject to an income-test. It will be offset by 60 per cent of private income, with a modest 'free zone'. While the benefit payment won't be subject to an asset test, the income test should be as broad as possible, applying to underlying returns from all assets of an investment nature.

The most efficient way to deliver the benefit is an unfunded scheme with no identified contribution, but with a watch kept on the pension scheme's future liabilities through the provision of proper annual accounts. This information will provide notice of any need for change well in advance of that need occurring.

For reasons of objectivity and public confidence, responsibility for monitoring the scheme needs to be taken out of the hands of the elected government and be given to an independent body.

****

If something can't go on forever, it won't.
Herbert Stein, Chairman of Council of Economic Advisors, 1972-74.

Tier I is Inevitable

I've already talked about the reasons that states have become involved in delivering at least some of most citizens' retirement incomes. Unless a government is prepared to intervene in the *total* process by aiming to deliver 'adequate' provision to all earners (such as in Chile or Singapore), there will always be at least some publicly provided income.

The last two chapters concluded that neither tax incentives nor compulsion seems a good way forward for Tiers II and III. However, before we look at a preferred route, we first need to settle the shape of Tier I (basic, universal state pension) and reach a consensus on everything that matters about the design of the benefits to be delivered at that level. That agreed scheme will then become the foundation for the discussion in chapter 7.

Around the world, the number and scope of Tier I schemes have grown like topsy.[1] Designs are complex, contradictory and expensive. The demographic pressures faced by all developed countries mean their Tier I schemes are now contracting in the same rapid, haphazard way in which they grew, and are now covered in sticking plasters and bandages. No one would run a company like this and it's no way to run a retirement income scheme.

Decision Strategy

For the moment, I'll concentrate attention on a suggested long-term framework for a New Zealand Tier I scheme. That's partly because I'm most familiar with my own country. Looking at New Zealand's needs will, however, show that, despite having what now seem to be fiscally and politically sustainable arrangements, aspects of our Tier I 'New Zealand Superannuation' can and should be improved. For the reasons I've already set out, the issues that New Zealand faces are echoed to a greater or lesser extent in all developed countries.

My strategy for looking at a new generation scheme will be to begin by assuming there's no existing scheme, no existing pensioners and no-one on the point of retiring. We start with a relatively clean sheet of paper. The first step is to agree on Tier I's objectives. The next is to look at what other countries have done, for two reasons: first, to learn from their experiences—to gain from their good experiences and learn from their bad; second, other countries are our competitors for labour, or more accurately, for the price of our labour.

Information about our own people then needs to be gathered: housing patterns and costs; the cost of food, clothing and services at the older ages; the availability and cost of support services like health and sheltered accommodation. Tentative decisions can then follow on each of the key elements, along with suggestions on the transitional arrangements that move the country from here to there. The results need to be tested for long-term fiscal and political sustainability. Only then can public debate and a process to gain political consensus on the whole structure follow.

All this is pretty much how an employer goes about deciding what it wants from a new employee pension scheme and how it goes about getting what it wants. A country is in many, but not all, ways an employer writ large.

Most of these steps can only be started within the confines of a single chapter of this book, while others are either beyond my resources (the information gathering) or control (public debate and political consensus). Nevertheless, you'll get a sufficient flavour from the next few pages to see how a debate on Tier I arrangements might be started.

---

[1]   The most complicated Tier I schemes among OECD countries are in Norway and Spain, though the US runs a close third. In this last case, the Social Security system confesses to failure when it advises contributors to call their local office if they want to find out how much their retirement income will be. If people can't figure that out for themselves, you've lost the plot at Tier I. The US authorities also suggest that 'everyone—near retirement or not—request a [personal earnings and benefit estimate statement] every three years. That way, the records you'll need to double-check your account will be close at hand...'

Tier I's Objectives

Poverty in old age is much the same as poverty at other ages and, although usually children won't be involved, health issues are much more important. Even if the poverty were self-inflicted (by the 'free-riders' of chapter 5), what could a democratically-elected government do about that by the time someone got to retirement age? So, if there were to be some form of protection against poverty at younger ages, similar justifications would see that protection continue on into old age. That then becomes the minimum objective of Tier I—to do something about inevitable poverty among some of the old.

There can be higher—and increasingly expensive—objectives. The full range was summarised by Susan St. John and Toni Ashton[1] from bottom to top as:

Grade 1: alleviation of poverty

Grade 2: prevention of poverty

Grade 3: belonging and participation so that retired people feel part of the community, and

Grade 4: continuance of economic status so that the standard of living relates to pre-retirement levels.

You can't look at Tier I's objectives in isolation. Design decisions will have knock-on effects on other parts of the economy. The more expensive the scheme, the more that has to be taken out of the community's resources to pay for it. Taxes would have to be higher (if the scheme were unfunded) or more would have to be put aside ahead of retirement (if funded).

If a country thought it was important for people to save and to make their own decisions as to what might be the best ways of doing that, adopting either the 'belonging and participation' or 'continuance of economic status' objectives for Tier I would limit people's capacity to deliver on the personal saving objective. That's because more of today's resources would be needed to deliver that higher state benefit.

We can't assume that everyone can achieve their retirement income objectives from their own resources. The sick, the disabled, those who leave paid employment to care for children and the unemployed all lose varying periods of income and potential saving capacity. It would be good if the shape of Tier I could take account of this. One size cannot necessarily fit all.

My own preference for this key decision lies between 'prevention of poverty' and 'belonging and participation' say, at about Grade 2½. That preference is influenced by a number of considerations:

First, in a democracy, poverty (even if self-inflicted) is unacceptable. It tends to produce irrational, national political outcomes that eventually leave everyone worse off, including the poor. That's why I think the debate in the US about getting rid of 'entitlements'[2] is a distraction. Let's just accept that starving the old isn't a sensible national strategy.

Second, governments tend not to know best. Public policy instruments tend to be blunt because they can cope easily only with the average or the

---

[1]   *Private Pensions in New Zealand : Can They Avert The Crisis?*, Institute of Policy Studies, 1993, pp. 114-15. The grade references are mine to make it easier to place different schemes in the range.

[2]   Where the state pays money based on a legally defined eligibility, for example the age-based Social Security pension.

standard and bulk condition. Governments tend to be unresponsive, of limited vision and, in this area at least, to operate within too short a time frame.

Third, Tier I shouldn't 'crowd out' private provision. In principle, everyone, even at the lowest pay levels, should be encouraged by the relatively low level of Tier I into doing something about retirement saving for themselves. Participation in private saving schemes, even at modest levels, has all kinds of benefits.

Many of the discussions about saving issues and the accompanying economic debate 'out there' concerns big picture issues. There seems to be very little analysis of what's actually happening to individuals and how they might behave. The economics profession doesn't seem to have proved that unfunded benefits at Tier I reduce individual savings, but that may only demonstrate that citizens have no faith that the government will eventually deliver the current level of benefits. If they could see that Tier I was sustainable, why wouldn't they allow for the state benefit when planning what to do at Tiers II and III? It just doesn't make sense to ignore it.[1] If then our citizens started to believe that the benefit would be there, a link between a larger benefit and a smaller need to top that up with private savings would make sense. The result would be smaller household savings.[2]

Ownership of the Retirement Income Issue

However, I think there's a gap between individuals' perceptions of what the 'government' can do and reality. People do not accept (because they have been trained out of it over the decades) that the 'government' has no greater capacity to solve problems or provide services than individuals can collectively allow or deliver.

Some think that it's more economically efficient for the government to provide retirement incomes from tax collections, but that argument ignores the impact on individual behaviour of the ownership of the retirement income issue. That's why there should be a balance between what the government does and what society should expect individual savers to take responsibility for.

---

[1]   Kotlikoff, L.J., 'The Adequacy of Savings', in *What Determines Savings?*, with Spivak, A. and Summers, L.H., The MIT Press, 1989, chapter 17, looked at the US Social Security Administration's *Retirement Income History Survey* and concluded that: 'no strong case can be made for or against Social Security and other forced saving programs unless and until one pins down the exact response to those programs'. Their conclusions were that '...Social Security significantly raises the level of retirement consumption. Likewise ... the crowding out of private savings is significantly less than dollar for dollar'.

[2]   In fact, there's a new theory that annuities and other government transfers (like health benefits) lasting until a pensioner dies, are the problem. J. Gokhale,J., Kotlikoff, L. and Sabelhaus, J., 'Understanding the Post-war Decline in US Saving', *Brookings Papers on Economic Activity*, 1996, argue that state pensions reduce the fear of running out of money and that health benefits reduce the need to be frugal against the possibility of medical catastrophe.

It's then the collective strength of all those individual 'behaviours' that will determine the success of any policy.

Private savings can never replace state provision, but persuading everyone to save (even only relatively small amounts) has the potential to change things for the better, regardless of theoretical economics. This is part of what Horace Brock[1] describes as 'the incentive structure of society'. In one of the paradoxes that seem to afflict the modern world, Brock thinks that, to ensure security for everyone, you have to make life less secure. It's only when people have something at stake that they look seriously at changing their behaviour. Brock also said we should watch what we wish for—developed societies wanted cradle-to-grave security and they thought they had got it. In the long run, however, what they really had was the lack of security now afflicting most developed countries—another unintended consequence of the best of intentions. When individuals put all their eggs in one basket, they and their country increase their collective exposure to risk. It also raises anxiety levels among older citizens who happen also to be voters.

Advantages of Private Savings for Individuals and the Economy

However, the issue of ownership isn't the only reason saving is a good idea for everyone. Financial education is a good thing. We're all part of the economy, so the more that more of us know about its workings, the better for us all. Apart from anything else, that knowledge will help stop governments getting away with the fiscal mirrors that marked the performance of most developed countries over the 1970s and 1980s. Inflation is bad for savers if it means they can't earn a real return on their money. It follows that the more savers there are, the bigger will be the part of the electorate against inflationary policies, unless those policies produce real growth and improvements in real returns to savers.

Financial education is also good for employers as the financial pressures they face have similar characteristics to those faced by savers. Concepts of the present and future values of money, the need to earn a real rate of return, the impact of competition, both local and international, are all issues that even the smallest shareholder should be taking into account. Aligning the interests of employees and shareholders is good for employers and the economy.

Advantages of Limiting the Scope of Tier I

Corresponding to the benefits of private savings for individuals and the economy as a whole, there are good reasons for limiting the extent of Tier I provision.

Affordability and Sustainability

A smaller Tier I is more affordable, and more sustainable. This makes Tier I more stable and provides a firmer foundation for savers to build provision at Tiers II and III.[2]

---

[1]   In a speech to the GAM Conference in Jerusalem on 13 June 1995.

[2]   A more affordable scheme also costs taxpayers less and so means that less tax will be needed. Collecting tax is a costly affair. Not only are there the direct costs but higher taxes discourage additional work effort, training,

Limiting Costs Limits Increases in Unemployment

We mustn't price our labour out of international markets. The more expensive we make Tier I relative to our international competitors for labour, the more expensive we make employment and the goods and services that employment produces. Eventually, that will lead to higher unemployment relative to our competitors, unless we can compensate for our uncompetitive pension scheme through higher productivity.[1]

Unemployment hurts retirement saving schemes in three ways. First, a smaller number of employed people imposes a greater burden on them to support the already retired (and everyone else who depends on a government-provided pay cheque, including the unemployed). Secondly, periods of unemployment reduce the number of years that a person has to build up private resources for retirement. Thirdly, unemployment leads to dissaving as the unemployed run down financial resources when their incomes reduce. Unemployment tends to leave people further behind than ever.

Generally, Tier I should aim to reduce the external costs imposed by the government on employment to the greatest extent possible, consistent with achieving its other objectives.

However, there are at least two problems with applying a single grade for Tier I to a whole community. You'll tend to miss 'deserving' cases that most will agree need some special attention. Should the parent who takes 15 years out of the paid workforce be given a Grade 3 benefit (participating and belonging), while the single employee who free rides all the way to retirement deserve a Grade 2 benefit (prevention of poverty)? To treat them alike sends a bad signal to both. The parent who loses years of earnings needed for saving for retirement will pay the financial price twice over: once through reduced family income while the children grow up and again through a lower retirement income. For the free riders, we would signal that we'll look after them when they retire, even though they could have done something about it for themselves.

The traditional answer to the deserving cases is to have some kind of income-tested benefit on top of the basic state provision. In that way, if the parent had actually been disadvantaged by the years out of the paid work-force, it would show up in a lower private retirement income. However, income-tested benefits are complex and expensive to administer. Apart from anything else, the community needs to agree the qualifications for that special

---

investment and saving. These are called the 'dead-weight costs', see chapter 4, pp. 76-77. Identified social security contributions can create a similar effect if contributors doubt whether they will get the 'promised' benefits.

[1]   According to Gary Becker, *Business Week*, 8 April 1996: '...European social welfare policies ... financed by high taxes and costly mandates on business, are mainly responsible for the enormous increase in European unemployment during the last decade and a half'. He called it the 'European disease ... that badly infects their labour markets'. He noted that about half of the total labour costs in France and Germany result from social security, health, unemployment benefits, disability and other taxes.

treatment—no easy task. Income-tested benefits also tend to encourage anti-social financial behaviour (*homo economicus* again).

If we could come up with a neat solution to this problem, I would probably reduce my overall assessment for Tier I to Grade 2 (prevention of poverty) and leave the top-up benefit to boost the minimum to Grade 3 for the deserving cases. Until someone can solve the problem, I'm relatively content with a Grade 2½ for the whole retired community—more than enough to prevent poverty, but not enough to allow retired people to feel part of the community. For that, they'll need to do something for themselves.

The next issue with a single national grade is that the various objectives of the different benefit grades become relatively imprecise in different parts of New Zealand. A single benefit level might prevent poverty in a small country community where the cost of housing is low by national standards but won't achieve the same objective in a larger community. In New Zealand, the median price of a home in Auckland (a largish city) is about 2.8 times that in Southland (a relatively unpopulated area at the other end of the country).[1]

It's not practical to deal with this issue other than through tightly targeted housing assistance.

A single measure also ignores the different measures of poverty that might apply to someone who is chronically ill by comparison with someone who is fit and who could perhaps undertake part-time work to fill a temporary shortage of money. Again, targeted medical help could fill this gap.

So what would Grade 2½ mean in New Zealand? In 1997, the New Zealand Superannuation benefit paid to a married couple was (after tax[2]) about 66 per cent of the after-tax national average, ordinary-time wage. The equivalent benefit for a single person living alone was about 44 per cent of the national average wage. By contrast, the net benefit paid to a married couple where the earner is unemployed was 44 per cent and, to a single unemployed person, only 27 per cent. According to the measures suggested by St. John and Ashton, New Zealand Superannuation would probably rate something a little short of Grade 3 while the amounts paid to the unemployed would be Grade 2 benefits.

If we split the difference roughly between these two benchmarks (to achieve my objective of Grade 2½), we would have a married couple's net New Zealand Superannuation sitting at about 55 per cent of the net national average wage (a reduction of 17 per cent), with the single person's entitlement at about 35 per cent (down 20 per cent).

There's no real science to this assessment. It can only be a judgement call, but I think a reasoned discussion is possible once everyone understands the rules of the debate and the trade-offs required, particularly if the debate takes place in the presence of quality information and in the absence of immediate implementation.

With a 55 per cent/35 per cent benefit, New Zealand would still be treating its citizens relatively well. As Table 1 on p. 14 of chapter 2 shows (albeit for 1980), a 35 per cent benefit would place New Zealand sixth of the nine countries cited. However, we should make such comparisons with care—the income delivered by Tier I may not be the only form of state-funded benefit.

---

[1] According to the Real Estate Institute of New Zealand, 19 June 1996.

[2] In New Zealand, all state benefits are taxed as ordinary income.

Property tax and transport subsidies are common and the different ways that the state delivers medical services also distort international comparisons. Differing tax treatments of the state benefit itself (or of low earners, which covers most retired people) can also change the net spendable position.

The Key Design Issues for Public Provision

Having established an interim target for the benefit, there follow a number of key design issues for a new Tier I scheme for New Zealand:
- How is the benefit calculated?
- Who qualifies?
- The qualifying age.
- How to protect the benefit against inflation?
- Should the benefit be reduced if a person earned an income and/or had assets of a certain level?
- How should extra dependents, like a partner, be treated?
- What happens when a pensioner leaves New Zealand permanently?
- What happens when the beneficiary needs full time medical care?
- Should the programme be funded or unfunded? Identified contribution or from general taxation?
- What is the review process? What might justify change and how might that happen?

These decisions will, of course, impact on private provision at Tiers II and III. That's the essence of any foundation—the strength and shape of any superstructure will depend on it.

How is the Benefit Calculated?

If New Zealand wanted a Grade 4 benefit (continuing economic status) it wouldn't have a choice about the way the benefit was calculated—the benefit would have to be worked out in relation to each employee's pay—either at retirement or over some period. That's used by many of the OECD countries—11 of the 24 base their social security pension directly on pay, at least to some extent.[1] Another six countries have a flat-rate scheme but supplemented by a benefit that's also based on pay.

However, my Tier I scheme aims for something less than continuing economic status for New Zealand's retirees. This Grade 2½ scheme is aimed at all citizens and pitched at a level that avoids poverty in old age by a margin. That implies we need a flat-rate benefit of the kind I've already suggested—55 per cent/35 per cent of the national average wage. Before settling on those amounts, I would want to be sure they actually achieved their objective. Detailed surveys of the spending patterns of the presently retired over time are the only way of finding that out.

I want my proposed scheme to deliver a message that the state will save individuals from retired penury, but that, if they want to participate and

---

[1]   Unless otherwise stated, all the OECD statistics are based on information from the *International Benefit Guidelines 1995* published by William M. Mercer. Choosing 1995 as the benchmark means I've missed Singapore as a participant in the OECD round-up—it was recognised as a developed country (along with three others) only in 1996.

belong or to maintain the economic status they have achieved while in employment, that would be their responsibility, not the state's.

A flat-rate benefit also carries the significant advantages of simpler (and less expensive) administration, ease of understanding and clearer, more easily communicated objectives. These are desirable attributes for any state-run arrangement. It also removes concerns about equity. If my scheme achieved its Grade 2½ objective, pay and contribution records wouldn't need to be maintained to make sure that contributors get a fair deal for the amounts they paid while they were in work. Nor would there be a concern about allowing for people who haven't worked for a period for whatever reason—sickness, unemployment or child rearing.

We would need to know only that the individual was alive at the age of entitlement.

Recommendation: A flat-rate benefit equal, after tax, to 55 per cent of the after-tax national average wage for a married couple and 35 per cent for a single person.[1]

Who Qualifies?

Developed countries have different ways of working out who gets the benefit. Of the 24 OECD countries, only five base eligibility conditions on residence—the rest all use contribution records or periods of employment as the measure.[2] Mostly, that's driven by the style of benefit. With flat-rate benefits, periods of residence tend to test eligibility. In three countries that have flat-rate benefits (Ireland, Japan and the Netherlands), eligibility is driven by contribution or service records,[3] while the four other flat-rate countries base eligibility on periods of residence before being entitled to receive the benefit (for example, Australia and New Zealand).

If the benefit is related to a contributor's pay, then both contributions and entitlements would be driven by individual calculations. This would shut out new arrivals and those who for whatever reason haven't earned or been part of the formal economy. The scheme would also need complex provisions for the partner of an earner who may not have a complete contribution record.

Countries that mix flat-rate benefits with contribution eligibility conditions (for example, the Netherlands, Ireland and the UK) make things unnecessarily complicated for themselves. Complete contribution records may mean that people have to earn their benefits by being responsible citizens, but requiring

---

[1]   A country that has a progressive tax system and that taxes the Tier I pension must include the 'after-tax' requirements otherwise the differences between the average tax rate paid by someone on the national average wage and a pensioner will see more than the objective delivered to the pensioner.

[2]   Denmark uses a mix for its two-level flat-rate scheme—residence is the test for the basic provision while employment drives the supplementary benefit.

[3]   Japan also has a compulsory, pay-based, partially-funded Tier II scheme for private sector employees (Employees' Pension Insurance) but not teachers or employees in the agriculture, forestry and fishing industries—an interesting group of exceptions.

that could mean that our proposed scheme may fail to achieve its objective (Grade 2½). The financial gaps would then need to be plugged by other parts of the welfare system (where's the saving there?). The enormous cost of tracking contributions from deduction to receipt and then maintaining that record for each contributor's full working life (39 out of 45 years for males in the UK) reduces the savings from providing smaller benefits for those without a complete record. Then there are the compromises that have to be made for the sick, the unemployed and those who have the unpaid responsibility for looking after children. Most contribution-related schemes allow credits to the contribution record for those kinds of people. Contribution-based benefits (or those based on pay) find it difficult to cope with those who are in and out of the workforce—for example Ireland gives credit for periods during which the Department of Social Welfare pays a benefit but no personal contributions are due. Then you have to worry about people who immigrate/emigrate and so on. And then you need to see what can happen when 'entitlements' have to be divided between partners to a failed marriage. Switzerland has a state of the art mess that I can't hope to explain here—but it's fairness personified.

Having to contribute towards your own retirement benefit has a Calvinistic ring to it. It forms the basis of calls in the US for the 'privatisation of Social Security' with arguments such as 'you only get back what you put in'. However, looking around the world at countries that have contribution-based systems, it's clear that contributions aren't paying, or won't pay, for the benefits that the systems promise. Germany and Japan face the largest disconnection in this regard. In both these countries, contributions will pay for less than half of the expected outgoings on pensions by the second half of the next century.

In reality, there's little present connection among OECD systems between the values of contributions paid and benefits received. Though it's sometimes described as 'social insurance', it's insurance in name only. It also carries with it the ultimate, and in my view fatal flaw for a Tier I scheme—a *contributory*, flat-rate scheme creates 'entitlements' in the minds of the voters. When times were good, those 'entitlements' steadily improved—now that times are not so good and benefits need to be wound back, the concept of 'entitlements' is a real impediment to reform. How do you explain to contributors that, when they made their contributions, they weren't really buying for themselves the protection that existed for the then-retired? It doesn't matter that today's contributions are simply paying for today's retired. Voters either don't understand that, or are knowingly myopic when it comes to their turn to retire or to vote.[1]

---

[1] In *The Good Life and its Discontents*, Times Books, 1995, Robert Samuelson argues that entitlements are one reason that voters are so grumpy these days. Because governments really can't fix much without endless resources, Americans are complaining and blaming other people (or the government) for their troubles. Samuelson argues that Americans should recognise that nobody is 'entitled' to anything and embrace a new ethic of 'responsibility', cited in *The Financial Times*, 29 January 1996. According to *Business Week*, 20 November 1995, 'entitlements' already consume 61% of the US Federal budget and, without change, will increase to 80% by 2005. In the UK almost half of state spending goes on welfare 'entitlements'.

For reasons I'll explain shortly, state schemes need to be flexible and need to change as conditions change. Entitlement-based regimes, particularly of the flat-rate kind, are much more difficult to change. Needed reforms tend to happen by stealth (such as will happen over the next 20 years or so with the UK's Tier I benefit) rather than in the open. When change has to happen, change by stealth is a bad thing.

Recommendation: I propose a flat rate scheme. Residency is therefore an appropriate test, but the benefit shouldn't be paid to everyone. A criterion of a relatively brief period of residence of the kind New Zealand already has (10 years after age 20 with at least five of those after age 50) is a reasonable hurdle for immigrants to jump before they dip into taxpayers' pockets.

Such a relatively simple qualification has the great virtue of coping with the different career patterns that are now a feature of women's working lives and will increasingly become the pattern for men. There are signs in the US of greater equality of financial contributions to the family's income from each spouse.[1] Basing a couple's Tier I entitlement on one of the partner's work or contribution history is no longer appropriate.

As now, reciprocal arrangements can be made with other countries that have similar state provisions.

What is the Qualifying Age?

The 'Normal' Age

Choosing the age from which the benefit will be 'normally' be payable is a trade-off—there's no particular reason (physiological, physical or gerontological) to pick *any* age because the appropriate age for any individual will be driven by a whole raft of issues including health, availability of work, family circumstances and wealth. When the state chooses a 'normal' age, it must balance social issues, labour market efficiencies, voter satisfaction and fiscal considerations.

The practice among developed countries varies but has a consistent theme: from about age 60, people start qualifying for some form of state-provided income. The average 'normal' ages among the 24 OECD countries are 63.1 for women and 64.3 for men.

Though the ages for men and women are now evening up,[2] the lower age for women was part of early scheme design because of the tendency for men to partner younger women. Once the man qualified for a state pension, it was convenient if his younger partner also qualified at or about the same time. That leads us into one of our first trade-offs.

From a benefit perspective, we need to decide whether our focus is the individual or the domestic unit. When social security systems first started, the

---

[1] A study by Aimee Dechter and Pamela Smock of the University of Michigan, reported in *Business Week*, 24 April 1995, shows that, in 1963, the husband earned at least 70% of the family's income. By 1992, almost half of all marriages in which the wife was aged 18-44 and the husband was present were 'co-provider' unions. Each spouse contributed 31%-69% of their joint earnings.

[2] Of the 24 OECD countries, 17 now have the same state pension age for men and women.

working man earned the rights to the age benefit—his wife qualified only because she was married to the man. In a number of countries, that still tends to be the case. In the UK, the non-earning spouse 'earns' rights to the basic state pension from the National Insurance contributions made by the earner. In those older, 'simpler' times, the benefit was delivered to the family and so the lower age for women made domestic, if not financial sense.[1]

Our focus should be on the individual so there's not much sense in having a younger starting age for women. Family-based entitlements will continue to become less relevant as the shape of the domestic unit changes and becomes more varied. In any event, human rights legislation around the developed world will eventually eliminate the distinction. This is one area where men have been consistently discriminated against: having to wait longer to receive the full benefit and then living for a shorter time once the benefit started. The answer, however, is not to reduce the qualifying age for men (that would be too expensive), but to increase the age for women.[2] The European Court of Justice now requires equal state pension ages in Europe.

Demographic pressures will also force the age higher for both. The US will increase the qualification age for Social Security progressively from 65 to 67 between 2002 and 2027. Italy, behind as ever in these things, is currently increasing its qualifying age from, now, 61 for men and an unbelievable 56 for women to 65 for men and 60 for women by 2003.[3]

New Zealand's state pension age is also increasing from 60 for both men and women in 1991 and will reach 65 for both by 2001.[4]

In setting the age for my proposed scheme for New Zealand, I have allowed for:

The signal the chosen age will send both to employers and employees. Even though our human rights laws will, after 1999, prevent New Zealand employers from forcing someone to retire at any particular age, the state benefit's availability eases people into retirement. That may not be good for the country if it happened at too young an age for the population as a whole.[5]

---

[1]   Women live longer than men on average, so starting their benefits earlier increased the value of their already more valuable entitlement.

[2]   That's happening in four countries—Australia, Portugal, Switzerland and the UK. However, even when the ages have been equalised, men will still receive a less valuable benefit because they don't live as long as women.

[3]   The 1996 changes that introduced the new defined-contribution scheme will eventually see the ages harmonised at 65.

[4]   In fact, according to Robert L. Brown in 'PAYGO Funding Stability and Intergenerational Equity', *Transactions of the Society of Actuaries*, Vol. XLVII, 1995, lifting the state pension age is the most powerful potential change governments can make to restore 'balance' to the funding of 'pay as you go' state schemes. As you will see, that's not the only thing that I think should be changed in the New Zealand Tier I scheme.

[5]   Australian research (by Angela Ryan 'Early retirement and the optimal retirement age', Third Annual Colloquium of Superannuation Researchers, University of Melbourne, July 1995) shows that Australians respond rationally to a combination of age- and tax-based signals and the value they put on leisure. Ryan demonstrated that, using hypothetical approaches to retirement for people on varying income levels, the optimal

Not only will the skills of older workers be lost to the economy but the state benefit will cost more; people will save less as they leave the workforce and accumulated savings will fall as they are drawn down.

Our scheme's design should try not to drive employment patterns. As baby-boomers move towards retirement, we'll need to retain their skills.

The cost of an earlier rather than a later age. A given annual pension payable from age 60 falls in value by about 35 per cent if it starts from age 65. Part of the point of this whole process is to prepare tomorrow's taxpayers for retiring baby-boomers—it makes no sense to design a scheme that won't survive the known, relatively immediate future.

The scheme's objective—to prevent poverty plus a margin. That doesn't necessarily mean the state needs to finance fit people who are still making a significant contribution to the economy into a long and expensive retirement.

When the age of entitlement for New Zealand's 'Universal Superannuation' was first set at 65 for men in 1938, the average expectation of life for men at 65 was only 12.6 years. It's now increased by 19 per cent to 15.04 years.[1] If 65 were the 'correct' age in 1938, there would be a case to increase that for a new generation New Zealand scheme by two or three years.[2]

Life expectancy continues to improve throughout the developed world and there are signs that some of the advantages women have had in the past are reducing.[3] A number of OECD countries have, it seems, responded to improving mortality by setting the state pension age at 67.[4] Three countries have done this (Denmark, Iceland and Norway), while a fourth (the US) has decided to make the move although the higher age will apply only to those born after 1959.

Given our new scheme's objective, the state pension age should be set at an age when people are 'naturally' contemplating retirement. As far as practicable, the state should be aiming to 'prevent poverty plus a margin' at about the time the average older person is about to encounter poverty. In a way, that's a Catch 22 objective, because people may 'naturally' contemplate retirement when the state benefit starts. We saw that in New Zealand, when the state pension age reduced to 60 from 65 in 1977. We will probably have

---

ages were between 55 and 59. Ryan raised the possibility that a continued downward trend in retirement ages could undermine the prosperity required to finance that and other social goals.

[1] New Zealand Life Tables 1992-94 (estimated).

[2] In the US the story is much the same. When Social Security first started in 1940, a male had an average expectation of life at retirement of 12.7 years—it's now (1995) 17 years.

[3] A US study by Buck Consultants Inc., reported in *Business Week*, 27 November 1995, found that the life expectancy of a typical 65 year old male worker increased by 15 months in the period 1989 to 1995. Over the same period, the expectancy for women increased by only 9 months. The study's 65 year old women can expect to live to nearly 87 compared with 83 for men. The average for the population as a whole is lower. People who retire from work at or about age 65 tend to be healthier than average.

[4] Though it could be a response to increasing costs rather than to life expectancy. Increasing costs are, in part, driven by the fact that old people are living longer.

to find out from the currently retired when they would have preferred to stop work and, from the about-to-retire, when they would like to retire. That information should be kept up to date.

Recommendation: I suggest age 68 for men and women as the state pension age for New Zealand. Based on today's statistics, that will give men an average retirement of 13 years and women 16.5 years. However, by the time the new age becomes effective (see p. 148 for more on that) the average length of retirement will probably be longer than now.

Early Payment

The next thing to consider is whether the benefit should be available before the state pension age. Again, in principle, the design of the state scheme should try not to influence employment patterns. Employees should be as free as possible to choose the date of their retirement so that the country continues to benefit from their skills and experience for as long as they are making a real contribution to the economy. Equally, the system shouldn't encourage early retirement by placing financial incentives in the way of people who are approaching state pension age. On the 'third hand', there needs to be some co-ordination between the state's disability provisions and the retirement benefit. There's no sense in having an elegant work/retirement transition if the disability benefit is more generous than that paid by the state on early retirement. People aren't stupid and neither are their employers.

It's a balancing act, but it does imply the need for some flexibility in the age from which the benefit is payable, something that's not presently available.

While the state scheme shouldn't try to influence employment patterns, they will inevitably be affected by the state scheme. The 'success' of flexibility (both for early and late payments) should be measured by the degree of satisfaction retirees have with their retirement decisions, assuming, of course that they have some choice on timing. Private provision, a flexible state pension age and outlawing specified retirement ages would give New Zealanders and their employers sufficient room to reach mutually agreeable arrangements.

Practice around the OECD varies—of all 24 countries, 12 don't allow for early payment and a further two (Canada and Denmark) with basic /supplementary schemes have a varying practice between the two elements of the state scheme. Denmark allows early payment for the basic but not for the supplementary scheme while Canada doesn't allow it in the basic scheme but does for the pay-related supplementary scheme. For those combined schemes, it doesn't make any sense to have different rules between the two elements—each section is sending conflicting signals to contributors.

None of the seven OECD countries with single-level, flat-rate schemes allows early payment. If the driving force behind having flat-rate benefits were simplicity, then I could understand their wanting to keep life as simple as possible—by paying the same benefit to everyone from the same age. However, that has a cost in a relatively less efficient 'work/retirement' decision. It's also more difficult for people to ease their way into retirement by 'partially retiring'.[1] The Western tendency is to work full-time until you retire full-time.

---

[1]   Sweden has a 'partial retirement' benefit between ages 60 and 65 as long as the retiree works at least 17 hours and has reduced working hours by at least five. Administering that must be a bit of a handful.

That's probably bad both for employers (who are 'forced' to give up the retiree's skills in one hit) and employees for whom retirement is sometimes a fatal disease.

My proposed flat-rate scheme has a benefit paid from a qualifying age of 68. The same benefit paid from an earlier age is more valuable. If we allowed payment from, say, age 60, the benefit should reduce to reflect the number of additional years. The terms would need to be stated and to be actuarially fair, by being based on up-to-date mortality and interest data. That means the terms would change as those conditions change.

An OECD comparison isn't useful in this case as, with three exceptions, (Denmark, Sweden and Japan), the only schemes that allow early retirement are nine pay-related schemes where shorter membership and normally lower pay at the earlier age would impose their own natural reductions. However, I'm not talking about either of those 'reductions'. There should be a further reduction for the early start.

In the three countries (Canada, Greece and Germany) where the actuarial reduction is stated,[1] it was 0.3 per cent in Greece and 0.5 per cent in the other two for each month of early payment before the 'normal' age of 65. In both Canada and Germany, the benefit is revalued in payment in relation to community pay increases, so even a 0.5 per cent reduction factor (six per cent for each year; 30 per cent for five years and 48 per cent from age 60) is probably not enough for actuarial equivalence, particularly at the younger ages.[2] However, there are administration and communication virtues in using that factor as a relatively simple formula so I would like to adopt it for my proposed scheme.

Recommendation: Under my scheme, a person could choose to receive the Tier I benefit from age 60. The 'normal' age 68 benefit would be reduced by 0.5 per cent for each month of early payment (48 per cent reduction for retirement at age 60). The state scheme should then be relatively indifferent, from a financial perspective, to whether or not a person chose the early retirement option.[3] The income testing rules, described later, would apply from the date the pension starts.

---

[1] According to *International Benefit Guidelines*. See note 1 on p. 122.

[2] It's important that the reduction factor is as close to actuarial equivalence as practicable. According to a *Reuters* report of 23 January 1996, 'public coffers [in Germany] have been hammered by companies using the social welfare system [not just the age-related benefits] to cushion the cost of redundancies and to get rid of older workers. The government says that is an abuse of a system intended to help workers, not subsidise rationalisation.' The German government obviously has a schizophrenic notion of what helps workers and is apparently surprised to see employers behaving like *homo economicus*. The German Federal Labour Ministry, quoted in *The Wall Street Journal*, 2 February 1996, says that each of these redundancies cost the government $150,000 and the employer only $12,000. What did the lawmakers expect?

[3] The country can't be as indifferent, however, because of the 'knock-on' economic consequences of early retirement already mentioned (loss of skills, reduced saving and so on).

Late Payment

For reasons similar to those for allowing early payments, people should be able to start their benefit after the 'normal' age of 68. A benefit starting after that age and set at the same level is worth less than the 'normal' benefit because, on average, it will be paid for a shorter period. The annual pension should therefore be increased to reflect the later starting date.

Of the 24 OECD countries, 14 allowed for late retirement with at least some recognition for the deferral. In five countries, late payment was allowed, but not early payment. That's just about as illogical as the three countries that allowed early payment, but not late.

Among the seven single-level, flat-rate schemes, however, only one (Japan) allows for late retirement by increasing the 'National Pension' at Tier I as long as the retiree has a complete contribution record at age 65.[1] Denmark's flat-rate supplementary scheme allows for increases of 10 per cent for each year of deferral; Germany's pay-based scheme allows six per cent for each year; Sweden, 7.2 per cent and the UK, 7.5 per cent.

Recommendation: In the interests of simplicity and ease of communication, I think the increase factor for late retirement should be the same as the reduction factor for early retirement. Accordingly, I suggest a benefit that increases by 0.5 per cent for each month a person defers receiving the benefit after age 68 (12 per cent at age 70, 42 per cent at age 75). That's probably a smaller increase than might be actuarially justified; but this part of the design needs to recognise the potential advantage accruing from deferral for someone who might lose some or all of their entitlement through the income and/or asset testing regime that will apply (see below for more on that). Keeping the increase for late retirement the same as the decrease for early retirement also has communication advantages.[2]

There's no reason to impose a maximum deferral age although the regulators would probably prefer one, out of tidiness. If people want to defer their benefit, they should be allowed to do so. On average, they will probably miscue the start date, so the state will save money.

What About Inflation?

Protecting the Tier I benefit against inflation is vital. The state is the only body that can reliably promise to protect anything against inflation. Nothing needs greater protection against falling purchasing power than retirees' Tier I incomes.

Because my proposed scheme is a Grade 2½ benefit, its objective to prevent poverty plus a margin must be constantly reviewed against the backdrop of inflation. If inflation-proofing a Grade 2½ benefit is too much of a commitment for the country, then the objective should be dropped to, say, Grade 2, to ensure that the inflation-proofing objective can be met. A stable (in real terms) objective is more important as a planning base for our citizens

---

[1]   It's difficult to see the logic of the contribution record requirement. If it were a good idea to allow for late retirement then it shouldn't matter how much of your potential benefit you have built up.

[2]   Canada has the same 0.5% rate in the state's Tier II benefit for each month of both early and late payments.

than one which aims too high and has then to be reduced by losing its purchasing power. That's dishonest and unsettling. The state has an absolute obligation to be up front on this.

Of the 24 OECD countries, six either don't state their objective or express it in ways that don't fill me with confidence. Two (Belgium and Switzerland) have a special index, while seven increase the benefit by a measure related to increases in prices. Seven countries relate increases to average pay rises while the final two (Luxembourg and New Zealand) lift them in relation to a combination of pay and price increases.

For my scheme, I propose a two-pronged approach to the issue of increases. The Grade 2 'prevention of poverty' objective will probably be driven mainly by prices though, as and if the community becomes richer, the definition of 'poverty' would probably drift upwards. Lifting the objective to Grade 2½ and relating that measure to a proportion of the national average wage means that some regard must be given to the living standards of the wider community, including those in employment. This means that wage increases have to play a part in the formula for increasing the benefit.

Increases in the present New Zealand Superannuation are linked to prices, but the value of the after-tax married couple's benefit must be maintained within 65 per cent to 72 per cent of the net national average wage. If wages increased at a faster rate than prices (as they should), the married couple's benefit would fall to 65 per cent and then increase in line with wages.

Recommendation: My proposal is that the benefit should increase in line with national average wages but should be regularly tested in line with the Grade 2½ benefit's objectives against the living standards of the community and, particularly, the retired community. Some form of Pensioners' Cost of Living index[1] will be an essential part of this last process.

Income and Asset Testing?

Should we pay a Tier I benefit to people who don't need it? As a taxpayer, my answer must be 'no'. The need to prevent poverty dominates the Grade 2½ benefit's objective. Why should the state pay anything to someone who isn't poor? The trick is to find out who doesn't need it or who isn't poor.

This is a sensitive issue. Much political blood has been spilled in New Zealand on the subject—we are probably the country most experienced at income testing. We haven't touched asset testing, possibly because of the problems caused by income testing.

Given my Grade 2½ objective, it makes sense to pay the benefit to those whose 'other income' puts them below the 'poverty plus a margin' threshold but, arguably, only to the extent needed to put their *total* income, including the state benefit, up to the 55 per cent/35 per cent target. That implies a dollar-to-dollar offset of public income for after-tax private income up to the target. Once a married couple had net private income of 55 per cent, no state benefit would be payable. If, at any time during retirement, net private income fell below 55 per cent, the state scheme would top it up to the target.

---

[1]   Such as the one New Zealand has already—it's a subset of the Consumer's Price Index.

That's a pretty severe test—certainly a lot more severe than the income test that currently applies in Australia or Canada—the only OECD countries that operate a direct income test on Tier I benefits.[1]

Until 1 April 1998, New Zealand Superannuation was reduced by 25 per cent of 'other income' that exceeded $NZ15,400 for a married couple (about half of the national average wage) and $NZ10,300 for a single person. That had at least some New Zealand Superannuation being paid to a retired couple with pre-tax income of $NZ84,000 a year or 2.7 times the national average wage[2]—a level that doesn't remotely approach any definition of poverty. Despite this, the new (1996) coalition government decided to abolish the income test from 1998. However, we've not seen the last of the 'surcharge'. For our present purpose, we should ignore what recently happened in New Zealand.

While an income test for my proposed scheme logically follows the establishment of a specific objective (delivering a Grade 2½ benefit) and will save the government money, such a test has a number of difficulties:

Administration

Income tests are complex to administer[3] though a 100 per cent offset would be easier to understand and easier to administer than the one we had recently in New Zealand. An income test requires beneficiaries to report their income each year and may mean that some of the state benefit has to be repaid at the end of the year.[4]

Sending the Wrong Message

Income-testing can signal that the state is penalising thrift. On the one hand, it says that people should look after themselves but, on the other, it says that, if you do, we'll take some or all of your state benefit away. Until a married couple's net 'other income' exceeds the 55 per cent level, the effective marginal rate of tax is 100 per cent—the couple is no better off by saving. That apparently severe treatment leads on to the next problem.

---

[1]   The Australian Tier I pension is reduced by $1 for each $2 of income that exceeds $3,146 for a married couple ($1,815 for a single person). Other OECD countries, such as Denmark and Finland, have income-tested supplements to the basic Tier I entitlement while the Danish Tier I benefit is income-tested for pensioners who retire early.

[2]   Because of complex provisions relating to counting only the interest component of pensions or annuities, the equivalent amount for a married couple who receive their retirement income as a tax-free TTE pension is more than $127,000 a year (four times the national average wage)—see below for an explanation of 'after-tax calculations' for more on this.

[3]   The needs-based benefits for the aged, blind and disabled in the US cost $273 a year to administer for each beneficiary while the 'universal' social insurance benefits, administered by the same agency, cost $71 for each beneficiary, according to Lawrence H. Thompson in 'Principles of Financing Social Security Pensions', July 1995.

[4]   The more generous the state scheme, the tighter the income-testing regime has to be. The less generous it is, the less we have to worry about people 'gaming' against the system and the simpler the administration of the state scheme.

People Work Out How to Avoid or Minimise It

Homo economicus starts to respond in sensible but anti-social ways—we have seen this in New Zealand. People either invest in ways to minimise their taxable incomes (or their incomes generally) or they simply fail to report amounts that would reduce their state-provided benefit. Generally, you would expect that behaviour to become more extreme as the income test becomes more strict.

In all respects, the state benefit is paid to people who wouldn't otherwise qualify, so taxpayers spend more on the Tier I scheme than they have to. Also, the kind of investments that report no taxable income to the pensioner tend to be made for that reason rather than because they might produce the best overall return. Tax-driven investment policies often don't produce the best returns, so that's bad for the saver and, eventually, for the country.

Political Impact

State benefits can easily become the *raison d'être* of a potentially powerful lobby group. The 'unfairness' of a 100 per cent effective marginal tax rate ('we've done our bit for the community, now it's time for the community to do its bit for us') is much easier to explain than a scheme that tops up a person's income to a community-agreed objective.

Part of the problem with New Zealand's income test was that the 'surcharge' (as it was known) was introduced by one political party in the face of solemn promises that it wouldn't do so, and then not taken away in the face of equally solemn promises by the other political party that it would be abolished, but only once they were elected (which they were).

Welfare 'Stigma'

One advantage of a universal entitlement is that you avoid the stigma that's often associated with state-delivered benefits. That argument says that, on the one hand there's a need to be addressed but, on the other, society shouldn't be seen to be delivering it. That isn't a major problem with retirement benefits any more—we've moved on from the poorhouses of the nineteenth century. Financial life is now more clinical and a lot less public—automatic bank deposits deliver the benefit and tax returns administer the income test.

The Advantages of Income-testing

An income test has advantages—it makes the Tier I scheme more affordable because it only goes to the people who actually qualify for the benefit. Making the scheme more affordable makes it more sustainable and more stable—all these are essential elements of my suggested Tier I scheme.

It also makes the scheme fairer by limiting the income transfers from poorer taxpayers to the rich retired who, according to our Grade 2½ objective, don't need the benefit.

Having said that, there are at least two reasons for having a 'free zone' of private income that doesn't count in the income test. First, the cost of administering the offset for very small amounts of private income could easily be greater than the amount saved in reducing the state benefit. That doesn't make economic sense.

Secondly, I think we should encourage all citizens to have at least some private retirement income and a relatively small 'free zone' would help achieve that objective.

That free zone could be, say, a net 10 per cent of the national average wage for each person. That means a married couple's total net income would be about 67 per cent of the after-tax national average wage[1] (about 40 per cent for a single person), before the income test started to reduce the state benefit. However, the main reason for the free zone is administrative convenience, not improving the after-tax lot of the less well off.

An alternative approach to the 10 per cent free zone with a 100 per cent offset is to reduce the benefit by a proportion of the pensioner's private income, say 60 per cent, rather than the full 100 per cent offset that I have suggested. Everyone could see they would be better off by saving. That could then be combined with a smaller free zone (say, five per cent of the national average wage) that would deal with those with very small private incomes where the cost of calculating and collecting the offset will be more than the saving. However, having something less than a 100 per cent offset above the free zone means that at least part of the state's expenditure for the old will be directed at people who, according to our 'prevention of poverty plus a margin' objective, don't need it.

This more loosely targeted combination has the following principal advantages.

First, it doesn't matter how much someone saved—their total retirement income (state plus private) would always be improved. By contrast, the 100 per cent offset would see no improvement in total retirement income for amounts of a married couple's net private income of between 20 per cent and 55 per cent of the national average wage (10 per cent and 35 per cent for a single person).

Secondly, people would be less likely to arrange their incomes so that they fall just below the maximum free-zone amount. For example, using available cash to buy a more expensive home rather than see the extra investment income lost to the income test will leave a pensioner worse off under this alternative approach. Having a 100 per cent offset would encourage sensible but anti-social financial behaviour.

The price to achieve these benefits would be to overshoot the Grade 2½ objective for married pensioners with net private incomes between 10 per cent and 102 per cent of the national average wage. This is because at least some of the benefit would be paid to married pensioners with net private incomes between those amounts. The equivalent amounts for a single pensioner would be five per cent and 63 per cent.

Recommendation: I prefer the 60 per cent offset rather than the 'purer' 100 per cent. Notwithstanding the difficulties I have summarised, it's simply not possible to have a state benefit with a Grade 2½ objective without at the same time having an income test. Calling it a 'top up' to private provision rather than a 'benefit that's income-tested' may help the problems of presentation, but doesn't really change the fundamental issue.

Some of the political difficulties associated with introducing income testing will be reduced by the transition provisions discussed below, at p. 148.

---

[1]   In New Zealand, the state benefit is taxed at 15% (the lowest income tax band) reducing the 55% gross to 47% net. 47% + (2 x 10%) = 67%.

Tables 5 and 6 show the patterns for abatement rates of between 20 per cent and 100 per cent of net private incomes above the 'free zone' of 5 per cent for each recipient:

I think the tables show that, for my proposed scheme, the 60 per cent offset, combined with the five per cent free zone for each recipient, gives a reasonable mix of public and private provision while at the same time preserving the incentive that makes those who do something for themselves better off. For a single person the state will still pay some benefit to someone whose after-tax income is 1.8 times the state benefit itself (it 'runs out' at 63 per cent of the net national average wage by comparison with the state benefit itself of 35 per cent). For a couple, the state benefit 'runs out' at 1.85 times the state benefit itself so there is reasonable symmetry between the two treatments.

I concede that the overall design will tend to encourage recipients to structure their affairs to avoid the income test. The scheme's administrators will need to be open in their efforts to limit such arrangements. They should make it clear that the law will be changed, and changed again, to preserve the design's integrity.

I think tables 5 and 6 show that abatement rates of less than 60 per cent produce total retirement incomes, subsidised by taxpayers, that are too generous.

Income-testing Provisions and Tax

If there were an income test, there would be two complexities to allow for. First, in the TTE tax environment that I recommend for private savings,[1] you will have a mix of taxable and tax-free private incomes, because private pensions and annuities won't be taxed in the hands of the recipient. My proposed new Tier I scheme will be taxable. That means the income test for the state benefit should be an after-tax calculation. The after-tax benefit from my scheme would be reduced by 60 per cent of the after-tax private income from all sources.

In any country, the reduction will depend somewhat on the average marginal tax rate pensioners pay. In New Zealand that's now 24 per cent and will fall to 21 per cent in 1998. The 'effective marginal tax rate' (EMTR) with a 60 per cent after-tax offset would then be 69.6 per cent with tax at 24 per cent and 68.4 per cent with a 21 per cent rate. That's probably at the outer end of bearable EMTRs. The higher the average tax a country's pensioners pay, the lower will be the bearable income test against the Tier I benefit.

The second consideration is the capital component of annuities. Over the average lifetime of a pensioner or annuitant, about half of the total amounts received are a return of capital while the rest is interest earned on the assets that support the pension during its payment. In the TTE regime, the pension provider has paid tax on that interest. So, in the hands of the pensioner, that's tax-paid income and should count in the income test as deemed income. The actual proportion depends on the underlying interest rates[2] and

---

[1]   See chapter 4.

[2]   A higher average return means that each pension instalment has a higher proportion of interest than capital and so more than half should count in the income test. If interest rates fall, a smaller proportion should count.

should be reviewed from time to time. Dealing with overseas-sourced pensions is not so easy and will remain so while there are still some EET systems left. Because they have grown up in highly tax-favoured environments, the tax-paid capital element of the annual retirement pension will be somewhat less than half.

Table 5
Total Net Retirement Incomes as Percentages of Net Average Wage

Single	State benefit reduction as percentage of net private income				
Net private income	20%	40%	60% (suggested)	80%	100%
5%	40%	40%	40%	40%	40%
10%	44%	43%	42%	41%	40%
20%	52%	49%	46%	43%	40%
30%	60%	55%	50%	45%	40%
40%	68%	61%	54%	47%	40%
50%	76%	67%	58%	50%	50%
60%	84%	73%	62%	60%	60%
70%	92%	79%	70%	70%	70%
80%	100%	85%	80%	80%	80%
90%	108%	91%	90%	90%	90%
100%	116%	100%	100%	100%	100%
State benefit runs out at	**180%**	**93%**	**63%**	**49%**	**40%**

Table 6

Married	State benefit reduction as percentage of net private income				
Net private income	20%	40%	60% (suggested)	80%	100%
10%	65%	65%	65%	65%	65%
20%	73%	71%	69%	67%	65%
30%	81%	77%	73%	69%	65%
40%	89%	83%	77%	71%	65%
50%	97%	89%	81%	73%	65%
60%	105%	95%	85%	75%	65%
70%	113%	101%	89%	77%	70%
80%	121%	107%	93%	80%	80%
90%	129%	113%	97%	90%	90%
100%	137%	119%	101%	100%	100%
State benefit runs out at	**285%**	**148%**	**102%**	**79%**	**65%**

Source: Author for both tables.

Notes to tables 5 and 6:

1 All percentages are expressed in relation to the net national average wage calculated using tax rates that apply to a single person. The state benefit, being taxable, is grossed up so that the net rate is 35% (single) or 55% (married) of the net national average wage.

2 The shaded areas show where no state benefit is payable.

The same deeming principle could be used if pensioners started 'hiding' their assets in family trusts to avoid the income test. There are perfectly good reasons to have a family trust that have nothing to do avoiding a welfare benefit income test. However, if that's what actually happens then there could be an assumed 50 per cent tax-paid income element (or whatever the current proportion is) applied to any distributions of tax-paid 'capital' and it would be up to the pensioner to prove that another proportion is more appropriate.

If pensioners start 'hiding' assets in the tax-paid funds of institutions like life insurance companies (this has happened in New Zealand), the solution is easier. All financial institutions could be obliged to report the pre-tax income element of assets managed and pensioners would then be obliged to include that income (and the tax paid by the institution as the pensioner's proxy) for the purposes of the income test on the state pension.

Although all this sounds complicated, just go back to the reason we're having any state pension at all—it's to prevent poverty, plus a margin. Once we've achieved that, the state shouldn't have a role and should start backing out—that's why we need an income test.

The test must be fair and rigorously applied, otherwise there is a risk of losing credibility in the objectives of the overall structure. This is now happening in New Zealand, despite the 1993 Accord,[1] as the fringe parties start influencing the political process in our new proportional representation electoral system.

Asset Testing

Asset tests introduce another layer of administrative and political difficulties. Australia is the only OECD country that looks at a pensioner's assets to assess eligibility for Tier I benefits. In Australia, financial assets are broadly caught under the income test where the state assumes that interest is earned at 'deemed' rates, even if it isn't. Because of what is now called the 'extended deeming' rule, even the income test is an asset test in disguise. This is because the state decides what you should have earned from investing your financial assets—four per cent on the first $A50,000 for a married couple ($A30,000 for singles) and six per cent on the balance. The actual income doesn't matter, even if it's more than the deemed amount.

Then, in a parallel test, all a pensioner's assets over a threshold of $A10,000 (excluding the principal home and other limited assets) are valued on an open market basis. The state pension reduces by $78 a year for every $1,000 (7.8 per cent) of assets above the threshold.

After both the income and asset tests are run, the one that counts is the one producing the larger reduction in the state pension.

The advantage of an asset test is that, assuming that the community has agreed on the 55 per cent/35 per cent targets in my scheme, the asset test should prevent people behaving in economically sensible but anti-social ways. There would be no point (as is the case in New Zealand) in 'hiding' assets in trusts or investments that may produce poor but tax-paid returns.

There are, however, disadvantages. The assumed four per cent/six per cent in Australia's 'extended deeming' provisions that apply to 'financial assets'

---

[1] An agreement signed by the three main New Zealand political groups in August 1993 that settled the principles of both public and private provision for retirement—more on this in chapter 7.

implies a hurdle rate that may not bear a reasonable relationship to what's happening in investment markets. For that reason, it needs reviewing on a regular basis.

First (and this happened in Australia), the asset test might change the nature of banking. Indeed, this seems to have been one of the Australian government's objectives in introducing deeming principles. All of a sudden, saving bank deposits that produced only three per cent a year became loss makers in 1991 when the reduction in the state benefit was taken into account. Money crossed over into term-deposit accounts that produced a return which was closer to the underlying rate assumed in the asset test (then a single rate of five per cent).

Next, assets that ran the risk of producing no return (like gold) would fall from favour. In fact, for ordinary income-producing assets, the pressure is on fund managers to produce a return that beats the government's implied rate. If it didn't, a pensioner could pay the price of a lower state benefit, but without the compensation of the private income to fill the gap.

Another disadvantage is complexity. Requiring pensioners to report all their financial assets and then checking up on them will create a new army of bureaucrats and expenses. In reality, the test relies heavily on the honesty of pensioners. However, the gains from cheating the system are large enough to justify taking some risks.

A third disadvantage of asset-testing is that exempting the principal home from the test encourages pensioners to spend more on their homes than they might otherwise. That's because an expensive home doesn't affect the asset test (or the income test) by comparison with having a cheaper one and the rest invested in financial assets at about the deemed rate of return. This problem is borne out by the Australian experience.

Recommendation: On balance an asset test has more problems than advantages. However, because of the significant potential gains from avoiding the proposed 60 per cent offset for my new New Zealand Tier I scheme, I suggest that the proposed income test should be spelled out in considerable detail and should apply to returns from all assets of a financial nature, such as the underlying returns (not just those that are taxed as income) from unit trusts, insurance policies, family trusts and personal assets (other than a car, the family home and its contents), such as other vehicles, second homes, businesses and collections of art, stamps, antiques and the like.

What About an Inheritance Tax?

If, when a pensioner died, the state recovered the whole cost of all benefits delivered during the pensioner's lifetime, you wouldn't need to worry about either an income test or an asset test while the pensioner was alive. If the state delivered more than it needed to, it would all be recovered from the estate at death.[1] The pensioner's beneficiaries would therefore pay for the amount spent by the state through lower inheritances.

Though I understand the argument that inheritance taxes are more efficient economically than income and expenditure taxes, recovering the cost of all age-related expenditures would change behaviour significantly. Asset protection would become an industry overnight and hiding assets from the taxman would start at much younger ages than now. Different ways of

---

[1]   An idea proposed by *The Australian Financial Review*, 1 May 1996.

passing assets from one generation to the next would emerge and existing techniques would become more popular.

I think there is scope for the use of an inheritance tax to recover specific expenses at the end of a pensioner's life (like the cost of rest-home care where the government's contribution is asset-tested), but I don't like the idea of including the cost of the Tier I benefit.

A Pensioner's Dependents

My proposed new Tier I scheme for New Zealand would give a married couple a net 55 per cent of the after-tax national average wage with 35 per cent (or 64 per cent of the married rate) going to a single person. That means each recipient would have to qualify in his or her own right—there would be no dependent's benefit *per se*. However, the different rates mean that each qualifier of a couple will get 21 per cent less than the single person's benefit. How does this relate to other countries?

Flat-rate Benefits

The practice among OECD countries tends to be driven by the way the retirement benefits are worked out. All seven single-level flat-rate schemes, including New Zealand, give less to single pensioners than to a married couple. On average, the single pensioner's benefit is 60 per cent of that paid to a married couple. The other way of looking at this, of course, is that each partner of a married couple gets less than a single person—on average, 17 per cent less.

Pay-based Benefits

Ten of the other countries have a single-level, pay-based scheme. Six of those don't offer a married supplement to the income-earner's entitlement. That's to be expected because the entitlements are based on the earner's own pay records. Three of the other four with single-level, pay-based schemes (Austria, Belgium and Spain) have a less than pure, redistributive approach—they all have minimum benefits, regardless of the contribution period, and those minimums include a lower pension for single contributors (70 per cent of the married couple's benefit in the case of Austria, 80 per cent for Belgium and 85 per cent for Spain). The US goes its own way with another type of redistribution—a married contributor simply gets 150 per cent of the single benefit unless the two spouses' own contribution records would produce more.

Two-level Benefits

Four of the seven two-level schemes have married/single benefits for the basic benefit and no special treatment for the supplementary benefit. That's logical because the state is entitled to have a view on the base benefit and to specify who gets what. Another two (Norway and Switzerland) apply a uniform 67 per cent to both levels, despite the fact that the supplementary scheme is related to the contributor's own pay—that seems illogical. The last one (Japan) pays a dependent's supplement that makes a single person's benefit 78 per cent of the couples' benefit.

My suggested level for a single person of 64 per cent of the level for a couple is therefore in tune with current international practice.

Originally, the difference in the benefits between married and single pensioners emerged from an era when the married couple was the benefit focus (and the single person's benefit was a subset of the main benefit). The justification is now different. It's now related mainly to the relative cost of housing; relative, that is, to the amount of the benefit. A single person spends a greater proportion of the pension because the cost of housing for a single person is probably about the same nominal amount as for a married couple.

Recommendation: If single people were living together, each person's benefit should be half of that paid to a married couple (a net 27½ per cent of the net national average wage each). The higher single-person's benefit (35 per cent) should be paid only if that person were maintaining a separate household. Using this test, there would be no need for concern about whether the couple were married, in a *de facto* relationship or simply sharing accommodation.

In my proposed scheme, the income test already suggested would apply to each person on an individual basis, regardless of whether they were married.

Emigrants

If a New Zealander left to live in another country, any entitlement to the state benefit should disappear. That's because the scheme's objective is to prevent poverty in New Zealand. Any measure of poverty, or of living conditions in general, can only be in relation to New Zealand conditions. People would have no 'entitlements' to a state benefit in New Zealand, in part because they wouldn't have made identified contributions to pay for it. That makes it easier to make rules about emigrants that suit New Zealand rather than individuals.[1]

Full-time Medical Care

The scheme design needs to consider what would happen to the benefit if a pensioner went into full-time care and that was likely to be permanent.

Under my scheme, if the care were paid for by taxpayers, then the portion of the benefit that is designed to prevent poverty should stop. With food, clothing and shelter being provided by the state, there would be no need to pay that part of the income to the pensioner.

Recommendation: However, the 'plus a margin' portion could still be justified so that the difference between the normal Grade 2½ benefit and what would otherwise have been a Grade 2 benefit would continue. This would allow the pensioner some discretionary spending and some economic dignity at what is an extremely difficult time of life.

If the pensioner is in full-time care that is not government-provided, then the benefit should continue as before.

Financing the State Pension
Should the Scheme be Funded or Unfunded?

Should the Tier I benefit be pre-funded so that, when a person retires, there's

---

[1]   However, if there are reciprocal social security arrangements with another country, the New Zealand government will probably have to pay a proportion of the New Zealand benefit to the other government even though it wouldn't pay anything to the individual.

a pot of money that meets the estimated value of the retiree's expected pension payments?

A country has three choices on the way it finances its Tier I obligation:

Compulsory private provision
It can force its citizens to pay for the benefits in advance and invest those financial resources in compulsory arrangements that deliver retirement income in ways and at times the government demands to meet the Tier I obligation.[1] Forcing people to save implies access to financial resources to pay—there will always be some who can't save, even in a compulsory environment.

Those who don't or who can't work will always depend on the state for Tier I. Because of the need to accommodate those who can't save (or can't save much), compulsory private provision implies an income-testing regime that fully offsets the compulsory scheme's benefits against the state's residual Tier I obligation.

Unfunded[2]
The second option pays benefits as they fall due, the so-called 'pay as you go' system. Social security systems that require contributions from employers and the employed/self-employed fall into this category.

Once the community has agreed on Tier I's objectives (in my scheme 'preventing poverty, plus a margin'), the unfunded regime also implies an income test against a retiree's other private retirement income.

State fund[3]
The third choice is for the government itself to build up a fund ahead of time just like an employer does for a defined-benefit scheme. This would be managed centrally and invested in much the same way as a private fund. Taxes would need to be higher today than otherwise required, so the fund could build up to pay for tomorrow's benefits as well as today's.[4]

You will have gathered from the last chapter that I don't support compulsory private provision. So, of the other two alternatives, what's a country to do?

Practice among OECD countries is consistent on this point. No country (including the US) pre-funds its Tier I obligations. The US Social Security 'Fund' is no more than an arrangement of fiscal mirrors that helps paper over some of today's budget deficit. There are no real assets—just the promise of today's governments that tomorrow's taxpayers will pick up the bill for today's and tomorrow's retirees.

So are the OECD countries right? In short, yes. It's simply not sensible for a government to pre-fund its liability for a Tier I scheme, particularly of the kind I'm proposing for New Zealand.

---

[1]   Such as in Chile and the Retirement Savings Scheme put to a referendum by New Zealand's Coalition Government in 1997 (and heavily defeated).

[2]   Such as New Zealand's current Tier I scheme, New Zealand Superannuation.

[3]   Such as proposed by the New Zealand Labour Party in the 1996 election.

[4]   As proposed by the privately organised 'Retirement Income Inquiry' in the UK for the earnings-related Tier II state benefit.

The proposal currently being debated in the US[1] that would see part of the Social Security contributions diverted into private securities, still owned by the 'Fund's' trustees, is an unbelievably woolly piece of thinking. The presence of a Social Security 'Fund' with trustees, assets and accounts encourages that kind of wrong headed 'logic'. It's true that shares have given better returns than bonds over the years (and should do in the future) but that's not the issue. The government bonds that are in the Social Security 'Fund' at the moment shouldn't exist because there shouldn't be a 'fund'. That means the comparison between the two classes of asset over any number of years shouldn't matter.

Then there is the other notion that some of the current contributions should go into personal accounts in the name of the contributor. Letting beneficiaries have individual accounts under the aegis of the overall 'Fund' is like having a bit of Chile and a bit of the US. It's the worst of both worlds.

The government is in a different position from employers in deciding whether to put money aside for future pension obligations. Employers *should* pre-fund the future liabilities of their employees' retirement benefits for only one reason—employers might go out of business and leave their employees without their retirement benefits. Pre-funding is all about the security of employees' entitlements, not about delivering defined benefits more cheaply or encouraging 'sensible' financial investments.

The government will never go out of business—its capacity to deliver retirement incomes to its citizens in any year is limited only by its ability to dip into taxpayers' pockets, to readjust the balance of the division of economic production between workers and pensioners.

This comes back to a point I made in chapter 3 that the annual state pension in any year for an individual pensioner has been, and *should* continue to be, the total figure that taxpayers as a whole are prepared to pay in that year divided by the number of pensioners eligible in that year to receive it. Having a pool of money that the government can draw on to pay for today's benefit doesn't change that basic principle. However, it does dilute the connection between the community's fiscal obligation to older citizens and its tolerance for fiscal pain, while, at the same time, keeping control firmly lodged with the central bureaucracy and political process.

Once the government has decided on its Tier I obligation, it should be in the business of getting benefits to their intended recipients as quickly and as efficiently as possible. Mixing social commitments and administrative efficiencies (both proper government responsibilities) with saving and investment objectives (principally the concern of citizens and businesses) is like mixing oil and water. That's not to say that the government has no interest in saving and investment. A strong community is better placed to deliver on the government's social obligations, and a well run bureaucracy that invests in effective technology reduces the cost of governing. Governments should concentrate on doing the things where they have a

---

[1]   A report by the Technical Panel (of the 1994-1996 Council on Social Security) on Trends and Issues in Retirement Savings, January 1997. All 13 members thought that at least some of Social Security contributions should be invested in private markets while a majority (7 out of 13 members) thought that individual accounts should be set up within the overall system.

competitive advantage and stay away from activities where they have a dismal record. History shows that governments which try choosing winners in capital markets or forcing citizens to behave in ways that don't suit them will eventually lose. That leaves to one side some of the problems faced by a government-run investment fund—the huge sums involved in any sort of pre-funded Tier I would ensure that the government becomes the largest player in investment markets. How would voter-sensitive politicians and bureaucrats deal with some of the hard issues faced every day by private investors? With ownership comes control and with control comes responsibility.[1]

However, for the sake of the argument, let's assume that a government can set up a funded regime that's protected from political interference and, through competitive performance, achieves something akin to a market-related performance.[2] Does that make it a good idea?

The cost of *any* retirement benefits scheme, including pre-funded arrangements run by employers, is the amount of the benefits paid.[3] That cost can't be known until the last person entitled to a benefit has died. That could take 50 or 60 years and may never happen if you keep allowing new people to enter the system as potential beneficiaries. This rule holds good for any arrangement, no matter how you pay for it. If an employer chose to put money aside into a defined-benefit scheme ahead of the time when its employees retired, that still wouldn't change the cost of the scheme. The benefits haven't been changed as a result of the decision to pre-fund them.

However, the cost to the *employer* will change as a result of a decision to pre-fund—now the amount needed from the employer will be benefits paid, less investment income.

If an employer weren't worried about the security of members' benefits, the only reason for it to pre-fund its future pension obligations should be that it thought the investment return on the scheme's assets is likely to be greater than the return the employer could generate in its own business. If that were the case, the employer should seriously think about changing its business or getting out of it altogether. That, however, is not relevant to the pre-funding issue.

So, giving employees the security of knowing that their benefits are likely to be there at retirement no matter what happens to the employer in the meantime has a cost to the employer in any year that is calculated as follows:

---

[1]   For more on this, see Ostaszewski, K.M., 'Privatizing the Social Security Trust Fund? Don't Let the Government Invest', *Cato Institute Social Security Paper Number 6*, 1996.

[2]   The Quebec Pension Plan (that province's mirror of the Canada Pension Plan) has assets built up to meet at least part of the government's Tier II, earnings-related pension. Apparently, its performance is competitive with private schemes. The Canadian government's latest proposal to partially fund the Canadian Pension Plan (see 'Securing the Canadian Pension Plan: Agreement on proposed changes to the CPP', February 1997) will see the country's plan develop assets invested in a diversified portfolio of assets equal to five years' benefits.

[3]   In this discussion, I'll ignore administration costs which are a given no matter how the scheme is funded, although they will be higher if there is a pool of money to look after and track.

Return on the employer's funds less return on the scheme's funds.

Employers should therefore make a decision on pre-funding on grounds of security for employees, not on grounds of cost.

Turning now to my proposed new Tier I scheme for New Zealand, the same principles apply. For the reason explained, a government doesn't, from a financial perspective, have to worry about the security of pensioners' future benefits.

So, what about the issue of cost? If the government puts aside money into a special fund to pay for its Tier I scheme, it would be making a judgement on a comparison between the fund's investment return less the costs of running the separate fund, and its own cost of money plus the cost to the community of collecting tax money ahead of the time it was actually needed (including the dead-weight cost of income tax).

While there may be some advantages in having a fund of retirement savings benefit, the monolithic nature of a large central fund would dissipate a number of those advantages. I covered these issues in chapter 5.

And, at the end of it all, what would have been achieved? A more secure retirement pension? No. While the whole process remains in central control, change is inevitable. More savings? Possibly, but, as I've already said, what matters is not the amount that's in the fund, but what happens to it once it's there and what has been done with the rest of the government's finances to get it there. Again, a central fund does no more than re-arrange the claims on today's economy between the productive and the retired. Having the fund doesn't and won't change things by itself.

A close look at the Provident Funds of Singapore, Malaysia, India and a number of the small Pacific Island states shows that the investment performance of central funds has generally been poor. According to the World Bank[1] the average annual real returns (after inflation) for the 10 years to 1996 were 0.3 per cent for India and -3.8 per cent for Kenya. The better performances of Singapore (3.0 per cent) and Malaysia (4.6 per cent) came at a high regulatory price.

> Funding and PAYG both offer individuals a measure of security about their future, but ... no method ... can insure against common shocks. The future is full of uncertainties (about rates of inflation, output growth, birth rates and the like), which affect pension schemes as they affect most other institutions. Thus it should not be surprising that there is little to choose between PAYG and funding in this respect. To imagine that funded schemes are substantially better in the face of aggregate uncertainty is to fall for crude mythology.[2]

The fact that pre-funding a state scheme is a bad idea doesn't mean the state shouldn't know what the scheme might cost in the future and be able to express that cost in today's money. I think the US Financial Accounting Standards Board's Statement 87 (FASB 87) gives governments a good model to monitor their costs year by year.

FASB 87 requires companies to work out the cost of their defined-benefit schemes within their profit-and-loss accounts. The company disregards the

---

[1]   *Averting The Old Age Crisis*, Oxford University Press, 1994, p. 95.

[2]   Barr, N., *The Economics of the Welfare State*, Stanford University Press, 1993.

fact that an external trust owns the assets and requires the company to treat the assets and liabilities as if they belong to the company. The company is forced to make best guesses about inflation, pay increases, investment income and the discount rate, and to report to their shareholders directly on the state of the scheme. There are rules about the way actuarial gains and losses are amortised (or spread) over longish periods, recognising the long-run nature of the liabilities. The standard also regulates the way that future costs of benefit improvements are accounted for.

FASB 87 has two main purposes. First, the people who pay for the benefits (the employer's shareholders) keep an accounting watch on a defined-benefit scheme's liabilities—those that have built up in the past and those that will accrue in the coming year. The second purpose is to work out how much the employer should be allowed to claim as a deductible expense for tax purposes. That second purpose has no relevance to a government's monitoring the future costs of a defined-benefit welfare arrangement.

Advantages of Applying the FASB 87 Principles to a Tier I Scheme

Applying the principles of FASB 87 to social welfare arrangements like my proposed scheme will have a number of advantages:

Confidence
Knowing that the government was maintaining a watch on year-by-year changes to the long-term liabilities would give voters and beneficiaries confidence in the sustainability of Tier I.[1] A good foundation for Tiers II and III is one of Tier I's main objectives.

Flexibility
Tier I needs to be flexible because some change is inevitable over the decades. FASB 87 allows decision makers to see the long-term implications of changes, and not just as beneficiaries are about to collect their changed entitlements.

Political constraint
FASB 87 would impose financial constraints on the political process so that the true, long-term costs of this year's political 'bribes' would be known when change happens rather than, as now, when the crisis is about to strike.

In fact, there's a good case for governments to run proper balance sheets (with assets and liabilities identified for the country as a whole) along with

---

[1]   That way, voters wouldn't be surprised to learn the size of unfunded pension liabilities. In Canada, they are estimated at 100% of GDP in today's money (about the same level as its 'official' debt). Italy's total is 113% and Japan's is 110%, while, in the US, unfunded pension liabilities amounts to 'only' 31% of GDP (from an OECD report cited in *Business Week*, 28 August 1995). Those levels may or may not comfort voters but they would probably affect their behaviour in any debate about change. They could see that pensions that are promised in exchange for social security contributions are quite like government bonds bought by today's investment, see Laurence J. Kotlikoff's *What Determines Savings?*, chapter 8, 'Economic Impact of Deficit Funding', The MIT Press, 1989 for a discussion on the various ways that governments dress up taxes, funding and deficits. They are quite like bonds but not the same—governments can change the rules on Tier I promises and the 'bond holders' have to reach state pension age before they start to collect on them.

expenditure and income accounts.[1] Nearly all developed countries use cash flow statements—and that's no way to run a country any more than a business.

Applying the FASB 87 principles is not the only way a country should look at its future pension liabilities. Generational accounting and fiscal sustainability exercises should also be carried out on a regular basis—chapter 3 explains how they work.

Identified Contribution?

Most OECD countries have an identified social security contribution that often pays for more than just the retirement benefit—it usually covers death and disability benefits as well. In some cases (for example, the UK) it also includes the cost of the national health scheme and Tier II arrangements such as in France and Japan.

One thing stands out—the size of those contributions. The average is a total (employer and employee) of 23.3 per cent of covered pay among the 22 OECD countries with a separate contribution. Admittedly, some of the contributions are based on pay that is capped, but that usually covers nearly all employees' total pay.[2]

Some countries deserve special mention. France topped the poll with a total contribution of 62 per cent[3] of pay (42 per cent from the employer and 20 per cent from the employee). Italy was a close second with a combined contribution rate of 50 per cent of pay—40 per cent from the employer and 10 per cent from the employee.

Germany, the Netherlands, Portugal, Spain, Sweden and Turkey were also top performers—in each case, the total social security contribution rate is more than 30 per cent of covered pay.

Only two of the 24 countries (Australia and New Zealand) don't have a separate social security contribution. Their retirement pensions are simply paid out of current tax revenue. That's appropriate for a flat-rate benefit, although the other four countries that have a single-level, flat-rate scheme seem to want an identified contribution and all have a completely separate collection system to pay for social security benefits.

Let's get one thing clear: if a country operates an unfunded retirement income system (as do all of the OECD countries) it doesn't matter how that country sets up the system that pays for the scheme. Its citizens are not setting aside money for their own benefits, they're paying for the benefits of today's retired. It's money in and money out, all in one go. Requiring identified contributions on the grounds that this changes the state

---

[1]   New Zealand is the only OECD country that has accounts prepared in accordance with Generally Accepted Accounting Principles (GAAP) and audited by a private firm. It doesn't, however, use FASB 87 for its pension liabilities and should.

[2]   In fact, capping pay imposes a barrier to part time employment because it might be cheaper to employ one full-timer (whose pay exceeds the cap) rather than two part-timers whose total pay is the same but where both fall under the cap.

[3]   Based on a salary of $50,140 a year and including the contributions to both Tier I (17.16% of earnings to $55,400)and Tier II.

intervention from welfare to something that looks like co-operative self-provision is playing to the deliberately myopic, deeply self-interested older voter.

A completely separate system to collect and record contributions has no real justification.[1] It's just another tax with the disadvantages of being expensive to collect and a tendency to being regressive—the low paid pay relatively more than the high paid. Social security contributions are often paid on more of an employee's pay (and with fewer deductions) than income tax itself. On its own, that will tend to encourage employers to shift compensation from pay that would have attracted social security contributions to benefits that don't.

It also leads to illogical rules to cope with the infinitely variable working lives of our citizens. In the UK, for example, if you've missed years of contributions through education or absence overseas and you want to retire early, you can make up for the years that you would have contributed between retirement and state pension age. The bargain struck in 1995 was that, for a lump sum of £1,446, you can buy five years' worth of the inflation-proofed basic state pension of £349 a year—an absolute snip!

Recommendation: Benefits under my proposed new Tier I scheme for New Zealand should, as now, be paid out of general tax revenue.

Reviewing New Zealand Superannuation

This chapter has suggested a design for a new Tier I scheme for New Zealand. It is designed from a 1998 perspective, using, for example, 1998 definitions of poverty and 'participating and belonging'. Those definitions will change as the community becomes more or less wealthy. The affordability of any scheme will also change, as will the way people work and businesses operate.

All this means that the design, if agreed to by the community, must adapt to changing conditions. The process of change should be quite formally established.

The responsibility for monitoring the scheme should be taken out of the hands of the elected government and be given to an independent body. That body would be given the mandate to ensure the scheme's objectives are met. It would also act as the focus for studies on possible changes and the short- and long-run cost implications of change. I have more to say about this new body in the next chapter at p. 186.

Information gathering to ensure the scheme is meeting its objectives and to allow appropriate modification through informed, reasoned debate would be a vital role of the review body. New Zealand must never again endure the kind of changes that were proposed in the National Government's 1991 Budget. That introduced, overnight, a severe income test (dubbed the 'clawback') based on deeply inadequate data. Because that change was in the Budget, it

---

[1]   The theoretical justification for separate contributions comes from the 'insurance' side of the social insurance argument. Social security 'contributions' are not supposed to be like a tax, they are supposed to deliver protection and so are like the price of any good. That argument tends to fall apart because of the increasing disconnection in state schemes around the world between contributions and benefits and the apparent disbelief contributors have in the benefits they will eventually receive.

became a matter of parliamentary 'confidence' that it be passed into law without effective debate even among the opposition's politicians. It also nearly caused a revolt within the government's own ranks once voters started to bend the ears of their representatives. Changes of that kind need never happen to a retirement income scheme if objectives are properly set and monitored. The concept of 'overnight crisis' is oxymoronic in the retirement income context.

Overall, the review body's role would be vital to the financial plans of all New Zealanders.

So, if the Grade 2½ objective were agreed by the community, information must be gathered on a regular basis to ensure the scheme is doing its job. That information should be published at least annually.

The review body should be able to receive submissions on possible changes from any quarter, including politicians. The responsibility for the scheme's community acceptance should not be confined to our elected leaders. Everyone should have access to the process of change and therefore to the scheme's long-term acceptance and viability.

Transition—Moving from Here to There

As discussed in chapter 3 the present New Zealand Superannuation and future governments' accounts look in passable shape. So we don't need to replace the existing scheme immediately, or even in the medium term, at least from fiscal and political perspectives.

Because my suggestions for New Zealand Superannuation significantly change the government's involvement in New Zealanders' retirement incomes, I want to ensure that all current earners (over the age of 20) will not be affected by the new regime—in other words their existing plans need not be disturbed.

We should say to New Zealanders who are now coming into the workforce from, say, age 20 that they will have 48 years' notice of change as far as the benefit itself is concerned. I suggest two exceptions to that general principle. First, I think that the state pension age should be increased to age 68 before 2045 (48 years from now). Along with most developed countries, New Zealand will face significant skill shortages as the baby-boomers move through to retirement, and the state scheme should not be encouraging those skills to be lost through retirement.

Baby-boomers start retiring in 2011 (based on the current 'normal' age of 65) so I think we should aim to have the new age-68 state pension age effective by 2014. That gives 13 years (the age-65 change being fully effective by 2001) to shift the additional three years to 68. That's time enough.

Second, I think the early and late retirement payment provisions should be introduced relatively soon. Forced retirement on account of age will be outlawed from 1 February 1999. The new payment provisions should be in place by then.

Choosing age 20 for the first New Zealanders to run by the new rules introduces a significant discontinuity between those who just qualify for the old benefits and those who 'suffer' from the new. Discontinuities in benefit provision of any kind should be avoided if possible but, in this case, that can happen only at the expense of complexity, administrative costs and communication problems. Despite the discontinuity, I think the simpler the rule for a change of this kind, the better. Lifting the state pension age for everyone by the time my proposed scheme starts will have eliminated a major issue.

Recommendation: In summary, I propose that by 2014 the state pension will be increased to age 68; the early and late retirement provisions would be introduced by 1 February 1999 and all the other changes will take effect 48 years from now.

Why Look Just at OECD Countries?

In this chapter, I have concentrated on 24 OECD countries for international comparisons. From New Zealand's perspective, that's potentially dangerous because it assumes that international competition for the price of our labour, including the cost of the Tier I scheme, will come only from those countries.

Of the 24 OECD countries, only Australia, Japan and the United States could be said to be of particular importance to our economy. So, is my proposed scheme likely to make us uncompetitive? Before looking at this, it's as well to realise that there are signs of the practices of developed countries appearing among the Asian tigers.

Of eight East Asian countries,[1] only one (Thailand) has no present Tier I retirement scheme, although that is shortly to change. Of the other seven, compulsory funded schemes are the order of the day—five have this type of arrangement.[2] Of these, Singapore's is by far the largest (in terms of the way that it dominates the economy). Only Korea has the pay-related, defined-benefit scheme that grips most European countries. The cost of the Korean scheme increased by 50 per cent in 1997 to a total of nine per cent of covered pay.

Each of these countries will be facing its own version of the demographic deluge and there are few signs of any detailed preparation among most of them. In the context of the issues that our near Asian neighbours will be facing over the next 20 to 30 years, I am confident my proposed new scheme for New Zealand will not affect our competitiveness.

I feel even more comfortable when I look at New Zealand's four main trading partners—Australia's Tier I is at roughly the same level as my scheme, though its asset- and income-testing regimes are nominally more severe. However, Australia's Tiers II and III need radical reform, as do Tiers I, II and III in Japan. Its horrendous problems mean no competition for New Zealand on that issue at least—no problems from that quarter for several generations. The US is in reasonable trouble as well at all three levels, though not to the extent that tomorrow's Japanese taxpayers face.

The Philosophy of Change

I hope you have seen a consistent theme to the recommended changes. They reflect my preference for market-based incentives as the way of reducing

---

[1] China, Hong Kong, Indonesia, Korea, Malaysia, Singapore, Taiwan and Thailand.

[2] The position in China is in significant flux—China faces a doubling of the over-60s as a proportion of the population by 2025 as the old state-run companies' obligations to the retired are slowly transferred to the central government. The government has said that a unified retirement pension system will be introduced by the end of 1998. Apparently, these funds 'should be invested in government bonds or special pension savings accounts' (according to *Dow Jones News* , 27 October 1997).

developed countries' involvement in the provision of retirement incomes.

Speaking for New Zealand, I return, again, to the behavioural aspect. For a lot of reasons (high inflation, general economic mismanagement, an absence of agreed national objectives) New Zealand, as a country, has treated New Zealanders like children as far as retirement savings are concerned. I think New Zealanders have considerable potential for greater independence on this issue. However, that won't happen without continued low inflation, a commitment to economic and financial education and an improvement in the efficiency of savings institutions.

I think everyone should be aiming to reduce the risks of dependence on the state, because those risks are considerable. Before they can do that, they have to understand what those risks are and that they can be managed.

We must recognise that for most the state will continue to provide a significant slice of their retirement income needs.

I am convinced that most New Zealanders can afford to save for retirement and, given the right environment and information, I believe they will. Why wouldn't they?

7

So Whose Responsibility Is It?

Summary

In terms of choice, equity, cost-effectiveness and optimum returns, individuals and the economy in general are likely to benefit most from a voluntary, unsubsidised regime. However, the arguments that make tax incentives and compulsion unsatisfactory answers to retirement income provision at Tiers II and III do not let governments off the hook when it comes to private retirement provision.

The key attributes of a private retirement income system are to achieve a good return on savings, financial security, fairness, flexibility and affordability. Governments have a substantial role to play in achieving these things, without needing to be directly involved as a provider or sponsor at the level of private provision.

Governments can and should control inflation; ensure fair tax treatment, including tax neutrality on employer contributions and investment income; create clear signals for investors and markets through consistent public policy; establish a straight-forward process for resolving disputes between savers and providers; facilitate the provision of comprehensive and useful information on saving, saving rates and retirement trends for the use of individuals and investment markets; create a regulatory environment that opens up the flow of information rather than prescribing what providers and investors can and can't do; encourage diversity by facilitating the provision of products such as inflation-linked bonds, reverse annuities and home equity conversions; and ensure a consistent reporting regime, so savers can compare like investments and understand exactly what's happening. As with Tier I, the regime should be monitored by an independent body. There also needs to be a process built into the system that allows for measured rather than radical change.

****

After decades of experience with income redistribution and spending programs, we know for a fact that the liberals' claims were unfounded. Promised benefits did not materialize, but many unpromised problems and costs to society did. The 'Great Society' ended in failure and left a legacy of almost intractable problems.

Paul Craig Roberts writing in Business Week, 6 November 1995.

So, Where are We?

The last chapter sets out a sustainable, flexible Tier I scheme offering an inflation-proofed Grade 2½ benefit designed to prevent poverty 'plus a margin', that is, a benefit set above the 'poverty line', from age 68. This chapter looks at what the state should do about Tier II (employer-provided schemes) and Tier III (all other private savings).

Chapter 4 argues that tax incentives for Tiers II and III are a bad idea, despite their global popularity.

Chapter 5 concludes that compulsion at Tier II has both advantages and disadvantages, but the disadvantages significantly outweigh the advantages. A country has to be in real trouble with Tier I before the disadvantages can be put to one side for the greater and immediate good.[1]

By the end of this chapter, you will see that there are many ways in which a government can facilitate and encourage private provision without resorting to direct intervention.

Macro Versus Micro

Before we look at what a country as a whole can do about the saving habits of its citizens, I want to return briefly to the general points about savings, growth and intergenerational equity arguments made earlier. Chapter 3 (pp. 30-33) briefly summarised current thinking on the relationship between savings and growth—growth seems to come first. Chapter 5 (pp. 107-8) looked at Nicholas Barr's analysis of the fallacy of composition and the possibility that forced saving could actually hurt an economy's ability to cope with the demographic deluge. It could also widen the political divide between the producers and consumers of the country's economic wealth.

This chapter suggests that the government must separate its attentions between 'macro' and 'micro'; between, on the one hand, understanding its responsibilities to today's and tomorrow's economy as a whole while, on the other, helping its citizens to make sensible decisions about their individual needs. These are two separate issues and I'll look first at what can be done about the economy as a whole.

Demographers predict that tomorrow we will have relatively fewer producers and more consumers. If governments could do anything about that, they could alter the balance only through policies that increased production and reduced consumption. Policies would need to reduce consumption by workers (because that will leave more for pensioners) and by pensioners (because that will leave more for workers). If the policies achieved all three (increased production and reduced consumption for both workers and pensioners) then perhaps the changing shape of our population wouldn't matter much.

As Nicholas Barr pointed out,[2] the country as a whole can do several things about increasing production:

- increase capital stock and its quality
- increase investment in labour by education or training—this can be done (or facilitated) by the state, by employers or by individuals on their own account

---

[1]   Chile's 1981 welfare crisis is a case in point. For a compulsory scheme introduced for the wrong reasons, see Australia in 1986. Its underlying philosophy was a trade union-government axis aimed, in part, at securing the union movement's relevance in a declining market for its traditional services.

[2]   *The Economics of the Welfare State*, Stanford University Press, 1993, p. 232.

- reduce unemployment and encourage those who choose not to work to return to the workforce[1]
- import more labour through immigration, and
- increase the retirement age—increasing the state pension age to 68 (as I suggested in the last chapter) will probably lead to an increase in the age at which people tend to retire. This both increases the size of the workforce and reduces the period that people are retired, so reducing the cost of supporting the old.

Of these five policy options, only the first (increasing capital stock and its quality) could potentially benefit from more financial savings. These savings would presumably be of the voluntary, unsubsidised kind I have already suggested.[2]

Barr concludes that storing up financial resources at the behest of the government isn't the best basis on which to prepare for an ageing population. Voluntary unsubsidised savings, however, do have a positive role to play at a macro-economic policy level. Private markets supported by the voluntary, unsubsidised private savings of our fellow citizens are important to the effective operation of capital markets. In a number of areas that matter, free markets have a greater potential to achieve the increase and improvement in the national capital stock than the other main alternative—state control.[3] Voluntary, unsubsidised savings also provide a way that individuals can shift consumption from their working lives to their retirement. In this case, what's good for the individual is not necessarily, but could be, good for the community as a whole.

Should Individuals be Left to Their own Devices?

If you accept the arguments in chapters 4 and 5, we can't bribe or bludgeon those of our fellow citizens who don't seem to know what to do into behaving appropriately. On the other hand, can we really expect them to do whatever it is they should be doing, all by themselves?

The answer to that is 'yes and no'. In developed countries, we aren't used to making these sorts of decisions for ourselves. We need to be introduced to a new era where there are no 'entitlements' without demonstrated need and

---

[1] So childcare policies and barriers to work like the minimum wage can be seen as part of a long-term retirement income strategy.

[2] 'Funding is clearly irrelevant to [the other four policies] which can all be pursued by direct methods. If funding makes any difference, it can only be if it (a) leads successively to an increase in saving, in investment and in output ... and (b) does so more effectively than any other method of garnering resources and channelling them into productive investment ... The evidence on (a), both theoretically and empirically, is mixed, inconclusive and highly controversial, and that on (b) is unlikely to be less so', Nicholas Barr, p. 233.

[3] Though there are also areas of the economy where, perhaps, the government has a role that can't be easily matched by the private sector. Obvious candidates are investments that maintain the quality of the environment, law and order and defence. More controversial candidates include infrastructure (roads, national power and telecommunication grids) and the education of our children.

where governments will show how, but not try to do more than keep a friendly eye on events from the sideline.

So, what's to be done?

Meet *Homo Economicus* Again

We've already met *homo economicus*. We've seen him (and her) most recently in the bad light either of:

- **tax induced savings,** where *homo economicus* wants to take advantage of the tax breaks but tries to avoid the returns that society demands through paying tax on the emerging benefits or,

- **compulsory savings,** where *homo economicus* tries to avoid doing what's required because he/she has better ideas than the command-and-control driven bureaucracy.

Those who favour tax incentives or compulsion won't like *homo economicus* very much. Individuals will always seem to be doing the things people don't want them to. That means they have to be controlled. Control means regulation and regulation means more regulation and it starts to get out of hand. It could be said that it's all the fault of *homo economicus* for failing to follow instructions.

But that misses the point. If people should be doing what's in their own best interests then *homo economicus* should be seen as the true north; as the force for good. We need to find ways of capturing that force; of showing them what would happen if they kept doing the things they were doing and then leave them to decide the best way to get to that point, wherever that might be.

I believe that people want to do the right thing if given the choice—they need to be shown why, what and how. The information barriers must be broken down. Governments can help a lot in this. The government's greatest challenge is to help make information accessible, relevant and comprehensible to savers, not specialists.

Then everything needs to be tested against that true north; tested and retested as events unfold.

'Partnerships' with Private Provision?

When the state decides on its involvement with Tiers II and III, I think it should stay away from 'partnerships' with private provision. The UK shows what's wrong with the idea

Having decided in 1975 that the flat-rate basic state pension should be supplemented by an earnings-related top-up (the State Earnings Related Pension Scheme or SERPS), the UK government then let private schemes 'contract out' of SERPS by agreeing to provide private pensions that were at least as good. There are several reasons why 'partnerships' such as this are unsustainable:

Partnerships would mean rule changes for all partners. Private schemes are for the long term. I've stressed that public provision at Tier I must be for the long-term otherwise private saving arrangements can't take sensible account of the state's role. However, state schemes must also be adaptable and that means they may have to change. If the state scheme were in 'partnership' with private schemes to achieve an overall objective, then change to the state scheme would mean rewriting the partnership's rules, probably with retrospective effect. No one likes rules being changed part way through a game and so it has proved in the UK. A partnership with a state scheme is like dancing with elephants.

Such partnerships would be heavily regulated. Though private schemes won't normally be *required* to join the partnership (that's the case with 'contracting out' in the UK) if they did, there would be books of rules needed to regulate the 'partnership' and armies of bureaucrats to police them. That's expensive and not particularly productive—it doesn't add to the nation's wealth.

The objectives of public and private providers will usually conflict. In the UK, private schemes usually contract out to save money, not to 'join with the state in the provision of a decent standard of living' or some such noble cause. Partnerships should be about moving together towards a common goal, not about worrying who's walking behind you.

There would be a tendency for 'gaming' at the margins. We must expect that individuals (including financial institutions) will want to maximise their benefits, preferably at the state's (all other taxpayers') expense.

The UK again shows why. The government, for ideological reasons, allowed individuals to leave what were, until then, normally compulsory occupational schemes,[1] and take out 'Personal Pension Plans' that remained contracted out of SERPS. The financial services industry saw this as a potential bonanza. Misleading selling techniques saw more than 550,000 defined-benefit scheme members leave in favour of expensive personal plans that were going to leave their owners magically better off despite the loss of the employer's subsidy to their previous defined-benefit scheme. Anyone who knew anything about pensions could see a disaster in the making, and so it turned out. Now the sellers of these products are faced with the costs of the negligent advice—(estimated, in May 1996, at £1 billion). The defined-benefit schemes are now being asked to let the wayward members back in. All in all, an unmitigated disaster.[2]

'Partnerships' can also blur the state's responsibility for delivering on Tier I. I think that's one explanation for why the UK government is getting away with the long-term reductions to both the basic state pension (Tier I)

---

[1] They were compulsory, not by government fiat but through the terms of private employment arrangements.

[2] Now the UK government is allowing compensation for mis-sold personal pensions to be paid tax free (UK Budget 1995). This applies to anyone who was advised wrongly to transfer from, opt out of or not join an occupational scheme but, instead, to take out a personal plan between 29 April 1988 and 30 June 1994. Then there is the generous offer extended by public sector schemes to 'allow current employees to rejoin schemes and buy back pension rights for previous service at reasonable cost' reported in *The Financial Times* 22 November 1995. Mrs Angela Knight urged 'the private sector to follow the example of public sector schemes'. That's all right for Mrs Knight because her schemes are ultimately paid for by, guess who?

and the earnings-related addition (SERPS) that started only in 1978. Over the last 20 years, by reducing the real net value of state benefits and therefore the number of people that depend on them, governments have reduced the size of the electorate that's needed to keep them honest—by that I mean, being up front with what they're doing. The more people who look to the private sector for benefits that the state has decided to provide (SERPS), the better the chances of the electorate tolerating the reduction of the state benefits for everyone, including those who participate in the state's own earnings-related top-up. Though 'contracting out' applies only to the earnings-related addition, it seems that cutting back on the basic state pension at Tier I is easier because the whole picture (state + private) is now so complicated that few have a clear grasp of what's happening.

Overall, experience like the UK's demonstrates that, while the idea of the state going into 'partnerships' with private schemes may sound great in theory, in practice it leads to confusion, cost and some disastrous outcomes.

The World Bank's Solution

Before looking at what I think the government's role should be at Tiers II and III, I want first to address the recommendations of the World Bank's report *Averting the Old Age Crisis.*[1] In summary, the report proposed:

At Tier I,[2] a benefit that should 'reduce old age poverty' at the relatively modest level of about 20 per cent of the average wage.[3] It should be tax-funded and paid from an age that is 'high enough so that it is a good proxy for the inability to work for the majority of people'. These are somewhat more limited objectives than the benefit I suggested in the last chapter. However, the World Bank's benefit would be paid to everyone, even those who didn't need it. My suggested Tier I would reduce if private resources achieved the 'prevention of poverty, plus a margin'.

At Tier II, a compulsory, funded but privately-managed savings scheme, much as in the Chilean mould. However, occupational schemes and personal accounts could all participate along with:

> extensive government regulation ... to compensate for market failures such as a lack of information by workers and socially inefficient restrictions imposed by employers.

The report thought that Tiers I and II might together deliver up to 40 per cent of an employee's final pay.

At Tier III, anything more that people might want to provide for themselves.

There's no point retracing the reasons for my suggested Tier I. The balance I have suggested is that the state should ensure its citizens are delivered from 'poverty, plus a margin' and they should then be left to get on with the rest of their economic lives. The World Bank can justify its stinginess at Tier I (20 per cent of the average wage *vs.* my suggested income-tested 35 per cent)

---

[1]   Oxford University Press, 1994.

[2]   The report actually referred to the more traditional 'pillars'.

[3]   According to the measures I used in chapter 6 the World Bank's Tier I would be about Grade 1½ for New Zealand, or somewhere between alleviation and prevention of poverty.

because of the huge intervention in private markets that it proposes at Tier II, with a compulsory savings scheme.

The overall balance between intervention, regulation and freedom is a matter for each country to resolve. I think the balance should simplify the state's involvement at Tier I and stay away from direct intervention at Tier II. That favours my income-tested Tier I scheme rather than the World Bank's mandatory, two-level arrangement proposed for Tiers I and II.

The World Bank's justifications for interventions were as follows:

> Depending purely on voluntary actions by individuals to provide for their own old age security leaves several problems:
>
> - Short-sightedness—some people may not be farsighted enough to save for their own old age and may later become charges on the rest of society.
>
> - Inadequate savings instruments—capital markets are underdeveloped and macroeconomic conditions are unstable in many countries.
>
> - Insurance market failures—adverse selection, moral hazard, and correlations among individuals make insurance against many risks (such as longevity, disability, investment [income], inflation, and depression) unavailable.
>
> - Information gaps—people may be unable to assess the long-term solvency of private savings and insurance companies or the productivity of alternative investment programs, and cannot reverse their choices when large mistakes are discovered late in life.
>
> - Long-term poverty—some people do not earn enough during their working lives to save for their old age, so redistribution is necessary to keep them out of poverty (pp. 5-6).

The report gave a lot of interesting data in its summary of the world's retirement income systems but, when it came to the piece that really mattered (why governments should intervene to fix all these problems) the authors produced a bureaucratic leap of faith:

> How should a country choose among these alternative financing and managerial arrangements [Tier I: funded or unfunded; Tier II: compulsory or voluntary and Tier III] and develop a coherent strategy for providing old age security? Any strategy should have the basic goals of helping the old and helping the broader economy. That is, old age programs should be both a social safety net and an instrument for growth (p. 233).

As chapter 6 pointed out, only governments can deliver on Tier I, but there are choices at Tier II. The World Bank mentions only in passing the significant distortions that a compulsory saving regime creates (detailed in my chapter 5), but they are not analysed with any rigour. I agree that old-age programmes should be a safety net, but the second goal needs to be re-expressed. Rather than be 'an instrument for growth', the goal should be that those programmes shouldn't impede growth. The World Bank's report glosses over the real dangers of one policy having more than one objective and missing both (or, more likely, failing to deliver optimal results for both).

Several of the problems the report uses to justify massive interventions at Tiers II and III, even if true, have no particular relevance for the developed countries that are the subject of this book. Inadequate savings instruments, unstable macroeconomic conditions, information gaps and long-term poverty among the old are all things that most developed countries have largely under control. These, however, are the countries that have the biggest problems with their retirement income systems.

The report doesn't review the problems created by tax incentives—another extraordinary gap. In fact, I wasn't sure whether the report recommended that the compulsory savings at Tier II should attract tax relief or not.[1] Forcing people to save in a particular way and then rewarding them with their own money for doing it is absurd.

The combination of a modest but reasonable Tier I plus voluntary private provision[2] was not suggested by the authors as a possible way forward. I had the feeling that the authors started, rather than finished, with a solution and then developed their arguments to fit their case. The main problem seemed to be current levels of tax and internal deficits and how to get these under control relatively quickly. This is not what might constitute a 'successful' system, however that might be defined in a particular country.

I was dissatisfied with the World Bank's report; in fact, it motivated me to get on and write this book. I felt that the report let its readers down.

Key Attributes of a Private Retirement Income System

Enough about the policies and ideas I don't like or disagree with. Let's talk about what it takes to make a successful private retirement income system. Those who are familiar with the recommendations of New Zealand's Task Force on Private Provision for Retirement will be familiar with some of what follows.

The Task Force identified the five key attributes of a successful *private* retirement income system:

- good return on savings
- financial security
- fairness
- flexibility
- affordability[3]

From the country's perspective, the first two key attributes are related to the issue of getting the economy 'right', protecting the value of money (one of a government's most sacred duties) and creating an environment that protects property rights. The last three are related to letting people choose and allowing them the freedom to succeed and fail.

All the things a government might do in relation to Tiers II and III must in some way be related to these five key attributes—either helping achieve them or helping find out about them so that individuals can make appropriate decisions in relation to them. Individuals will know what's ahead and, if they

---

[1]   Because countries that have compulsory saving schemes also offer tax incentives on those savings, I assume the report's authors are relaxed about that. One of the authors (Estelle James) gave the Australian arrangements a tick, reported in *The Australian Financial Review*, 14 July 1995, without apparently mentioning the curious case of the incentivised compulsory contributions.

[2]   With no tax incentives—New Zealand's position on this was mentioned but more out of puzzlement. There was no discussion of New Zealand's reasons for removing tax incentives to save for retirement and whether they might be sound.

[3]   *The Way Forward*, the final report of the Task Force, December 1992 from page 15.

could and did decide to save, they would lower their retirement 'affordability risk' by spreading their sources of income in retirement. Because they'll be making their decisions with knowledge, our citizens will feel a greater sense of security about the whole business of retirement provision. That would be a change in most developed countries.

Then, with our income-tested Tier I pension, tomorrow's governments will also gain by reducing their outlays on tomorrow's retired, and every-one—savers, taxpayers, politicians and the financial service providers—will feel happier.

As the New Zealand Task Force on Private Provision for Retirement pointed out, the first two key attributes are closely related. Saving can't and shouldn't be risk-free and people need to appreciate the level of risk (security) that suits their circumstances and their objectives. They can't do that without reliable and usable information. They also can't do it unless the economy gives them an appropriate reward for risk and some reasonable certainty that they will actually receive that reward.

The test of fairness is subjective, so different people and different groups of people at different stages of their lives will give it different interpretations. I've already spent time on this important issue from the state's perspective[1]— political and fiscal sustainability are important elements of achieving fairness in any state-sponsored retirement income programme. It's also important for the private Tiers II and III.

Flexibility and fairness are also linked. A flexible system lets people achieve a degree of fairness to suit their different circumstances. That then leads us into the issue of individual affordability—another subjective and sometimes emotive topic.

If a retirement income system depends on a healthy response from private savings at Tiers II and III, it must incorporate realistic objectives. That can't be done without good information.

The Starting Point for Developing a Strategy

The New Zealand Task Force's five key attributes provide the starting point in developing a strategy for a government's policies at Tiers II and III. Leaving people to make their own decisions doesn't let governments off the hook.

A Good Return on Savings

Let's look first at the objective of a good return on savings.

A government can help its citizens with this in many ways. In what I think is their approximate order of importance to this key objective, they are:

Inflation
If savers are to be encouraged to defer consumption from today until retirement, they must be confident that they will get back real money. The long periods involved with saving for retirement make this a special responsibility for governments. It is one that only those who are in charge of public policy settings can have any hope of managing, if not actually controlling.

---

[1]   See the discussion in chapter 4 on fiscal affordability and generational accounting.

Tax treatment

A government's tax policies shouldn't favour one form of saving over another. Different treatments tend to attract savings for the wrong reasons (the tax break rather than the return). They also insulate the manager from the effect of relatively poor returns.

Regulators should treat all private savings on a common basis - one type of saving shouldn't be favoured over another (as is the case with tax incentives) and no market should be guaranteed to a particular group of suppliers (as is the case with compulsion). This should, in the long run, produce the best returns on savings.

Consistent public policy

Savers need to be confident that Tier I is sustainable and that it will be there when they reach state pension age. They also need to know that their own savings will be available when they need them and that directionless changes in policy won't interfere with their long-term plans.[1]

Information

Governments need to gather and monitor accurate information on issues relevant to retirement incomes. They then need to convert that information into digestible material that savers can use to understand their own positions and to set their own objectives. Not only savers need this—researchers will play an important part in the development of successful Tiers II and III. The information should also feed into the education system, so that saving becomes part of our culture—not something that only other people do. Financial education should be part of the mathematics syllabus.

A lot of this kind of information is already available, much of it from financial institutions that want to invest our savings. A potential problem with market supplied data is that those who manage our money have a direct and immediate interest in getting us to change our behaviour. Though governments have a long-term stake in our decisions to save (smaller and more secure future Tier I benefits) their short-term motives can be seen to be less prejudiced. Data supplied to savers directly by governments is potentially more believable and influential than the 'shock horror' stories about the coming demographic deluge that seem favoured in financial advertising campaigns.

Governments' greatest challenge is to make information accessible, relevant and comprehensible to savers, not specialists.[2]

---

[1]   Commenting on a book that reviewed the relationship between the wealth of nations and their economic freedom, *Economic Freedom of the World* by Gwartney, Lawson and Block 1996, *The Economist*, 13 January 1996, noted: 'Before individuals and companies will respond to new won freedom, they must believe that it is likely to last. It is no coincidence that the six countries that had persistently high ratings throughout the 1975-95 period (Hong Kong, Switzerland, Singapore, the United States, Canada and Germany) were also in the top 10 in terms of GDP per head in 1993-95.' So it is with retirement income policies.

[2]   The Financial Information Service in Australia (part of the Social Welfare office) is an example of the practical sort of thing that governments can do. It provides unbiased advice on how to choose a financial planner, the sorts of questions to ask and the effect of investments on state entitlements. The

Good market data
Governments also need to satisfy the information requirements of those who manage their citizens' money. That will help financial institutions understand their markets and develop products that best satisfy needs. Through their ability to regulate, governments are uniquely placed to make sure all relevant information is available to everyone who needs it.

Debates as to what constitutes the 'true' rate of inflation are running in a number of countries, most notably the US. Because of the very long periods that retirement saving need to build up (and then run down) these issues have to be resolved. For that, we need much better, believable data on the Consumer's Price Index.

Rule of law
When things go wrong in saving arrangements, the processes for settling disputes should be quick, effective and inexpensive. This is an important part of encouraging continued confidence in the system and of the trust we must have in the institutions that have our money.

A level playing field
If the various types of institutions that look after our money are treated on similar terms, those that do best for their customers will prosper for the best reason of all. It's not for regulators to say where individuals should (or shouldn't) put their savings or how they should then be invested.

Reporting
The regulatory environment should encourage the institutions that manage our money to tell us what's actually happening on a basis that lets us compare them with other opportunities for saving. A consistent reporting regime that treats all providers on a like basis should be a major objective.

Encourage variety
The ways that best suit our need to save at Tiers II and III will be varied. Traditional financial instruments may suit many but they won't suit everyone. The government should encourage diversity and promote different ways of achieving retirement income security, but it shouldn't actually do it.

The Five Key Attributes as a Benchmark for Policies

The need for citizens to get a good return on their savings captures most of what governments should be doing to encourage private provision for retirement at Tiers II and III. Achieving the other four of the five key attributes will also be helped through a range of these activities.

Table 7 summarises the position for all five. Although it might be possible to attribute each of the five key attributes to all nine government activities, the table shows the ones that I think really matter.

The five key attributes should be the reference points for governments. If a suggested policy were likely to have an effect on private provision at Tiers II and III, the question should be asked: 'What positive contribution is this change likely to make to one or more of the five key attributes?' Then list the positive contributions. If that can't be done, or if the change is likely to have a negative overall impact, then it should be abandoned.

Service also runs education programmes and provides a contact point between the government and industry groups.

This sounds like more 'market'—abandoning our citizens to the ravages of capital markets so they can lose their savings in the ways they choose for themselves. However, I like 'markets' because they send the best and most believable signals to savers about the things that really matter. As *The Economist* said, there is:

> ... a strong presumption in favour of markets—not because they always work perfectly (they never do) but because the alternative is usually worse ... [and] not because classical economic theory says so, but because experience seems to agree.[1]

This doesn't mean abandoning savers—remember there's already a Tier I scheme in place and there's quite a lot more that needs doing.

Table 7
Five Key Attributes and Nine Government Objectives

Government activity	Good return on savings	Financial security	Fairness	Flexibility	Affordability
1 Control inflation	✔	✔			
2 Tax neutrality	✔		✔	✔	
3 Consistent policy	✔	✔	✔	✔	✔
4 Good information	✔	✔	✔	✔	✔
5 Institutional data	✔		✔	✔	✔
6 Rule of law	✔	✔	✔		✔
7 Level playing field	✔			✔	
8 Reporting rules	✔	✔		✔	
9 Encourage variety	✔		✔	✔	✔

Source: Author
Note a ✔ indicates that the government can help achieve that key attribute through policies designed to achieve that 'column item'.

More on Tax—Income and Expenditure Taxes

Chapter 4 argued against a tax-subsidised saving regime. However, deductions for contributions and/or tax-favoured accumulations and/or tax-favoured distributions are not the only way that tax policies affect retirement saving plans.

What is 'Income'?

First, there is the issue of what counts as income. If there is to be income tax on income derived from employment, then all income should be taxed. That includes wages, benefits in kind supplied by employers (like cars, medical

---

[1]   'State and market', 17 February 1996.

insurance and private services like financial advice), the value of retirement benefit accruals, the income earned by those holding assets on behalf of individuals and the benefits that come out at the end of the day. If some types of income weren't taxed, or some were taxed on a favourable basis by comparison with others, then *homo economicus* would exploit those differences.[1] Even if the tax system were 'neutral' on the issue of saving for retirement (my recommendation), the tax playing field could be easily tilted by less than neutral treatment of some forms of income. That has the potential to damage the retirement saving system.

Tax Neutrality under the TTE Tax Framework

Chapter 4 suggested a TTE tax framework for formal retirement saving arrangements like pension schemes. That's all right as a starting point but, to be truly neutral, there are some subtleties.

We need to look at each of the 'tax points' in the movement of money into, around and out of the scheme, to ensure scheme members are treated as closely as practicable to the regime that would have applied had they saved the money in their own names, rather than through the scheme.

Money in

Personal contributions aren't deductible for tax purposes in a TTE regime. Contributions by an employer should be taxed as a proxy for the members in respect of tax they would have paid had they received the contributions as income. That sounds fine but, unless you have a flat personal income tax with no personal deductions (no country does, though Hong Kong gets close), what tax rate should apply to the employers' contributions? New Zealand has adopted the top personal rate of 33 per cent (which is also the corporate tax rate) but, as personal tax rates are now falling, that 'withholding tax' on the employer's contributions is becoming less appropriate.

The answer is 'imputation'—continue charging initial withholding tax at the top personal rate, but give the member a certificate specifying the contributions and the amount deducted. The contributions will be imputed taxable income in the member's return while the withholding tax will be shown in the end of year return as a tax credit. That way, a member with a lower marginal rate will get a refund.[2] That's relatively easy to follow for

---

[1]   Some argue that one of the problems the US faces with the cost of the health system is that the amount spent by employers on health insurance is tax-favoured income whereas, if an individual bought insurance, it wouldn't be deductible. The 'solution' is to make all of it (employer and individual premiums) available for a tax credit (David Kendall and Mark Pauly in *The Wall Street Journal*, 10 June 1996). I'd prefer to make the premiums paid by employers taxable income in the hands of employees—that would create a level playing field and force employers and employees to consider whether they were getting good value.

[2]   New Zealand has a similar system for company tax and the taxable dividends that are distributed to shareholders. The company's income is imputed to the shareholders and the tax paid by the company is an offset to the shareholders' own liability.

defined-contribution schemes,[1] but there are problems with defined-benefit schemes.

These arise because the employer's contributions can't be attributed directly to any individual member or to their benefits. They're usually expressed as a percentage of all members' pay. There are two ways to handle this—the first (rough and ready) way is to assume that the amount paid for each member is the average rate for all. That will advantage younger members over older and also those who get a smaller rate of pay increases over those with a faster rate of pay progression.[2] The second, more precise technique would estimate the amount the employer contributes for each member each year using the same actuarial assumptions that were used to work out the employer's average overall contribution in the first place. While that sounds complicated, the computer programme that produces the annual benefit statements for members can include such a procedure. It still won't be precise because the actuary's assumptions as to what will eventually happen to the member will almost certainly turn out to be wrong.

Investment income

Imputation is, once again, the only practicable answer for true neutrality. In this case the investment income attributed to the member will be the share of the scheme's income that relates to the member's vested benefits, including those built up in earlier years. The same principle will apply both to defined-benefit and defined-contribution schemes. As the member becomes vested in more valuable benefits, so too will the size of the attributed income grow. However, not all of the scheme's investment income will be attributed among the beneficiaries because not all the scheme's benefits will be vested.

Imputing the investment income to beneficiaries will create 'leakage'—that's because the member will end up with any advantage that a personal tax rate, lower than the scheme's rate, will produce. If the scheme paid a higher rate than a member paid at the applicable marginal rate, the member would get the refund, not the scheme. I don't see this as a problem, but if scheme members are not to benefit from membership of the scheme before they withdraw, imputation would need to be accompanied by a mechanism that saw the scheme recovering the overpayments. However, I think the issue is not about the appropriate tax rate for the scheme but what's fair for the member. Leakage should not be a concern.[3]

Benefits

Benefits paid to the member on leaving the scheme are exempt under TTE, as are continuing benefits like pensions. However, imputation would still play a

---

[1]   Where the contributions can be identified to each member. However, imputation should strictly be applied only in respect of contributions that become vested in the member's name during the year.

[2]   That's because younger members and those with a slower pay progression cost less than their counterparts. The average rate for the scheme is reduced by the rate for those members.

[3]   New Zealand proposes adopting a 'tax credit' system from 1 April 1998 that is imputation but with measures to prevent 'leakage' and impose the administrative burden on schemes (rather than individual savers) to impose the appropriate tax rate.

role for pensioners because the assets held by the trustees (or the insurance company, in the case of an annuity) would still be earning investment income. In most cases the underlying interest rate would be set when the pension starts (a profit-sharing annuity would be in a different position). Each year the pension provider would attribute the underlying investment income rate to the then value of the pensioner's benefit. That would reduce as the pensioner got older. The investment income imputed to a given annual pension for a given rate of investment income would fall as the pensioner ages.

Tax Policy and Housing

Although this isn't the appropriate place to talk about housing policies in general, a country's housing policy is an important element in a sustainable Tier I because higher proportions of owner-occupied housing makes Tier I arrangements potentially more robust. Put simply, the more retirees who own their own homes debt-free by the time they retire, the less pressure there will be on state-delivered incomes.

In fact, some argue that private housing also has advantages for individuals as well as the state. It lets people make rational decisions about private provision for retirement:

> ... home ownership is the perfect vehicle of privatised life-cycle redistribution. It ties long-term saving for old-age and other risk contingencies to the acquisition of equity in a real asset, on which the individual would, in any case, need to spend very substantial resources over a lifetime in order to procure shelter.[1]

I don't support the state bribing its citizens to buy their own homes through tax subsidies, government-funded programmes or state subsidised 'affordable' housing projects.

It's no accident that a lot of countries with real pressure on state-delivered incomes have lower levels of owner-occupied housing among the retired population than others that have less pressure.[2] On the other hand, private housing is favoured as an investment compared with saving through direct investment (like shares or bank deposits) in most developed countries. That favour can be:

---

[1] Francis Castles and Deborah Mitchell in a 28 February 1996 piece on the Pension Reform Interest Group, an Internet discussion group run out of 'prig@mailer.fsu.edu'.

[2] Deborah Mitchell of Australia (in another 28 February 1996 piece on the Pension Reform Interest Group) showed the home ownership rates among age 55+ retirees in nine countries as: Australia: 81%; US: 79%; Belgium: 74%; Canada: 73%; the Netherlands: 67%; Austria: 49%; Norway: 45%; Germany: 45% and Sweden: 41%. New Zealand's rate is about the same as Australia's. According to a survey carried out in New Zealand for the Retirement Commissioner in mid-1995, 84% of all retired respondents owned their home outright. Francis Castles and Maurizio Ferrera in 'Home Ownership and the Welfare State—Is Southern Europe Different?', *Southern European Society and Politics*, 1996, extended this argument to a general proposition about rocks and hard places— '...the gap between the need for a government to spend and the capacity of a government to induce its citizens to pay tax is likely to be at its greatest where pension spending is at its highest and home ownership is at its most widespread'.

- direct tax relief for mortgage interest payments (the US and the UK)
- favourable treatment on capital gains (Australia and New Zealand)
- exclusions from asset-tested state benefits (Australia again), or
- reducing dividend and interest income by tying up more money than necessary in the retirement home.

The danger of unfocused favours is that the state signals to *homo economicus* where money should go, thereby driving up the value of the housing stock relative to other sectors of the economy. An economy that carries a larger than optimal value in housing stock places itself at a disadvantage relative to its competitors for the goods and services that the economy produces. If this imposed pressures on the taxpayer-provided Tier I pension, then it would be taxpayers of the day who were asked to pay for the consequences of the mismatch between housing and retirement income policies.

One possible answer is to treat private housing, for tax purposes, in the same way as all other savings. That would see realised increases in values taxed as income.[1] It could also see the value of a house above an agreed level counting in the income test for the Tier I pension. Australia's 'extended deeming' principles[2] suggest a model for the way that could work. I'm not against pensioners living in houses that are more valuable than they 'need', but if they wanted a Tier I pension then, as a taxpayer, I might be entitled to a view on their standard of accommodation.

To run any sort of debate on a sustainable retirement income system, we need as much good information on where our fellow citizens live and how they pay for it as we need on their other saving habits.

Income vs Expenditure Taxes

Governments have to collect taxes—the mix of those between income and expenditure taxes (for example, Value Added Tax in Europe or New Zealand's Goods and Services Tax) has an indirect effect on savers. For a given level of required revenue, changing the mix from a largely income-based measure (where 'income' includes the money earned by savers on their investments) to one where spending is taxed more will let the government reduce taxes on income. Savers would then get a better after-tax return.

If the government had to increase taxes then, from a retirement saving perspective, it would be better to increase consumption taxes rather than income taxes.[3]

---

[1]   That will raise at least two issues—inflationary gains shouldn't be taxed and, if they were excluded for private housing, they should be excluded for other assets as well. The other issue is that taxing gains will distort the allocation of housing because owners will be reluctant to move out of houses that no longer suit their needs, particularly at retirement. However, if house values generally kept up with inflation and inflation were excluded from the tax calculation, perhaps this wouldn't be such a problem.

[2]   Explained in chapter 6 on p. 137.

[3]   The regressive tendencies of consumption taxes mean they have a bigger impact on the poor because they spend a greater share of their income on essentials than do the rich. That should be fixed through the welfare net

Consumption taxes, aside from being more difficult to avoid, are less likely to distort economic activity than a higher rate of personal tax which tends to discourage effort, make the black economy more attractive or increase the attraction of tax avoidance.[1] They are also an efficient way of raising money and, if designed well, tend to be self-policing.

We pay consumption taxes when money is spent rather than when it's earned, so that, on its own, tends to favour saving rather than spending—that's also good for the retirement saving regime. Because the retired population tends to spend more than it earns, consumption taxes also help ensure that retirees pay their share of the costs of running the government.

For similar reasons, if the government wanted to reduce overall tax receipts, it would be better, from a retirement saving perspective, to reduce income taxes rather than consumption taxes. That will tend to favour the wealth-producing, working population rather than the wealth-consuming retired.[2]

More on the Need for Good Information—Saving and Saving Rates

Politicians usually leap on the latest household saving statistics. In developed countries in recent years, they have usually shown reducing saving rates and have encouraged our leaders to discuss intervention because 'something has to be done'. Most recent international calls for a compulsory Tier II scheme have been founded, at least in part, on a feeling that our citizens aren't saving 'enough'. They need to be forced into changing their ways on the assumption that this will somehow fix the problem.

Recent New Zealand work[3] emphasises the importance of meaningful data and proper comparisons. This is important because people want to know if the country's voluntary saving regime at Tiers II and III is actually working. Popular wisdom has it that New Zealanders aren't responding.[4]

As often happens, official measures are not all that they should be or seem to be. First, we need to understand that what the economists call 'savings' are not necessarily what ordinary savers might call them. Generally, they are the

---

rather than through the tax system.

[1]   Particularly if the tax system treated retirement savings favourably as in all OECD countries except New Zealand.

[2]   It would also tend to reshape the intergenerational transfers of wealth that happened when developed countries introduced their unfunded, 'pay as you go' pension schemes earlier this century.

[3]   *Westpac·FPG Household Saving Indicators*, 'A Comparison of Household Saving Rates, NZ and the OECD', June 1995

[4]   In a voluntary regime, it's difficult to know how to measure 'success'—does it mean that New Zealand's household, private or national saving rates are up there with the best? Does it mean we have more money flowing into saving institutions; or that home owners are paying off their mortgages more quickly; or that more New Zealanders are starting small businesses? Or is it that when New Zealanders reach retirement, they have the living standard they were expecting? That last test appeals to me, but it's less easy to measure than the traditional savings rates.

difference between all kinds of income[1] and all kinds of expenditure.[2] The household saving rate is then worked out as a 'residual' by expressing what's left as a proportion of the household's *disposable* income (income less taxes and social security contributions etc). This is the so-called 'flows approach' because it follows the destination of money, not what happens to it once it gets there.[3]

The treatment of housing is a major gap in this process. Most New Zealanders' wealth is in their home. At September 1994, housing comprised 71.2 per cent of all households' wealth.[4] I've already cited the difference in the house ownership statistics among the retired in different countries (see footnote 2 on p. 165). If the official saving statistics ignore changes in the value of a New Zealander's most important asset, they miss an important element of a saver's preparation for retirement.

Table 8
OECD: Household and Corporate Saving Rates

	Household saving	Rank	Household + corporate	Rank	% points increase and (ranking)
Italy	21.0%	1	21.3%	1	0.3% (10)
Japan	17.1%	2	20.0%	2	2.9% (5)
Germany	13.4%	3	14.7%	4	1.3% (8)
Canada	11.5%	4	14.5%	5	3.0% (4)
France	10.8%	5	13.1%	6	2.3% (7)
Australia	9.5%	6	10.6%	7	1.1% (9)
New Zealand	8.2%	7	16.8%	3	8.6% (1)
US	7.7%	8	10.1%	8	2.4% (6)
UK	6.4%	9	9.7%	9	3.3% (3)
Sweden	2.6%	10	9.3%	10	6.7% (2)
OECD average	10.8%	-	14.0%	-	3.2% (-)

Source: Westpac•FPG study.
Notes: The saving rates are the averages of the following years: 1972, 1977, 1982, 1987 and 1992, measured on the 'flows approach'. The OECD average is unweighted.

The *Westpac•FPG* study showed up another shortcoming with the traditional flows measure. It first pointed out that the data are collected in different ways and so can be regarded as only approximations. It then went

---

[1]   Wages, welfare benefits, income from property, the 'entrepreneurial income of unincorporated enterprises' and overseas transfers.

[2]   Consumption, direct taxes, social security taxes and levies, interest payments and overseas transfers.

[3]   The other method is the 'stocks approach' because it looks at what people actually have and captures the 'wealth effects'. For example, economists don't count realised (or unrealised) capital gains as 'saving'. To me, the stocks approach seems more sensible because a person's capacity to survive in retirement depends more on what they have when they get there rather than where they put there money on the way there.

[4]   The *Westpac·FPG* study. Of total household financial liabilities, 83.1% were housing-related.

on to look at what would happen if corporate savings were amalgamated with household savings. The study thought that, of all possible adjustments to make to the raw numbers, amalgamating the corporate sector and household savings made the most sense because, in the end, households are the ultimate owners of the corporate sector (both listed and unlisted).[1] Table 8 shows what happened looking at five-yearly snapshots for 10 OECD countries over the period 1972 to 1992.

Several conclusions can be drawn from Table 8:

First, superficial comparisons of data across countries (for example, by just looking at household saving) can be misleading[2] and can be used to mislead deliberately.

Second, looking only at household savings ignores an important part of a country's capacity to deal with an ageing population—the corporate sector. Again it's the economy as a whole that matters, not one particular section of it.

Third, cross-country comparisons are very difficult when they ignore the different ways that countries organise their affairs—the superficial treatment of 'house saving' data (and other capital assets) is a significant gap. The cross-country differences in this area alone make information in Table 8 significantly less useful than it should be.

Fourth, Table 8 summarises a series of snapshots of the countries at five-yearly intervals. Most are 'slices' through the economy at a particular point in time. Even if the numbers were done every year, they would lose the subtleties that trace particular changes through time. In a long-run business like retirement saving, that's not good enough.

The question is, at the end of it all, how important are household saving rates, whether you include the corporate sector or not? They are a starting point but, on their own, they won't make a country more or less able to withstand the demographic deluge.

What matters is where those savings are invested, not how much they were in the year they were identified. However you can't start to look at the former if you don't have the latter. Saving large amounts and then lending it to the government which spends it on current consumption, rather than investment, doesn't prepare the country. Saving large amounts and then letting the corporate sector waste it on real estate that fails, or on speculative investments that evaporate, doesn't do much for the country either. Saving

---

[1]   It also avoids one of the measurement problems caused by people who accumulate their savings in the corporate sector but then retire and run down their savings in the household sector. Also, retained corporate savings remain in the corporate sector whereas dividends go to the household sector.

[2]   For example, they're affected by a population's age profile—an older or younger population changes the proportions of people in work. They're also affected by labour force participation rates—New Zealand's, at 65%, is relatively low by international standards and that reduces households' capacity to 'save' as economists define that. They are also affected by the different ways that governments collect their income—'disposable income' counts direct taxes but not indirect, like expenditure taxes. The higher the proportion of indirect taxes, the more the disposable income because, for a given level of total taxes, households' post-income tax incomes will be higher.

can grow in two ways—by increasing the amount that's put away each year *or* by increasing the value of existing savings.[1]

Measuring Saving in New Zealand

Comparing New Zealand's 'official' saving figures with what's actually happening on the ground further emphasises the need to get good, believable information. Figure 9 shows 'national savings' over the last few years:

Figure 9
New Zealand: Gross National Savings as a Percentage of GDP

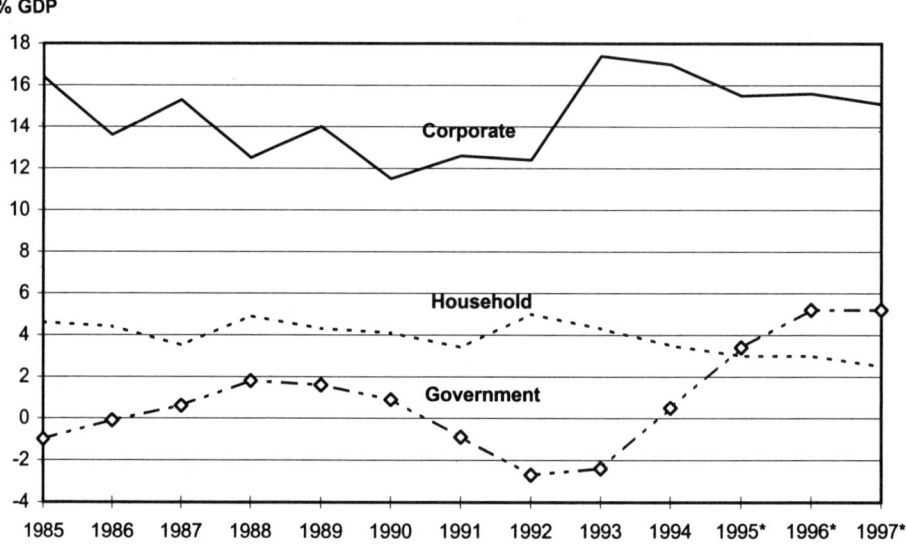

* Estimates

Source: NZIER Quarterly Predictions—depreciation is excluded from each component.

You would be forgiven for thinking that New Zealanders haven't responded to the calls by their government to look after their own retirement saving. Figure 10 however, suggests a different conclusion:

---

[1]   Australian calculations by Tony Makin, 'The Wealth Cycle and Macroeconomic Policy', *Agenda*, 1995, p. 494, show that annual changes in Australia's wealth are dominated by changes in capital values rather than by what the economists call 'savings'. Annual changes in wealth also tended to coincide with changes in GDP, though the fluctuations were 'considerably more severe.' McKinsey & Company in the US showed the importance of the quality, rather than the quantity issue. In a 1996 study by its Global Institute, reported in *The Economist*, 8 June 1996, the fact that the US fared poorly in national saving comparisons stood in stark contrast to productivity levels in a number of sectors. Superior productivity from a better use of capital seems the explanation. Again, it's not how much you save, it's what you do with it that matters.

Figure 10
New Zealand Households: Total Assets and Liabilities

Source: Westpac•FPG Net Worth Index

Note: The length of each column represents households' gross assets. From those, the liabilities should be deducted to produce net assets. Closing values at March 1997 for each category were 'other assets' $86bn; 'housing' $217.9bn; 'liabilities' $52.8bn.

The official 'national saving' statistics look at where money comes from—whereas the Westpac•FPG chart looks at what households actually do with their money, still on an aggregate basis.[1] In the aggregate, the Westpac•FPG chart gives a better idea of changes in New Zealanders' wealth in the context of a discussion about retirement incomes than do the official numbers about 'household savings'.[2] However, the producers of the index emphasise that care needs to be taken with these numbers. This is because they indicate changes in net worth but don't distinguish borrowings for business, consumer goods or house improvements.

The Westpac•FPG Index of Net Financial Worth (excluding housing assets and liabilities) gives observers a similar idea of movements in the more traditional forms of saving. Figure 11 shows New Zealanders' behaviour in this more traditional measure:

---

[1]   The All Elements Net Worth Index includes the value of houses, deposits with M3 institutions, holdings of government bonds, unit trusts, retirement schemes, shares, life insurance policies and privately held accounts by trustee companies and solicitors.

[2]   A call for a similar shift of thinking in the US context was made by Arthur B. Laffer, writing in *The Wall Street Journal* on 16 October 1996: 'The "savings" that government measures have almost nothing to do with the type of national savings we need for economic growth ... For the purpose of analyzing growth the relevant concept of savings has to be the increase in wealth, not the absence of consumption.'

Figure 11
New Zealand Households: Indices of Financial Assets and Liabilities

September 1993 = 1,000

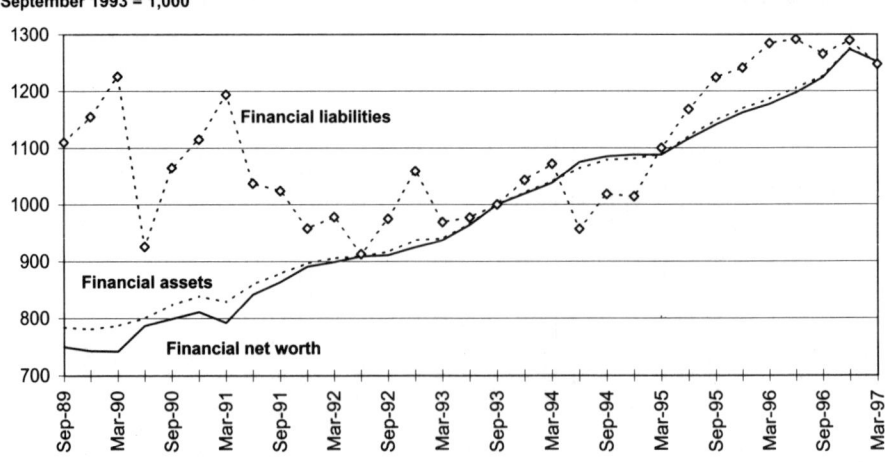

Source: Westpac•FPG Net Worth Index.

The indices show that the financial liabilities of New Zealand families rose over the 7½ years by 12 per cent while net financial worth (excluding housing) rose by 67 per cent.

Figure 12
New Zealand Household Assets Excluding Housing and Mortgages,
Annual Change

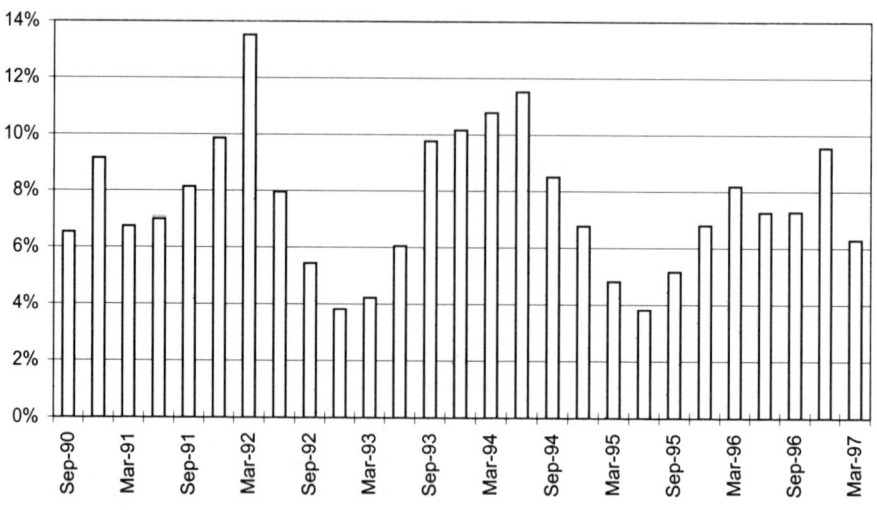

Source: Westpac•FPG Net Worth Index.

Figure 12, from the same series, shows the annual rate of change in the net financial assets of New Zealanders (disregarding housing and mortgage liabilities) and again, the picture looks promising.

These new measures are in their infancy. However, the analysis of what households are doing with their money seems to show that New Zealanders aren't in denial: that, in the aggregate at least, they are responding 'sensibly'. We need more of the kind of information that will enable us to assess this.

The long-term positions for both the government's own finances (fiscal affordability) and the relative equity among different generations of taxpayers (political sustainability) also need constant review, publication and explanation as a country's circumstances change.

The Place of Good 'Micro' Information

It's just as important for us all to know what individuals are thinking and doing as it is for us to have good data on what the country as a whole is up to. If we are to maintain Tier I's objective as 'prevention of poverty, plus a margin', we must know about the living standards of the retired and those near retirement.

We must also know when people retire and/or when they want to retire. Why do they want to retire?

Is it really the ill health that so many say is the reason? Or did the employer initiate termination when performance was no longer all that it should be or because the employer was cutting back or simply wanted new blood? What have people done themselves about saving and what have others, like employers, done for them? How much do they own and owe? How do all these things change over time and through changing circumstances?

A private survey has been carried out in New Zealand—'The Westpac•FPG New Zealand Savings Profile'.[1] The results from face-to-face interviews with 3,350 individuals will help New Zealanders understand their current savings behaviour and the distribution of savings. It will also shed light on the level of the awareness of the need to plan for retirement, how people go about planning and what might stop them. As results from this are released they will help us to understand what the macro statistics actually mean 'on the ground'. That will help suppliers to the industry to target their services more effectively and will make the decision to save easier to implement.

This work should look at people as they pass through the various phases of their lives. Economists call these 'longitudinal studies' because they follow particular groups of people over a long period rather than look at 'snapshots' of different populations at given points in time. Longitudinal studies can follow not only the preferences that affect individuals' behaviour but also the effect of changes in government policies on those preferences.[2]

---

[1]   Initial results were released in July 1996.

[2]   For example, Rand Corporation released a report in July 1995 on the assets owned by different groups of US citizens. This showed a growing disparity in wealth among white and minority families. For every dollar of assets held by white families, black households held 27 cents and Hispanic households 30 cents. The survey also showed how the median household was likely to get the expected 69% replacement income in retirement—the sources were likely to be Social Security 24.1%; pension

Publishing the results of these kinds of studies gives the government good information on the effects of its policies on private provision for retirement. They will form part of the information and education programme to help individuals make informed choices on their possible options. Finding out what people know will also help the information campaign focus its efforts.

Other studies will also help us understand the things that matter to potential savers and show them where they can get help. Two thirds of respondents to the 1996 Westpac•FPG study just described said that they would be prepared to pay for advice, but thought it shouldn't cost more than $24 an hour (about the same as a car mechanic). That's unrealistically low and an education programme should explain why. The fact that one third of respondents in the same survey thought it was too late to do anything about saving for retirement shows up another information gap. New Zealanders are probably no different from others in this regard.

More on the Rule of Law

Resolving Disputes

A good legal system and a respect for property rights and the law of contract are all an important part of society's 'glue'[1]—they're vital for retirement saving particularly as, in the voluntary regime I'm proposing, the amount accumulated for retirement will, for most, probably be their second most valuable asset after the family home.

With particular regard to retirement saving arrangements, there's a need for a cheap, quick and effective means of resolving disputes between financial institutions or advisers and individual savers. When arguments arise, the balance of power between the two parties usually means that the institution, with more at stake than the particular saver's dispute, has more resources at its disposal.

That imbalance can be corrected by allowing disputes to be referred, at least initially, to a Savings Ombudsman who could settle issues of fact between the parties and resolve the argument quickly and at low cost. That should help consumers have confidence in the system. Either party could take questions of law to a higher authority, but not questions of fact.

That process would sideline one of the reasons for industry bodies that represent special interest groups (like financial planners, insurance brokers, investment houses and the like) whose role often includes the policing of its members' practices. If the playing fields were level and no particular favours were conferred on one form of institution over another, the question of whether the 'industry' should regulate itself or be regulated would go away. The government's role should see that all information relevant to a saver's decision is out in the open. The regulators of securities are there to see that it is. Beyond that, it's for the market to say what it needs and to show whether those needs are satisfied.

21.3%; real assets 13%; and financial savings 10.9%. Researchers plan to track the sample of more than 13,000 households over the following ten years, reported in *The Wall Street Journal*, 25 July 1995.

[1]   In the already cited *Economic Freedom of the World* by Gwartney, Lawson and Block, 1996, respect for property rights is one of the four 'freedoms' that seem consistently to be associated with prosperity.

Micro-regulation of the Savings Industry

Regulators should get involved in the micro-regulation of the saving industry as little as possible. Regulation about the information that's given is better than regulation about what can or can't be done.

For example, US rules say that an employer can't hold on to an employee's saving scheme contributions for more than 90 days once they have been taken out of the employee's pay. The US government thinks that should reduce to 30 days.[1] I can't see any justification for an employer holding on to the money even for 30 days, let alone 90. However, it's not the government's role to say what's acceptable. It should make employers report how long they've held the money and leave it to the employees, whose money it is to decide whether that's acceptable. That way, employees might be concerned if they knew their retirement savings were mostly invested in their employer's own shares[2] or in buildings occupied by the employer.[3] They might not worry but, unless they knew, how could they judge?

UK pension schemes now have a new set of rules to worry about—the 'Minimum Funding Requirements'. They are supposed to control funding risks in a defined-benefit scheme by imposing benchmark portfolios (driven by the scheme's liability profile) related to UK equities and bonds. This is intended to make the Pension Act's compensation scheme manageable. However, because they concentrate on only two asset classes, they will actually increase risk and expected returns. The problem is the presence of the compensation scheme, but the effect, again, is to impose the regulator's view of an appropriate set of behaviours. That's not the government's role.

Micro-regulation should emphasise opening up information flows, not the regulator's view of lawful or appropriate behaviour.[4]

---

[1]   As reported in *The New York Times*, 9 December 1995.

[2]   This is common in US 401(k) schemes. *The Wall Street Journal*, 15 July 1996, reported the proportions in a number of companies: Banc One, 60%; Bell Atlantic, 58%; Cooper Tire & Rubber, 77%; Disney, 63%; Ford, 58%; McDonald's, 71% and so on. A study by the US Institute of Management and Administration, reported in *The Wall Street Journal*, 13 September 1996, found that 42% of 401(k) money is invested in the shares of the member's employers. For the informed saver, that might be acceptable if their other retirement savings were diversified away from their job, but members should get clear information so they can understand the risks to make that kind of judgement.

[3]   The 1,362 members of the Color Tile Inc 410(k) scheme in the US discovered that their employer leased shops that were worth 82% of the scheme's assets. When the employer collapsed, rent stopped as did all benefit payments while the company tried to sell the shops, reported in *The Wall Street Journal*, 5 June 1996.

[4]   Good information can have unexpected outcomes. In the UK, life offices are obliged to disclose how expenses might affect returns on the products they sell including what happens if the policy were lapsed early. *The Financial Times*, 6 January 1996, quotes the Personal Investment Authority's report that costs are coming down now that investors know what they are. With better pre-sale information, policies are staying on foot for longer and commentators were predicting that the more competitive market will lead to smaller companies being taken over by larger, more

Given the often snail-like response to changing conditions, the bureaucracy's view of what should (or shouldn't) happen is usually a long way behind the market's (for example the New York State Insurance Department hasn't reviewed the basis on which life insurance agents' commission is calculated since 1929). A rigid attitude to regulation will ossify information channels and distance savers from markets.[1] Rigidity often produces unintended consequences, such as a failure to protect where protection was the objective, or a failure to inform where information was the requirement. The regulator's responsibility is to link savers to markets—to make sure people who have money know where it's going, when it's going to come back and in what shape it's likely to be.

The five key attributes of a successful retirement income system provide a useful test. If any particular regulation wasn't likely to help achieve or maintain one of the five key attributes, then it should be forgotten.[2]

More on Encouraging Variety

Inflation-linked Bonds

Governments shouldn't intervene directly in the saving decisions of their citizens, but there are ways they can help savers, and there's one form of assistance that can only be provided by governments.

Government bonds that promise a real rate of return are an established part of the UK investment scene, but are relatively uncommon elsewhere.[3] Governments that introduce them will help remove a significant roadblock for their citizens' retirement saving—they could save future taxpayers some money as well.

I've rated the fight against inflation as one of the most important things a government can do to help savings at Tiers II and III. Issuing inflation-linked bonds will give the government an important financial incentive to keep inflation in check. It will also give some confidence to savers either that they will get real money back when they need it or that the government is serious about inflation. In the bad old days, inflation was great for politicians, as they didn't have to worry about their growing need for tax revenue. The progressive

---

efficient companies.

[1]   Regulation is also expensive. Just as there is a dead-weight cost of taxation, there's also a dead-weight cost of regulation. According to an estimate quoted in The Economist, 27 July 1996, the cost of complying with US federal regulations has risen to 47% of the whole federal budget in 1995, up from 40% in 1988.

[2]   In this, we must remember that regulation has indirect (as well as direct) costs. In a study ('Market Opening, Regulation and Growth in Europe', Economic Policy, October 1996, cited in The Economist, 12 October 1996) K. Koedijk and J. Kremers ranked the 11 European Union countries according to output and depth of regulation. They found a startling correlation between heavy regulation and low growth.

[3]   Australia, Canada, Sweden, Chile and New Zealand have also issued them (but New Zealand's are not fully inflation-proofed because the inflation element is taxed). The US is now dipping its toe in the inflation-proof pond. In the UK, inflation-linked bonds are now 15% of total government debt.

tax structures used in developed countries meant that, as the nominal incomes of taxpayers grew, they paid a greater proportion in tax by moving into higher tax brackets. Had all debt been financed through inflation-proofed bonds, the politicians wouldn't have been able to get away with as much as they did.

With the inflation risk removed, investors should expect the rate of return on the bonds to be less overall than with the traditional issue. That's because one of the unknowns (the cost of future inflation) will be removed from the pricing process—buyers won't need to include a margin in the interest rate against the possibility of inflation being more than expected. And so it has turned out in the UK. Since their introduction in 1981, inflation-proofed bonds have returned an average 7.9 per cent a year to 1995 compared with 14.2 per cent a year for conventional bonds.[1] Lower costs for tomorrow's governments means lower taxes for tomorrow's taxpayers. It doesn't, as some commentators in the US have suggested, stop savers from worrying about inflation (the real return will be modest) or encourage the government to be profligate by shifting the risk for debt from savers to taxpayers (many of whom belong to both groups).

The retirement saving industry will also get an advantage. Inflation-proofed bonds will give institutions more flexibility in the design of saving products that are suited to the long-run nature of their business. At the moment, the government is the only institution that can reliably promise to inflation-proof a retirement pension.[2] It's been said that one of the reasons civil servants are attracted to work for the government (central or local) is the prospect of an inflation-proofed pension at the end of their careers. For reasons that I will look at in chapter 8, that's a bad reason for anyone to stay with an employer. But everyone should have access to an inflation-proofed pension from a private provider, if they want it. The cost of such a product would be too high in the absence of an inflation-proofed bond because the pension provider has to allow for inflation over 15-20 years.

Reverse Annuities and Home Equity Conversions

I've already commented on the relationship between sustainable, state-provided retirement incomes and the prevalence of owner-occupied housing. It's important that people understand the advantage of having mortgage-free homes when they reach retirement. That helps the state because if people had to pay for accommodation, the state is under some obligation to deliver income to help them out. That is because Tier I is designed to prevent poverty 'plus a margin' regardless of the reason for the poverty.

---

[1]   PDFM's 'Pension Fund Indicators', reported in *The Financial Times*, 18 May 1996. However with currently much lower rates of inflation in the UK, the present annual saving is estimated at 1% a year after allowing for inflation (according to *The FT*).

[2]   According to Nicholas Barr, *The Economics of the Welfare State*, Stanford University Press, 1993, unexpected inflation in retirement means that private annuity markets can't operate in the same way as other forms of insurance. Inflation, when it happens, affects all private pensioners and so there can be no risk sharing in this crucial area. If inflation-proofed bonds underpinned private annuity markets, they would provide insurance against unexpected inflation at the expense of taxpayers of the day.

Given the private wealth that's tied up in New Zealand housing, it's perhaps surprising that the financial institutions haven't been more innovative in turning that asset into income. In fact, there are some good reasons why they have avoided this type of product.

Income testing
An income test on the state-provided pension, such as exists in Australia and existed in New Zealand, is an immediate disincentive to converting an asset into income, particularly one that's ignored in the asset test as is the case in Australia. The heavier income test in my Tier I scheme suggested in chapter 6 will increase that disincentive.

The inheritance effect
Parents want to pass money on to the next generation—the family home is the principle source of that. Reducing its value by securing some form of retirement income contract over it may improve today's income but at the expense of tomorrow's bequest.

State adequacy
As most state systems deliver an adequate and, in some cases, a generous income, there simply hasn't been the need to convert equity in the home into income.

Risk aversion
Older people are naturally more risk averse than younger. In New Zealand, complete control of your shelter is an important part of a retiree's risk strategy. Trading down to a less expensive (but still fully owned) house in retirement is likely to be a preferred way of raising retirement capital rather than losing control of even a part of the family home.

At least one of these reasons (adequate state benefit) will disappear when New Zealand's new Tier I benefit is fully effective by 2055.[1] If retirees want to 'participate and belong' in their society, they will need to have at least some private income. For some, converting equity in the family home may be their only choice.

So how can the government help develop a market for reverse annuities (where the home-owner borrows to buy an income) or for home equity conversion (really a drip-feed loan)?

First, and most importantly, the state shouldn't actually do it. It should, however, be a source of good information on the advantages and disadvantages of these services: who is doing it, who shouldn't and why, what alternative suppliers are offering and how to rate one against the other.

Second, the rules for disclosure should be clear and informative. Finally, there should be an inexpensive and rapid means of resolving disputes. Disclosure and disputes resolution procedures should apply to all investment products, but they have particular relevance for the elderly home-owner where there is significant potential for abuse.[2]

---

[1]   As explained in chapter 6.

[2]   Disclosure rules on reverse annuities in the US include the requirement to show: all costs (interest, all fees, closing costs) as a percentage of the loan; what happens to the costs if you paid the loan off after two years, if you stayed in the home for the average life expectancy or if you lived for 40% longer than average; and then what would happen to the costs if your home appreciated by 4% or 8% a year or not at all.

Home equity conversions are unlikely to be a major source of capital because the lender wants to be sure that the growing value of the loan never passes the value of the home. However, they can deliver cash on an as-needed basis to pensioners who are asset rich but income poor. They will be particularly useful where the Tier I benefit is income-tested, because the amount borrowed each year would not be income. Much the same kind of regulatory considerations apply to this type of transaction as to the reverse annuity.

More on the Reporting Rules—an Approved List of Assets?

I've suggested governments should make savers sure that institutions managing investors' money report on a consistent basis so savers can compare like investments and understand what's actually happening. Governments should stay away from telling individuals or institutions where that money should be invested. Lists of approved assets shouldn't be part of a retirement income regime. As long as investors know what's going on, it's for them to decide whether or not they like what they are told.

There's a great temptation for regulators to think they know what constitutes an appropriate investment so they can protect the general public from themselves. There would be some point in this if all taxpayers had a stake in a scheme's assets through the tax that will eventually be collected from the eventual pension. But there's little other justification, or even evidence, that a group of politicians can pick winners. In the tax-neutral environment I propose, the state cannot justify intervention.

In fact, most of the rules used by countries fail to achieve their objective of protecting savers. Requiring schemes to invest in government bonds (as in France, where at least 34 per cent must be so invested) may actually increase the scheme's risk because they may require over-exposure to the bond market, to one currency and to one country, when that may not be a sensible strategy. Work done by the European Federation for Retirement Provision[1] shows that requiring approved schemes to increase their risk in this way harms returns. Table 9 summarises some of that.

Ireland had no investment restrictions and the highest real returns in the study. The UK followed very closely (you need the second decimal place to see the difference of 0.02 per cent). The controls imposed on pension fund investments in the countries listed are at their most detailed in Switzerland—so the outcome is no surprise.

The returns achieved by pension fund investors matter in countries where there are tax incentives. This is because the greater the returns, the larger the pensions at the end of the day (or the cheaper the pensions are, in a defined-benefit environment), and the more tax future governments will collect (or the less governments will have to pay in tax bribes along the way). However, good real returns also matter, even where there are no tax incentives, such as in New Zealand. That's because, the bigger the pensions, the less will be the pressure on state-provided benefits when the wave of retiring baby-boomers reaches its peak from about 2025 onward.

---

[1] Reported in *The Financial Times*, 24 June 1996. The Federation (or *The FT*) made a mistake in simply deducting inflation from the return to get the real return. That doesn't affect the rankings though it does affect the results.

The European Federation for Retirement Provision demonstrated the power of good returns by working out the annual amount that would be needed to pay for a retirement pension equal to 35 per cent of pay at retirement after 40 years' employment, based on the returns shown in the Table 9.

Table 9
Pension Funds' Real Returns: 1984 to 1993

Country	Average return	Inflation	Real return
Ireland	14.0%	3.8%	10.2%
UK	15.5%	5.3%	10.2%
Belgium	11.8%	3.0%	8.8%
The Netherlands	9.5%	1.9%	7.6%
Germany	9.4%	2.2%	7.2%
Denmark	10.0%	3.7%	6.3%
Switzerland	7.6%	3.2%	4.4%

Source: European Federation for Retirement Provision

Table 10
Paying for a Tier II Pension: 35 Per Cent of Pay

Country	Required contribution (as % of pay)
Ireland	5%
UK	5%
The Netherlands	10%
Germany	13%
Denmark	19%
Switzerland	19%

Source: European Federation for Retirement Provision

Table 10 demonstrates that governments should want to leave investors alone to make their own decisions on where their money goes.[1]

Requiring schemes to invest in a particular type of institution or in a particular type of contract is no better—Japan has at long last discovered the truth of that.[2] Prudence should be encouraged and, possibly, even required,

---

[1]   It's curious to see that, in some countries where there are no restrictions, funds adopt very risky strategies all on their own. The study identified the Netherlands and Spain in this camp. Spanish funds, for example, put 96% of their money into fixed-interest investments. The European Commission now seems to be on the war-path in this regard. The Economist Intelligence Unit, 1 August 1996, reports that the Commission warned the Belgian government of action in the European Court of Justice over a requirement that Belgian pension funds invest 15% of assets in state government bonds.

[2]   In a paper published in NRI Quarterly, June 1996, cited in The Australian Financial Review, 17 October 1996, N. Tokarama and H. Tanaka looked at the pension liabilities of 16 Japanese companies that disclosed data to the US Securities and Exchange Commission. Using the US FASB

as is the case with the English law on trusts. Beyond that, savers should be free to put their money where they, not regulators, decide.

You may say that's all very well for someone who is reasonably well versed in investment matters—what about those who aren't? That doesn't change the case—regulators still don't know more than the markets. If the financial reports told everything then it would be up to the financial press or the rating agencies to convert that into digestible material for those who are less familiar with the intricacies.

Stifling innovation is a sure way to harm savers' interests in the end. Just look at the state of Japan's financial system—regulators thought they knew how to protect savers, but were unable to. Now Japan's politicians face the unpleasant task of convincing voters that taxpayers' money is needed to rescue the failed lenders.

Insurance against Failure?

Some governments think they need an agency that insures savers against various forms of loss. The Pension Benefit Guarantee Corporation (PBGC)[1] in the US is one of the better known in retirement income circles. It's government-run and insures private pension schemes against the possibility that they won't deliver on their promises. Private schemes pay risk-related premiums so those in better financial shape pay less proportionately than those in worse shape. There are similar arrangements in Japan (Workers Compensation Insurance Fund and a modest guarantee provided by the Employees Pension Fund Association) and another in Germany where an agency protects the vested benefits promised by book reserved Tier II pension schemes.

The UK has just set up a different type of insurance plan that came out of the aftermath of the Maxwell affair.[2] Rather than collect premiums in advance of the disaster, the UK scheme collects from other private schemes only once disaster has struck and the losses are known.

So, are any of these approaches a good idea? Should the state be involved, even if it didn't cost taxpayers anything (only other savers)?

I don't think so. The test for me is whether a private organisation would be prepared to offer that kind of insurance on a private, profit-making basis. If not, then, in principle, neither should taxpayers. The question is whether, by intervening, the government's 'insurance' adds value to the saver's decision.

---

accounting standard, the authors found an average shortfall of 34% of available assets and, in some cases, it exceeded 50%. I wonder if the schemes' beneficiaries and the companies' local shareholders get that information?

[1] It covers about 55,000 pension schemes with nearly 42 million beneficiaries, according to a press release of 14 March 1996. In the same release, the PBGC said that 'the agency receives no funds from general tax revenues.' That's true, but irrelevant. Presumably the 42 million are taxpayers—the amounts collected by the PBGC as 'premiums' from, effectively, the beneficiaries, are a tax by another name because there's no choice about paying and no competition for the insurance business.

[2] In which Robert Maxwell stole large amounts of money from the pension schemes of the companies that he ran.

Insurance normally protects a policyholder against unexpected events. With pension schemes, the 'policyholder' (the person who benefits from the insurance) is the scheme's beneficiary, not the person who is in charge of the risk (the trustee). The mere existence of the insurance may persuade trustees (and has done so) to take risks with the assets under their management that they wouldn't have taken in its absence.

It doesn't seem appropriate to cover failure resulting from fraud or mismanagement—or to cover for general market failure, which is a risk in any kind of saving.[1] You can't get private insurance to cover the consequences of money you might steal yourself. Asking the rest of the industry to make amends for the fraudulent few is charging a tax to the better managed funds for doing things properly. That sends a terrible message.

As private saving arrangements move away from defined-benefit promises and toward defined-contribution (or cash accumulation) principles, the need for this kind of government intervention will diminish anyway. Defined-contribution schemes tend to be more transparent financially. They require assets and liabilities to match at least once a year (at the balance date). Defined-benefit schemes need never have a balance between liabilities and assets because a lot of the security for future benefits depends on the employer's (or other underwriter's) strength. Defined-benefit schemes need someone to agree to pay the balance of the cost of the benefits (after allowing for regular contributions and investment income). They usually get into trouble when their sponsor gets into trouble.

Defined-benefit schemes aren't easy to understand—neither the benefits nor their financial condition make gripping bedside reading. That seems to be why governments are becoming more and more involved in the mechanics of the way they operate, presumably as proxies for bemused beneficiaries. The US rules are an absolute minefield and the UK and other countries are all falling into step. The UK Pensions Act 1995 even gets into such details as how trustees must make and publish decisions on investment strategy; they're told that they must take account of the need for diversification of investments and that they must even consult the employer on this!

This is all absurd—the principle that governments can somehow require savers to be advised of every imaginable problem is misguided and imposes large transaction costs on what is, in essence, a private contract.

In any event, probably the best form of insurance that a government can deliver to saving schemes is a sound economy.

> ... Almost every financial catastrophe can be traced back to some failure or other of economic policy. There is a simple lesson in that. The greatest single contribution that any government can make to better banking is to create a stable macroeconomic environment in which banks can flourish.[2]

---

[1]   When the whole market falls out of bed (just when this type of insurance would be most needed) what value will any so-called insurance have anyway? The good old taxpayer will ride to the rescue again, just like the bail-out of the US Savings & Loan organisations. At least one US commentator (Zvi Bodie reported in *The Economist*, 3 June 1995) thinks the PBGC, by investing 30% of its assets in equities, exposes the US taxpayer to losses from the very event that could call on its funds—a sharemarket fall that makes its customer schemes insolvent.

[2]   *The Economist*, 27 April 1996.

And so say I, for retirement saving schemes at Tiers II and III.

Impact on Capital Markets

If my retirement income strategy became popular then governments would gradually back out of delivering retirement incomes to their citizens. This would then be followed by a growth in private savings of all kinds and you could expect some major changes in capital markets round the world. At about the same time, governments would also be backing out of the ownership of trading enterprises by privatising them—a happy coincidence. Institutions would be coming by investment money at about the same time that governments needed it.

Pre-funding Pension Obligations

Pre-funding pension obligations is relatively uncommon in Europe, even among private employers. In part, that's because of the state's huge intervention at Tier II. In Germany's case, it's also helped by the practice of book reserves supporting private pension promises. Table 11 shows the practice in Europe.

Table 11
Population and Pension Assets

	Population (millions)	Pension assets ($bn)	Assets per capita ($'000)	Assets (% of GDP)
The Netherlands	15.4	380	24.7	124
Switzerland	7.1	187	26.7	80
Denmark	5.2	105	20.2	77
UK	58.4	721	12.3	76
Ireland	3.6	15	4.2	32
Finland	5.1	28	5.5	21
Germany	81.2	285	3.5	16
Belgium	10.1	17	1.7	8
Portugal	9.9	5	0.5	7
France*	58.1	41	0.7	4
Averages	-	-	10.0	45

Source: NRJ Research cited in Marathon London's *Investment Review*, 30 September 1995. The figures on France were not in the original NRJ table and come from a similar table in *The Economist* of 22 April 1995.

* *The Economist's* article from which the French numbers were taken described these kinds of statistics as 'ropey'—some of the numbers quoted by NRJ Research are a bit different from those in *The Economist* but that doesn't change the point I am making.

The mix of public and private provision (and, in Germany's case, its attachment to book-reserving to support pensions) underpins Table 11's disparities. If developed countries adopted my suggested mix, the pension assets per head of population would trend toward the practice in the Netherlands and away from Belgium, France and Portugal.

Even if the countries in Table 11 that had less than the present average of $10,000 *per capita* increased their pension assets up to that level, that would imply an extra $1,290 billion (an increase of 72 per cent) to be invested. If the nine countries did as well as the 'best' in Table 11 (in relative terms), the number would become $4,410 billion extra (up 247 per cent from the present total of $1,784 billion). And these wouldn't be the only countries in the world where this change would be happening.

This movement implies some fundamental changes both to investment markets and the way they are regulated.

Changes of Ownership

For Germany, it assumes a gradual change of ownership for companies and a shift away from debt and towards equity as a means of raising new capital. The beneficiaries of other employers' schemes will become significant ultimate owners as the essentially unfunded book-reserve schemes of $183 billion[1] 'come out' into the trusteed arrangements favoured in English-speaking countries.[2] The internationalisation of funds management will grow as countries' pension schemes become increasingly dependent on the strength of other countries' businesses to support their own retirees' incomes.[3]

The changes in the ownership of businesses in Europe will impose new demands on the managers of those businesses who will come under increasing pressure to perform by comparison with their international peers. Businesses that meet the expectations of their new owners will find it easier to finance their expansion while markets will give the message to those that don't. Corporate governance will also trend to the practices of the more demanding jurisdictions and away from the old cosy clubs of France, Germany and Japan. 'More market' means more transparency and with transparency comes accountability.[4]

Pressure on Regulators

Regulators will come under increasing pressure from investors who are already demanding changes to reporting requirements as the standards of the

---

[1]   The book reserves are equivalent to about one third of Germany's stock market capitalisation according to *The Financial Times*, 29 May 1996, and comprise about 56% of Germany's pension scheme assets.

[2]   *The Economist*, 22 April 1995, calculates that the book reserves held by German companies are probably about $20 bn short of the estimated value of the pension liabilities they are supposed to support. In large part that's because of the rules that run the tax deductibility of additions to those reserves. Book reserves really amount to self-investment because employees are doubly dependent on the financial security of the employer. Self-investment is frowned on in the English-style, trusteed arrangements.

[3]   Ireland is an example as more than 40% of the average pension portfolio is in overseas' equities (from a report in *The Financial* Times, 4 December 1995).

[4]   Japan is particularly vulnerable on the transparency issue—70% of listed shares are 'cross holdings' between other companies and banks and so aren't traded. On top of this, the government intervened directly by spending $200 billion to support the values for insurance companies, pension schemes and banks. There's also the practice of institutions valuing investments at book (or historical) cost rather than current market value.

most rigorous regulators become the benchmark. The well publicised changes to the accounts of Daimler Benz (turning 'profits' of $155m into 'losses' of $875m) following its listing in the US are an example. The corporate governance programmes of very large investors (like the California Public Employees' Retirement System or CalPERS) are another type of influence.[1] Those kinds of changes will also illuminate the opaque institutions of Japan as the savings of Japanese citizens are allowed to earn market returns instead of the rates agreed by cosy cartels.

Initially, there will be a tendency for financial chauvinism as the countries with the largest pools of capital dominate the reporting standards. The US 'Generally Accepted Accounting Principles' or GAAP prevail even though they are not generally accepted. However, there are signs of co-operation through the International Accounting Standards Committee (IASC) that may even be accepted by the powerful Securities and Exchange Commission (SEC) in the US.[2] As more companies issue IASC statements, international demand for their securities will increase. That will be good news for retirement savings around the world.

Impact on Governments

The next trick will be to get governments reporting on their own activities with equivalent transparency. Even if they didn't, life would become more demanding for them. That's because, although governments will be able to finance their own borrowings more easily from the increased pools of capital, their own performance will also be monitored by markets in the same way as businesses. And they will be punished more quickly if more private savings are riding on the outcome of those decisions, especially if those savings belong to the less forgiving and less regulated citizens of other countries.[3] If a government decided to loosen the monetary shackles and have a bit of unexpected inflation, everyone would start to pay for that through higher interest rates even before the inflation actually happened. A government's riskiness will be under constant watch.

Does that mean that non-elected, and ever-more-powerful, financial markets pose a threat to democracy? There is no evidence that they do; indeed in some ways, capital markets, driven by the decisions of millions of investors and borrowers, are highly 'democratic'. They act like a rolling 24-hour opinion poll. Moreover, they increase politicians' accountability by making voters more aware of governments' economic performance. Financial markets have much sharper eyes than voters.[4]

---

[1] However, the jury is still out in the US as to whether shareholder activism (what The Wall Street Journal has called 'pension fund socialism') has improved performance, see 'Not awakening the dead', The Economist, 10 August 1996.

[2] As reported in The Financial Times, 1 February 1996.

[3] James Carville (an election adviser to US President Bill Clinton) said 'I used to think that if there was reincarnation, I wanted to come back as the president or the pope. But now, I want to be the bond market: you can intimidate everybody', reported in The Economist, 7 October 1995. As a taxpayer, I'm happy about that.

[4] From a survey 'The World Economy', The Economist, 7 October 1995.

While some xenophobes fret about the apparent power that now rests with international financial markets, governments can't short-change their citizens the way they used to. Savers (and particularly savers for retirement, given their long-term focus) should cheer that the world's financial markets are keeping a watching brief on every move that politicians make.

Measures will Change

Another consequence of the regime I'm suggesting is that the kind of statistics shown in Table 11 (p. 183) will become increasingly difficult to produce. The concept of 'pension assets' depends on a regulatory framework driven mostly by tax concessions. The removal of concession-driven investment strategies will challenge investment managers to maintain their existing business without depending on the 'lock-in' demanded by the tax system. Statistics will still be needed to monitor the health of the whole retirement income regime, but the numbers will start to flow from untraditional areas like the growth in value of owner-operated businesses and household wealth statistics.

Freeing up markets has the potential to do more for honest and open government than all the regulations that any politicians in the 'best' command-and-control mode could devise.

Monitoring and Maintaining the Retirement Income Regime

Who's Going to Look After All This?

There's a lot for governments to do over very long periods of time. It's unrealistic and unfair to expect politicians to have the kind of vision and patience needed to let the markets adjust to a new way of doing things. Their focus is just too short-term—the next election is never more than four or so years away.

Although I'm not a fan of increased bureaucracy, I think the retirement income business is important enough to demand its own specialist and apolitical team. The New Zealand Task Force on Private Provision for Retirement, of which I was a member, recommended the appointment of a Retirement Commissioner—that has now happened. I think all countries should have an equivalent body.[1]

The Retirement Income Act 1993 (section 6) states that the Retirement Commissioner's role is:

- To develop and promote methods of improving the effectiveness of the retirement income policies from time to time implemented by the Government in New Zealand, which function shall include promoting education about retirement income issues and publishing information about such issues:

- To monitor the effects of retirement income policies that are being implemented in New Zealand:

- To advise the Minister of the tasks that need to be undertaken, and the information that needs to be collected, to enable the preparation of each [six-yearly] ... report ... and to monitor the undertaking of those tasks:

---

[1]   That body can also be the focus for Tier I's reviews and information requirements, see the previous chapter under the heading 'Reviewing New Zealand Superannuation' at p. 147.

- To advise on retirement income issues, when requested to do so by the Minister:...

- To collect and publish information for the purpose of enabling the fulfilment of any of the functions referred to in this section ...

I have already talked about the role of monitoring the objectives and effectiveness of the Tier I benefit—that role should, as now in New Zealand, encompass private provision as well. Though a Retirement Commissioner would be on the public payroll, I don't see the Commissioner as one of the normal team of civil servants. That's because the services of the office should be open to all. If someone—particularly a politician from outside the ruling group—wanted to propose a project that might help us understand why one part of the new regime wasn't (or was) working, they should be able to put that proposition direct to the Retirement Commissioner, rather than through the government.[1] This openness would be essential if the office were to help create public confidence in the whole retirement income regime—both state and private provision.

An important part of the New Zealand Retirement Commissioner's role is to gather good information on the effects of implementing all the changes proposed by the Task Force and formalised by the 'Superannuation Accord'[2] and Retirement Income Act. I see this as a useful model for any country that wants to maintain political and public consensus on retirement income policies. Gathering good information and interpreting that for the public will require the development of a small expert team to help fulfil the Retirement Commissioner's responsibilities.

The Commissioner's office will be a vital part of any successful regime. It's no small task: a survey carried out in July 1996[3] showed that New Zealanders think saving for retirement is a personal responsibility (71.5 per cent thought so) rather than the government's (15 per cent), the employer's (3.2 per cent) or something the family, partner or spouse should do (12.9 per cent). But 61.7 per cent either agreed or strongly agreed with the proposition that no-one can predict how much will be needed in retirement and 53.7 per cent thought the government wasn't helping people to plan for their retirement. That says, either that there's a receptive audience out there waiting for good information or that we haven't yet weaned New Zealanders off their state dummy. Either proposition is a challenging prospect.

Allowing for Change

As with the philosophical underpinning for Tier I, the regime I propose for Tiers II and III is a 1998 picture of how things should look for the next 50-60 years. I'm realistic enough to realise that a single piece of public policy hasn't a hope of surviving unscathed for 60 years. We don't know what anything will look like in 60 years time—the only thing we can be certain of is that things will be different, in some respects very different, from what we know today.

---

[1] Though, if the government controlled the Retirement Commissioner's budget, that would allow indirect control, but it would have to be exercised publicly.

[2] An agreement between the three main political parties, explained at p. 191, note 2.

[3] The 'Westpac-FPG New Zealand Savings Profile' described earlier in this chapter at p. 173.

For the proof of that, we need only look back to 1938 and try to put ourselves in the position of trying to guess how 1998 might have turned out.

That uncertainty isn't an excuse to avoid a single, long-term strategy for a sustainable retirement income system, but it does mean we need to build a process into that system to allow for change. If we don't, the pressure will build for change until radical reform becomes inevitable. Major changes in retirement income policies must be avoided because they create uncertainty and are the ideal excuse for our citizens to wait and see, despite an obvious need to do something.[1] If we knew where we were heading, and circumstances put us off course for any reason, trimming the sail would be better than changing tack.

Regular Reviews

In New Zealand, a system of regular, formal reviews of retirement income policies (both public and private) will provide a vital pressure valve. The Retirement Commissioner will give New Zealand the information the review team needs to see if the regime is working. The Commissioner will be under the spotlight, along with the policy, and so shouldn't be part of the review team.

The reviews should be timed to avoid elections. In New Zealand, we have elections every three years, so the reviews will take place every six years and not in an election year. Any country will need at least six or seven years to see how people react to a hands-off strategy of the kind I'm suggesting.

There are many ways a review team can assess whether everything is going according to plan. It would need lots of information and all of that should be in the public domain. It would need to see whether Tier I is achieving its objective of 'preventing poverty, plus a margin'. The income test should be checked to make sure it's working and that the ever-inventive financial services industry hasn't found a way through the net. It should find out how people (individuals and employers) are reacting to issues like the state pension age, late and early retirement, disclosure requirements, interest rate changes, inflation and investment returns. It should also look at what other countries are doing, to keep up with innovations. And then it should review the fiscal sustainability and intergenerational equity of the whole system of taxes and benefits.

Major changes won't result in New Zealand from any one review, but in 60 years' time the system will look a bit different from the new Tier I scheme we launched in New Zealand in 1998. I also hope that citizens and politicians will be taken along with the process, because political consensus will be an essential element of the new regime.

Getting Started—the New Zealand Experience

The process for getting started will vary from country to country. I want to describe briefly what happened in New Zealand because that seemed to work well for us.

---

[1]   The final report of the Task Force said (at page 84): 'We found that people "know they should save more" in the same way that they "know they should eat healthier foods", or "know they should exercise more". Unless they are educated to know what action is appropriate in their own circumstances, they will simply feel helpless when faced with conflicting viewpoints, and will therefore be inclined to avoid the whole issue'.

First, I should note that the retirement industry was battle-weary by 1991. When the National Party's government finally committed *hara-kiri* on the retirement income issue in its 1991 annual Budget,[1] even its own backbenchers threatened revolt. Something had to be done, so someone thought of the traditional New Zealand way of deferring difficult decisions—set up a committee and hope that it will all go away.

And so the Task Force on Private Provision for Retirement was born.

It was a disparate group—headed by Jeff Todd, the senior partner of a major accounting firm (an inspired choice for reasons I will shortly explain). There were four public sector members and four private (including me).[2] The group was supported by a talented secretariat.

The chairman's role turned out to be vital because one of the first and most important jobs was to win the confidence of all the major political groups and persuade them that we weren't the government in disguise. Also, he had the job of turning the group into a team that worked. Jeff Todd performed those jobs with patience and persistence. If another country went down the same track, I couldn't emphasise enough the importance of that public face to the initial review group. Retirement incomes had become a highly charged issue in New Zealand. The distrustful public had to be brought alongside.

We developed our own process as to how we were going to complete the job. We had no direction from our political masters and no precedents because, as far as I have been able to tell, no other country had ever tried it before (or since). We published three reports: *The Issues*, *The Options* and *The Way Forward*.

The Issues emerged in December 1991. This tried to put in one place, for the first time in New Zealand, all the things that seemed to matter in a review of policies on private provision. This wasn't a long document (80 pages) though we also produced a pamphlet that summarised the main points in eight pages. We spent a lot of time on the language we used, employing a specialist editor for the purpose. We wanted our reports to be accessible to everyone who had an interest in the topic—not just the 'experts'. *The Issues* made no recommendations.

We then took *The Issues* to the people, running workshops in 12 cities and making presentations to interest groups, the press and anyone else who asked. We weren't looking for submissions though we would have welcomed suggestions as to any issue we had missed. There weren't any significant gaps.

We built up our own mailing list, including any group or person we thought might have a role in our work of building community consensus. That included all the groups who were involved with the elderly, with employers, the unemployed, unions, with young people, service organisations, the churches and ethnic groups. We needed to go back to them with the next stage of the process and in the meantime tried to keep in touch with newsletters that told people what we were up to.

---

[1] Proposing, among other things, to lift the effective marginal tax rate for existing pensioners with modest amounts of 'other income' from 53% to 92.8% in one hit and overnight, and also without debate and based on deficient data.

[2] A fifth private sector member was added later.

The Options was a more ambitious affair. It emerged in August 1992 in three versions: the main version (378 pages), a reduced version called 'an overview' (129 pages) and, again, a summary pamphlet of nine pages.

The Options produced detailed designs of the three main alternatives for private provision at Tiers II and III in New Zealand (tax incentives, compulsory and voluntary). We wanted to provoke debate, but we wanted that debate to be informed. To that end, the main report included supporting documents covering such diverse topics as fiscal affordability; individual affordability; adequacy of saving and its role in growth; neutral tax and saving; inflation; annuities; the role of employers; home equity conversion; saving products and the then current regulatory regime.

We described the three options even-handedly, pointing out the advantages and disadvantages of each. We made no recommendation as to which of the three we preferred—in fact, we had been careful in our own internal discussions not to say which one we preferred individually. If the public debate that followed *The Options* was to be of any help, we had to have open minds on the possible outcome.

We took to the road again, this time presenting in 13 cities and to all kinds of groups, including those with which we had made contact in the first round. This time we were looking for submissions and we got them—104 in all—not as many as I had expected, given the white-hot nature of the debate that preceded our appointment. I was reasonably satisfied on one aspect—we tried to present the 'best' models for the three main ways forward and we didn't get much argument on the detailed aspects of each of the three designs for private provision.

However, it became obvious that there was a major gap that our title made clear and that had made our work relatively uncontroversial. Most people were cross about the to-ing and fro-ing on *public* provision and our brief specifically prevented us from looking at the Tier I arrangements—we were the Task Force on *Private* Provision for Retirement. From the emphasis I've given in this book to the role of Tier I in the private saving decision, that gap was a major impediment to the completion of our work.

The discussion on public provision was supposedly the responsibility of a joint committee of both Cabinet Ministers and backbenchers (the ones who had threatened revolt). In fact, not a lot happened on the review of public provision in the 12 months or so that we took for the first two stages of our work. In retrospect, that was probably a good thing. If we were to finalise our recommendations, we had to make the first move. Politically, that was a sensible strategy, as it meant the suggestions could emerge from an independent body before they went through the political process.

The Way Forward emerged in December 1992 in two editions—the main report of 129 pages and a 13 page pamphlet. Once again, we took great care with our language because we wanted the message to be loud and clear on both public and private provision. We didn't, however, take it to the people but left it to the press—our role was over. We disbanded ourselves on the day the report was released.

In summary, we recommended some specific changes to public provision[1] and came down in favour of the voluntary option for private provision.

---

[1] We had, fortunately, discovered that Tier I was broadly affordable over the next 50-60 years with some potential fiscal risks so we could generally support the status quo which was 'good news'.

Probably the most controversial aspect was that we didn't support the compulsory option over the voluntary alternative. If you've read this far, I don't need to explain why.

I felt pleased with the process and the outcome—I had started with the belief that something had to be done and that that 'something' was probably compulsion.[1] I didn't understand why tax incentives were such a bad idea. My views changed over the 15-month life of the Task Force. I hope it doesn't take everyone as long as it took me.

What else did I learn?

There was (and still is) a low level of public understanding of the issues so that, at least on that point, we didn't achieve everything that we should have. People who should know better don't take the trouble to inform themselves before making public pronouncements on the issues. That doesn't help public understanding.

The role of the press is vital in the whole process. The daily (or weekly) realities of meeting deadlines mean that it's very difficult (especially in a country the size of New Zealand) to build knowledge among reporters and, through informed comment, to build public knowledge. This lack of sophistication is in fact a world-wide malaise, even among the specialist financial press.

A task force should spend a long time with the press—not to 'snow' them, but to build up knowledge and to engender confidence in the process.

There should have been an information programme built on the release of our final report. Public opinion could have been moulded in the aftermath of the debate that followed. The reason for the gap was that the government then had to get political consensus on our recommendations, something that emerged spectacularly with a tripartite 'Accord'.[2] However, it was a shame to lose the knowledge that the Task Force and its secretariat gained over its 15-month life.

Retirement income is an emotional issue and it's very difficult to shift entrenched opinion or even to get an informed debate going. Opinions are, understandably, most entrenched among those who are most dependent on current policies (the currently retired and those who are too close to retirement to do anything meaningful about a changed policy). Paradoxically, they are the people for whom any new policies should have least effect, if the transitional arrangements are well designed.

So we did some things reasonably well and other things middlingly so. There's no need for other countries to learn these things afresh. If a government thought a version of the New Zealand Task Force would suit its country, it could do worse than taking the time to read the three reports.

---

[1]   As my views were relatively well known, I suspect that's why I was put there.

[2]   This was signed in August 1993 between the three major political groups National, Labour and the Alliance. Since then, a new party (United) has joined but one (New Zealand First) remains outside the Accord. Regrettably, the run up to the first proportional representation election in October 1996 produced some intellectual backsliding among the politicians. However, the points of difference weren't on the big picture issues (apart from the suggestion of a compulsory Tier II scheme from two minor parties) but they're annoying all the same.

Should You Ask the People?

I believe in democracy because, as Winston Churchill observed, despite all its imperfections, no-one has thought of a better way of running things.[1] Having said that and despite the need for community consensus, I don't think that the people should be asked for their direct blessing to our new pension arrangements. A referendum[2] is an inappropriate vehicle to deal with such a complex and multi-faceted issue. Just imagine, for a moment, what single question a government would put to its citizens to gauge their views—and that's one of the reasons why the 1997 referendum in New Zealand on compulsory private provision was such a bad idea.

I have suggested that wide and representative groups of citizens should be involved in the review which, at its initial stages, should not be part of the political process.

Political consensus is the next stage. In the end, elected representatives must make the decision but, because of the review procedures and support programmes I suggest, the final decisions should be relatively uncontroversial, especially with the long lead-time proposed. In a way, a formal vote wouldn't be needed, because I hope that the whole subject would be depoliticised by the review process. Getting consensus among politicians may sound a daunting objective, but it's an essential one.

... And In Conclusion

I've presented what I hope is a strong case for 'market-based incentives' to drive a government's role in the development and promotion of a sustainable retirement income system. I want the government to steer but the markets to row. The state will deliver Tier I but will signal its wish for savers to replace Tier I with private provision at Tiers II and III. The state will no longer be the unquestioned provider; nor will it be the savers' protector—though they won't be left entirely on their own. They will be helped to make informed decisions and allowed to see what will happen to them if they chose to do nothing (which might turn out to be an acceptable and sensible decision).

If we needed to force people into saving for retirement, I think we would all have failed in our communication job and that includes the government, the education system, employers, advisers and anyone else who has any influence on the flow of relevant information to help savers make sensible decisions. The fact that I want people to make their own decisions does not mean I don't care what people do; it means that I trust them to make decisions that are in their own best interests.

People want to do the right thing. If you present them with a good idea and help them see, in ways that are relevant to their needs, how they might benefit, you would empower them to do the 'right thing', whatever that might be in any given country. I'm sure of this and we won't need to pay them, or

---

[1]   He said, in fact, that: 'No-one pretends that democracy is perfect or all-wise. Indeed, it has been said that democracy is the worst form of Government except all those other forms that have been tried from time to time.' (Speech to House of Commons, 11 November 1947).

[2]   Of the kind carried out in Switzerland in June 1995 on the 10th Social Security (AHV) Revision.

force them to do it. But, in the end, there's only so much that a government, distant from the individual saver, can do. That doesn't let the saver off the hook. Saving for retirement is an individual responsibility.

There is, however, another important part in the retirement incomes puzzle—we look at the role of the employer next.

8

Why Involve Employers?

Summary

Employers can make a significant contribution to a relationship with the government at Tier II to create a mutually beneficial public policy. The present pattern of employer involvement in retirement schemes reflects a complicated 'pay + benefits' patchwork. This has evolved in the absence of an understanding of the role employers' retirement schemes perform within the general retirement savings framework, or of their costs and benefits both to the employer and employee.

Changes in employment patterns and in employer/employee relationships contribute to a need for change in approaches to compensation. A 'total compensation' approach provides a simplified environment in which the employer and employee agree on the total price to be paid for a job and where the employee decides the ratio of cash to benefits (including retirement savings) in which payment is received.

The employer can also provide a means of communicating with employees and an efficient point for the collection of contributions, and group schemes that have the advantage of scale. These are both valuable roles in ensuring the success of Tier II arrangements.

Changes in the relationship between employers and employees will change the focus of policy makers and advisers, as the employee becomes the primary customer for information on savings and retirement income policies.

****

With a sustainable safety net at Tier I, along with a supportive information and education programme, we could ask why governments should be concerned with what employers think or do about their employees' retirement income provision at Tier II. Shouldn't they be left to get on with the serious business of being an employer—to make money, provide a service, keep their owners happy or whatever?

There are several public policy reasons for the government and employers to co-operate. Such a relationship can operate to their mutual benefit to achieve three main public policy objectives.

Efficiency of Tier I

The government wants people to understand how its Tier I scheme fits into the retirement plans of its citizens. It also wants employees to have confidence in the sustainability of the regime. Employees are probably the best placed to do something about retirement saving and the government wants to help employees make the best economic decisions for themselves at Tier II. With the retirement income strategy I'm proposing, the aggregate decisions of all employees are likely to be in the best economic interests of the country as well.

Employees must also understand the reason for Tier I's income test to minimise the 'savings trap' where people refuse to save more because they think they'll miss out on benefits. They must understand the trade-off between, on the one hand, a tested, secure, fair benefit and, on the other, higher tax rates, higher debt and insecurity.

Making the Communication Programme Work

Employees get a lot of economic information from their employers, either directly or indirectly. They are more likely to believe information they get from their employer on retirement incomes compared with information from self-interested providers of financial services, or from politicians whose main objective may be re-election.[1] The new retirement income regime will be more credible if employers get behind it; also, the cost of getting that information to its ultimate consumers (savers) would be significantly lower—there are many more employees than employers. Adding employees' families to the potential audience further improves the efficiency of that information channel.

Promoting Action

It's easier to get employees to do something about the need identified in the information and education campaign if you can convince them to divert some of their pay before they actually get it.[2] It's also more efficient and cheaper to tap into the flow of money between the employer and its employees—in the same way as we have deductions at source for income tax and social security contributions. Governments have learned the lesson on mandated collections—the same principle applies to voluntary ones as well.

In most developed countries, employers play an important role in helping their employees save for retirement. This chapter looks at why a successful private Tier II (employer-sponsored schemes) will help create a sustainable retirement income system, and how governments can help build that successful Tier II. Successful Tier II arrangements will also wash over into Tier III as employees' knowledge and demands for more and better information is fostered and then rewarded.

---

[1]   In a survey carried out by Putnam Investments, reported in *The New York Times*, 25 February 1996, three quarters of the 1,000 adult participants said they get retirement planning information from their employers and prefer to get it that way.

[2]   According to the Putnam Investments survey mentioned in the last note, 93% of respondents wanted employers to deduct savings from their pay before they got it. Another survey, this time by the US Employee Benefit Research Institute, found that 64% of employees preferred retirement savings to be deducted at source rather than first going to the employees (even if the tax treatment were the same, which it isn't)—reported by *Dow Jones News*, 31 May 1996.

The Things that Matter to a Government

A fiscally sustainable public retirement income system depends on the government first getting the economy right. Until that happens, nothing much else matters—only the government can set that economic scene. After that, two issues really count—the age at which people retire, and the mix between those who are earning and those who have retired.

Retirement Age

Put simply, the later an employee 'retires',[1] the shorter, on average, will be the retirement period and the lower will be the risk of dependence on the state for income. From a national perspective, the retirement age is an important ingredient in the sustainability of retirement income policies. Both public and private pensions become less expensive if the retirement period is reduced. At the same time, privately-provided income becomes more affordable for both employers and employees because savers have a longer period of time to achieve target retirement incomes.

When do people 'retire' in New Zealand? We don't have good information on this, but we do have some numbers that show a pattern repeated, to a greater or lesser extent, around the developed world. Table 12 shows the rates of male labour force participation over age 65:

Table 12

Men over age 65 working in New Zealand

Census year	% of men working over age 65	% change on previous census
1936	34.5	-
1945	30.7	-11
1951	26.5	-14
1956	26.0	-2
1961	22.0	-15
1966	24.0	-9
1971	21.5	-10
1976	16.0	-26
1981	14.0	-31
1986	11.7	-16
1991	10.0	-15
1996	13.9	+39

Sources: New Zealand Yearbooks and Statistics New Zealand
Note: Labour force participation rates for women have changed so much over the last 50 years that comparisons of the participation rates for older women are less meaningful than for men.

The pattern in the US is more dramatic—the percentage of men over age 65 who worked fell from about 50 per cent in 1950 to below 20 per cent in 1980. Ten years later it had fallen to 16 per cent.[2]

---

[1]   When an employee's main paid employment ceases and reliance on private savings or state-provided income begins.

[2]   Monthly Current Population Survey data in the US cited in *Passing the Torch* by Quinn, Burkhayser and Myers, W.E. Upjohn Institute, 1990. Participation rates at younger ages have also fallen in the US. Today, only

In developed countries, participation rates for men fell on average from 33 per cent in the 1960-66 period to 11.1 per cent in the 1986-90 period.[1]

A number of things, including health and availability of income and work, affect an individual's retirement age. The availability of income is particularly important. Because I define retirement in the context of dependence on savings and state-provided income, replacing employment-derived income is a key determinant in fixing the retirement age.

Table 12 shows that fewer older New Zealand men now participate in the workforce with the rate of retirement picking up since the 1970s. That change in New Zealand was influenced by the introduction of 'National Superannuation' in 1977. This saw the Tier I benefit's entitlement age reduce overnight to 60, while the benefit itself was increased in both nominal and actuarial value (because of the younger age from which it became payable). These changes had two effects: first, individual employees found they could afford to retire at earlier ages and chose to,[2] and second (in most cases), employers reduced their *compulsory* retirement ages from age 65 to age 60.[3]

Until recently, New Zealand employers could choose their own compulsory retirement age. In 1990, the government finally grasped the connection between the cost of state age-related benefits and the impact of employers' retirement age policies. Its response was to change the Human Rights Act to outlaw compulsory retirement before the now increasing state pension age.[4]

However, increasing the allowable compulsory retirement age won't necessarily change the retirement age for employees as I have defined earlier. Although the change in the age of entitlement for the Tier I pension was probably an important element in the fall in employment participation (shown anecdotally by the table on male labour force participation rates) it wasn't the only influence. Participation rates were falling long before the state pension age fell to 60.

Further change has now been made to the Human Rights Act outlawing *any* compulsory age. This could even produce a perverse outcome—falling ages of

---

65% of men aged 55-64 are in the labour force, down from 83% in 1970 (from *The Wall Street Journal*, 6 May 1996).

[1]   From *Averting the Old Age Crisis, op. cit.*, page 322.

[2]   The US work cited in *Passing the Torch* by Quinn, Burkhayser and Myers, W.E. Upjohn Institute, 1990 demonstrated particular decreases in participation rates at ages 62 (the earliest age of eligibility for Social Security) and 65 (the age of maximum entitlement for Social Security).

[3]   One regular survey (carried out by the Association of Superannuation Funds of New Zealand) saw schemes with a compulsory age of 60 increase from 42% of participating schemes in 1979 (two years after the state pension age reduced) to 65% in 1992.

[4]   This became age 61 on 1 April 1992 and increases gradually until it reaches age 65 on 1 April 2001. Many employers' compulsory retirement ages in New Zealand are increasing with the increasing state pension age. This explains the increased participation rates for males shown for 1996 in Table 12.

retirement from *career* employment.[1] From no later than 1 February 1999, New Zealand employers will be forced to replace age-based retirement policies with performance-based policies where the age of retirement will be determined by the capacity to do the job.

Once the new rules are in place, New Zealand may see increasing numbers of older people becoming reliant on state-provided incomes before the state pension age, like the unemployment or disability benefits, rather than the Tier I scheme, as in the past. New Zealand may also see lower levels of saving at Tiers II and III (as a consequence of the new anti-age discrimination rules) rather than the expected increasing numbers of older people still at work.[2] That's because employers presently use the concept of a compulsory age as a humane (or non-confrontational) way to address failing performance. Knowing that the employee will go by no later than age 65 tends to encourage employers to hold off asking the employee to resign. The possibility of having to keep the employee until age 70 or beyond should force employers to address failing performance earlier rather than later. Older employees are often the first to be made redundant and, once out of work, usually find it more difficult to get another job.

However, this influence may be offset, to some extent, by the shortage of skilled employees that many commentators seem to expect over the coming 20-30 years. Employers may want to retain the skills of older workers rather than pay for the costs of training new ones.

The nature of the process of retirement itself may also change. The traditional pattern of the main full-time 'career' employment being replaced quickly by full-time 'guillotine' retirement should give way to a longer process. This would involve an earlier end to full-time, 'permanent' employment followed by a 'bridge' of part-time or temporary periods of work until the retirement age is reached.

Earners and Retirees Mix

The government's capacity to deliver anything directly depends on its capacity to tax. A lot of its income comes from taxes on personal income and, in particular, from the taxes paid by employees.[3] The mix between those in employment and those who are retired is therefore an important element in the fiscal sustainability of the Tier I scheme and the success of Tiers II and III.

---

[1]   Another unintended consequence of outlawing age discrimination will be the ultimate death of the defined-benefit retirement benefit scheme. The cost to the employer of defined benefits increases with age. If an employer couldn't refuse to take on an older employee because of age (or to reduce the employee's pay on that account), defined-contribution benefits, where a fixed amount is contributed regardless of age, would become the norm.

[2]   The US experience with a similar law (Age Discrimination in Employment Act) is similarly discouraging. The US Congress says that age discrimination remains an obstacle to employment for older workers and that 'statutory provisions ... remain incomplete and somewhat ineffective', reported in *The Economist*, 27 January 1996.

[3]   In New Zealand, 48.4% of total tax came from individual incomes in 1995/96. These incomes include welfare beneficiaries and the retired but most would belong to those in the workforce.

The importance of these two factors—the retirement age and the mix between earners and retirees—means that countries must have much better information on retirement ages, their interaction with the state pension age and the part-time employment patterns which ease the transition from full-time employment to full-time retirement. Countries need this more detailed information on a regular basis as patterns develop in response to social and economic change.

Although public policy can influence these issues, it can't, by itself, change behaviour. The economic needs of employers and employees are probably the most important influences. They are like the tide to the state's King Canute. The state can no more demand that people be employed up to a given age than can an employer demand that the state delivers a retirement income from the age it wishes to retire its employees.

The Things that Matter to Employers

To understand how the interests of employers can be served under the banner of public policy, we first need to understand why employers are involved at all at Tier II and how they express their interest in the financial welfare of employees.

Chapter 2 discussed why employers first got into the retirement income business. In our new environment (income-tested Tier I—no tax incentives or compulsion at Tiers II and III) those reasons don't go away.

Employers have a demonstrated interest in helping their employees provide for periods of financial dependency. The fact that many employer-sponsored retirement income schemes started in New Zealand and then survived the withdrawal (during 1987-90) of tax incentives seems, at least anecdotally, to support the idea that tax-avoidance wasn't the real or only reason for their existence. In some ways, it's remarkable that employment-related schemes still exist in New Zealand, given the constant, disruptive and expensive changes they experienced between 1975 and 1995.

From an employment perspective, there are three main reasons that an employee becomes financially dependent: death, disability, and retirement. Financial dependency can also follow redundancy.

An employer often has programmes that help its employees provide for these dependencies, even though they may seem the employee's private concern. The reasons for the employer's traditional involvement include concepts such as being a 'good' employer, competitive pressures and maximising value through group purchases. For retirement, however, there is the very real advantage of helping to implement a retirement policy; of being able to part with employees, knowing that they can have a reasonable standard of living in retirement. If the employer knows that an employee can afford to retire, the decision to part company is easier and cheaper, at least at the actual retirement date.

An employer's interest in its employees' retirement schemes goes further—when the employer wants someone to retire, there's a great temptation to pay the employee money to help make it happen, especially if the employee hadn't, until then, contemplated the possibility. The economic cost of keeping the employee until a later age could be greater than the economic cost of paying money now. Those *ad hoc* payments have a similar role to the regular subsidy to a formal pension scheme during the employee's service; it's just that the employer can't plan for them. The fact that the circumstance and the payment are both, by definition, unplanned means the employee can't count on it either.

The Spectrum of Employer-based Pension Programmes

The way the employer regards all its obligations to employees is reflected in the way it pays employees, including both *ad hoc* payments and regular subsidies to formal programmes, like pension schemes. The different types of pension programme run in a spectrum from full involvement at one end through to 'hands off' at the other end. In descending order of value to employees (and cost to employers) they are :

Defined-benefit scheme where the employer pays the full cost and bears the investment and mortality risks. The employer bears both the investment risk in the build-up of assets as well as the mortality and investment risks inherent in a long period of retirement. Defined-benefit lump sum schemes have a slightly lower priority in this spectrum as they leave the investment decision, and possibly also the mortality risk, to employees at the point of retirement.[1] These defined-benefit schemes are often compulsory (or effectively so—who in their right mind would give up the opportunity of a 'free' benefit?) where they cover more than the most senior employees.

Defined-benefit schemes that require employees to contribute towards the overall cost. Requiring the employee to contribute saves the employer money in two ways—first, the employer isn't carrying the full cost of a meaningful benefit; second, the contribution 'hurdle' means that a proportion of employees will decide not to join. They might not have the money or might not see the point of spending their own money on retirement benefits.

Defined contribution, with no employee contributions. Because the employee assumes the investment and retirement mortality risks in a defined-contribution scheme, the employer has put some distance in the financial relationship.

Defined-contribution schemes that require employee contributions. As with the defined-benefit contributory schemes, these save the employer money over their non-contributory counterparts.

Group saving vehicles. These are internally administered or managed by a third party and operate on a defined-contribution basis, where there is no direct subsidy to the employee's contributions, though the employer may pay for the costs of administration.

No employer-linked scheme. Employees make their own arrangements.

Why Does Tier II Exist?

New Zealand employers play a relatively less significant role in helping employees prepare financially for retirement than is the case with most developed countries. Information on participation rates in formal retirement saving schemes is fairly sparse but fewer than 20 per cent of all employees in New Zealand belong to a Tier II scheme. The proportions are much higher in

---

[1]   Whether lump sum or pension benefits emerge at retirement is usually driven by the requirements of the tax system that gives concessions on the contributions and build-up.

other countries.[1] In the UK, for example, where the employers' contributions are about nine per cent to 14 per cent of the payroll,[2] more than 50 per cent of employees are involved in a Tier II scheme. In the US, 63 per cent of employees in 1993 worked for employers that sponsored some type of retirement scheme, though only 50 per cent of all employees had actually joined a scheme.[3]

I suggested in chapter 3 that Tier II is the second most powerful weapon in a government's retirement income arsenal, so it's important for us to understand why employers have retirement saving schemes. If we want to change things we need to know the likely impact of such changes on employers.

So why do employers continue to help their employees in this way? In some countries, there's no choice (or no effective choice)—compulsion is becoming quite common. In other countries, multi-employer agreements may take the decision out of the individual employer's hands.

But what if the employer has a choice and still decides to set up a scheme and to pay for, or subsidise, employees' retirement savings? Is it altruism? In a profit-driven market place, that seems an unlikely explanation. In fact, surprisingly little is known of—or written about—employers' motives. Asking employers doesn't seem very illuminating. A 1992 survey of 66 employers[4] from the north west of England tried to shed light on this question. Table 13 summarises the responses from the participants to a list of reasons presented:

Retaining staff is the standout reason on all three counts.[5] Taylor and

---

[1] The main reasons for the low New Zealand participation rates are almost certainly due to the combined effects of a relatively generous Tier I and the high ratio of owner-occupied housing among retirees. Our 'poor' performance by comparison with other countries will also be exacerbated by the absence of tax incentives in New Zealand.

[2] According to P. Moore in 'The company pension scheme; a boon or a burden?', *The Journal of General Management*, 1987 cited in 'The provision of occupational pensions in the 1990s', S. Taylor and J. Earnslaw, *Employee Relations*, Vol. 17, No. 2, 1995.

[3] From 'Caught between the Demographics and the Deficit', Gerald Cole and Marjorie Taylor, Compensation & Benefits Review, Special Issue, 1996— data from US government sources—of those who hadn't joined 39% hadn't met the eligibility requirements and 31% had chosen not to join.

[4] Conducted by S. Taylor and J. Earnslaw, cited in 'The provision of occupational pensions in the 1990s', S. Taylor and J. Earnslaw, *Employee Relations*, Vol. 17, No. 2, 1995. The survey covered 367,755 employees with 164,258 scheme members who mostly (90%) belonged to defined-benefit schemes that were contracted out (85%) of the State Earnings Related Pension Scheme. The authors concluded that the 66 schemes were a typical cross section of UK schemes.

[5] A 1994 survey carried by the Confederation of British Industry (CBI) (covering employers of 2.2 million employees with 1.5 million scheme members and 2.4 million other beneficiaries) rated retention as the most significant justification (33% ranked it most important) while paternalism ranked second at 28% and aiding employee motivation was third at 21%. Interestingly, these last two didn't feature in the Taylor and Earnslaw survey.

Earnslaw then asked whether the considerable regulatory interventions that had taken place had affected the employers' costs or their attitude to pension scheme provision. Most couldn't (or wouldn't) say how much changes had affected costs—a surprising result.[1] The authors then concluded:

> ... very little work has been carried out, either by the companies themselves or by external bodies, which seeks to question the extent to which any of these objectives are in fact met.

Table 13
Employers' reasons for having pension schemes: UK

Objectives	Significant	Very significant	Most important
Retaining good employees	95%	73%	60%
Attracting new staff	95%	51%	12%
Improving industrial relations	86%	38%	6%
Improving company's image in the labour market	76%	26%	6%
Managing the time and manner in which employees retire	71%	23%	16%
Tax and financial advantages	65%	20%	0%
The opportunity to promote younger members of staff	39%	5%	0%

Source: Taylor, S. and Earnshaw, J.

Given the cost of pension schemes, this is curious. However, it may be explained by the slightly circuitous logic captured by the process most employers go through when they look at Tier II saving schemes—'we must have one because everyone else has one so what sort of scheme do they have? We'll have one of those.' That's the retention justification—how can you retain people if you aren't doing what other employers do? Pensions are all pretty complicated so we had better leave it to the experts.[2] The employers' surveys that follow the decision to have a scheme then compare, in the minutest detail, the individual aspects of all the schemes but don't ask the question (because it can't be answered): 'Is what we are doing in total for our employees enough to retain them?'[3]

---

[1] However, in the 1994 CBI survey just cited, over 70% of respondents would have chosen a defined-contribution scheme—81% had some form of defined-benefit scheme so they obviously felt that they would prefer to change if they could.

[2] The fact that longer-serving salaried staff tend to benefit most from employers' schemes probably helps them to stay the way they are. Schemes do tend to be administered, reviewed and managed by those who benefit most from their continuation.

[3] US research recognises that firms with pension schemes have employees who tend to stay longer but can't tell us if that's because of the presence of pension schemes, the financial penalties from leaving early or because those firms pay more in total (cited in *Passing the Torch* by Quinn, Burkhayser and Myers). Alan Gustman and Thomas Steinmeier in *Pension Incentives and Job Mobility*, W.E. Upjohn Institute, 1995, suggest that the financial penalties aren't large enough on their own to explain the lower

If employers find it difficult to justify what they are doing, then from a public policy perspective, we must be very careful not to make life too difficult for employers. They might start to wonder why they are in the pension business when they make cars or computers. They're more likely to be totally put off by interventionist policy makers—the goose responsible for those golden eggs will quietly expire.

That's what makes so damaging the process of constant change that afflicts most developed countries in the regulation of Tier II schemes. If the 'retention of staff' argument really is a bit like the emperor's new clothes, there's a danger of employers calling it quits and saying to employees that it's their responsibility. Once that trend starts, change will be quite quick—fashion will be a catalyst and will also undermine what seems to be the main present justification for having the schemes at all—other employers have a scheme so we must have one to retain our staff against our competitors for labour.

The demographic deluge and the fiscal limits now faced by most developed governments mean they have limited ability to pass the responsibility for retirement incomes on to employers, though that won't stop some from trying. It's important therefore for employers to continue seeing retirement saving schemes as a significant part of their personnel policy armoury.

The Compensation Patchwork: 'Pay + Benefits'

How employees are paid is important for a successful retirement income system.

Over many years, the compensation practices of employers in New Zealand and other developed countries developed into a 'pay + benefits' patchwork. The price for a job was divided into direct cash (which could include 'at risk' or bonus elements), and indirect benefits such as retirement benefits, car, insurance (health, life, disability), loans, subscriptions, and so on.

Indirect benefits grew in number, significance and complexity, driven by:

- tax laws that favoured benefits over cash and some benefits over others

- personnel policy favouring certain types of behaviour over others

- competitive pressures for labour from other employers

- the historical need to distinguish between waged employees (represented by unions) with benefits such as overtime, special payments and allowances, and salaried employees (non-unionised) who tended to receive fixed amounts of pay, and

- the employer's access to benefits at a cheaper rate than employees were able to obtain.

The 'pay + benefits' approach to compensation has many problems. The main problems in New Zealand are:

---

turnover and thought that a better explanation was that employees in pensioned employment get more in direct pay even before the value of the pension benefits is taken into account. Given the undoubted early leaving penalties and the difficulty in measuring 'total compensation' in the presence of pensions, firms probably don't really know why they have pension schemes other than that everyone else who matters does.

The Different Tax Treatments of Various Benefits

These have been gradually eliminated since 1985. The introduction of Fringe Benefits Tax and Withholding Tax on retirement scheme contributions (both of which are imposed on the employer) coupled with the removal of tax incentives for retirement saving and life or disability insurance means that cash and indirect benefits now have similar overall tax treatments.

Complexity

Employees tend not to understand (or know how to calculate) the total value of their compensation. Some schemes are so complicated that even professionals have to draw breath at the detail.[1] Employees tend to undervalue non-cash benefits or even not to value them at all. As a result, the amounts spent by the employer are, in part, wasted. Employers have not necessarily communicated with or educated their employees well so part of this waste is self-inflicted.[2]

Lack of Linkage Between Fringe Benefits and Performance

Fringe benefits can only be indirectly related to an individual's own performance. Benefits that are based on pay (like retirement benefits) have an indirect linkage but other benefits do not (like cars and medical insurance).

Over- and Under-provision

Benefit schemes can be designed only for the average condition or for the average employee. They will over-provide for some and under-provide for others. Over-provision can also result from duplication where two different employers are providing similar coverage for the same family (like medical insurance).

The Impact of Tax Changes on the Value of Total Compensation

As tax laws change, the pre-tax equivalent of total compensation changes, particularly if inconsistent changes occur across various types of benefit. The employer has no control over tax changes but may end up paying for their

---

[1] According to a survey of working Americans (by Towers Perrin called *Preparing for Retirement*, 1995) of the 71% of employees who said that their employer had a pension scheme, 67% didn't know the pension formula, 55% didn't know what percentage of pay the pension would replace, 25% weren't sure of the early retirement age and 21% weren't sure of the full benefit age. Now wonder how employees could put a realistic value on their benefits and also why the employers were spending money on those benefits.

[2] Typically, neither the employer nor the employees understand the actual cost of employment. In a Noble Lowndes survey in the UK, *Attitude Survey on Flexible Compensation*, October 1991, 68% of covered employers acknowledged that they communicated their benefits package in a way that prevented employees from valuing it fully. However, 81% of employers said they wouldn't abandon all benefits and just give employees cash.

impact if the taxes are (as has happened in New Zealand and Australia[1]) imposed on the employer not the employee.

Lack of Fairness

Benefit schemes tend to be unfair, particularly those that require employees to contribute. These interpose a hurdle so that an element of compensation (in some cases, a large element) is available only to those who can afford to jump that hurdle (or who think it important enough to jump). Similarly, schemes that base their benefits on age, gender, habits and health (such as insurance) are inherently unfair.

Inability to Accommodate Individual Needs

Some schemes are not relevant to the needs of an employee so the price paid by the employer is therefore wasted (like life insurance for a single employee with no dependents). In fact, the individual needs of employees cannot be accommodated in single level benefits delivered in bulk.

The Employment Contracts Act is also transforming relationships between employers and employees in New Zealand. The emphasis is now turning much more towards individualising the employment relationship and, therefore, the contract itself. Collective, multi-employer, union negotiated agreements are less important than they used to be. Traditional benefit schemes are more difficult to adapt to the new types of individual relationships that will eventually be of infinite variety. For example, one employee can easily have a variety of relationships with more than one employer.

Difficulty of Fitting Pay-related Benefits into a Variable Pay Environment

Pay-related benefits don't fit neatly into a pay environment that includes performance-based pay such as commissions or profit-sharing. Artificial definitions of pay for benefit purposes are usually needed to make both the employer's and employee's exposure to risk reasonable and to preserve relativities.

Employees' Tendency not to Assess Their Own Needs

Because the responsibility for delivering benefits essentially lies with the employer in the traditional environment, employees tend not to assess their own needs. Adequacy of coverage tends either to be assumed by the employee or, at least, not questioned, especially where the employee is not required to contribute directly.

'Golden Handcuffs' Syndrome

Traditional benefit schemes can act as 'golden handcuffs' and reward service rather than performance. They can become a disincentive to leaving, creating

---

[1] Both countries have Fringe Benefit Tax that imposes a tax obligation on the employer as a proxy for the employee. It's cheaper and more effective to impose the tax on the fewer and more easily tracked employers than on the people who actually receive the indirect benefit.

situations that suit neither the employee nor the employer.[1] Examples here include the defined-benefit retirement scheme and medical insurance where the employee has an indifferent medical history and would have trouble replacing the cover after leaving.

For employers, this reduces flexibility and so their capacity to respond to change. It also means they may keep employees who have to stay, rather than want to stay. The unintended consequence of rich, indirect benefit programmes is that employers find it more difficult to shed unsuitable labour.

Benefits that depend on the employee's pay at or near retirement (like defined-benefit schemes) also restrict employment practices such as reduced responsibilities, part-time work and other ways of easing the transition from full-time work to full-time retirement or independent contracting. Again, this potentially disadvantages both the employer and employee.

Retirement benefits, particularly in defined-benefit schemes, also reward service because the value conferred on employees by the employer's contributions is significantly skewed in favour of *older* employees. Two employees of different ages doing the same job on the same direct pay will receive very different total compensation because of the favour conferred by the defined-benefit scheme on the older employee. Fortunately for employers, most employees don't understand that imbalance.

The skew also imposes a barrier to the hire of older people. Their total compensation is more, by reason of the retirement benefits, than for younger employees.[2] Employers that understand may not only avoid older prospective employees, they may also want to encourage older scheme members to leave ahead of younger because of that higher annual cost.

Requirement for Cost/Benefit Analysis of 'Pay + Benefits'

The 'pay + benefits' patchwork needs professional expertise to value the variety of benefits and determine their costs to the employer and benefit to the employee. That adds further cost and makes it difficult for the employer to explain to employees what the benefits actually are.

The patchwork also consumes significant management time and incurs substantial external fees. Dealing with international transferees is an

---

[1]   They may help to explain why average tenures in US companies were so long. Robert Hall, cited in *Passing the Torch* by Quinn, Burkhayser and Myers, W.E. Upjohn Institute, 1990, estimated that in 1978 about half of men aged 40 or more were in jobs that would last at least 20 years. John Addison and Alberto Castro (cited in the same report) found a similar result and thought that the longer tenures were associated with unionised, rather than non-unionised employees. The employee benefits' link could therefore be with union-based schemes. Over the last 20 years, the position has stayed fairly static—according to a report in *Business Week*, 15 April 1996, average job tenure in the US has hardly changed in the 1980s and early 1990s.

[2]   This led a correspondent in *The Financial Times*, 23 September 1995, to suggest that the tax breaks for defined-benefit schemes should be restricted to help develop non-discriminatory schemes—another example of how the tax system can fix anything, given unlimited bureaucratic resources.

administrative and taxation nightmare.[1] This is a real issue for multinational companies in New Zealand because our tax authorities treat benefits very differently from most—taxing benefits when other countries don't, and not taxing them when others do.

Difficulty in Making Accurate Comparisons with 'Market' Remuneration Practices

It's difficult to compare remuneration practices in the compensation 'market' in the presence of schemes with voluntary membership. Whose 'pay + benefits' are measured when the employer (or the employee) is trying to understand the market position for the total cost of employment? Those who belong to the scheme or those who don't? Or is it the unreal average? Because of this, the value of membership attributable to the employer's contributions is often deliberately disregarded in pay comparisons.[2]

Most of these problems apply in all developed countries. If employers wanted to rationalise some of their present practices, this needn't be a move towards less of a commitment to the welfare of employees or be seen as a breach of faith. It doesn't need to make employers less 'family friendly'. I don't think policymakers should intervene to establish minimum standards.[3] Getting rid of fringe benefits, by itself, should be seen as a positive, not a negative move.

That's because the 'pay + benefits' approach tends to be complex, inflexible, misunderstood, undervalued, inappropriate and unfair. That's why I think it should change, not because there is some international conspiracy among employers to make the lives of their employees less secure and, therefore, cheaper.

Total Compensation—a New Way of Paying People

I think paying employees what they are worth and then letting *them* decide how they want to receive their pay is a better way of doing things. The so-called total compensation approach to remuneration has some important implications for Tier II arrangements. But before we look at those, it's worth understanding what this means.

Total compensation is the total price of pay and benefits that the employer pays for an individual's services as an employee. It includes the obvious elements such as:

- direct wages or salary
- a car (or a car allowance that compensates the employee for *private* expenditure, such as travel to and from work)

---

[1]   The European Community has had several goes to sort this issue out even among themselves. They haven't managed it so far.

[2]   Or taken into the survey by using an arbitrary top-up to base pay. This at least allows employers that have schemes to be distinguished from those that don't—it can't pretend to get close to the value actually conferred.

[3]   As argued by Robert Kuttner, in *Business Week*, 10 July 1995—he was concerned by the fact that: '[c]orporate America is littered with companies that once prided themselves on generous fringe benefits and no-layoff policies ... if we believe as a society in pro-family workplaces, lifetime learning, pay for performance and other enlightened principles, these norms must be anchored in national policies'.

- representation allowances
- retirement benefits
- medical insurance
- life or disability insurance, and
- personal planning (such as preparation for retirement).

It also includes the direct costs associated with the provision of those benefits, like the Fringe Benefits Tax and Withholding Tax that are due in New Zealand if benefits are paid for by the employer. It should also include other amounts that the employer pays to the state in respect of the employee, such as social security taxes.

Total compensation means that the employer and employee agree on the total price that will be paid for a job. There are then no restrictions on the way in which that price is delivered. It can be all cash or a mixture of cash and benefits as the employee chooses. The price calculated can also include 'at risk' or variable amounts depending on employee performance.

A cynic might suggest that employers who move to total compensation want to avoid the additional costs of employer subsidies to traditional employee benefit schemes. Total compensation does imply a move out of subsidised schemes. Some might see this as a backward step, particularly if you wanted to make retirement incomes more affordable for employees by subsidising their contributions.

In fact, appearances are deceiving. When an employer fixes total compensation for a position, it must have regard for individual performance *and* the market (as well as its capacity to pay), otherwise it cannot expect to attract or retain employees. If survey data accurately measured the *whole* market, including what other employers are delivering in subsidies to traditional benefit programmes, that would be factored into the employer's decision.

The employer doesn't then impose any barrier in the delivery of the piece of pay that is delivered as a subsidy elsewhere. If the employees wanted it in cash, that would be their decision. If they preferred it to be delivered as benefits, as may be the requirement in the external market, that would be their choice, not the employer's.

Also, the employer will deliver that element to *all* employees not just those who choose to join the scheme or who qualify after some eligibility period to become a member. In a typical voluntary retirement benefit scheme, New Zealand experience has shown that only about half of eligible employees choose to join (mainly because they are usually made to contribute when they do)[1] so only about half have the chance to benefit from the employer's contribution to that scheme.

Those who join tend to be better informed employees who appreciate the value of the traditional subsidised arrangement. An education or information gap therefore influences the way in which an employer's total compensation

---

[1]   This is irrational behaviour because, despite the fact that the employee usually has to contribute, the employer will also contribute. By deciding not to join, the employee misses out on part of the potential pay for the job.

is actually delivered and how much that amounts to.[1]

These gaps in understanding actually save employers money in the typical subsidised environment. Installing a total compensation policy won't cost the employer any less than the 'pay + benefits' approach (assuming the total amounts paid were calculated correctly by reference to external indicators) and could indeed, depending on circumstances, cost more.

Under a total compensation approach, the employer is, in theory, indifferent to whether the employee takes all cash, all benefits or a mixture of both. In practice, however, the employer cannot be indifferent, because it will have human resources' objectives (like a retirement policy). These objectives can still be achieved in a total compensation environment by adopting one of the following strategies:

a) compulsory coverage, with the price of that coverage being charged to the employee's total compensation;

b) convincing employees to behave appropriately, however that might be defined, through an information and education campaign.

Of the alternatives, the first is more direct because it forces the employer to justify its policy to employees— 'I'm taking this amount out of your pay packet because...'. The second is more demanding but, if successful, would be more likely to produce an enduring outcome. It's also more risky because employees may not see things the way the employer does.

If employees had a choice about where their money went and when and how they got it back at the end of the day, there would be investment return and expense implications that a traditional subsidised environment tends to disguise. Even employer schemes that operate on defined-contribution principles, where returns (and expenses) are more visible, tend to disguise these implications.[2]

The same applies to subsidised saving schemes where savers are rewarded for saving by, say, a dollar-for-dollar subsidy from the employer. The investment manager could, in theory, lose 50 per cent of the combined amount before savers ran the risk of being worse off by losing some of their own money (forgetting about any tax subsidy). Alternatively, the seller of an employer-subsidised saving product could charge 50 per cent of the amount invested for setting up the deal before it touched the saver in the pocket. In both of these cases, the saver is relatively less sensitive to poor returns or to high administration costs than would be the case if the first dollar of net returns went into the saver's pocket or if the first dollar of costs came out of the saver's pocket.

---

[1] The gap can be illustrated in reverse by looking at what happens when the employer tries to bridge it—a survey of 2,055 US households sponsored by Merrill Lynch & Co found that 88% of workers who take employer-sponsored financial education courses sign up for section 401(k) saving plans by comparison with 64% of co-workers who don't attend the courses, reported by *Business Week*, 9 September 1996.

[2] I've already talked about the buffer that tax incentives put into the relationship between investment managers and savers. See chapter 4 p. 71. Briefly, the argument is that subsidies from other taxpayers mean that a manager has to lose quite a lot of money before the saver is actually out of pocket, allowing for the tax subsidies.

However, in a total compensation environment, the saver will pay 'instantly' for poor returns (and possibly also administration expenses) so the market will become less forgiving for fund managers and administrators. It could also mean that savers become more risk averse.

Tax and Regulatory Conditions

There's one final implication for an employer that adopts total compensation as a way of paying its people—it may help the employer to limit its financial exposure to any adverse tax or imposed compulsory saving regime. Looking at the kind of talk that's going on in most developed countries, this could be an important protection. Additional costs arising from such a tax or compulsory scheme would be passed directly on to its employees through reducing their total compensation.

In theory, the employer will be indifferent to the varying tax/regulatory treatments which are imposed by central authorities on different benefits. If a government decided to reward retirement savings by giving a tax concession then the value of the dollar ultimately delivered to the employee at retirement will be higher (other things being equal) than a dollar delivered as taxable pay.

If the government also decided that a tax-favoured dollar must comply with certain conditions (for example, it could emerge only as a pension from a particular age) then the employee would allow for the 'cost' of those restrictions in assessing the value of the tax concession, before deciding to spend a dollar of compensation on that benefit.

In both cases, the employer is indifferent to the employee's decision, as any costs will be 'passed through' the scheme directly to the employee's benefits.

However, employers cannot be completely protected because, in the end, they must retain employees in a competitive labour market.

What Does All This Mean for Policy Makers?

If employers change the way they pay employees, the most important implication for policy makers would be a change in customer focus. In the traditional environment, the policy maker's first customer is probably the employer, next the trustees of the schemes offered by the employer and last, the ultimate object of all this attention, the schemes' members. All the rules that the policy maker's customers must comply with to achieve current policy settings in most developed countries focus on the financial institution (the pension or savings scheme) or the employer. In part, that's because the financial institution and the employer are effectively the agents of tax collectors, and a great deal of the regulation is about protecting the tax base.

In the total compensation environment, the employee/member becomes the policy maker's customer.[1] The test of Tier II's success will be in the use to which *employees* put it. If the policy maker can't communicate effectively with

---

[1]   According to the Towers Perrin US survey of employees already cited (see note 1, p. 204) 81% believed it was the employee's primary responsibility to save for retirement. Only 10% thought it was the employer's responsibility and 5% thought it was the government's responsibility. The equivalent responses to a New Zealand survey ('Westpac-FPG Savings Profile' described in the last chapter p. 173) were personal responsibility, 71.5%; government, 15%; employers, 3.2%.

employees through the system then Tier II may fail to satisfy the long term needs of the country's citizens.

Having the taxpayer-employee as the customer means politicians will get good, instant feedback on the potential political sustainability of change. It will also make employees much more aware of the 'big picture' changes which policy-makers within social security systems are facing throughout the developed world. Employees will see the immediate consequences of a government's attempt to impose additional costs on the employer.

What Can the Employer Bring to the Partnership?[1]

Why should governments be interested in what employers can bring to the relationship that might create a successful Tier II? In fact, employers have a vital role to play in ensuring the success of Tier II. There are several aspects to this.

A Mechanism for Informing and Educating Employees

All countries have a very much smaller number of employers than employees. Table 14 shows a profile of New Zealand employers by the number employed:

Any change to public policy on retirement incomes will be easier to implement if it is targeted at employers. The cost of getting the message to 1.4 million employees will be significantly greater than for 199,000 employers. That's not to say employers have to pay for the cost of implementing public policy but having employers behind the policy and helping communicate it will make change much easier.

Table 14
Employers by Numbers of Employees, New Zealand

Number of employees	Number of employers	(%)	Total employees (full & part-time)	(%)	Average employees per employer
0 to 5	158,152	79	352,969	25	2.2
6 to 9	18,384	9	149,490	11	8.1
10 to 49	19,495	10	419,239	30	21.5
50 to 99	1,868	1	146,770	11	78.6
100 or more	1,183	1	319,860	23	270.4
Totals	**199,082**		**1,388,328**		**7.0**

Source: *Business Activity*, Statistics New Zealand, 1995—the number of employers in the table as at February 1994 are what the compilers call 'activity units' as opposed to the less numerous 'enterprises'.

Table 14 shows that, in February 1994, 66 per cent of New Zealanders worked in what Statistics New Zealand calls 'activity units' of fewer than 50 employees. Only 23 per cent worked in activity units of 100 or more employees. These are very significant statistics in a retirement income policy context, as small employers tend not to have the resources to cope with

---

[1] Readers who are familiar with the New Zealand Task Force's report *The Options*, August 1992, will recognise some of what follows.

constant and complex change. Part-timers, not specialists, are usually responsible for setting pay and conditions of employment. For Tier II to be successful, government policies should focus on the small, not the large employer. If they work for small employers, that will cover most employees. And larger employers will find those policies a breeze.

The position in the US is much the same as in New Zealand (97.5 per cent of US businesses employ fewer than 100 employees), and there are calls for Washington to pay more attention to small employers. A study carried out over 1994-95[1] found that only 22 per cent of small businesses had a 401(k) saving scheme for their employees' retirement saving. The study singled out complex legislation as a major impediment to small employers' improving that count.

In New Zealand, the presence of employment-related retirement saving schemes has been correlated to the size of the employer. Figure 13 shows the position:

Figure 13
Presence of Corporate Schemes: New Zealand

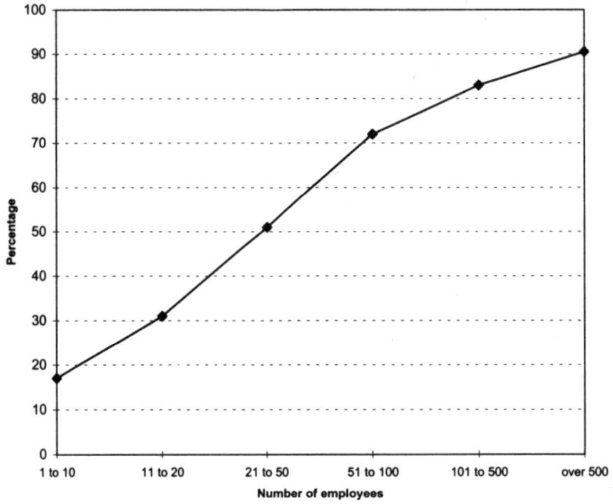

Source: From a Department of Labour and Employer's Federation survey cited in *Workplace Superannuation* by Vanessa Lidgett, 1996.

Economies of Scale: Group vs Individual Schemes

It's easier for employees to achieve a retirement saving objective if their own savings are subsidised by the employer. However, even where the employer does not directly subsidise employees' contributions, there are still advantages to employees (and, therefore, to the government) in having access to an employer's scheme.

Employer-based retirement saving schemes offer significant economies of scale. These economies extend even to quite small groups (say, down to 10 individuals). Schemes for individuals cost a lot to establish—in part, that's to do with commissions paid to the people who sell new schemes or who renew them. Also, the costs relating to sale and documentation, collecting and

---

[1]   By the Public Agenda Foundation in collaboration with The Employee Benefit Research Institute, reported by *Dow Jones News Service—Business Wire*, 4 May 1995.

remitting regular contributions and reporting to members, are all spread in group schemes, so that they will be significantly lower for each member. Coping with regulatory change is less expensive for a group.

The cost of some services that are in the long-run interests of a saving scheme also become more practicable for a group of savers rather than a number of individuals. Larger schemes can buy asset consulting services and comparative performance statistics rather than relying on the institutions that are running the money to tell them how the investments are performing. Such things are beyond the individual saver.

Effective Means of Collecting Contributions: Pay Deduction

Most advisers in the retirement income area say that regular savings should be deducted from pay before it's received. There's a large body of anecdotal evidence supporting the power of this facility in helping people save for retirement.[1] Net income defines our standard of living, even if part has been stopped at source on a voluntary basis to provide for our ultimate retirement. It seems easier to regard whatever we receive directly in cash as our total weekly or monthly income as being available for current consumption. Lowering today's standard of living in that way also lowers the target for retirement income purposes and makes it easier to achieve the target.

If the voluntary, tax neutral Tier II is to achieve its objectives, employment-based schemes should be readily available. Having to persuade a saver to invest from income already received places another obstacle in the way of encouraging citizens to do something about saving for retirement.

Education

Only a small proportion of New Zealand employees belong to an employer-based retirement scheme. Information on actual participation rates in formal schemes is very poor. The best information we have[2] shows that in 1995 only 18.5 per cent of New Zealander employees belonged to an employer's retirement saving scheme. To this can be added those employees who save in other ways for retirement (such as the 11.5 per cent of all New Zealanders who belong to a retail retirement saving scheme) and the business owners, including farmers, who save by building up business assets. However, this leaves a large group that is yet to be persuaded of the need to put money aside for extra retirement income.

The campaign of persuasion should ideally be directed, through the employer, to the point at which pay is delivered. This campaign should cover such issues as the future sustainability of Tier I, the amount of savings needed to support a particular standard of living throughout retirement, the different saving vehicles available, risk and return along with the impact of inflation and tax on returns.

These and the other reasons described earlier in this chapter demonstrate that there are advantages for all New Zealanders if public policy encourages

---

[1]   According to the US Public Agenda Foundation study already cited (see note 1, p. 212) 79% of the public participants in the survey said the best way to save for retirement was by pay deduction.

[2]   From the Government Actuary's office, the regulatory authority for New Zealand retirement benefit schemes.

(or, at least, does not discourage) the establishment of employer-based retirement saving schemes.

And there are some other, quite compelling reasons for employers to help the government build a sustainable Tier II. If Tier II doesn't work, future governments are bound to look to employers to help solve the problem. Doing something because you want to, and because you think it will actually help, beats doing it because you have to—an employer can be *homo economicus* as well as a citizen.

Future Patterns

The relationship between employers and employees is changing throughout the developed world. Some of those changes have considerable significance for Tier II schemes and their place in the retirement income system.

Careers vs Short Term

The role of the employer is undoubtedly changing. Tom Peters believes employers should change from offering new employees a career, to undertaking that the employee will be more employable at the end of their relationship. This in part is a consequence of the flattening of structures within organisations—there simply aren't the career opportunities that there used to be. It means that employees now have to take more responsibility for their own careers.

> It is not enough for companies to tear up the old unwritten contract with their workers, which promised security and automatic promotion in return for loyalty. Far better, with the demise of lifetime employment, to switch to the notion of lifetime employability. ...[Employers] will be rewarded too—not just with less anxious employees but with higher quality ones, as the best people queue to work for firms that offer not just the illusion of security, but an opportunity to stay employable.[1]

This implies shorter periods of employment and more employers in an employee's working lifetime. That prospect seems to have particular relevance to employees with fewer qualifications and less marketable skills.[2] Organisations themselves won't survive for as long and will change shape over time. Project teams have always existed inside organisations and they are now common outside as well, as bits of employers are drawn together for specific projects and then disbanded.

Implications for scheme design: It follows that employees won't belong to the same retirement saving scheme for long periods. This has implications for the design of employment-related retirement saving schemes:

Relevance of defined-benefit schemes: Defined-benefit schemes will face

---

[1]   *The Economist*, 16 March 1996.

[2]   Paul Gregg and Jonathan Wadsworth of the London School of Economics reported a 19% decline in the average years in a job for UK males (from 7.9 years in 1975 to 6.4 years in 1993) but a 10% increase for women over the same period, cited in *The Financial Times*, 29 April 1996. However almost all the rise in job turnover came from the under-25s and over-54s. The pattern in the US was more stable. According to Henry Farber, reported in *Business Week*, 15 April 1996, job duration has remained relatively unchanged since the early 1970s.

another obstacle to their continued relevance. The total compensation approach to paying people already means that employees want more say over where *their* money is invested. Empowerment means they will be less interested in having other people like employers and trustees say how and when they can get their money.

Staying with an employer for relatively short periods means that employees won't be interested in benefits that are worked out in relation to their pay near retirement. That may have been relevant in times when there was a reasonable prospect of getting there, but not anymore.

Vesting schedules: Employers will find it even more difficult than now to justify vesting schedules. These say to scheme members that they don't qualify for the most valuable of the benefits (at retirement) until they complete a minimum period of service or membership. The better (more expensive) schemes let members build up their entitlements to the retirement benefit, while the worst have what Americans colourfully call 'cliff vesting'. (You get nothing, or not very much, if you have done four years and eleven months' membership, but collect if you survive the extra month.)

There are two reasons for this kind of practice: first, the US regulations specify the maximum vesting period;[1] second, the longer the vesting period, the lower the cost of the scheme to the employer.

If the employer wants employees to have relatively short 'careers', vesting periods will have to go or at least be significantly reduced. Employers will be unable to justify different 'total compensations' for an employee's 'career' of four years by comparison with one of ten years.

Retained benefits: Defined-benefit schemes are not portable[2] and employers will be even less willing than now to retain benefits in their scheme for employees who may have left decades earlier. Apart from the design problems that long periods of deferral present for defined-benefit schemes,[3] there are the administration costs involved in keeping track of people.

Investment decisions: If the money 'belonged' to the employees in defined-contribution schemes, scheme trustees would find it increasingly difficult to prevent the owners from saying where their money should be invested. Different owners will have different risk preferences and someone (probably the employer) will have the job of explaining what those preferences might be and why employees might choose one over another.

Communicating the results of those investment decisions will also become more important than now.

Increase in Part-time, Temporary and Self Employment

A further pattern, that flows from the freeing-up of the nature of the

---

[1] There is also a years of age + membership test in the US.

[2] Without significant changes to the nature of the promise or deliberate cross subsidies.

[3] How should the benefit be revalued during the period of deferral? Had the employee remained in the scheme, that would usually be taken care of by pay increases up to the retirement date. In a number of developed countries, the regulators have books of rules to tell schemes what they allowed to do and what not.

employment relationship, will be an increase in the proportion of temporary[1] and part-time employees and also the self employed.[2] It's already happening and will increase because it makes economic sense. In New Zealand, 29 per cent of all filled jobs are part-time, an increase of 76 per cent over 18 years.[3]

For part-time employees, the growth will impose its own strains on the nurturing of Tier II. These changed patterns mean that families can expect more fluctuations in their incomes than used to be the case 30-40 years ago.[4] Job uncertainty and unexpected changes in incomes are the enemies of settled retirement saving plans.

However, part-time work can also help the retirement process—savers can use it to ease themselves from full-time work into full-time retirement.[5]

Self employment is now an important part of the work patterns of developed countries—David Blau estimated that 12 per cent of US men were self employed in 1982.[6] That number has almost certainly grown since then with the de-layering, re-engineering, out-sourcing and lay-offs that have characterised the last 15 years in the US.

An increasing number of self-employed both helps and hinders a government. It helps because those people probably have more choices about when they retire and may be able to lower their saving requirement by maintaining work until they can afford full-time retirement. It hinders by creating a challenge for governments to get to the self-employed in the information campaign—about the need to save and the ways that can happen.[7]

---

[1]   Temporary employees in the UK increased by 350,000, or 30.2% between 1990 and 1995 (data from the Central Statistical Office). Over the same period, total employment (including temporary employees) fell by 720,000, reported in *The Financial Times*, 1 February 1996. In the US, temporary and contract workers represent 10% of the workforce, Labor Department statistics reported in *The New York Times*, 18 August 1996.

[2]   The self employed are not really part of Tier II, though that will make them part of Tier III.

[3]   *Quarterly Employment Survey*, Statistics New Zealand, November 1995.

[4]   In the US, the Census Bureau reports that 54% of US workers 'experienced serious wage and salary fluctuation, up from 49% a decade earlier', reported in *The New York Times*, 18 August 1996.

[5]   In 1989 in the US, 44% of men aged 65+ in work in non-agricultural industries had chosen to work part-time (cited in *Passing the Torch*, Quinn, Burkhayser and Myers, W.E. Upjohn Institute, 1990—statistics from Employment and Earnings, January 1990). An extra 4% over age 65 had to work for economic reasons. The equivalent figures for women were 53% voluntary and 5% for economic reasons. The authors noted only a modest increase in all part-time work over the 1968-1989 period—up from 15% to 18% of all employees.

[6]   Cited in *Passing the Torch*.

[7]   In the US, the government faces a further challenge—the company that hires an independent contractor isn't responsible for Social Security contributions or unemployment taxes and doesn't have to provide health insurance, sick leave, holidays or other benefits. For the government, collecting amounts due will be more expensive and the absence of

Personal Financial Plans

The traditional regime tends to present the 'one-size-fits-all' solution to retirement benefit planning. That must change in the new environment. The only practical way for employers to give employees information and support is to offer tailored solutions to their individual needs. There is no reason why each employee couldn't have a personal financial plan based on the employee's own aspirations and financial status.

Computer-based modelling tools have the potential to change the face of the saving information business—I'll have more to say about this in chapter 9.

Implications for Advisers

These changes will also have far-reaching implications for the different types of advisers that inhabit the employers' financial services food chain. Actuaries, asset consultants, investment managers, custodians, benefit advisers, communication specialists, lawyers, accountants and trustees will all have to change their games in much the same way as policymakers when they face more knowledgeable and more demanding customers.

Throughout the developed world, the growing complexity of compensation, tax and regulatory requirements has given rise to an industry of advisers on these issues. If we see more individual understanding and responsibility by employees and shorter assignments with individual employers, it won't mean the loss of existing customers (employers will still need help), but it will mean that the nature of the services offered will change.

For example, if we don't have defined-benefit schemes, we won't need regular, expensive actuarial valuations. But we will need software that helps an employee figure out the weekly or monthly amounts that need to be put aside to fill a saving gap. Same skills; different ultimate users. Again, we won't need expensive and regular asset/liability modelling followed by expensive and detailed consulting advice on appropriate investment strategies for a large defined-benefit scheme. But we will need to help employees understand risk, volatility of returns and to hold their hands through the building of a portfolio that meshes with their existing financial assets and achieves their saving objectives. Same skills; different ultimate user.

We have to convince an employee to part with money that could be spent today on more immediate needs. This requires a different mind set from the professional communicator whose job, at the moment, is simply to show that employees get paid more if they join the subsidised scheme. Same skills; bigger challenge.

Each of the disciplines linked to the present large pools of capital associated with employer-sponsored schemes in the developed world will face similar challenges.

Large vs Small Employers

It's unrealistic to suppose that only large employers will be able to offer the more demanding total compensation approach to compensating and counselling their employees. With the costs of communication still falling in real terms, a small employer will be able to dial into a total compensation

---

employer-provided benefits could see the contractor falling back on the state's safety net in due course.

system run by a scheme administrator for a number of small employers. Such an administrator will assume some significance in the delivery channels between service suppliers and ultimate end-users (the employees). Just as with a stand-alone, tailor-made system, an individual employee/customer will have direct access to the 'wholesale' markets and could be taken through the decision process on a computer screen. The results of a counselling session will be communicated to suppliers, employee and payroll.

The scheme administrator could just as easily be a bank, life insurer, money manager or a department in an employee benefit adviser. The large firms of benefit advisers have, over the years, been shut out of the small end of the market because of their preference for delivering tailored (and, therefore, relatively expensive) advice to their employer clients. That kind of advice will be no longer required in a total compensation environment. The new challenge will be to create a way of delivering access to wholesale markets for the retail employee.

As a matter of practical necessity, most small employers already have a total compensation approach because they pay employees and aren't able (or aren't interested) to offer them the often dazzling array of fringe benefits that big employers with large support staffs can offer. The world I describe and the shift to total compensation by large employers will reduce the employee benefit gulf that presently separates the large from the small employer. Technology has the potential to eliminate it.

Tier II is Vital

This chapter acknowledges the importance of employers in the success of New Zealand's future strategy on Tier II. Such a strategy is more likely to be successful if citizens have the committed support of their employers.

The voluntary, neutral regime is now the prevailing treatment of Tier II retirement schemes in New Zealand. But employers need time to respond to the new environment and there are some signs that change is starting after the turmoil of the last 13 years or so.

But if we want a successful Tier II, governments will have to win the hearts and minds of employers as well as of voters. Of the two groups, voters generally are probably easier to satisfy. Employers are more sanguine—I don't see a major problem with the larger employers but it will be a major challenge to win over the smaller employers that employ most New Zealanders.

New Zealanders won't change their behaviour overnight—we've taken 60 years to get to where we are today[1] and, according to future projections of government expenditure, we have about 22 years to turn the ship around. If the government wants to use employers as a major provider of information it will take time to build trust, because the supply of this kind of information has not been a traditional role for employers in New Zealand. It will also take time to convince employees that they can make these decisions if they are empowered with the appropriate tools.

I am convinced that, if employees are provided with the tools and information to take charge of their own financial futures, they will respond appropriately.

---

[1]   Since the major reform of social security in 1938 that marked the real beginning of the welfare state.

9

The Information Age:
Linking Savers and Markets

Summary

Retirement saving issues are complex and require far-reaching, long-term decisions. However, international surveys show that many savers do not have an adequate understanding of the issues and do not make appropriate decisions. This could be due to a failure to understand financial relationships or because people are simply overwhelmed with the weight of information and changing conditions, and so defer their decisions.

Computer programmes, with the aid of a neutral 'facilitator', would allow the individual to enter personal information and gain an understanding of specific individual requirements for retirement saving and the consequences of different decisions and other variables.

Such programmes would allow the individual to develop a sound 'micro' retirement policy which, in turn, should lead to a sound 'macro' policy for the nation as a whole. So, governments should facilitate this educational process and then stand back and allow the individual saver to analyse the information and come to a decision.

In terms of the employer-employee relationship, the facilitation of information and education by the employer reinforces the 'total compensation' approach where the employee is empowered to make personal decisions about savings and the way in which each employee would prefer to receive compensation.

The availability of such software also allows for more extensive, rapid, updated and relevant information, all the more so with the use of CD-ROM and Internet technology.

****

Chapters 6, 7 and 8 suggested an overall structure for New Zealand's new retirement income system. The issues are complex whether viewed from the state's perspective or from that of employers or individuals, whether as employees or tax paying citizens.

However, the issues affect everyone in individual ways. About 80-90 per cent of citizens (in developed countries) will make it to an age when we will be seriously thinking about retirement. Saving for retirement means making some long-term plans and sticking to them over long periods. How do we go about it? Do governments and employers have a role in helping individuals to form and reach their goals?

The answer to these questions is 'yes' and this chapter aims to explain why.

How Did it Happen Before?

Workers in the past had a simple way of collecting information and deciding how to finance their retirement:

> ...they do their retirement planning by looking around. They look at their parents, siblings, and other acquaintances and discern how Social Security [the US Tier I benefit] treats people who are much like themselves. They look at their older co-workers and discern how their employer-sponsored plans treat people who are also much like themselves. They see these acquaintances move into retirement and observe how their standards of living change. They conclude that if they behave as their acquaintances who participate in the same kinds of retirement plans do, then they will be able to retire in a comparable lifestyle.[1]

That may have worked in the past when life was more straightforward, when the concept of career employment still tended to mean 'one employer', when most citizens thought that a demographic problem meant too many children and too few teachers, and when governments didn't face the cash constraints that are now forcing most of them to cut back public programmes.

This book suggests quite modest changes to the New Zealand retirement income system. However, in most other developed countries, much more revolutionary changes are needed, and planning by 'looking around' would be no use at all. Nothing in the present experience of retired people in those countries would give the individual anything to go on.

How Does it Look Now?

There are two ways of looking at present practice—one way is to ask employers or individuals what they think, the other is to see what people are actually doing.

In the first case, most surveys of what people think produce discouraging results. One after the other, they seem to show that savers don't understand the issues or do understand them but aren't behaving 'sensibly'—however we might define that. Some examples:

Rogers Casey (US)

Executives responsible for making decisions about retirement plans were asked how successful they thought their schemes would be in helping their employees save for retirement. Fewer than one third of respondents thought that employees would fund their retirements 'adequately'. They weren't joining the schemes, they weren't contributing enough, and they weren't allocating their savings to investment sectors that would get the best long-term returns.[2]

Employee Benefit Research Institute (US)

According to a Public Agenda report (sponsored by the EBRI)[3] only 34 per cent

---

[1]   Sylvester Schieber, 'The Sleeping Giant Awakens: US Retirement Policy in the 21st Century', *Compensation & Benefits Review*, special edition 1996.

[2]   *The Wall Street Journal*, 27 March 1996, the survey covered 520 employers with 2.6 million employees.

[3]   D. Bryant, and J. Sullivan reported in 'Promises to keep: how leaders and the public respond to savings and retirement', in 'The 401(k) Plan and the Retirement Planning Revolution' in *Compensation & Benefits Review*,

of Americans have even tried to work out how much they need to save for retirement.

Putnam Investments (US)

A survey of 1,000 adults found that asking people to work out how much they must save 'doesn't work because the numbers are too overwhelming and retirement seems too far away'.[1]

Merrill Lynch (US)

In the seventh annual survey of employee benefit managers of 400 companies, fewer than 20 per cent of respondents felt their employees were well prepared for retirement, despite 'the growing number of planning choices and more need for employee responsibility'.[2] Merrill Lynch also runs an annual review of what it calls the 'Merrill Lynch Baby Boom Index'. The fourth review (1996) confirms that Americans born between 1946 and 1964 need to triple their savings rate, using 'optimistic' public policy assumptions. The review found no evidence that the rate of saving by baby-boomers was accelerating as their households moved into their late forties.

MRL Research (NZ)

The New Zealand Retirement Commissioner commissioned a survey in 1995.[3] New Zealanders appeared to be much like Americans—38 per cent of the non-retired weren't making any financial provision for retirement. However, 85 per cent of the non-retired thought it was very or quite important for them to make provision and only 42 per cent thought their current level of provision at that time was adequate.

Flemings Investment (UK)[4]

A 1996 survey in the UK found that 49 per cent of people (excluding students) were set to receive a retirement income of less than 40 per cent of their expected pay near retirement. From the same report, 16 per cent could expect an 'ideal' retirement income (two-thirds of their final pay or more) while another 14 per cent could expect a 'comfortable' retirement of between half and two-thirds of final pay.[5]

---

special edition 1996.

[1] Reported in *The New York Times*, 25 February 1996.

[2] *Hoover News Alert Article*, 29 February 1996.

[3] 'Retirement saving: public awareness, attitudes and behavior', a survey of 1,000 New Zealanders of whom 250 were retired, June 1995.

[4] Commissioned by Fleming Investment Management Trust and reported in *The Financial Times*, 4 May 1996.

[5] A Barclays Life survey (again, in the UK) of 1,579 working and 945 retired adults found that 77% of people in work thought their retirement standard of living would be at least equal to (or better) than in their working lives. However, 70% of the retired participants thought their retirement planning was inadequate, reported by *The Financial Times*, 21 October 1996.

Perpetual Funds (Australia)[1]

Most respondents didn't think their existing retirement savings would be enough but doing something about it didn't seem a priority. The survey estimated there was a gap of $1,120 a year, on average, between what people actually saved and what they thought they should save. Though retirement planning wasn't on the agenda for the 30-50 age group, on average they wanted to retire at 57. It is no surprise that the average retirement age had gone up to 61 by the time respondents reached age 50.

All these figures present problems. For a start, it's no surprise that they tend to be paid for by a company involved in the financial services sector. Secondly, the raw numbers are usually misleading—it would be useful to know if those who are in relatively good shape tend to be older (children no longer at home and mortgage under control—and an awareness that it's time to pay some serious attention to retirement saving), and whether those who seemingly don't stand a chance are in the midst of family, career and nest building. However, if we do take these figures at face value, the question is: what is to be done with these impecunious people?

People know they should be saving more, just as they know they should eat better and less food and exercise more than they do. Asking them what they think is therefore unlikely to reveal much that is new. Government statistics can partly fill the void, but they are mostly about 'macro' issues (such as how much is invested in mutual funds, how much in banks, how money moves around the system). Also, where information tries to capture what these figures mean for citizens and their families, it tends to be 'snapshots' or slices through the population at frozen points in time.

On the other hand, finding out what people are actually doing as opposed to what they are thinking is much more difficult (and expensive). That's because the first step is to find out what each respondent's expectations are. For example, if a respondent had a mortgage-free home and was content to live on the Tier I benefit, there would be no need to save any more for retirement. Not saving would be a rational response.

Once respondents' aspirations have been identified, the next step is to look at their assets and liabilities, income and expenditure patterns, and try to work out whether they have a reasonable chance of achieving their expectations.

Fletcher Challenge of New Zealand[2] tried such a survey in 1989. Fletcher Challenge identified a randomly selected 10 per cent of its then 15,000 New Zealand-based workforce. 54 per cent of them chose to participate. They were asked to complete a detailed questionnaire including their assets and liabilities, retirement saving plans, family situation and other profiling information, and they were asked what they thought about a number of propositions. The whole exercise was analysed by an independent research firm so that the information remained confidential.

---

[1]   The first of a series of benchmark surveys of savings behaviour and retirement planning by Australians, reported in *The Australian Financial Review*, 13 December 1995.

[2]   From the period 1988 to 1997 I was the Employee Benefits Director for Fletcher Challenge (New Zealand's largest employer).

We estimated how much the respondents would actually receive when they retired if they kept doing what they were doing. It was evident that most were fairly reliant on the Tier I benefit for their retirement income, though they didn't seem overly concerned about retirement. Table 15 shows what they thought were the most important reasons to save:

Table 15

Fletcher Challenge Employee Benefit Survey

Most important reason to save	All respondents	Those aged 26-35	Those aged 55+
Buying/improving a home, including paying off mortgage	48%	66%	31%
Providing a retirement income	17%	5%	45%
A 'security cushion' for expenses	11%	8%	11%
To pay for a special purchase	10%	8%	-

Source: Fletcher Challenge Ltd., 1989.

So, the view that financial saving for retirement is important doesn't seem to fit with what people think, even when retirement is bearing down on them. Most people (48 per cent on average in the Fletcher Challenge survey) thought buying and paying off the home was the most important reason to save. That's a major contribution to retirement saving but it might upset some who think shares and bonds are more important.

If we keep asking people what they think and then sensationalise the results, we run the risk of turning people off and making the whole subject seem just too daunting. A 1995 Australian survey[1] illustrates my point. Respondents were asked how much they thought they needed to have saved up by the time they retired to have 'an income for the rest of your life'. The answer was an average of a lump sum of $475,000, enough to provide an income of about 140 per cent of the national average wage.[2] For the profile of respondents covered by the survey, that was far too much. So, given the ambitious target they had set themselves, what were they doing about getting that amount saved? The answer was not much more than what was revealed in the American surveys already described.

Is this irrational behaviour? There are two possible explanations—the first is that people simply don't understand the relationship between capital and income and find it difficult to visualise what their retirement needs might be and how they might achieve those.

The second, and more likely, answer is the 'possum in the headlights' syndrome. People understand that they should be saving more (they mightn't

---

[1]   Carried out by ASSIRT and reported in *The Australian Financial Review*, 29 April 1996.

[2]   The surveyor assumed a 7% interest rate with no capital withdrawn and with no protection of the income against inflation. For a retiree, that's an unrealistic basis. However, a more realistic lifetime, inflation-indexed annuity (that depleted the capital over the retiree's lifetime) would still leave the retiree with a pension of 138% of the national average wage.

understand exactly how much, so there is an element of the first answer in the second). However saving is difficult for a lot of reasons, including constant changes in public policy, uncertain investment returns, deferring today's consumption and then deciding when and how to save.[1] Thus, in a way, it's easier to stay on the road, frozen to the spot by the headlights of impending retirement and be eventually mown down by financial reality when it all actually happens. It's just easier not to think about difficult things even when it's in our own (and no-one else's) best interests that we should do so.

The Importance of Information

I've already suggested that employees like getting financial information from their employers—they prefer to get it that way because the employer's information tends to encourage, not discourage, saving and investment. In the 1995 Towers Perrin survey, three-quarters of respondents said the information they got from their employers on retirement planning was either very helpful (26 per cent) or somewhat helpful (50 per cent).[2] Participation in employer-sponsored saving schemes tends to be associated with employers that help out with information and guidance. As many as 32 per cent of all respondents said they didn't belong to a plan because they couldn't afford to save. But where there was a 'great deal of employer assistance' with information, only 19 per cent of respondents said they couldn't afford to save. So, employer help with information seems to convince employees that they can find some money to save if they look hard enough.

Let's look at a typical example: a 40-something employee whose children are starting to leave home; whose mortgage is largely under control and who belongs to an employment-related saving scheme and contributing the minimum amount needed to belong. This individual (a male) has no idea when he wants to retire, whether he might work after his 'career' is over, how much he'll need in order to have a reasonable standard of living, how long he'll need that for and how to take account of the likelihood that his wife will survive him. He has no idea how much the state might pay but has a feeling that, if social 'security' were still there when he retired, it wouldn't be as much as it is today and wouldn't be enough.

Sound familiar? So, where will he go for help?

The Fletcher Challenge Model

Let me answer this by explaining what happens to an employee of Fletcher Challenge in New Zealand, because I think it provides a model for how countries and companies can bring the 'big picture' down to the level of the individual saver. We should all be turning 'macro' information into relevant, understandable, 'micro' hand-holding or guidance.

---

[1] The calls for tax incentives by some in New Zealand (and the calls for more generous incentives in other countries) again give savers the excuse to defer a decision—'we'll wait and see what the government might do'.

[2] Though the Merrill Lynch survey (cited earlier) showed that only about 40% of employers provide financial planning services to employees, so perhaps some of the Towers Perrin respondents had a lower expectation of what information was very or somewhat helpful.

Before we look at the saving decision, I should explain that Fletcher Challenge is heading down the 'total compensation' path. The last chapter explained that compensation philosophy but, in summary, it means that the employer sets the total price that it is prepared to pay to get a job done and then says to the employee that it is indifferent to how that price is delivered—all benefits, all cash or a mixture of cash and benefits. It's for the individual employees to decide; based on what they think is important for their families; depending on where they are in their financial lives and where they want to be by the time they get to retirement. The employer can't know those things and the employees don't want it to know. It's their personal business.

Let's return to our model (male) employee, who has now joined Fletcher Challenge. He likes the freedom to choose but needs support to make decisions. He's finding it difficult to get unbiased advice on 'appropriate' decisions in the saving and insurance areas. He's bombarded with propaganda from self-interested suppliers in the financial services sector.

The employer has stepped into the gap. Within a week or so of joining the company, the employee can take part in a personal financial planning programme. This will let him carry out a needs analysis on his saving and insurance needs.

He's not used to making these decisions. In his old job, he didn't even think about them—all he had to do was join the schemes his employer offered and hope it knew what it was doing. However, he's comforted by the fact that he'll find out about these things in a non-threatening environment (success won't be measured by whether a sale occurs). The employer says he'll be able to have a look at these things with his wife and that there'll be constant support for the decisions he makes.

The first step in the process is to go to a presentation session that introduces the employee to the programme. It also tells him what information he needs to bring to the second stage—a personal session with a trained facilitator who's paid by the employer but who isn't on the regular staff, so the employee needn't worry about sharing personal information. He makes an appointment with the facilitator for his wife and himself.

He soon finds out that at the heart of his employer's financial planning programme is a software programme that Fletcher Challenge has developed and is giving to employees for nothing. The first time they see it is with the facilitator who helps them run the software by inputting all their own information and then seeing what their retirement will look like if they keep doing the things they are doing. The software covers retirement and other saving needs as well as life and disability insurance needs.

The retirement module suggests that the couple first works out how much they want to live on in retirement, even though that's nearly 20 years away. They build themselves a retirement spending budget—by then, they'll have the mortgage paid off but will want to travel overseas every 2-3 years. All that is put into the budget which gives information in today's money and tells the couple they will need $45,000 a year in today's money to give them the retirement they want. That's the target their saving plan will have to aim for over the next 20 years.

Now for the scary part—piece by piece, they put in all the information about themselves and their financial lives—assets, liabilities and anything that might be relevant to the retirement saving issue: part-time work in retirement, how long and how much, any future inheritances, cash needs at retirement, and so on. The couple puts the information in themselves—the facilitator is there to get them going, answer questions, encourage them to key in the information themselves, and make sure they are getting the messages the software delivers.

Once they've answered all the questions, the computer processes the information and starts giving them some answers. They get a view of what the state will deliver them at Tier I (the employee's wife's benefit will start two years after his), how much their current saving plans will deliver, and then, what the saving gap might be in after-tax, real dollars and how much they need to put aside each month for the next 20 years to fill that gap.

Let's say the answer for this couple is $650 a month, which is a bit more than they expected. The software then paints a picture of what their retirement will look like—all in real terms and right through to the time the employee is expected to die, based on average statistics, and then how long his wife will have to depend on their savings after he dies.

Then they see how sensitive the whole calculation is to the financial guesses on which it is based—the facilitator explains that their expected retirement income is worked out on the basis that it increases in line with inflation. Changing the inflation guess from two per cent to four per cent makes a big difference to the answer—the $650 becomes $920 a month. They can see that if four per cent became the long-term inflation rate and there weren't compensating adjustments to their pay and the rate of return on their savings, they would have to lower their retirement sights and give up some of the things they wanted to do. They can see this even though the retirement date is 20 years away.

Then the facilitation moves through the possibility that the employee might die tomorrow or might become disabled and be unable to work. At the end of each section, there is a printed summary showing the family's financial position if they kept doing the things they are doing and showing them the things they can do to achieve the goals they have set themselves. There is no pressure from the facilitator—she just makes sure they understood the messages and, at the end of the session, gives them her business card so that they can get in touch with her if they still have any questions. The session takes about two hours but, at the end of it, they feel confident that they would be able to install the software on their home computer and run it for any updates to their personal or financial position.

Why Should the Employer Do This?

With the right sort of support and with a commitment from an employer to deliver this in a non-threatening way to the employee and the employee's family, I think that a sound retirement income policy for the country as a whole (as explained in chapters 6 to 8) can become a sound policy for an individual as well. The successful 'macro' will become a successful 'micro' policy.

Why Fletcher Challenge Did It

The personal financial planning programme, among other things, highlights for employees the consequences of their decisions at an early stage. The programme will continue to remind employees of those consequences so that the actual amount of retirement income won't be a surprise when retirement age is reached. It's designed to show employees what their financial futures would look like if they keep doing the things they are doing.

What mattered to Fletcher Challenge, initially, was its commitment to 'total compensation' as a way of paying its employees. That was a change in the way things have been done in New Zealand but, because the new policy had the potential to cost the company more than the traditional 'pay + benefits method' (for the reasons explained in chapter 8), Fletcher Challenge wanted to make sure that it didn't pay twice—once in the 'total compensation' and then again at the end of an employee's career, when the economic cost of keeping someone on after the optimal retirement age was more than the cost of paying a retirement allowance to ease the person out of employment. All this meant that Fletcher Challenge wanted its employees to make decisions about their pay that suited their circumstances best. But it also wanted them to see, in ways that were relevant to them, what would happen if they kept doing the things they were doing.

'Total compensation' means a shift in decision-making responsibility but it doesn't mean the withdrawal of Fletcher Challenge from involvement in employee-benefit schemes. At the same time, part of the new programme saw the introduction of three unsubsidised schemes, for saving, life insurance and disability insurance.

Employers, like governments, should get out of the bribery business and let people make their own, unsubsidised decisions about saving for retirement. I'm very much in support of 'total compensation' as a policy. However, 'total compensation' is unlikely to be a successful long-term strategy unless the employer provides the kind of support to employees that is offered by the Fletcher Challenge process.[1] There's a real risk that, despite all the written warnings, the employer will end up paying twice. The personal financial planning programme is a kind of insurance policy against employees not responding appropriately to the new flexibility. There will be no surprises: if the employee arrived at retirement and things turned out much as expected, the employee alone would be solely responsible if there weren't as much retirement income as would have been preferred.

Other Education Objectives

The kind of personal financial planning process outlined above can have other objectives as well.

Testing Tier I

Most employees, especially the younger ones, will say that Tier I benefits won't be there when they get to retirement age. Even if an employee thought otherwise, trying to work out what those benefits might be isn't easy, especially in countries like the US and the UK where the rules are so complicated.

---

[1]   Research from the US supports this—the Employee Benefit Research Institute has found that employees respond to education efforts by their employer, reported by *Dow Jones News*, 27 February 1996. 40% of employees who attend a seminar on retirement planning increase their pension contributions and 46% reallocate their assets into different sectors.

Tier I benefits may reduce in years to come (though not, I suggest, my recommended Tier I scheme for New Zealand), either by postponing the age of entitlement or by reducing their real value. Most employees are probably not acting on their beliefs though the time will come when they will have to face up to their expectations. However, if they did indeed base their decisions on a scenario of no Tier I benefit, they would save too much.

Employees need to be able to test their opinions about the future of Tier I. The issue should be to decide what's realistic and it's in the interests of employers that employees arrive at 'sensible' conclusions based on provision and analysis of appropriate information.

Buying Services

Computers and the information they process can help employers help employees find the answers to their individual situations. They can let employees design their own mix of benefits and direct pay on a computer screen, taking account of what the state might deliver at Tier I. The employee will decide whether to buy services from the employer's plans (if there were any) or to take cash. Decisions can be based on information delivered from an 'expert system'[1] that lets employees work out for themselves how much they need to save for retirement and where that money should be placed.

It also lets them see what changes to make to their financial arrangements if their circumstances changed—as they will over the life of their retirement saving programme. They can simply go back into the software when the event occurs (rather than wait until they receive the next annual advice) make the changes and play with the suggested outcomes.

General Communication

Software is very likely to overtake print-based services as a means of communication. Scheme booklets and newsletters, advice and reports will still be needed, probably mainly to satisfy regulatory requirements. However, their significance will reduce. The power of on-line communication will supersede the slower, more expensive and relatively unread print medium. Employees will be able to go straight to areas of particular interest and avoid others of no or little interest.

Communication is about delivering information—computers will significantly enhance the communicator's power and the array of information delivered will expand. If the information source already knew the saver and knew what the saver was doing, computers could focus the communication in ways that print communication can't.

Risk Assessment

Asset services, which are currently seen as a separate service delivered by investment strategists to wholesale users of information for large pools of capital, will merge into communication as a discipline. Trustees will no longer

---

[1]   So called because the rules used by the software are the rules that an expert would use if the expert, rather than the computer, were sitting in front of the user. It's like having the expert inside the computer—everything the expert knows is incorporated in software that doesn't need an expert to use it.

be interested in the investment performance of their scheme's total assets (by comparison with other equivalent schemes) nor in their risk profile nor investment strategy unless they wish to deliver defined benefits as part of the benefit menu (defined-benefit accruals during contributory membership or annuities in retirement).

The people who are now interested in this are the employees. They will be able to assess on the screen their own risk profile for investing their savings and the risk/reward relationship.[1] Investment performance statistics can be delivered directly to them and used to explain the 'efficient frontier'.[2] Employees will be empowered to understand issues through access to information which presently needs an 'expert' to translate. The system will become the expert and the customer will be driving the process, not the expert as is the case now.

The impact on asset allocation shows the effect of giving employees at least some information—called 'participant advisory services' in the US. Table 16 shows what has happened so far:

Table 16
Impact of Member Advisory Services on 401(k) Asset Allocations: US

Allocations	National average[1] (%)	Average with advisory services[2] (%)
Equities	19	51
Bonds	7	9
Balanced portfolio	14	5
Money market, GIC[3]	32	15
Employer's own shares	23	18
Other	5	2

Source: From 'The DOL 401(k) Guidelines: How Employers Can Separate "Information" from "Advice"', Compensation & Benefits Review, special edition, 1996.

Notes:
1 source: Access Research
2 source: Smith Barney plans
3 'guaranteed investment contracts' that offer protection on the capital invested at some cost by way of a lower long-term return.

Table 16 shows that, once employees are shown how to invest rather than how to save, they respond by giving a longer 'look' to their portfolios.

---

[1]   If there is any doubt about the need for that kind of information, consider this: according to the Towers Perrin survey, three quarters of respondents felt very comfortable or somewhat comfortable about making savings plan investment decisions (83% of men vs 67% of women). However, 39% of participants in 401(k) plans (that usually offer choice) didn't know where their savings were invested, 17% of participants didn't know whether buying company shares or 'guaranteed' investments would produce higher returns over 20 years, half the remaining respondents thought that guaranteed investments would perform better (35%) or the same (15%) as shares, and 32% of participants thought there was no risk associated with investment in bonds.

[2]   At which, according to Harry Markowitz (the developer of the efficient portfolio theory), the optimal return in a portfolio for a given level of overall risk (measured in terms of the volatility of returns) occurs.

Regulatory Changes

Information on changes to tax or regulatory structures can be delivered electronically and their implications to an employee's own circumstances can be available instantly. Providing information will become a bulk or wholesale business—the successful providers will be at the hubs of the wheels which are the various employers' 'total compensation' programmes. The users of that information will be the scheme's beneficiaries and not their administrators, as is the case now.

Financial Education for Employees

Once employees get used to the idea of making these kinds of decisions for themselves, there will be another advantage for the employer. Many of the issues faced by employees in their own financial lives have an echo in the financial lives of their employer. Knowledge about concepts of present and future value, budgeting, the impact of financial markets on the cost of money and on the value of financial assets, risk protection and the effect of inflation on financial decisions is all information that will help employees plan their financial futures. It will also help employees understand the pressures that mould the employer's future and determine its success (and, in fact, whether the employee will have a job in the future).

Acquiring these skills will also help employees understand the ebbs and flows of business life: that part-time work for a number of employers might not be so frightening, that redundancy is part of business life and can be the start of a new and brighter one, that planning for resignation need not be intimidating, and that all this should be part of an employee's career plan.

Employees should be in control of their financial lives and not controlled by them. That control can then extend into the pre-retirement period when employees have to start thinking about how they will run their financial lives once the regular salary or wages stop. By then, they will know a lot more about financial markets and will hopefully see the virtues of risk-taking and budgeting.

Change in the Employer-employee Relationship

All this is part of a new development in the future relationships between employers and employees. Charles Handy[1] believes that employers can't offer stability to employees and yet the employer's most valuable asset is its employees—a dichotomy he sees as being resolved through a commitment by employers to training and a change in the nature of company ownership. All that reduces the relevance of the corporate pension scheme which he sees as dying within the next decade.

I don't believe that the corporate pension scheme will die but its shape will be revolutionised through education, empowerment and choice.

Some employers, particularly in the US, would be concerned about the potential legal liabilities that might result from the involvement to such an extent in the financial lives of their employees. However, the process of converting an employee's own data into an amount that will fill the 'gap'

---

[1]   Author of, among other books, *The Age of Unreason, The Age of Paradox.*

between their chosen objectives and what they now have in place is actually quite mechanical. The 'art' is in the economic guesses on which the processes are founded. If the employee could make those guesses and was able to see their implications, that would actually remove the employer from the process. It's about empowering employees and reducing the importance of 'experts'—or, at least, cutting through the arcane processes typically used at present.

Current thought in the US (the most developed world market in this area) is that the more individualised the information becomes, the more it looks like advice and the less it looks like information. I disagree with this. If we went down the route of personal empowerment, the only issue then becomes what guesses are embedded in the software that either we don't tell the user about or don't allow the user to modify or understand.

The rules that govern employer-sponsored pension schemes around the developed world are complex. That makes the process remote and engenders suspicion in consumers. Perhaps that's one of the reasons why employees irrationally turn down the opportunity of increasing their overall compensation by joining a subsidised scheme. The kind of personal financial planning process I have described can cut through the regulatory complexity—users won't have to understand the rules, only how those rules might affect their objectives.

There is one impact on employers that mustn't be ignored: under a voluntary, subsidised retirement saving scheme, when employees are educated on the need to save for retirement and the amounts of money they need to have by the time they retire, it is most likely that more employees will join the scheme. Not only will the employer be spending money on the advisory services but also their pension costs would go up.

Future Developments in Information Provision

The future potential for computer-based communication of personal financial planning processes is substantial. Subsequent versions of the software might include CD-ROM-based kiosks that, for new employees, could replace the group-based presentation style with a seminar-style tutorial. Employees can then pick the topics of greatest interest to them rather than go through the whole programme. This could, over time, replace the facilitation process currently used by Fletcher Challenge and so reduce the cost of introducing personal financial planning to employees.

These CD-ROM kiosks could then be linked to the employer's central administration system to give employees an interactive service. The software could initiate responses to events like the birth of a child, the death of a spouse or divorce/separation, better (or worse) than expected investment performance, children reaching an assumed age of independence, and so on.

Such a service could encourage employees to leave their personal details and aspirations on the central administration system (something that doesn't happen at the moment with the present Fletcher Challenge programme). That central administration system could then be linked to each employer's payroll processes. Employees could make their saving and insurance decisions on screen. The system would first check them on-line for compliance with the schemes' rules and then communicate the implications of any changes to the employer's payroll. Decisions could be implemented automatically and confirmed to the employee.

While that level of service sounds ambitious, there will be significant savings for Fletcher Challenge in the costs of administering a five-plan (saving, life, disability, medical and general insurance), multi-employer, infinitely flexible, paper-based system with, say, 12,000 members (employees and partners) being paid through about 100 different payrolls, all making and changing decisions on a regular basis.

Consideration should also be given to the Internet.

There are clear advantages in making the whole business of information processing, 'hand-holding' and regular advice available on the Net. At least initially, this should be seen as just another way of distributing power to the consumer. The software, or the parts of it that are of interest, could be downloaded to the saver's own computer with decisions flowing back the other way. The chosen suppliers of financial services could report back on progress, all without the usual piles of unread paper that accompany manual systems. Money transfers don't yet seem to be secure on the Net and, until that happens, the Net would be swapping only information and decisions. However, it's not too difficult to imagine the information system's completing the loop by issuing an instruction to the saver's bank (or the money manager's bank) to implement a decision. No money need actually flow through the Net; until that were secure, it would continue to pass down the usual banking networks.

Keeping software up to date would be easy in this environment because the user would download the required programmes only when they were needed. That means only one version of all the latest investment information, product details, tax rates and economic statistics. They would all be up to the minute and kept that way.

Based on the experience of Fletcher Challenge with its personal financial planning programme, I don't see the Net putting real people out of business for a while, but I do expect that to happen in due course. People think personal financial planning *is* a great idea but it's still a task they'll put off—a bit like going to the dentist—until, eventually, it simply can't be ignored. And then there are those millions of households or employees who don't have access to a computer and who even feel threatened by the business pages of a daily newspaper. This majority of our citizens should at least first be introduced to the principles of self-help in the non-threatening environment of their workplace and with a real person alongside, before thinking about letting them loose on the Net.

Even for non-employees, there will still be a need for the services of a facilitator, like one of the Fletcher Challenge variety; the role will be the same: to make sure the individual enters the correct information into the computer; to ensure that the messages that come back to the individual are understood; and, finally, that the choices are understood. For example, the current cost of a Fletcher Challenge facilitator is only $32 an hour. The facilitator will not be threatening—as there is no sale involved—and the cost will be low.

A Realistic Future?

The Chairman of Bankers Trust, Charles Sanford, predicts the empowerment of individual savers at the expense of the traditional banks, planners and other financial intermediaries (like actuaries, lawyers and accountants).[1] He thinks that computer programmes will sort useful from useless information and will deliver it straight to the person who really matters—the saver. The costs of this more personal electronic attention will be substantially less (despite its tailored nature) than the salesforce-driven distribution system that tends to characterise the retirement saving industry in most developed countries; and it will be a lot less than the main-street money shops of the traditional banks.[2]

In due course, savers won't need to understand how the whole electronic network works; they won't need to know, for example, whether they're dealing with an investment bank or a commercial bank—they'll have the equivalent of financial 'private eyes'[3] looking out for and after their individual interests, reporting back to them when there is a decision to be made and guiding them through that decision.

At present, as savers, we face a real danger of information overload—there's so much out there that might be relevant to our needs that we need the help that tailored technology can give us. Personalised software will act as a filter and could even be sensitive to users' difficulties in understanding what they're being told. That could call up a simpler explanation of the issue or could go back and start again.

That should be the preferred future scenario. Governments should get out of the bribery business and into opening up the information channels. We've seen only a fraction of what computers will do to our industry. They will pierce the veil and put money managers, wherever they are based, directly in touch with savers. Governments should facilitate that process—open up the regulatory channels and then step back. They should then stand on the sideline, acting as touch judges, not mixing it with the players on the now level playing field as referees. All this is in the best interests of today's and tomorrow's governments (and their taxpayers).

---

[1]   *The Economist*, 26 March 1994.

[2]   Even normal banking transactions are being transformed by electronic processing—an over-the-counter transaction in Australia costs about $1.97, while its electronic equivalent costs only $0.16. (David Amdal in *Business Review Weekly*, 29 April 1996.) The same kind of change can be expected in the costs of doing retirement saving business.

[3]   The computer industry's buzz word for this is an 'agent'. It's software that helps people and acts on their behalf after the user tells it the parameters it has to work under.

10

What Do We Do Now?

Summary

There are important structural problems faced by developed (and developing) countries in implementing a logical, consistent, affordable and sustainable retirement income system. These can be summarised as one or more of the following:

- *a tax-favoured retirement saving industry*
- *unrealistically high state provision*
- *excessive government regulation*
- *compulsory private savings for retirement.*

A suggested strategy for change is proposed and recommendations are made for employers and the state, using examples of countries which exhibit different aspects of the main structures used around the world. The countries examined are the US, UK, France, Australia, Germany and Chile. The final question posed is: can compulsion ever be justified as the solution to a country's retirement income policy problems? The answer is—only as a last resort. Change of some sort will be inevitable for all developed countries, but the most important first objective is to achieve consensus on what is required.

****

I can hear you thinking: the themes of this book are all very consistent and the proposals may even be logical; but[1] we have a particular problem in our country that makes these proposals impracticable.

Let me predict some of those problems:

- People wouldn't understand or accept them—they'll think something's being taken away from them, even if it weren't.
- We've paid our taxes (or 'contributions') and we're entitled to those benefits.
- We've done our bit for the country—you touch our pension at your electoral peril.
- Pensions are the original political football—the other side(s) will never go along with change even if they privately agree that it might be a good thing.
- The unions would never agree with the changes.
- We can't afford them.
- We don't trust so-called experts—we've seen them all before.
- We don't trust politicians—they'll make a deal behind closed doors that suits them but not us.

---

[1] It's a rule of interpretation that a reader should ignore everything in front of a 'but'.

Sound familiar? I thought they might, because the ways in which the existing structures in developed countries have the potential to block reform have a familiar ring to them, no matter what language they're said in.

This chapter takes some of the structural changes that have come out of the last few chapters and suggests a framework within which the debate in any developed country might kick off.

Strategy for Change

When an employer faces a complex employee benefit issue with many existing arrangements, it should adopt the following strategy for change:

Assume no Existing Schemes

The employer assumes it's starting a 'greenfields' operation with no employee benefit history. The employer then needs to decide what its philosophy should be, what it wants to achieve, and how it wants to express its objectives, starting with a clean sheet.

Review Existing Arrangements

Next the employer should look at its existing schemes so it can understand their objectives and existing members' expectations.

Transitional Provisions

Once the employer has decided where it wants to go, it's relatively straightforward to resolve how to reach the agreed future objectives, even if that takes some time.

The State's Strategy

The government should adopt a similar strategy when reviewing its retirement income system. Leaving aside current programmes and where we are at present, it should lead a debate towards consensus on where we *should* be. Having reached that consensus it should next direct the debate towards existing expectations and current structural inadequacies. The focus of that second debate should be on moving from where we are to where we all agree we should be.

We shouldn't be afraid of compromising our ideals in that second, transitional stage; nor should we be concerned if the new structure takes 50-60 years to reach full maturity, as long as the country concerned has got that amount of time. If the agreed future basis applied in full only to new taxpayers, that could be a satisfactory outcome.

Key Strategic Objectives

The main structural problems developed countries face in implementing a logical, consistent, affordable and therefore sustainable retirement income system can be summarised as one or more of the following (in approximate order of importance from the perspective of blocking change):

- a tax-favoured retirement saving industry
- unrealistically high state provision that tends to crowd out private provision (not just financial savings)

- excessive government regulation, often a consequence of tax incentives and/or compulsion
- compulsory private savings for retirement.

Some countries face all four problems.

I'm leaving out of this analysis the behavioural roadblocks discussed already in chapters 3 and 7. These include:

- a lack of believable information on what's actually happening
- a politicised environment that makes long-range policy formation difficult (if not impossible)
- a lack of agreed objectives
- no proper government accounts
- no commitment to keep inflation down, and
- no short term possibility of consensus among the people who matter.

I've already suggested some strategies that might help eliminate these. Those strategies, along with the education and information campaign I've also outlined, are given elements of the programme I think each country should now embark on.

To demonstrate what my suggested framework would mean in practice, I've chosen six countries and summarised what their retirement income systems could look like if they accepted my recommendations. The countries I've chosen show different aspects of the main types of structures used around the developed world.

The US—an extensive, contributory, unfunded Tier I, with complex tax incentives and regulatory requirements both for Tier II and the favoured part of Tier III.

The UK—the US structure with the added complexities of a Tier II state scheme and the need to harmonise its financial structures with EU requirements.

France—a contributory, unfunded Tier I coupled with a huge, unfunded Tier II and relatively low levels of private provision at Tiers II and III.

Australia—something of everything, including an increasingly complex, compulsory, funded, tax-favoured, (misunderstood) Tier II.

Germany—an unfunded Tier I and largely unfunded private Tier II arrangements.

Chile—an unfunded Tier I underpins a private, compulsory, funded, tax-favoured Tier II.

United States

Key Features of the Current Regime

The US has a largely tax-free,[1] contributory, unfunded state scheme at Tier I that relates its pension, in part, to the contributor's pay and contribution record and has a survivor's pension attached. Curiously, state and local government employees aren't included in the system. The Tier I pension is paid regardless of other income, though, at higher levels of other income, it

---

[1]   By weight of dollars paid to beneficiaries.

becomes partly taxed. The state pension age was 65 but is now rising to 67. Total tax for the Tier I benefit is 12.4 per cent of covered pay that, for individuals, comes out of after-tax income. The benefits represent 20 per cent of Federal expenditure. The Federal budget deficit is 0.4 per cent of GDP, the lowest in real terms since 1974.

An extensive, complex, tax-subsidised, private savings environment, operating through a variety of structures and aimed at employees and individual savers, produces taxed supplementary benefits at Tiers II and III.

Baby-boomers are the largest segment of the population, with almost 50 per cent more 30-50 year-olds, than 10-30 year olds and twice as many boomers as 50-70 year olds.[1]

Recommendations

Tier I

The present trust fund that nominally separates the 'Social Security' Tier I scheme from the government's general accounts should be dissolved. The current assets that are only government bonds should be wiped both as an 'asset' of the trust fund and a 'liability' of the government.[2] All separate contributions to Social Security (shared equally between employers and employees) should stop and the required amounts should be merged into the Federal income tax rates. Because all citizens pay Federal tax, this also means that the Tier I equivalents for state and local government employees will also disappear.

From, say, 1999, there will be only one budget deficit, not two, as is currently the case.[3] This means the contribution-based system of building up benefits will go and be replaced by a benefit that looks a lot like the Tier I

---

[1]   According to the Congressional Budget Office, reported in *The Financial Times*, 3 June 1996, the budget deficit will rise to between 26% and 37% of GDP by 2030 with Federal debt at 300-400% of GDP caused mainly by the promises implicit in existing entitlement programmes for the elderly. That assumes no increases in taxes or Social Security contributions. Increasing the Federal tax burden by 40% (from 20% to 28% of GDP) would avoid the debt blow-out.

[2]   A government bond is a promise by today's taxpayers to pay interest on a loan and by tomorrow's taxpayers to repay the loan. A promise to pay a pension is of a similar character with respect to the capital element. Also, the people to whom the US government is promising to repay the bond (the beneficiaries of the Social Security 'Fund') are similar to the body of people who will have to repay it (tomorrow's taxpayers). So, cancelling the bonds won't save any money (apart from some transaction costs) but simply converts a double payment (interest from general revenues to the Trustees then a pension from the Trustees to the pensioner) into a single payment. The change won't improve the government's balance sheet either—the liability will now be contingent rather than actual, but it will still be a liability.

[3]   Because Social Security contributions are more than the current benefit outgo, US governments over the last few years have included the excess when they are trying to make today's budget overspending seem less than it actually is.

state scheme I recommended in chapter 6.[1] The new benefit will be taxed as ordinary income and should reduce if the pensioner earns other taxable income above a relatively modest threshold. The benefit design details will need to be worked out in a similar way to the process described in chapter 6.

All benefits will now come from the government's general revenues, but this shouldn't stop the government (rather than the Trustees of the Social Security Fund, as now) from carrying out regular actuarial valuations of the its pension liabilities (explained in chapter 6).

Current entitlements should be preserved by the number of quarters of coverage earned up to the date of change. These will eventually be applied to the contributor's career-average, revalued earnings at retirement, as now. The contingent spouse's entitlement will continue to apply in respect of the protected entitlements. There won't be an equivalent entitlement in the new Tier I because of its focus on the individual pensioner's financial position and its disconnection from work-related entitlements.

There will be a strong case to introduce the new Tier I benefit for everyone, including the currently retired (to meet the 'prevent poverty, plus a margin' objective). If you didn't introduce it now, you would be failing on your objectives for at least part of the presently retired population, because the current state benefit is below the suggested target, especially taking account of the contribution record requirements.

If that happened, the gross amount of the new Social Security benefit should be reduced by the full amount of the current scheme's benefit[2] and the present income-tested supplement (the Supplementary Security Income) would disappear. Over time, because the present benefit is linked to prices and the new one to wages, the old pension will gradually disappear. The exception will be those whose other income means that the income-test free, largely tax-free, (but possibly smaller) Social Security pension will produce a higher benefit.

Where benefits are built up by identified contributions (as in the US), transition arrangements become necessarily complex. The income test will be particularly difficult politically, and so existing beneficiaries should be shielded from that unless their current benefit is less than the new. Based on our experience in New Zealand with the introduction of an income test for existing pensioners, a lot of political angst and electoral heat can be avoided with this transitional protection.

When fiscal circumstances demand change, transitions and transition periods should be as short as possible so that the objectives of the change process can be reached within, say, two to three electoral cycles. The design should allow a reasonable adjustment period, not insulate people from

---

[1]   35% of a figure that is accepted as a national average wage for a single person and 55% for a married couple (if that level 'prevented poverty plus a margin') indexed to that wage, payable after 10 years' residence to all citizens from an age that corresponds with the community's idea of an appropriate retirement age—say, age 70 for both men and women.

[2]   There shouldn't be any income test 'free zone' for the present benefit which would be topped up to the new level. The amount that's left should be income-tested against other income (with the agreed 'free zone' in respect of that other income) and the remainder would be taxed as ordinary income. The tax status of the current benefit should stay as it is.

required change. In the US, current Social Security benefit payments will overtake expected contribution levels by 2020, so there will be about 20 years[1] before something has to give.

My suggestions will eventually simplify the administration of the current scheme (though not in the short term). Once the new arrangements are in place, contributors will understand their benefits instead of, as now, being invited to telephone their local Social Security office to get a benefit estimate.

Tiers II and III

The present EET tax treatment of retirement savings should be replaced by TTE[2] within, say, two years of the decision to change. Let's say that date is 1 January 2000. From then, the following changes would be implemented:

Contributions
Contributions made by employers and individuals to retirement saving schemes will no longer qualify as a deduction for income tax purposes. For individual taxpayers and their personal contributions, that's quite simple to implement. Though, in order to remove other distortions and to prevent a shift in saving for tax reasons alone, the current deductions for interest paid on a home mortgage and local property taxes should also go, along with the tax subsidised interest paid on municipal bonds and other equivalent distortions (like the fact that the amount an employer spends on an employee's medical insurance isn't a taxable benefit).

For employers, it's a little more complicated.

In a progressive tax system such as in the US,[3] choosing the withholding tax rate isn't easy because the deduction should be as close as possible to the rate the employee would have paid had the contribution been received as regular pay. In the current environment, 30 per cent looks about the right number, adjusted for the increase created by merging Social Security contributions into the tax system. The alternative is to move to an imputation system of the kind I described in chapter 7.

From 1 January 2000, there will be no controls on the amounts that employers can claim as a deduction for contributions to their employees' schemes. All the present rules about 'top heavy' schemes will go—the government will no longer be concerned about the amounts paid in respect of more highly paid employees.

Investment income tax
Retirement schemes will pay tax on their investment income, again as a proxy for their members for whom the trustees are investing the money. Choosing the tax rate will result in a compromise rate that tries to match the tax rate

---

[1] If contribution levels to the Social Security system alone were held at present levels, retirement benefits would have to reduce 10% by 2010, 27% by 2020 and 41% by 2040, according to the Congressional Budget Office, reported in *The Financial Times*, 3 June 1996.

[2] See chapter 4.

[3] Personal Federal rates range from 15% to 39.6% though these will increase by the amounts that were called Social Security 'contributions' but will now be amalgamated into income tax.

the members would have paid had they been investing the money themselves.[1] Again, an imputation system could let members 'look through' the trust and pay tax on the trustees' income as though it were their own income.

There are still a couple more problems—the first and main one is the 'effective marginal tax rate' (EMTR) faced by members on income-tested welfare benefits and low-earner income tax supplements. In New Zealand, for someone coming off an unemployment benefit, the EMTR can be as much as 94 per cent when you allow for normal tax on pay and the reduction in the income-tested payments from the state. In the US, it can actually exceed 100 per cent. In New Zealand, we then have an additional problem—for someone on the tax-derived, low-income Family Support, the EMTR can be as much as 63 per cent.

In the end, New Zealand settled on a tax rate of 33 per cent for the income the trustees earn (without imputation[2]) which is our corporate tax rate and our top personal rate. Not perfect but a little on the low side for those with EMTRs that are higher than the top rate, which is probably a good thing—it slopes the tax field in favour of the low paid. Imputation would remove that slope and emphasise the high EMTRs. For the US something close to the top Federal rate for individuals should be chosen, say 35 per cent.

Benefits

Benefits paid will become free of tax, even if they are paid as a pension. All pension restrictions that currently apply to benefits will go—a scheme could even pay benefits as a tax-free lump sum.

There will be no limits on the value of benefits paid and no restrictions on when the benefit can start or stop. Now that the government has no investment in the build-up of assets through tax concessions, it no longer has an interest in whether the benefits are 'fair'.

All this will be a fairly traumatic period for retirement saving schemes, but the challenges won't end there. Requiring schemes to pay tax on their income and taxing the amount they receive in contributions from employers will mean that defined-benefit schemes must be given an opportunity to reduce their promised benefits. That's because those have been formulated, at least in part, on the premise of tax-free contributions and investment returns. The reductions for future service benefits will have to reflect the impact both of the investment income tax and the contribution withholding tax; past service benefits will need to be reduced only to take account of the investment income change. The reduction will also depend on the age of the scheme's members—the older they are, the closer they are to retirement and the less time that the contribution and investment return reductions have a chance to bear on the benefit accumulation. That means a smaller reduction for a given annual accrual of benefit for an older member than for a younger (or for

---

[1]   The flatter the overall tax structure, the easier it is to get a reasonable match between the rate fixed for the investment income and the rate the employee would have paid. Steeply progressive systems will be a real problem in that regard for defined-benefit schemes.

[2]   Though a modified form of imputation will be introduced in New Zealand for the 1999 tax year.

a pensioner compared with a member).[1]

The next challenge flows out of the investment the tax system has in the assets currently held in tax-favoured schemes. Future generations of taxpayers were expecting a return from the deductions that past generations of taxpayers have allowed. With the reforms I am suggesting, they won't now get that, so the tax system should get its return today by asking all tax-qualified schemes to pay a one-time charge in exchange for the tax they would have paid in future years.[2] The amount should be the present value of the tax on both present and future pensions.[3] From this vantage point, I can't make assumptions about what that charge should be. But it would be possible to work out, for a range of schemes, what their future pension and pensioner profile is and then estimate the present value of tomorrow's taxes as a proportion of today's assets. Once an average rate is settled on, it should be applied uniformly to all schemes. For the sake of the present discussion, let's assume that it's 15 per cent of the scheme's total assets at 31 December 1999.[4] By passing that amount over to the government, no-one is worse off on average—the government is collecting tax earlier than would have been the case under EET and the pension scheme is paying it earlier than under EET but the proportion of assets to be passed across should be roughly what would have been paid anyway.

With the amount of money tied up in tax-favoured schemes, the transfer of, say, 15 per cent[5] to the government has the potential to move markets.

---

[1]   When New Zealand defined-benefit schemes made the same kinds of adjustments in 1990, very few applied the full actuarial reductions. Mostly, they settled on a flat reduction for past service benefits along with a different (in some cases age-related) rate of reduction for future service benefits. In most cases, beneficiaries ended up better off on an after-tax basis than they were in the previous EET environment.

[2]   That didn't happen when the equivalent changes were made in New Zealand over the period between 1987 and 1990 so there was a transfer of wealth from tomorrow's taxpayers to today's beneficiaries of $2 - $3 billion. In the case of defined-benefit schemes, the transfer of wealth was from tomorrow's taxpayers to today's sponsors.

[3]   In the US that would also have to include the tax that states would have collected on the pensions, though, with the varying rates that apply across the US, that will generate some interesting discussions. However, it won't include an allowance for the tax that schemes will now pay on their investment income. The one-time charge relates to assets that have built up before the date of change in a tax-free environment and to the benefits that would have emerged in relation to those assets.

[4]   I'm aware that Alicia Munnell (in 'Current Taxation of Qualified Pension Plans : has the time come?', *New England Economic Review*, March/April 1992) also suggested a 15% charge on existing US schemes' assets when she recommended that the US go to the TTE regime for retirement saving. That's not why I'm making the same suggestion but it's a useful starting point. The vitriol that greeted Alicia Munnell's suggestion will probably be repeated.

[5]   Let's say $150 billion, or 15% of the approximately $1 trillion in pension schemes—and then there are the other tax-favoured vehicles like 401(k) plans (that have about $650 billion) and Individual Retirement Accounts.

Schemes should therefore be able to pass portfolios across, rather than cash. Changing the owner of those assets won't change their value in the same way as a sale would. The government could then contemplate cancelling bonds that it gets (just like cancelling the Social Security Fund's holdings) and holding the other investments in a special pool, realising them over time to maximise the return it gets from the pre-payment of tax. The government shouldn't contemplate holding those assets for any longer than it takes to realise them.

All the government's savings from the reduced costs of administration and withdrawal of tax incentives should be passed straight through to taxpayers by way of a reduction in income tax. Taxpayers can then make their own decisions on where and how to save. Social Security will eventually be much simpler to understand and the government will be obliged to report to everyone, not just the lobbyists, on the fiscal sustainability of the whole structure.

United Kingdom

Key Features of the Current Regime

The UK has a relatively low level, flat rate Tier I benefit that is built up by a lifetime of contributions by both employers and employees and carries with it a survivor's benefit. The benefit is taxed as income but is not tested against the recipient's other income. Increases are linked to prices not wages. There is also a state-run Tier II pension calculated by reference to earners' income above, roughly the level of the Tier I benefit over a minimum 20 year period. The total tax required for state pensions is about 18.8 per cent of covered pay. Government spending on pensions is 5.9 per cent of GDP and is expected to rise to 11 per cent of GDP by 2040.

As with the US, there's an extensive, intricate system of tax-subsidised private saving schemes at Tiers II and III. The annual loss of tax on Tier II alone is estimated at $18 billion.

Demographically, the UK is in better shape than many others but there is still a major potential issue when future retirees find out what the UK government has really been doing to their pensions.[1] Government spending is about 42 per cent of GDP (social welfare is 12.6 per cent of GDP), the budget deficit is about 0.6 per cent (falling) and debt about 60 per cent of GDP.

Recommendations

Tier I
As with the US, all separate contributions to National Insurance should stop and the required amounts should be merged into the income tax rates.

---

[1]   The 'basic state pension' was 20% of average male earnings in the 1970s, is now about 15% and is expected to be about 8% by 2030. The pension presently consumes about 10% of government spending. Somehow or another, *The Financial Times* (editorial, 30 October 1996) thinks that the UK's position is now sustainable. I think that the UK's 'improved ... balance sheet' because '... the government reneged on its implicit commitments' will last for only as long as voters don't really understand what's happened.

That means, again, that the contribution-based system of building up benefits will go and be replaced by a benefit that looks like the chapter 6 Tier I state scheme. The new benefit should now reduce if the pensioner earns other taxable income above a relatively modest threshold. The benefit design details will also need to be worked out in a similar way to the discussion in chapter 6.

Current 'entitlements' to the Tier I benefit should disappear with appropriate transitional arrangements. In the UK, the Tier I pension is actually in reasonable present and future financial shape because of its link to prices rather than wages and the relatively old average age of the working population. The Tier I scheme suggested in chapter 6 will improve the position somewhat for pensioners without much other income but, with the income test, that would change for richer pensioners. To avoid that electoral distraction, the transition for current pensioners could assure a minimum of the current payment (increased in line with prices, as now), regardless of other income.

Tier II—state
Benefits that have accrued to the date on which the new regime starts under the State Earnings Related Pension Scheme will be established as a percentage of pay that qualifies for benefit and will be preserved for payment at the individual's state pension age. The annual pension at retirement will be the accrued percentage at the change date applied to the individual's eventual career-average, revalued pay.

Contributions to the Tier II scheme will stop and there won't be any further accruals after the change date. Private schemes that are 'contracted out' of the state's Tier II scheme will also stop having to provide the 'guaranteed minimum pensions' that replace the state's Tier II benefit.[1] They will also lose the rebate they currently get from the National Insurance contributions because there won't be any contributions from which to get a rebate.

Tiers II and III—private
As in the US, the present EET tax treatment of retirement savings should be replaced by TTE within, say, two years of the decision to change.

All of the comments made about the process of change in the US apply equally to the UK. The amount paid by presently tax-favoured schemes to the government will again depend on calculations of the average pensioner and member profiles, but 15 per cent of total pension assets of $760 billion[2] is $114 billion.

All the present rules about when and how private benefits are calculated and paid will go, along with the rule that says pensions must be increased by inflation (or by five per cent a year if inflation is lower). Private schemes will only need to meet the consumer information requirements described in chapter 7. Rules about who should be trustees, compulsory transfer out and transfer in requirements and maximum benefit limits will all go.

---

[1] Though they will still have to maintain the contracted-out promises made for membership up to the change date.

[2] Source: NRJ Research cited in Marathon London's *Investment Review*, 30 September 1995.

Scheme administrators will stop spending their lives complying with rules[1] and will be allowed to get on with the serious business of helping members make sensible choices about where and how much to save for their retirement.

Chile

Key Features of the Current Regime

Chile has a low-level Tier I benefit ($1,370 a year or about 75 per cent of the minimum wage) paid after 20 years' coverage from general income tax. This is reduced by income from the compulsory Tier II scheme.

An extensive, compulsory, tax-subsidised, private, defined-contribution savings scheme produces a taxed pension at Tier II for an employee's contribution equal to 10 per cent of pay plus costs. (This scheme is discussed in considerable detail in chapter 5). Employer-sponsored schemes are rare but savers can use the compulsory scheme for voluntary, tax-subsidised, additional benefits. Very few do.

The population profile is relatively young but shows early signs of the changes now faced by more mature countries. 10 per cent of the population is categorised as 'absolutely poor'.[2] The government has a budget surplus of about two per cent of GDP.

Recommendations

Tier I

Unlike most countries covered in this brief review, there's not much that needs to be done to Chile's Tier I benefit, as long as the link to the minimum wage maintains the objective or 'preventing poverty, plus a margin'. However, the future of Tier I will need to be discussed in tandem with the decisions to be taken on the compulsory Tier II.

Tier II—compulsory private

The reasons for the introduction of the compulsory scheme (bankrupt and unreliable Tier I benefits) have now gone. The government should face the reality of a scheme where many of its members are seemingly 'delinquent' in their contributions, despite the tax bribes and high investment returns that it offers.

All future contributions should be made on a voluntary basis with effect from, say, 1 July 1999. The period between the decision and the effective date has to be short. The present delinquency rate means that, as soon as the change is announced, those savers who are still contributing will vote with their feet.

Balances currently held in an AFP (the approved saving institution chosen by the saver) will stay for a minimum period, perhaps even until the saver's

---

[1]   Like the more than 1,000 pages of regulations that have emerged from the Pensions Act 1995.

[2]   *The Economist Intelligence Unit*, 2 February 1996. According to Pilar Vergara, a Chilean economist, reported in the *Observer*, 20 May 1997, in 1993 the wealthiest fifth of the population received social spending twice that given to the poorest fifth.

retirement and may even still emerge under the current rules—payable as a pension with limited cashing rights. This decision will depend on the future viability of Tier I with which the compulsory scheme is currently closely linked. If the long-term future of Tier I looked secure without the compulsory Tier II scheme, members could be allowed to withdraw their savings from the AFPs on a controlled basis to limit the effects on financial markets and on inflation.

Tax incentives

The present EET tax treatment of savings at both Tiers II and III should go, but especially for Tier II (even if my suggestion about the fate of Tier II were ignored). There's absolutely no justification for encouraging people, through tax breaks, to contribute to a compulsory scheme.

The same considerations discussed in the US context for getting rid of tax incentives will also apply to Chile. But life will be a bit easier for the Chilean regulators in two respects—first, most of the tax-advantaged savings are locked into the compulsory scheme, so change can be forced on savers. Second, the private retirement savings environment, by weight of assets, operates on defined-contribution principles. It's a lot more complicated to withdraw tax concessions from a defined-benefit scheme.

As with other countries, that will still leave the government with quite a bit to do. Inflation is running at eight per cent or more—that's not good for savers[1]—and there'll be a lot of financial education needed for savers once the compulsory props are pulled out. In the new environment, it would be great if Chileans could maintain their high saving rate of around 28 per cent of GDP (in 1995). But I suspect that, like Singapore,[2] that statistic is at least partly reliant on citizens doing what they are told, not what they want.

France

Key Features of the Current Regime

France has an intricate, expensive, separately-managed social security system delivering at Tier I, from age 60, benefits equal to 50 per cent of covered earnings (average revalued earnings over 25 years of up to $26,900) after 40 years. The social security system is in serious trouble with an accumulated deficit of $23 billion, increasing at a current annual rate of $8.1 bn. The total tax needed to pay for Tier I is 19.8 per cent of covered pay. Government spending on pensions is 9.7 per cent of GDP but is expected to rise to more than 25 per cent by 2040. With government spending running at 55 per cent

---

[1]   At that rate, the value of money is halved in only 10 years.

[2]   Now that Singapore has been anointed by the OECD as a 'developed country', I should have included it in my 'solutions'. In fact, several of my suggestions on Chile also apply to Singapore. The Central Provident Fund will take years to unwind—the first thing that should happen is that all the assets the government has bought with CPF money (and that are financial investments, rather than infrastructure developments) should be passed over to the CPF and the underlying bonds cancelled. The government should then use its budget surpluses to repay the rest over time. Savers will then receive their balances over time in lump sum distributions as money becomes available.

of GDP on a budget deficit of three per cent and with debt at 60 per cent, immediate and extensive change is inevitable.

Tier II is also dominated by the state with mandatory, pay-as-you-go, defined-benefit pensions that supplement Tier I. The eventual pension here depends on the 'points' bought by the contributions and are skewed in favour of employees with a relatively flat salary progression.

Though both Tiers I and II are unfunded, they effectively operate under the EET tax principle. This is because contributions are deductible, the value of the accruing benefits isn't taxed in the beneficiary's hands and the eventual pensions are taxed. The government doesn't lose as much revenue in a pay-as-you-go environment because there are no assets on which tax-free income is earned.

Recommendations

Tier I

Again, the 'greenfields' process outlined in chapter 6 should produce a flat-rate, income-tested, inflation-proofed pension payable from, say, age 68 after, say, 10 years' residence. For employees, that will be a somewhat lower benefit than the present one so transitional provisions will be essential.

The government then has to complete the shift of social security's management from the present semi-independent process that involves the trade unions to one where proper recognition is given to the role of taxpayers in paying for the government's underwrite. The current contributors (employers and employees) are also taxpayers so responsibility for management of the whole system should be in the one place—with the elected representatives.

Current accrued entitlements under Tier I should be calculated and preserved. They will eventually be paid based on revalued pay at retirement from the present age 60. As people reach age 68, their entitlement under the new regime will be calculated and reduced by the benefit to which they are entitled under the present Tier I. In the case of a married couple, the entitlement to the new married couple's rate will be reduced by the present Tier I benefit received by either (or both) partners. Over time, the old Tier I will be replaced by the new.

It would be tidier if the old and the new regimes had the same way of working out increases to take account of inflation. If they didn't, the offset process would need to be done each year, which is messy. If the increase regime were the same, the offset need only be calculated at age 68 and the new Tier I benefit established as the net amount for the rest of the pensioner's lifetime.

The separate social security contributions will disappear and be merged into the normal income tax rates.

Tier II—public

As with Tier I, accruals under the two central Tier II schemes will stop. The points that each member has earned will be valued when the employee retires in much the same way as happens now.

The contributions will also stop and the amounts needed in the future to pay for the cost of past service entitlements will be merged into the income tax rates as with Tier I. The government will then pay from tax revenue the amount needed by the two schemes to meet benefit payments, including for the currently retired.

Tier II—private

While private Tier II schemes are less important because of the heavy state involvement, they do exist—mainly for top management—because of the relatively small pensions that emerge from the state schemes for the more highly paid. These are favoured for tax purposes and those favours should go.

The government has said that it wants to introduce what it describes as 'private capitalised pension schemes'. That sounds all right, but, unless the government sees these as a mandatory replacement for its existing involvement at Tiers I and II, it's difficult to see why the government should have a view on what it calls 'private capitalised pension schemes'. People should make their own decisions on these. The government certainly shouldn't be thinking of tossing taxpayers' money into the pot in place of the current Tiers I and II contributions. That won't stimulate long-term, sustainable change.

French governments have much future pain to endure on the pension front. Even the present government's first timorous steps have provoked anger. It's difficult to see how my suggestions could be implemented in the present environment unless the task were taken away from the political process. However, although change might be difficult for the French, change is essential. Depoliticising the pension policy review might help.

Germany

Key Features of the Current Regime

A complex social security scheme delivers Tier I from age 65 at a cost of 19.2 per cent of covered pay for pensions alone. It's difficult to summarise the benefit basis[1] but the full benefit is between 40 per cent and 45 per cent of covered earnings (of up to about $52,000). Government spending is about 50 per cent of GDP on an adjusted budget deficit of three per cent and debt is 60 per cent of GDP. However, spending on pensions is 8.2 per cent of GDP and is expected to rise to 30 per cent by 2040.

An extensive system of Tier II schemes pay, mostly, defined-benefit pensions that are meshed (or 'integrated') with Tier I and are often financed on a book reserve basis by the employer. Separate schemes (Support Funds, Pension Funds and Direct Insurance) also exist. An employer's contributions to Direct Insurance are now partially taxed. However, the general tax environment for separate Tier II schemes is EET.

Vested benefits in book reserve schemes must be insured through a state-run agency.

Recommendations

Tier I

The message is the same as for the other countries—introduce a new Tier I scheme, similar to the design described in chapter 6. As with France,

---

[1] Because it depends on a mix of 'individual career earnings, average pay, revaluation and insurance periods. Years of further education, military service, absence for raising children etc. count as insurance periods after age 16', according to William M. Mercer, *International Benefit Guidelines*, 1995. More than 80% of Germans' retirement incomes are delivered through Tier I according to a report in *Business Week*, 29 April 1996.

transitional arrangements will gradually replace the existing benefit with the new.

Current accruals will be calculated and paid in due course but will offset the benefits from the new scheme when they start at a, probably, later age than the present 65. Meshing the two schemes with respect to pension increases will be straightforward because the present Tier I increases its benefits in line with wages—chapter 6 recommended a Tier I scheme that took a similar approach.

Social security contributions will disappear and all income tax rates (company and personal) will increase to leave the government fiscally neutral.

Tier II
Most of the Tier II schemes, by weight of benefits, are unfunded, tax-favoured, book-reserved, defined-benefit pension schemes. Aside from the statutory insurance that covers only the vested benefits, the members of those schemes are dependent on their employer's continued existence not just for their jobs but also for their pensions.[1] A number of reforms to this seem necessary.

For a start, on consumer protection grounds alone, employers should not be allowed to accrue further benefit entitlements under the book-reserve system after a given date. All existing entitlements will stay where they are and will be protected in real terms to be paid by the employer from retirement. The existing benefit protection insurance regime should continue to apply for those past service benefits (which include pensions in payment) but will not cover benefits for service after the change date. If an employer wanted to continue promising defined benefits for future service, that would be allowed only if assets that are outside the employer's direct control support those promises.

Next, the existing tax treatment of *past* service benefits will change. Employers will continue to get a deduction for benefits that emerge from a scheme but they will no longer get special treatment for additions to the reserves held for past service benefits. Additions will be subject to a tax at a rate that reflects the average tax rate of the scheme's members. Income earned by the employer on the reserve (at, say, the average return on the shareholders' funds as a whole) will be taxed at the usual company tax rate.

The current tax-driven controls on the amounts that can be added to the reserve for past service benefits will go—employers will decide what's prudent. However, employers with such schemes will now be obliged to report to their shareholders on their unfunded, defined-benefit liabilities under a regime that will look a lot like the FASB 87 requirements in the US. They will also be obliged to report on a similar basis to the beneficiaries of those schemes.

Any tax favours enjoyed by funded Tier II schemes will, as for the US, go and be replaced by the TTE system. The same transitional arrangements will apply for existing benefits, assets and the investment income they earn.

All this means that (as with the suggestions I have made for funded schemes in the US) the past service benefits will cost employers more than they were expecting. They will therefore have the opportunity to reduce both the past and future service entitlements to allow for the new taxes. Anyway, they would probably want the chance to review future service benefits in the light

---

[1]   Though the state-sponsored insurance plan deals with employers that fall over.

of the changes I propose to the Tier I scheme. That's because a lot of them calculate their benefits as a top-up to the Tier I benefits.

More schemes will come out into the pre-funded type of environment that's typical in English-speaking countries. I've already commented on the implications of this for capital markets.[1]

Australia

Key Features of the Current Regime

Australia provides a relatively low-level, income- and asset-tested Tier I benefit ($6,260 single and $10,370 married a year) that is paid from general income tax. It represents about 26 per cent of the average ordinary-time wage for singles and about 43 per cent for the married. It is also largely tax-free so the pre-tax equivalent is higher.

An extensive, complex, compulsory, tax-subsidised private savings regime produces taxed benefits (lump sum or pension) at Tier II. These arrangements are discussed in more detail in chapter 5. Employer-sponsored schemes can participate in the compulsory Tier II (and often use their more generous benefits to satisfy the compulsory contribution obligations) but Tier II is dominated (by weight of members) by union-fostered, award-based, defined-contribution schemes.

Tier III can also qualify for tax incentives but, because some tax is collected along the way, the regime for both Tiers II and III is more accurately described as ttt[2] with concessionary rates paid on contributions, investment income and on the emerging benefits.

Australia is in reasonable demographic and fiscal shape and is ageing relatively slowly. Like Chile and New Zealand, that gives its citizens time to adjust to the financial consequences of new age patterns. The current budget deficit is 1.6 per cent and debt is only 37 per cent of GDP.

Recommendations

Tier I

As with Chile, there isn't a lot of work to do on Tier I. If the 35 per cent/55 per cent model suggested in chapter 6 were a fair reflection of a reasonable benefit level, Australia is about there on a pre-tax equivalent basis. However, it would be for the Australians to decide what Tier I's objective should be, in the context of the argument in chapter 6.

The government has already started to increase the state pension age for women from 60 to 65 which it will reach in 2013. I think the age for both men and women could then increase further to, say 68 or 70. There should also be more flexibility on the age from which the pension can start. This will remove some of the work/retirement distortions that are becoming apparent in Australia.

At the same time, the asset test for Tier I[3] should be dropped as the benefit levels gradually increase.

---

[1]   See chapter 7 from p. 183.

[2]   See Table 3, note 1, p. 55 for an explanation of 't'.

[3]   For more on this, see chapter 6 from p. 137.

Tier II

This is where the real work is needed, in the form of two key changes.

The first key change would be to withdraw the present tax concessions. The current tax on contributions of 15 per cent should increase to something akin to the average personal tax rate paid by Australians (unless imputation were introduced). The same rate should also apply to the investment income earned by the scheme's trustees and, for those changes, the current concessionary tax on benefits should go.[1] That would turn ttt into TTE in line with the suggestions in chapter 4.

As with the other countries, the government should allow defined-benefit schemes the opportunity to reduce past and future benefits because of the new tax regime.

The second major change would be to disband the present compulsory scheme. To avoid rattling markets, that could happen over two to three years rather than overnight. However, it hasn't been going long enough to rate the long transition period I suggested for Chile. Also, the fact that members can get their benefits as a lump sum before state pension age means that future governments don't have a significant investment in the present assets (through the savings that the Tier I benefits would otherwise have received from Tier II). Members could continue to save through their existing scheme if they wished, but, from a specified date (say, 1 January 1999), employers would no longer be obliged, as now, to contribute in respect of their employees.

All that can then be followed by the disbanding of the mountains of regulation that have characterised the Australian scene over the last 13 years or so. Australians can get on with the serious business of working out what sort of retirement they want rather than how to slide by the taxman.[2]

Cash Flow Constraints

Even if all future accruals under state-run Tiers I and II schemes were stopped, the momentum created by existing pensioners and the preserved rights of present contributors would mean that an improvement in the government's cash flows couldn't be expected for some years. If present estimates said that the social security contributions were on the increase and that future reductions to benefits might be needed, my suggestions wouldn't help a lot in the short to medium run. They may lessen the rate of increase but they won't make the problem go away. Burying the social security contributions in the income tax rates may help fudge the problem for a few years, but the problem of overly generous benefits or inadequate collections will have to be faced at some stage.

However, even stopping future accruals for baby-boomers 15 to 20 years before they get to state pension age will help, given that, in terms of the number of people affected, they are the biggest single generation in developed countries. This would leave the unenviable task of explaining to them why their overall tax rates (including the merged social security contributions)

---

[1]   The 'surcharge' on tax-favoured contributions for higher earners proposed in the 1996 Budget can also go.

[2]   One financial planner was reported to the effect that about 70% of financial planning in Australia is about tax planning. That's a terrible indictment of the whole system.

weren't coming down, despite the fact that they weren't earning any further pension entitlements.

There's no real answer to that—it's a natural feature of change in an unfunded scheme.[1] The present benefits still have to be paid for, even if no new benefits are being earned. However, with all the other changes I'm recommending to Tiers II and III, perhaps attention might be diverted from this issue.

So there you have it: a quick spin around the retirement income systems of five developed countries and one emerging one. My objective has been to provide a general impression of what can and should be done, and, in doing so, I'm sure to have missed some of the subtleties in countries that I am less familiar with. Also, all of the recommendations in this chapter will depend on costings of the proposals producing bearable numbers that eventually reach the future balance that consensus requires.

Is Compulsion Ever Justified?

I want to end by revisiting the question that cropped up early in this book. A number of countries have looked at or are looking seriously at compulsory schemes that force their citizens to save in a prescribed way for retirement. I looked in some detail at a selection of them in chapter 5.

I believe compulsion should be seen as a last resort—a solution to a much more fundamental set of problems than simply persuading citizens to behave 'sensibly', whatever is meant by that.

A country has to be in a real mess to justify compulsion and I don't think any developed country is. But there are some others where that would be a fair description—no capital markets of any consequence, undeveloped personal financial services, bankrupt Tier I scheme, a large underground economy, government budget deficits that are not for investment and a huge, seemingly unbridgeable gap between the 'haves' and the 'have-nots'. When a country gets to that stage, I think a compulsory saving scheme is probably inevitable but much more will be needed than just introducing such a scheme.

If a compulsory scheme could be justified because everything was in such a mess then it should have a limited life (say 10 years) to help get people going and help develop capital markets where they don't exist—which I think is compulsion's only real justification.

Change is Inevitable

The OECD estimated that, in 1990, 18 per cent of people in developed countries were age 60 or more. By 2030, the proportion will have grown to more than 30 per cent.

By 2006, baby-boomers will start to turn age 60 but, by then, nearly all developed countries will have a state pension age of 65 so 2011 now becomes the year when the reality check begins. That's only 13 years away—not long in the retirement income business, but time enough to make a difference if we really got stuck in. It's certainly sufficient time for those who will be retiring in 2030.

---

[1]   It's also the corollary of the easy times politicians had when they increased entitlements for voters in earlier times without also requiring those voters to pay for their own promises.

Change is inevitable—for many countries, dramatic change is inevitable. But we won't take even our first step if we continue to lob shells at each other from the trenches that seem to surround public policy on public and private retirement incomes.

I think consensus on the issues should be the first objective, even if we can't agree on the solutions. They will come, eventually, as long as we have agreed starting points and much better information.